The Politics of
Natural Disaster

edited by
Michael H. Glantz

The Politics of Natural Disaster

The Case of the Sahel Drought

PRAEGER SPECIAL STUDIES IN INTERNATIONAL ECONOMICS AND DEVELOPMENT

Praeger Publishers   New York   Washington   London

Library of Congress Cataloging in Publication Data
Main entry under title:

The Politics of natural disaster.

(Praeger special studies in international economics
and development)
    Includes bibliographical references and index.
    1. Sahel--Famines. 2. Droughts--Sahel.
3. Disaster relief--Sahel. 4. Economic geography.
5. Disasters. I. Glantz, Michael H.
HC591.S253F36   361.5'5'09611   75-8474
ISBN 0-275-01180-1

PRAEGER PUBLISHERS
111 Fourth Avenue, New York, N.Y. 10003, U.S.A.

Published in the United States of America in 1976
by Praeger Publishers, Inc.

© 1976 by Praeger Publishers, Inc.

Printed in the United States of America

To my daughter, Mica,
and my parents, Nathan
and Mary Zoller

FOREWORD
Walter Orr Roberts

This book tells a graphic story of tragedy in the Sahelian region of Western Africa. But it reaches far beyond the graphic. It is an example of the kind of transdisciplinary analyses that promises more mindful management of the future of the Sahel. The book emphasizes the interconnectedness of things. It reminds us that politics, history, cultural traditions, climate, range management, agriculture, population pressure, public health, energy, and many other factors enter essentially into the complex equations that govern the burgeoning of life at the perimeter of the desert.

The Sahel has generally been considered of secondary interest by the great powers. The dramatic history of the recent drought, however, has changed this. It awakened the world's conscience. More tangibly, it gave rise to large scale emergency relief programs. Over a longer time base, it has given birth to the projected U.N. Conference on Desertification, and to the World Plan of Action to Combat Desertification that will be developed by the Conference.

The Sahel drought is a poignant example of the effects of the ebb and flow of deserts, and their impact on the humans that live on desert borders—a problem not just of West Africa, but of increasing millions of the world's people. This book will help to show the global relevance of the disaster and the countermeasures that might have prevented, or at least mitigated, the tragedies it brought.

Research on the Sahelian drought will, I believe, point out ways for us to avert future drought disasters not just here but on all continents of the world. With their comprehensive range of disciplinary viewpoints, the essays in the book provide a glimpse of the new insights about the management of our planet that can only come from the holistic view. Guided by such insights, and sustained by cooperative international effort, we can, I am confident, create a future for humanity that brings quality, security and dignity to life in every region of the earth—and as a part of this, to the Sahel even in time of climate stress.

The essays in this volume are a collection of research papers on various aspects of problems related to the recent drought in the Sahelian zone of West Africa. They were selected to show the impact of climate on human activities (such as the implications of a failure of the monsoons in West Africa) as well as the impact of human activities on climate (such as the implications of overgrazing and of overpopulation).

The essays have been taken from several disciplines in the social and natural sciences in order to indicate the complexity of drought-related problems faced by the region's governments and inhabitants. Each author was asked to offer insight into the drought situation from the perspective of his or her discipline. The areas of research contributing directly to this volume—political science, economic history, range science, public health, climatology, and agronomy—represent only a partial list of those concerned with life in the Sahel.

One of the main objectives of this book is to show the widespread interest in the Sahel and to emphasize the need for comprehensive interdisciplinary and international cooperation in a search for ways to minimize the impact of recurring droughts in this region. The impact of and response to the recent Sahelian drought should serve as an important example to governments and inhabitants in other drought-prone regions. The time to deal with the perennial problems faced by those inhabiting drought-prone regions is before these natural disasters recur.

The book is divided into two parts. The first contains essays by social scientists. Chapter 1 introduces several of the problems faced by the inhabitants of the Sahel. It also challenges traditional thinking about natural disaster in general the the drought in the Sahel specifically. Chapters 2, 3, and 4 deal with questions surrounding international relief efforts to the drought victims. Chapter 5 presents new approaches to the area's long-term development and planning. Chapters 6 and 7 are concerned with the traditional way of life in the Sahel, with emphasis on the impact of the West on the traditional social systems.

Part II consists of contributions by natural scientists, covering a wide range of disciplines. Chapter 8 discusses the climate factor that must be considered in the population-food equation for the area. Chapter 9 continues along this line but also includes a discussion of the impact of man on his environment in this marginal climatic zone.

Chapters 10, 11 and 12 present the agricultural and grazing situations of the region. The impact of the drought on public health care systems in the Sahel is presented in Chapter 13. The final chapter presents some of the weather and climate modification schemes that have been presented by the science community since 1900. An alternative to weather and climate modification is suggested.

CONTENTS

Chapter	Page

LIST OF TABLES AND FIGURES

PART

I

SOCIAL SCIENCE
CONTRIBUTIONS

1

NINE FALLACIES OF
NATURAL DISASTER:
THE CASE OF
THE SAHEL
Michael H. Glantz

This chapter is concerned with misperceptions of the drought situation in West Africa. The Sahelian drought is analyzed through a discussion of nine statements that are generally accepted as true. The statements, here called fallacies, are of questionable value when applied to specific situations. It is suggested that the application of these fallacies to this drought tends to hinder rather than foster an understanding of the difficulties involved in any post-drought recovery program.

The chapter is intended to make the reader question these generalizations and others like them. In the long run, the unchallenged acceptance of such statements tends to confuse drought-related issues rather than to clarify them. Such generalizations, when applied uncritically to specific situations, not only fail to contribute toward a solution of the problem but become part of the problem.

The Sudan-Sahelian zone in West Africa has been adversely affected to varying degrees since 1968 by a major reduction in precipitation:

> The severity of the drought [in this region] was
> primarily a function of latitude. Rainfall during the
> period 1968-72 was in fact considerably above normal

The title for this article was inspired by Howard Zinn, Disobedience and Democracy: Nine Fallacies on Law and Order (New York: Vintage Press, 1968).

Michael H. Glantz was a fellow at the National Center for Atmospheric Research sponsored by the National Science Foundation.

along the Guinea coast and decreased to 60%
below normal along the desert fringe. . . .
Inclusion of 1973 data . . . merely increases the
predominantly north-south differences. [1]

A debate concerning the probable causes for this extended
drought has emerged in which the protagonists fall into two distinct
camps. One group strongly suggests that the current drought is the
result of a global cooling trend in the mid-latitude region in the
northern hemisphere. As the polar-equator temperature gradient
increases (that is, as the polar temperature decreases or as the
tropical temperature increases) the westerlies become stronger and
tend to suppress the monsoons that carry the precipitation on which
annual crops in the region are dependent.
        The other group contends that the current drought is a result
of random climatic fluctuations. Extended droughts in the Sahel
occurred before the current one (for example, in 1910-14 and 1941-
42), [2] but they were interspersed with extended wet periods; droughts
in the region are to be expected, as are favorable wet periods. This
group concludes that there is not enough evidence at present to indicate that the current drought in the Sahel is part of a global climate
change.
        Taking a neutral position between these contending views, the
World Meteorological Organization recently reported:

The unusually widespread reports of abnormal
weather in recent years are more than a reflection
of current wider dissemination of news. Their number
and some apparent correlation between them point to
at least a temporary climatic fluctuation which may
be global. [3]

Concerning sub-Saharan Africa it was noted that

Analysis of data on climate, river flow and lake
level over the past 100 years have brought to light
no real indication of a one-way trend which would
point to a long-term change being of current
importance. [4]

The two factions, however, do agree on two basic points. First,
climatic fluctuations are normal to the region, and in any event the
region will continue to be faced with occasional periods of prolonged
drought. The other basic point is the realization that human agricultural and livestock grazing practices have had a negative impact

on the ecologically fragile Sudan-Sahelian zone. Evidence has shown that the human input into the process of desertification has been a major one. Desertification (also referred to as desertization) has generally been defined as "the spread of desert-like conditions in arid and semi-arid areas, due to man's influence or to climatic change."[5]

Whatever the underlying cause (or causes) of the drought in the Sahel, it has been widely acknowledged that the impact of the harmful climatic fluctuations has, at the least, been greatly exacerbated by human misuse of the land in this region.

FALLACY 1: PEOPLE LEARN FROM THEIR MISTAKES

In a recent article in Science, Nicholas Wade wrote:

the primary cause of the desertification is man, and the desert in the Sahel is not so much a natural expansion of the Sahara but is being formed in situ under the impact of human activity. [6]

This view, recently reiterated in a Swedish study on desertification,[7] has been referred to for several decades and, as Wolf Roder noted, had some currency even in Biblical times.[8] Twentieth-century scientists and ecologists have been trying to get this viewpoint across to political decision makers. E.P. Stebbing, for example, wrote several articles in the 1930s on the nature of human impact along the southern edge of the Sahara. He used such provocative titles as "The Encroaching Sahara . . ." (1935), "The Threat of the Sahara" (1937), and "Man-Made Desert in Africa" (1938). "In spite of the scantiness of the vegetation," wrote Stebbing in 1935, "great herds and flocks were seen and the scrub forest and the grass is burnt, great fires crossing the countryside. Overgrazing and hacking in the forest that is left, annual burning, and sand invasion suggest the question: How long before the desert supervenes?"[9] In 1935 he observed, "It is curious to realize that up in this region the population is actually increasing whilst the means of supporting it are obviously and visibly decreasing."[10] And further, "But the end is obvious: total annihilation of vegetation and the disappearance of man and beast from the overwhelmed locality."[11]

More recently, J.L. Cloudsley-Thompson concluded:

The extension of the desert into tropical Africa is
primarily due to the deliberate action of man, in
many instances within living memory. Desert
encroaches over steppe, steppe over savanna, and
savanna over forest. Thus the increase of the
Sahara in recent years is part of a man-made,
large scale, shift of the vegetation belts. [12]

Human destruction of the ecological balance along the fringes of
deserts has not been restricted to the southern fringe of the Sahara.
For example, a South African Senate report issued in 1914 (at the
end of the 1910-14 drought) blamed the soil desiccation problem in
South Africa on land misuse. [13]

Similar observations were made in Rhodesia in 1967 by an
agricultural officer:

The degradation of vegetation and of soil as a
consequence of overstocking and mis-management
of veld grazing reaches its nadir in Rhodesia in
Natural Regions 4 and 5. . . . The reason for the
advanced stage of denudation reached in this area
is ascribed primarily to the type of utilization,
involving overstocking and mismanagement, and
secondarily drought which has added to the effects
produced by wrong utilization and has greatly
accelerated the process of degradation. [14]

It should be noted that the Rhodesian situation is a political and
racial one in which the Native Land Husbandry Act (1951) subdivided
Southern Rhodesia into halves. The white minority government "gave"
the African population of 2.5 million about 42 million acres for agricultural settlement, whereas the white population of 207,000 (70
percent of whom were urban dwellers) was given about 48 million
acres of the best land. For the most part, African lands were considered "unfit for agricultural settlement because of broken terrain,
poor soils, lack of water and tsetse infestation." [15]

As a final example, Chu Co-ching (also spelled Chu Ko-chen),
in his 1931 article about desertification in China, concluded:

The invasion of sand dunes into regions around
Yuling Fu is primarily due to man-made factors,
owing to the extensive cultivation of steppes beyond
the Great Wall, which began 200 years ago, and
new extends to 50 kilometers beyond the Great
Wall. [16]

The preceeding examples show that different governments have been aware of the negative impact that man has had on his environment, especially in semiarid zones. Historical evidence, however, tends to indicate that individuals, as well as governments, do not necessarily learn from past mistakes either directly or by analogy. Many of the proposals suggested in response to the drought crisis in the Sahel today are similar to those suggested 60 years ago, for example, in South Africa. The South African Senate report alluded to earlier, urging that attention be given to such destructive land management practices as erosion, overgrazing, misuse of water, grass burning, and deforestation, was issued in 1914. The Chinese comment on desertification was written in 1931, and the one on Rhodesia in 1967. An awareness of the problems faced by governments in semiarid zones is, therefore, geographically as well as chronologically widely distributed.

Awareness of the problems, however, is not necessarily translated into action that will rectify those problems. The complexity of the problem was recently suggested by an official from a major donor country who had interviewed a Fulani herder in northern Upper Volta in the spring of 1973. He reported that the farmer, asked how he had been affected by recent drought, said he had had 100 head of cattle and had lost 50. The farmer continued, "Next time I will have 200," implying that by starting with twice as many he would save the 100 cattle that he wants. Yet the land's carrying capacity is such that he will still have only 50 cattle, but his loss will have been much greater.

A recent article suggested that in some countries there may be an official ambivalence toward dealing with the known problems of land mismanagement, population growth, and overgrazing; the article also noted that decisions are needed on such problems as:

1) Whether it would be useful to restore the livestock herd to its pre-drought size, and, through its grazing, threaten the fragile ecology of the more marginal region once more.
2) How to solve the dilemma of the goat . . . .
   Such matters are being considered more actively by foreigners than by national leaders. [17]

A misleading feature of drought is that, following such a natural disaster, the population (human and livestock) is greatly reduced because of drought-related deaths or migrations. The land's carrying capacity will then be relatively more in balance with the drought-reduced populations that the land will have to support. What will have changed for the worse, however, will be the rejuvenative capacity of

the land. One must ask, as Stebbing did in 1935, "How long before
the desert supervenes?"

FALLACY 2: THINGS WILL HAVE TO CHANGE

People fear change. Eric Hoffer wrote about this theme in
Ordeal of Change:

> Back in 1936 I spent a good part of the year picking
> peas. I started out in January in the Imperial Valley
> and drifted northward, picking peas as they ripened,
> until I picked the last peas of the season, in June,
> around Tracy. Then I shifted all the way to Lake
> County, where for the first time I was going to pick
> string beans. And I still remember how hesitant I
> was that first morning as I was about to address
> myself to the string bean vines. Would I be able to
> pick beans? Even the change from peas to string
> beans had in it elements of fear.
> In the case of drastic change the uneasiness is of
> course deeper and more lasting. 18

There is a strong tendency for people to return to the known
way of doing things, to return to "normal." This is a feeling manifested by the Sahelian drought victims: nomads, sedentary farmers,
herders, and Sahelian governments. Yet, one must ask, what options
do they have? Each of the drought victims has only limited options.
For example, four of the six Sahel states are listed among the poorest
in the world. As for the sedentary farmers, they will want to return
to the land in spite of the general awareness that the land is in need
of a long post-drought fallow period. The options of the nomads are
somewhat more restricted. They can migrate to urban (sometimes
called pseudo-urban) centers within their own countries or in neighboring countries, or they can turn to a new but uncertain way of life
as sedentary farmers depending on land availability. However, to the
nomads these options are filled with the risks and fears of an unknown
future. Their only real options are, in fact, a return to a subsistence
way of life as nomads or to a less-than-subsistence way of life as
refugees in a camp or as migrants in a city slum. Such options are
apparently perceived as offering no favorable alternatives to returning
to the known way of life. Things apparently do not have to change.
They have to be made to change.

FALLACY 3: NOMADS WANT TO BE NOMADS

Nicholas Wade, commenting on social change in the Sahel, wrote: "unfortunately, there is no way short of a major social upheaval, that the nomads will consent to reduce their herds."[19]

What Wade failed to realize is that a major social upheaval is exactly what the nomads in the Sahel have, in fact, been subjected to. They have been forced to do things they would not have done in "normal" times. They have been forced to seek refuge in parts of the Sahel unfamiliar to them. They have been forced to sell off their herds. They have been forced to live in refugee centers.

At the recent Conference on Grazing in the Sahel held in Mali, C.F. Hemming stated: "The life of the nomad is an extremely hard one and there is little to suggest that he is unwilling to give up this hard way of life if an alternative is available."[20]

Reports from other sources indicate that at least some nomads in refugee camps did not plan to return to their former homeland. A Center for Disease Control report issued in the spring of 1974 recorded that

> results of an interesting survey conducted among
> a group of displaced nomads indicated that 66%
> of those interviewed stated they would remain in or
> near the cities even if they had animals again.[21]

These two points, among such others as the selling of herds and the decision by some nomads not to return to their home country, suggest that there may be an interest among nomads for what they perceive to be a better, or at least a different, way of life. Perhaps it is now, during this crisis (a time of great social upheaval), that the nomads could be persuaded to consider options other than the perennial ones of a subsistence way of life (as nomads in normal times) and the less-than-subsistence way (as refugees in camps).

The Somali government (in northeast Africa) has taken advantage of the drought situation to present its nomads with new options:

> Dislocations caused by the drought and famine
> besetting Somalia have been seized upon by the
> governing military council to speed up a timetable
> for resettling nomads. . . . Somali spokesmen
> prefer to see the resettlement plans . . . as the
> natural response to the disaster.[22]

It is now that nomads as well as displaced farmers and herders
of the Sahel should be most receptive to lessons, for example, pertaining to the necessity of and requirements for ecological balance in
the Sahel. For nomads, education might involve such important
matters as the necessity for herd size restriction, whereas for
farmers it might involve improved land management discussions.
Somalia faces similar problems today:

> The efficiently organized [Somali] refugee camps are
> being used not only to keep people alive and healthy
> but to indoctrinate them in the principles of the
> scientific socialism that is national policy . . . and
> to train them for new lives. [23]

The refugees also are being taught to read and to write, while in the
camps.

Apparently some nomads are not reluctant to make changes
when their options have been reduced—in this case by a natural disaster. Perhaps they would not be reluctant to consider changes in
their traditional way of life if the options made available by their
governments were to be improved. As Hemming noted,

> the key to this problem may lie in the answer to the
> question "What can be done in this predominantly
> grazing area which will provide alternative jobs
> and which will, in the long run, enable the improve-
> ment of the rangelands and subsequently their main-
> tenance at a high productive level?"[24]

FALLACY 4: WHEN THE RAINS COME, EVERYTHING
WILL RETURN TO NORMAL

In reference to the Sahelian states (Mali, Mauritania, Upper
Volta, Chad, Niger, and Senegal), what is meant by "normal"? On
this point a journalist wrote:

> For the villagers the end of drought, if the rains of
> this autumn [1974] return next year and the year
> after, means a return to "normal" life—on the edge
> of hunger, consistently malnourished, beset by
> malaria and hookworm and other parasites, having
> average life spans that fall short of forty years. [25]

Recall that four of the six Sahelian states are listed among the poorest in the world, with per capita incomes less than $100 year and with food production falling behind population growth. Malnutrition is widespread in the Sahel as well as in the rest of Africa, although the levels vary between countries, between regions, and between ethnic groups. In this respect, therefore, a return to normal means a return to a lesser level of malnutrition, that is, a continuation of malnutrition but at a more acceptable level. During abnormal times, malnutrition problems faced by the aged and the young are compounded: "During times of food scarcity, certain customs of West Africa culture may dictate that children receive less than their proportionate share of food" and are at a greater risk than adults to the effects of nutritional deprivation. [26]

Normal also means a return to pre-crisis political and social cleavages within the Sahel as well as with the Sahelian states: government versus nomadic populations, pastoralists versus sedentary farmers, recipients versus donors, recipients versus recipients. For example, many nomads who migrated to neighboring countries have been reluctant to return to their country of origin, often citing reasons of official discrimination against them. [27] Evidence of such discrimination exists. It was reported that there had been discriminatory food distribution within some of the refugee camps, a distribution that tended to favor the sedentary farmers over the nomads. It also was reported that the nomads in the camps were suffereing from higher levels of malnutrition than were others within the same camps. [28]

As an example of a political cleavage between a recipient and a donor state, in November 1974 President Tombalbaye of Chad cut off American food relief shipments because a New York Times reporter had exposed corruption in Tombalbaye's government. Is it likely that he would have done this if the rains had not returned to provide a relatively good harvest in 1974? Tombalbaye's unpopular government was eventually overthrown in mid-April 1975 in a popular military coup. [29]

Finally, one of the paradoxes of good news—that is, a return to "normal"—that is most difficult to accept is that with the return of near-normal rainfall, there will be a decrease of interest in the perennial problems faced by the inhabitants of the Sahel. As Randall Baker said:

> There is . . . a great danger that when the rains
> come in the Sahel, and the millet grows again, then
> the "problem" will be considered over until next
> time. [30]

FALLACY 5: EDUCATION IS THE ANSWER

What do we mean by education? In the 1950s and early 1960s
it was generally believed that, if the less developed countries (LDCs)
wanted to develop, their populations would have to be formally educated. They would have to become formally literate. Yet it is difficult
to accept the general proposition that formal education will cure the
ills of the LDCs. Government officials are educated, yet they often
fail to come to terms with problems. Often, the rationality of their
decisions is questionable. Why, for example, were relief trucks
from the Nigerian coast stopped at the Chad border so that relief
food could be transferred to Chad trucks? Why did some political
leaders (as in Ethiopia) fail to acknowledge the extent or even the
existence of drought in their countries? On formal education, a
recent U.S. Agency for International Development (USAID) report
noted:

> The legacy of education in Sahelian states has not left
> the countries particularly well equipped to address
> some of the key problems they face. Specifically,
> they still possess . . . overly formal education
> systems . . . ignoring for the most part the needs
> of the rural masses. [31]

It has been argued that traditional nomadic herding practices
in the pre-colonial era were extremely rational, given the ecological
system in which the nomads lived. As P. Lovejoy and S. Baier noted,

> the Tuareg trade network and commercial infrastructure
> not only formed a link between the economies of desert
> and savanna but also provided a safety valve for the
> desert during droughts, particularly those lasting more
> than several years.

Also,

> the desert [Central Sudan] played a unique role in the
> development of the savanna here, where integration
> enabled the desert sector to survive periods of
> crippling drought and to prosper in times of favorable
> weather. [32]

Yet it appears that the impact of colonialism and the establishment
of borders (such as those in the Central Sudan, between northern

Nigeria and Niger) along with a "redirection of overseas trade toward the coast" had a major impact on the viability of the desert-edge sector and on the way of the life of the nomads.[33] Another major undertaking that tended to upset the nomadic way of living was the digging of boreholes or wells. In the short run the digging of boreholes tended to relieve drinking-water shortages. In the long run, however, nomads often kept their herds by the boreholes instead of migrating to other waterholes, and the herds would destroy the vegetative cover in the area by overgrazing and trampling. The end result, as cited in an FAO/SIDA (Swedish International Development Agency) report, noted: "the cause of the heavy mortality of stock in 1973 was lack of forage, much more than lack of (drinking) water."[34]

In terms of functional (nonformal) education, the traditional nomadic migration, or transhumance, was a rational and logical system, given the ecology of the area. Yet factors external to the nomads established new ground rules by which nomads had to live: restriction of herd movements, uncontrolled use of boreholes, pressures to settle. Commenting on the value of the traditional nomadic way of life, a recent USAID report

> suggested that the only cost/effective and realistic
> approach to this critical problem is to recreate the
> necessary environment to permit the traditional
> management systems, with some improvements and
> adaptations to again function.[35]

What is needed is nonformal education. Also needed are reason and logic applied to questions relating to the ecosystem and man's impact on it. Reason and logic imply that the consequences of one's short, intermediate, and long term impact on the ecosystem will be looked at, thereby avoiding shortsighted decisions (such as the indiscriminate boring of wells).

In addition, continuing education would have to be undertaken so that individuals will not be permitted to neglect negative consequences of their activities. In order to encourage someone "to fix the roof after the rains have stopped," one must continually be reminded of what it was like while it was raining. On this point Garrett Hardin has written, "Education can counteract the natural tendency to do the wrong thing, but the inexorable succession of generations requires that the basis for this knowledge be constantly refreshed."[36]

FALLACY 6: SOLUTIONS CAN BE UNDERTAKEN ON A
PIECEMEAL BASIS (AND SEQUENTIALLY)

The problems associated with desertification in the Sahel must
be viewed systematically. Dealing with one problem in one place at
one time may only serve to exacerbate other problems in other places
at later times. A United Nations Food and Agricultural (FAO) report
noted:

> It is also easy to see how reduction or destruction
> of vegetation in one part of a nomad's yearly
> travels could have disastrous consequences on
> other parts of the range, on the animals and on
> the existence of nomadism itself. [37]

In addition, looking within the Sahel for solutions to current
Sahelian problems might foreclose the successful resolution of those
problems. The problems faced by Sahelian states (four of which are
land-locked) are numerous, but one step toward their resolution is
the awareness that their problems are regional West African ones in
that there exists an interrelationship between the Sahel states and
their coastal neighbors as well as among the Sahelian states. On this
point, a USAID report has stated:

> Africans and donors alike recognize that more
> planning efforts are needed if the problems of the
> drought stricken Sahel are to be eased. This
> planning must take into account the relationships
> between the arid and semi-arid lands of the
> Sahel itself and the wetter, generally more pro-
> ductive countries to the south. [38]

Technical examples of the need for a systematic approach are
plentiful. An FAO report succinctly stated a view supporting a systematic approach:

> It is true that, by putting down boreholes or making
> dams or conserving water by other means, it is
> possible to make water available to stock which
> could doubtless survive for a time if water were in
> fact the only limiting factor. However, as people
> in the African countries bordering the Sahara are
> well aware, making water available simply allows
> animals to exist long enough to destroy the remaining

vegetation which depends on rainfall. This artificial
condition of over-stocking cannot last for long, and the
animals inevitably decline in condition and eventually
have to be removed from the so-called drought areas,
once the basic vegetation has been removed.[39]

In light of all this, "France is considering new assistance programs
for well drilling in West Africa."[40]

At the end of the current drought the Sahel will function again
as an ecosystem, in part because of the return of the rains and in
part because the population, human and livestock, which had been
overtaxing the land, will have been brought into a relatively improved
balance with respect to the land's carrying capacity. A recent USAID
report confirmed this view:

> National herds, which may have been reduced to as
> little as half their pre-drought size, are presently
> thriving on abundant grass and water and are
> apparently in much better ecological balance with
> the environment.[41]

Unfortunately, this balance will have been achieved by drought-related
deaths and drought-related migrations—nature's means of control.
Yet the underlying causes for the destruction of land bordering the
desert region will remain: fluctuating precipitation patterns and land
mismanagement practices. The activities of the inhabitants will again
tend to reduce the resiliancy of the land, which in turn will subject
future generations of inhabitants to further droughts, the impacts of
which will be relatively more devastating. On this important point
W.C. Sherbrooke and P. Paylore have written:

> we have also focussed [our study] on climate
> fluctuation, short term weather patterns induced
> by uncertain rainfall and followed by cyclic droughts
> from which marginal areas may not recover if sub-
> jected to continued attempts at intensive use that
> cannot be sustained by a dry year or a succession
> of dry years.[42]

It seems that, after several downward spirals of drought and
less-than-perfect recovery, a functional approach to these problems
cannot succeed. The only approach is a systematic one, and such
problems as deforestation, grass burning, erosion, overgrazing,
overstocking, population growth, water resource mismanagement,
and the like must be looked at systematically.

Randall Baker proposed that

[it was most essential] to try and get the message
across to donor agencies, multilateral agencies and
recipient governments so that some structure of
integrated regional planning or coordination of effort
will ensure an holistic approach to change in pastoral
areas.[43]

FALLACY 7: POLITICAL LEADERS
SAY WHAT THEY MEAN

Not all political leaders say what they mean. A good example
recently was supplied by President Tombalbaye of Chad. When
corruption in his administration had been exposed by New York Times
reporter Henry Kamm, Tombalbaye said that if he had to take insults
in order to get American aid, then he would not eat.[44] What did he
really mean? In the terms used in transactional analysis, he was
saying that if American reporters continued to expose corruption in
his government (corruption in which his wife was implicated), then
he would cut off relief food shipments to his people and, therefore,
his people would not eat. American assistance was ended by the
Chad government as a result of the incident.

Ethiopia, too, demonstrates official neglect of drought victims.[45]
Government leaders at first ignored and later failed to acknowledge
the existence and scope of the drought, the famine, or the deaths
associated with this natural disaster. Some leaders who had pro-
claimed concern for their people's welfare while ignoring their plight,
such as those in Ethiopia and Niger, have been overthrown by military
coups.

Finally, it remains to be seen if the Sahelian states, which
have pledged to work together to cope with the impact of the drought,
will continue to do so, especially after the rains have returned to
normal. On this point Mohamed El-Khawas has written:

it appears that the Sahel governments are still
reluctant to work together in a joint regional
development plan despite public pronouncements
regarding their readiness to work collectively on
the drought problems. Even though interregional
committees and commissions have been created
there is no evidence of increased cooperation
among the Sahel governments.[46]

In fact, it is now, with the return of the rains, that the leaders of
these states should devote more attention to the underlying causes
of the desertification process by which their states' viability is
threatened.

FALLACY 8: THE MYTH OF INTERDEPENDENCE

Before discussing national interdependence, one must distinguish between what is and what ought to be. E.H. Carr, in Twenty
Years Crisis, discussed at length the differences between the realist
view (what is) and the utopian view (what ought to be) of international
relations. [47] It is important and useful to keep this distinction in
mind, especially when talking about humanitarian assistance and
national interdependence.
    An example of the utopian or what-ought-to-be school is the
following statement by Lester Brown:

> when one inventories the many kinds of ties now
> existing among nations, one begins to appreciate
> how rapidly our daily well-being is becoming
> irrevocably dependent on the resources and coopera-
> tion of other nations. [48]

About what ties is he writing? Are these ties more or less important
than areas in which ties do not now exist? Is dependence—economic,
political, military—irrevocable? In light of the view of the primacy
of politics, which contends that political decisions form the basis for
decisions in other sectors, the irrevocability of dependence is not in
fact a valid proposition. For example, in the 1960s Modibo Keita,
then president of Mali, destroyed his nation's only rail link to the
coast at Dakar, Senegal, because of a politico-ideological confronta-
tion with Senegal's leader, Leopold Senghor.
    What is meant by dependence—simply two states interacting
with each other? Prime Minister Pierre Trudeau of Canada once
mentioned that being a neighbor of the United States was like sleeping
in bed with an elephant, meaning that Canadian relations with the
United States involved dependence and not interdependence. There
is a difference between the two. Another example is U.S. Secretary
of State Henry Kissinger's threat about an eventual invasion of the
Mideast oil fields if the Arab pricing policy was no longer tolerable
to the United States. Interdependence accepted only up to a point is
not interdependence but dependence. Is it obvious, then, that one
should expect the developed nations (either the major powers or the

rich nations) to provide humanitarian aid to the developing countries or even to at-risk populations whose lives have been adversely affected by either natural or manmade disasters?

States apparently operate in their own national interest. Leaders make decisions intended to yield a payoff for their country. Humanitarian issues have only a relatively small input into their decision-making process.

U.S. Secretary of Agriculture Earl Butz recently let it be known that food for export was an important tool in the international negotiations kit. [49] This becomes obvious when one notes that in 1974 the pro-U.S. regimes of South Vietnam and Cambodia received 50 percent of U.S. food aid dollars while the six Sahelian states received about 12 percent. [50] "This is not a new practice, however. During the 1960s food aid was used to help South Korea finance its troop commitment in South Vietnam." [51] The Americans intend to use their food as a tool for influence as the OPEC (Oil Producing and Exporting Countries) nations use their oil against the developing as well as the developed countries:

> What has the oil cartel done to help the poorest
> countries? Last December [1974] [it was estimated
> that the oil cartel] had committed some $9.5 billion
> in development aid to the developing world during 1974,
> and disbursed about $2.6 billion. . . . In giving this
> aid the oil producing countries show a strong preference
> for the Moslem World. [52]

More than 74.4 percent went to Islamic nations, 3.7 percent to India, and 2.8 percent to all of black Africa. [53] This is the global system as it is, even though one might have differing views on how it ought to be. The harmony-of-interest concept referred to by Carr is currently interpreted as meaning that what is good for my country will be good for the global community. [54] Utopians or idealists should interpret this concept as meaning what is good for the global community will be good for my country.

There is, as Kenneth Waltz has written, a relatively low level of interdependence between most states. [55] To assert that there is a high level of national interdependence is to overlook that there also is a high level of noninterdependence. Misperception of the existing level of interdependence can lead to a crisis of expectations in that one would tend to match the actions of other states against this myth qua standard of interdependence.

States have linkages. The existence of such linkages indicates that states interact with one another but has no connotations of direction or degree of dependence. Major powers do not necessarily accept that they have obligations to render assistance, for example, to the drought victims in the Sahel. Some states give assistance but often they do so for less than altruistic reasons, as recently noted by Tom Wicker, who wrote that "the United States now is using its surplus food more nearly for international political purposes than for humanitarian assistance." He added that over half of the $1 billion Food for Peace Program was going to countries like South Vietnam, Cambodia, and Chile, none of which was acutely threatened by hunger.56

One should therefore question the belief that there exists an interdependent international order. The basic actor in the international political system is still the state.

FALLACY 9: TECHNOLOGY IS THE ANSWER

Because technology is neutral, technological developments can have an unfavorable as well as a favorable impact on society. In the Sahel, for example, technology can be used to dig deep wells to make water available for human and livestock consumption. As noted under Fallacy 5, however, wells dug in the Sahel often have led to situations in which water no longer was the limiting factor but vegetation near the water hole was.

Medical technology can be used to keep people and livestock alive longer in better health. Yet doing so would eventually mean an increase in population pressure on the land's carrying capacity. In addition, these surplus populations would drift further into the northern edge of the Sahel, the more marginal areas. Such population pressures in a climatologically marginal zone that is subjected to extreme climatic fluctuations would doom the herders as well as their herds to famine in times of drought.

Other technological breakthroughs, for example, would be irrigation construction and miracle grain development or protein enhancement of existing grains. Yet even these developments have their drawbacks. Technology is neutral. But its implications—social, economic, political, ecological—are not. Therefore, the implications of technological development must be assessed before the development is implemented, so that the downstream impact (unexpected side effects) of such developments might be pinpointed and prepared for. Failure to undertake technology assessments may lead to situations in which temporary gains through technology can lead to long-term losses of a more permanent nature. The problem is that

the man who drills wells [is not taught to] . . . ask
what will happen to all the animals which survive as

a result of his activities any more than a doctor
working in the Tropics questions the future of all
the extra babies he is adding to the population
problem.[57]

Kenneth Boulding commented on the potential dangers of
technology when he wrote about his "dismal theorem." In The Meaning
of the Twentieth Century he stated:

> there is a famous theorem in economics, one which
> I call the dismal theorem, which states that if the only
> thing which can check the growth of population is
> starvation and misery, then the population will grow
> until it is sufficiently miserable and starving to check
> its growth. There is a second, even worse theorem
> which I call the utterly dismal theorem. This says
> that if the only thing which can check the growth of
> population is starvation and misery, then the ultimate
> result of any technological improvement is to enable
> a larger number of people to live in misery than before
> and hence to increase the total sum of human misery.[58]

CONCLUSION: WHERE THERE'S A WILL,
THERE'S A WAY

Like the preceding nine generalizations, "Where there's a
will, there's a way" could also be considered a fallacy. One might
argue that sometimes when the will exists the way does not. For
example, the Sahelian region is vast in area but relatively sparse in
population. Therefore, in terms of cost-benefit or priorities analyses,
it may prove too costly to rectify the problems that plague the inhabitants of the Sahel. Whether the solution is the costly construction of
a tree belt across the Sahel, or an extensive irrigation project, or
even the resettlement of the nomadic population, the will to deal with
some of these problems may exist but the way may not.

On the other hand, after studying the Sahelian drought it becomes clear that ways of dealing with several of the drought-related
problems are known. For example, there are known solutions for
such problems as overgrazing, overpopulation (both human and
livestock), indiscriminate drilling of wells, uncontrolled use of
wells, deforestation, and other similarly destructive land management
practices. Yet for one reason or another—political expediency, lack
of resources, lack of concern—the will of governments to cope with

these pressing perennial problems of the Sahel surfaces only inter-
mittently. Their will is strong when a crisis is new but fades as the
crisis continues in time, especially when it becomes clear that solutions required to deal effectively with the problems are often difficult
to implement and not without sacrifice on the part of the recipient and
donor states. Overshadowing this thought is the paradoxical nature
of good news. When the rains return to "normal," interest in resolving the perennial problems in the Sahel will diminish.

NOTES

1. Derek Winstanley, "Climatic Changes and the Future of the
Sahel," in M.H. Glantz, ed., Drought in the Sahel (New York:
Praeger Publishers, forthcoming).
2. On previous droughts in the Sahel, see P. Lovejoy and
S. Baier, "Desert-side Economy of the Central Sudan," in Glantz,
ed., Drought.
3. World Meteorological Organization, "A Meteorological
Approach to the Problems of Drought in Africa" (Geneva, December
1974), p. 1.
4. Ibid., p. 2.
5. A. Rapp, A Review of Desertization in Africa (Stockholm:
Secretariat for International Ecology, December 1974), p. 3.
6. Nicholas Wade, "The Sahelian Drought: No Victory for
Western Aid," Science, July 19, 1975, p. 235.
7. Rapp, A Review of Desertization.
8. Wolf Roder, Department of Geography, University of
Cinncinati, comments during the African Studies Association meeting,
Chicago, 1974, panel on "Climate Change and the Future of the
Sahel."
9. E.P. Stebbing, "The Encroaching Sahara . . . ,"
Geographical Journal 86, no. 5 (1935): 510.
10. Ibid., p. 109.
11. Ibid., p. 110.
12. J.L. Cloudsley-Thompson, "Recent Expansion of the
Sahara," International Journal of Environmental Studies 2 (1971): 38.
13. The Senate, Parliament of South Africa, "Report from the
Select Committee on Droughts, Rainfall and Soil Erosion," (June 19,
1914), pp. v-vi.
14. Oliver West, "The Vegetation of Southern Matabele-
land . . . ," Abstracts of Proceedings of the First Rhodesian
Science Congress (Bulawayo, Rhodesia: The Teacher's College,
May 16-20, 1967), p. 99.

15. Barry N. Floyd, "Land Apportionment in Southern Rhodesia," in R.M. Prothero, ed., People and Land in Africa: South of the Sahara (New York: Oxford University Press, 1972), pp. 225-26. See also Wolf Roder, "Government by Technicians: The Case of the Nature Land Husbandry Act of Rhodesia," paper presented to the Third International Congress, Addis Ababa, Ethiopia, December 9-19, 1973.

16. Chu Co-ching, "Climatic Change During Historic Times in China," in Collected Scientific Papers: Meteorology, 1919-1949 (Peking: Academia Sinica, 1954), p. 272; Chu Co-ching was the vice-president of the Chinese Academy of Sciences until his death in 1974.

17. Henry Kamm, "Sub-Saharan Lands Are Hopeful of a Reasonable Harvest Soon," New York Times, November 10, 1974.

18. Eric Hoffer, The Ordeal of Change (New York: Harper and Row, 1967).

19. Wade, "The Sahelian Drought," p. 237.

20. C.F. Hemming, "The Need for a Wide Ecological Approach in the Planning of Future Rangeland Surveys," paper presented to the International Livestock Center for Africa's "Seminar on Evaluation and Mapping of Tropical Rangeland," Bamako, Mali, March 3-8, 1975, p. 3.

21. T.I. Kloth, Sahel Nutrition Survey, 1974 (Atlanta: U.S. Public Health Service, Center for Disease Control, March 1974), p. 15.

22. T.A. Johnson, "Somalia Resettling Famine-Beset Nomads in Socialist Communes," New York Times, March 22, 1975.

23. Ibid.

24. Hemming, "The Need."

25. Kamm, "Sub-Saharan Lands."

26. Kloth, Sahel Nutrition Survey, p. 1.

27. U.S. Senate, Disaster Relief: Senate Foreign Relations Committee Hearings on H.R. 12412 (Washington, D.C.: Government Printing Office, March 29, 1974), pp. 72, 73.

28. Center for Disease Control, Nutritional Surveillance in Drought-Affected Areas of West Africa, August-September 1973 (Atlanta: U.S. Public Health Service), p. 23.

29. Arizona Daily Star (Tucson), April 14, 1975, p. 6.

30. Randall Baker, "Information, Technology Transfer and Nomadic Pastoral Societies," paper presented to Joint Seminar of the Overseas Development Institute and Reading University, England, September 1974, p. 6.

31. USAID, "Briefing of the African Drought and Related Programs for the Senatorial Staff (Washington, D.C., February 7, 1975) Table 6, p. 10.

32. P. Lovejoy and S. Baier, "Desert-side Economy of the Central Sudan," paper presented at the African Studies Association 1974 meeting, Chicago, November 1, 1974, p. 24.

33. P. Lovejoy and S. Baier, "Desert-side Economy of the Central Sudan" in Glantz, ed., Drought.

34. Quoted in Rapp, A Review of Desertization, p. 48; see also the graphs depicting the relationship between the spacing of wells and overgrazing, p. 47.

35. USAID, "Briefing," Table 6, p. 6.

36. G. Hardin, "Tragedy of the Commons," in G. Hardin, Exploring New Ethics for Survival (Baltimore: Penguin Press, 1972), p. 225.

37. FAO Secretariat, "Food and Agricultural Organization and Sahara Reclamation," Unasylva 93, no. 23, p. 12.

38. U.S. Department of State, Bureau of Public Affairs, Bulletin, no. 10 (September 1974): 13.

39. FAO Secretariat, "Food and Agricultural Organization."

40. Baker, "Information."

41. USAID, "Briefing," Table 15, p. 1.

42. W.C. Sherbrooke and P. Paylore, World Desertification: Cause and Effect, Arid Lands Resource Information Paper no. 3 (Tucson: University of Arizona, 1973), p. 1.

43. Baker, "Information," pp. 8-9.

44. New York Times, November 1, 1974.

45. On the politics of the Ethiopian drought, see Laurie Wiseberg, "An International Perspective on the African Famines," in Glantz, ed., Drought.

46. M. El-Khawas, "An Analysis of International Relief Efforts in the Sahel," in Glantz, ed., Drought.

47. E.H. Carr, Twenty Years' Crisis (New York: Harper and Row, 1964), passim.

48. L. Brown, The Interdependence of Nations (New York: Headline Series no. 212, 1972), p. 3.

49. Quoted in Peter Wiley, "U.S. Food Policy Based on Profit, Politics," Colorado Daily (University of Colorado, Boulder), March 31, 1975, p. 3.

50. Ibid.

51. Ibid.

52. Paul Lewis, "Poor Nations Still Await Most of OPEC's Promised Help," New York Times, March 16, 1975.

53. Ibid.

54. Carr, Twenty Years' Crisis, pp. 41-62, 80-85.

55. K. Waltz, "The Myth of National Interdependence," in C. Kindleberger, ed., The International Corporation (Cambridge, Mass: MIT Press, 1970), pp. 205-23.

56. Tom Wicker, New York Times, November 16, 1974, p. 39.

57. Baker, "Information," p. 4.

58. K. Boulding, The Meaning of the Twentieth Century (New York: Harper and Row, 1964), pp. 126-27.

361.55   P759t
c.1

2

**DISASTER IN
THE DESERT**
Hal Sheets
Roger Morris

By the autumn of 1972, five years of relentless drought had
brought catastrophe to millions of people in the sub-Saharan region
of West Africa known as the Sahel. Though emergency international
relief over the following spring and summer saved many lives, famine
took a grim toll among the 22 million people of the area. In a nutritional survey in four of the six Sahelian countries, U.S. Public
Health Service experts calculated at least 100, 000 deaths from the
drought during 1973 alone. Most of the dead were children. On a
proportional basis, it was as if more than a million Americans had
been struck down by a natural disaster.

The human cost of the drought was not only in lives lost but in
the destruction of a way of life for two million pastoral people. Their
camels and cattle herds wiped out, their livelihood gone, the nomads
survived the famine only to face despair, disease, and still uncertain
food supply in squalid refugee camps and settlements across six
countries. For an already impoverished region, this mass of humanity
driven from its economy and culture would be yet another burden and
a potential source of social or political turmoil for generations to
come.

In 1973 the rains were again meager, the land barren. In the
words of the League of Red Cross Societies, the plight of the Sahel
was "desperate" and its needs "urgent and immense."

Engaged in drought relief in the area since 1968, agencies of
the U.S. government and the United Nations assumed major roles in

_____

Reprinted with the permission of the Carnegie Endowment for
International Peace.

international relief for the Sahel in 1973, much as they had led similar humanitarian efforts in such disasters elsewhere in the world for more than a quarter-century. In some measure, this emergency effort was generous and effective. By mid-October 1973 more than twenty countries had provided some $150 million in aid. The United States was the largest contributor with $50 million. American officials claimed early in August in a report to President Nixon that "mass famine had been averted." And it was clear that grain shipments rushed to Africa through the summer of 1973 prevented starvation deaths from mounting toward the even greater numbers many observers had earlier feared.

According to reliable sources, however, the drought in the Sahel also revealed serious flaws in the organization of the inter-national relief effort. Behind humanitarian intentions and official claims of success lay bureaucracies often unprepared, or unable, to take measures that might have further reduced the tragedy. Despite decades of international experience in dealing with mass famine, relief for the Sahel seemed haunted by rudimentary failures to heed early warnings, to plan in advance, and to monitor and coordinate the rescue efforts.

Drawn mainly from interviews with responsible officials and from several unpublished official documents, this study recounts from a Washington vantage point these and similar problems in the administration of drought relief by the U.S. Agency for International Development (USAID) and, to some extent, the U.N. Food and Agri-culture Organization (FAO), the leading participants in the relief effort in the Sahel. The role of one government or organization in this single tragedy, however, is only illustrative. Weighed against the humane purpose and accomplishments of the U.S. and UN relief efforts, and against the comparative lethargy of other governments, those failures might be overlooked—were not the stakes so high. But for thousands in the Sahel, the stakes were high enough. And the problems revealed in the drought seem likely to plague international relief efforts elsewhere in future disasters affecting untold numbers of people.

The catastrophe of the drought did not happen suddenly. For at least four years, scores of officials from the United States and United Nations were in the region, observing that the states of the Sahel were essentially helpless to deal with the drought, reporting the gathering disaster, and dispensing some relief. Yet neither the United States nor the United Nations had contingency plans to deal with the tragedy as it reached overwhelming proportions by the fall of 1972. Aid that American and European medical experts believed might have saved many and perhaps most of the lives lost, such as measles immunization for hunger-weakened children, had not been planned. For tens of thousands it apparently came too late.

Although U.S. reports since 1969 stressed the need for ready information on factors such as the specific transport capabilities of the needy countries, it was precisely the lack of such data that hampered vital relief efforts. There were also predictable bureaucratic delays in providing U.S. aid because of red tape in Washington that might have been avoided or counteracted. Even after food shipments began to move into the Sahel in major quantities, there was little capacity in the relief effort to monitor their proper use or measure their impact, despite evidence of waste and discrimination in distribution. Reports from several sources, for example, indicate that ethnic or political rivalries in some African countries had led to gross inequities in the provision of food to the nomadic peoples suffering most from the drought. In any event, authoritative information gathered by U.S. Public Health officers on the severe malnutrition of the pastoralists and on other crucial aspects of the famine and relief effort was poorly disseminated, if at all, within the American government or among the UN and private relief organizations.

Over the entire episode, in spite of the dedication of many officials at all levels, there was the shadow of bureaucratic factors in the United States or United Nations scarcely related to human suffering in Africa—programs continued or initiatives neglected out of institutional inertia, rivalries between offices and agencies, an unwillingness to acknowledge failures to the public or even within official circles. Seen in historical perspective, the drought not only raised doubts regarding the management of international disaster relief in 1973 but also left unanswered questions about the approach of the United States and other donors to the basic problems of world poverty and human needs over the last decade.

BACKGROUND

The drought thrust before the world countries largely forgotten in international affairs. A half-century of French colonial rule did little to develop the stagnant agricultural and herding economies of the area. Without the natural resources or possible value of other colonies, the Sahel remained, after independence as before, a relative backwater of French involvement in Africa, its states sovereign but its predominantly rural population among the poorest in the world.

Confidential French figures given to an international agency for the years 1968-71 show total government aid to the six countries as averaging under $60 million yearly—little more than half the amount of French assistance to Algeria alone in any one year during the interval, and less than one fourth of all French assistance to black

Africa over the same period. French private investment in the Sahel was also insignificant.

In the years following independence, there remained in the area substantial numbers of French governmental advisers, teachers, merchants, and military instructors. The regimes of the Sahel were made up of French-speaking African politicians and civil servants closely tied to France both culturally and politically. In Chad, French military aid was crucial in containing an obscure but bloody insurgency in the late 1960s. Yet by the 1970s French influence showed signs of waning in what President Leopold Senghor of Senegal called Franco-phone Africa's "second war of independence." The change had come in part from the internal political pressure of unemployed African graduates seeking jobs held by Frenchmen, in part as the product of anti-Western Arab initiatives in West Africa, and to some degree out of rising political resentment at either French interference or, conversely, the limited amount of French aid. As a result, the Sahelian countries in the last few years had joined other Francophone states in tangibly reducing Paris's influence by severing bilateral cultural and economic ties or moving to replace expatriate French employees with Africans.

"The French contributed to their own demise by creating African elites," said one scholar. "France stayed in the Sahel," another expert observed, "because she saw herself as a great power maintaining its influence, but the good times of the early sixties turned later to discontent on both sides and the realization that neither the French nor the Africans were getting much out of it." As the drought culminated in famine and social disruption in 1972-73, French support and involvement in most of the affected countries, never a major commitment, would be in many ways less than at any time since colonization.

While French help for the Sahel was limited and declining, other aid donors, particularly the United States, seem to have decided that the needy states of the region were to be France's responsibility in any case. There were several reasons for Washington's comparative indifference to the Sahel. For some of the countries, it seemed the United States had no choice. By the mid-1960s Mali was closely tied to the Soviet Union and vocally hostile to the United States at the United Nations and elsewhere. Mauritania was to break relations over U.S. support of Israel in the 1967 Middle East war. During the period of Franco-American estrangement under President de Gaulle in the 1960s, countries under major French influence such as Chad or Senegal seemed to many U.S. policy makers distinctly inhospitable to greater American assistance. Added to these obstacles in the political climate in the Sahel was a growing scarcity of U.S. foreign aid money for Africa in general. By 1966, foreign aid was already

falling an annual casualty to U.S. congressional resentment over the
war in Vietnam. There was rising political pressure in general to
quit international programs in favor of pressing domestic needs. The
African aid budget, always relatively small, presented an especially
tempting target for congressional cuts. It was in this setting that
U.S. aid policy toward the six countries was made, initially under
President Kennedy and then under subsequent administrations.

U.S. aid to the Sahel was marginal even when American
assistance to Africa was at its peak in the early 1960s. Total American assistance to the six countries in 1962-65 was approximately
$40 million, or less than half the support given Liberia for the same
years. By 1966-67, Washington had formally adopted an African aid
policy that strictly confined bilateral development assistance (which
constituted two-thirds or more of total American assistance to the
continent) to some ten emphasis countries.* U.S. bilateral aid was
ended for other African states, including the six nations of the Sahel,
for whom assistance would henceforth be limited to small "self-help"
programs averaging less than $100, 000 yearly for each recipient, or
to "regional" projects among two or more nations.

The policy document codifying this approach to U.S. foreign
aid for Africa was known as the Korry Report, after Edward M.
Korry, then U.S. ambassador to Ethiopia, who chaired a six-person
State Department and USAID task force that wrote the document.
Some 150 pages completed in July 1966, the Korry Report was
ostensibly the product of a searching official study of American
interests and economic needs on the continent. Former and present
officials recall the study less as a critical and innovative examination
of assistance and development, however, than as a bureaucratic
rationalization of decisions already made to maintain the existing
U.S. aid programs in Africa, particularly in the face of dwindling
congressional appropriations. "Every year was getting tougher on
the Hill," remembered one former policy maker. "The Korry Report
made a virtue of necessity and kept our hand in where it mattered."

How the U.S. government determined in the mid-1960s "where
it mattered"—the rationale for giving the bulk of available aid to ten
African countries—only reinforced neglect of the Sahel. As with other
aid donors, the United States gave foreign assistance in the 1960s on

---

*Liberia, Ethiopia, Ghana, Nigeria, Morocco, Tunisia, Zaire,
Kenya, Tanzania, and Uganda—the latter three combined in a regional
grouping of "East Africa." U.S. aid also "concentrated" on Sudan
before that country broke relations after the 1967 Middle East war.

grounds of development potential and diplomatic interests rather than
on the basis of human needs. A 1969 public report to Congress by
USAID justified the concentration solely in terms of such political
and economic self-interest: Morocco and Tunisia had "excellent
relations with Western Europe," and "a moderate independent policy
within the Arab world"; Ghana and the Congo (now Zaire) had "considerable capacities for economic growth" and "should exercise a
constructive influence in Africa"; Nigeria held "a fifth of Black
Africa's population" and the "promise of self-sufficiency in the mid-
to-late 1970s"; Ethiopia and Liberia had "long-standing relationships
with the United States"; Kenya, Tanzania, and Uganda had formed a
regional economic community that was "the most advanced example
of the potential benefits of regional integration and cooperation—a
major theme of U.S. aid policy in Africa." Beneath these reasons,
say several sources, was powerful bureaucratic inertia in USAID
simply to "keep its hand" where it already was, to continue on-going
programs in the ten "emphasis" countries that already amounted to
more than $1 billion in the period 1962-65.

Declassified in 1973, the Korry Report itself added little to the
policy justification for a particular concentration of aid. The "emphasis" countries were getting roughly 75 percent of U.S. aid. "There-
after," said the report, "the correlation between the amount of
assistance and the 'importance' of the countries becomes very hazy."

The figures reflecting these decisions and policies were no
accident. Over the decade 1962-73, U.S. assistance to the Sahel was
about $175 million; to the "emphasis" countries over $3 billion.
Moreover, assistance from other bilateral donors and from international organizations—the United Nations, World Bank, and European
Economic Community—largely followed the flow of French and American aid bypassing the Sahel. From 1953 to 1972, development support
from international organizations to the six Sahelian states was some
$800 million, while assistance to the African countries emphasized
in Washington's aid program was $2.2 billion, nearly three times
greater. Even after the drought had struck in 1969 and 1970, total
bilateral aid to the Sahel from the major donors—including the United
States, France, United Kingdom, Germany, Canada, Japan and other
Europeans—was little more than $50 million per annum, less each
year than the same donors gave to Ghana alone.

A decade after independence, the Sahel remained poor almost
beyond measure. When the United Nations Economic and Social
Council identified the thirteen least developed countries in the world
in 1971, four were in the Sahel. Mali, Upper Volta, Chad, and Niger,
the United Nations found, had per capita gross national products of
less than $100 and under 10 percent adult literacy. Three of the
Sahelian countries—including Senegal with the highest per capita GNP

in the region at $200—recorded no growth rate at all for 1960-70.
World Bank figures for the decade showed Upper Volta and Niger to
be suffering a negative growth rate.

There would be no simple cause-and-effect relationship between
the comparative lack of aid to the Sahel, its unrelieved poverty, and
the calamity of the drought. Experts would later assert that some of
the assistance that did go into the Sahel during the 1960s—such as well
drilling in marginal areas adjacent to the desert and augmenting
livestock herds without safeguards against overgrazing—may have
contributed to the worsening of the drought by lowering water tables
and stripping large areas of protective vegetation. More money for
such projects might only have compounded these effects. Nor are there
altogether clear lessons of policy for the donors. Whatever the official
rationale for aid, there existed authentic and pressing human needs in
the countries receiving more generous outside aid. Ethiopia and
Tanzania, two among the U.S. "emphasis" recipients, also appeared
on the U.N. list of the least developed nations.

But there seems little doubt that more proportionate international
assistance to the Sahel in some areas—transportation, training of
personnel, technical assistance, health services—might have eased
the worst human ravages of the drought, not to mention the daily plight
of countries where life expectancy in 1972 was still hardly forty. With
greater aid might have come, too, the added attention, the vested
interests of bureaucracies and governments, that could have led to
urgent new programs to combat the physical impact of the drought
before it became clamitous. As it was, the peoples of the Sahel faced
the deepening crisis of drought and hunger from 1968 until the spring
of 1973 almost entirely without help or attention that might have
alleviated the disaster. Their remote countries were of little moment
for international aid programs in which political, economic, or bureau-
cractic factors more often outweighed sheer human need.

President Diori of Niger would tell a visiting journalist in 1973
that aid policies had been determined by a simple dictum. "The
poorer you are," said the president, "the less you get."

The drought struck the Sahel with savage effect. From the
spring of 1968 there were ebbing water supplies, chronic crop failures,
and a recurrent need-for emergency food shipments to a million or
more people. The disaster was visibly etched in the ecology of the
region. By 1971, Lake Chad was reduced to one-third its normal
size. The great Sengal and Niger rivers were shrunken in many places
to shallow streams. Each year the wasteland of the Sahara moved
relentlessly southward across the 2, 600-mile belt. Ten miles here,
fifty miles there, the desert consumed the parched land without vegetation or moisture to hold it back. The flight of some pastoral people
began as early as 1968 as hunger hit various areas of Mali, Niger, and

Senegal. By 1972 the migrations were massive, ending in the refugee
camps, new urban slums, or death. USAID reports estimated the loss
of livestock, the livelihood of nine out of ten people in the region, at
33 percent at the lowest in Niger to virtual annihilation in Mali.
Governments of the Sahel, dependent mainly on tax collections from
this agricultural base, confronted the worst crisis of their history
with their sources of revenue wiped out for years to come. Commercial crops, primarily peanuts in Senegal and some cotton in
Mali, were also crippled by the drought. Early in 1973, the FAO
associate director-general for African affairs, Moise C. Mensah,
announced that the drought had slashed the gross national product of
the six states by an estimated 50 percent, leaving them by far the
most destitute countries on earth.

To some watching this sequence—the encroachment of the
desert, the crushing burden of the refugees, the portent of economic
collapse—ultimate tragedy in the Sahel seemed almost inescapable.
"We don't know if they will even be here in ten years," one U.S.
intelligence analyst said of the six countries and their 22 million
people. "It may be that all we can do is forestall the doom."

U.S. involvement in drought relief in the Sahel began in 1968
when Mali, Niger, and Senegal asked Washington for emergency food
rations for more than a million people suffering from crop failures.
The evolving role of USAID in the disaster over the next four years—
a role that would make the U.S. government a major influence in the
international rescue effort in 1973—was the result of several circumstances.

Whatever the deliberate limits on U.S. development aid for
Africa, there was and remains a standing U.S. policy to provide
emergency aid to help relieve disasters throughout the developing
world. The responsibility for executing that policy had routinely
gone to USAID as the bureaucratic offspring of the great postwar
recovery programs and as a farflung apparatus with observers and
administrators in or near virtually every poor country. In 1968
USAID was occupied in relief operations in half a dozen places in
Africa, dealing with problems ranging from local epidemics to the
massive famine caused by the Nigerian civil war. And despite the
relatively insignificant U.S. foreign aid to the Sahel in the 1960s,
there were nonetheless at that time substantial numbers of USAID
personnel in the U.S. embassies in the region. In fact, since 1967
USAID maintained a staff of between 35 and 75 full-time employees
stationed throughout the Sahel, with the exception of Mauritania,
which had broken relations with the United States following the Middle
East war of 1967.

Not least, the American role in the drought (as in other such
calamities) stemmed from the fact that the United States was a

principal source of surplus food for famine relief. No other country had given so much of its resources to emergency assistance or seemed so able and willing to continue. The policy and bureaucratic constraints that severely limited U.S. development aid to the area did not extend to the provision of disaster aid. As did their colleagues in the agency's African Bureau in Washington, USAID officers in the Sahel saw drought relief in their countries as a logical outgrowth of both established policy and USAID's considerable experience with disasters elsewhere. By the end of the 1960s, reliance on American relief seems to have hardened into habit in international affairs. There was an expectation of U.S. relief not only from the victims but also by potential donors, like the French, who apparently assumed that the relief of the Sahel was to be Washington's province, much as the United States had consigned the region's earlier development to the French. It was in this setting that the African governments first turned to Washington for food aid in 1968.

USAID's Foreign Disaster Emergency Relief Reports for 1968-71 chart a developing pattern of disaster assistance to the Sahel in which the United States was the major and sometimes sole contributor. Emergency food aid to the Sahel during 1968 amounted to some $2.6 million. A further $600,000 went to Chad, Upper Volta, and Mali in 1969. For fiscal year 1971, USAID instituted in Mali, Senegal, Upper Volta, and Niger a grain stabilization program that provided grants of grain costing $9.3 million. But by 1971 the drought would leave no respite for such resurrection of the battered agricultural economies of the area. After the shipment of the first 77,000 tons (of a projected 200,000), the remainder of the grain to be provided under the stabilization program had to be given simply as emergency grants. Of international drought relief provided the Sahel from 1968 through mid-1971, the United States contributed more than $13 million. Other donors supplied roughly $3 million, with Canadian grain accounting for half of that aid.

In addition to the USAID presence and the growing U.S. drought relief in the Sahel, there was another American involvement in the region during the late 1960s that would become important during the 1972-73 crisis. From 1966 to the fall of 1972, Sahelian states were included in the West African smallpox and measles eradication programs of the U.S. Public Health Service from the Center for Disease Control (CDC) in Atlanta, Georgia. More than one hundred U.S. physicians and other experts participated in that effort, acquiring in the process considerable experience and information with respect to the peoples of the area.

Outnumbering both the USAID and CDC observers in the region, however, were officials under field projects of the other leading participant in the 1973 international relief effort—the Food and

Agriculture Organization of the United Nations. One of the largest
and busiest of the U.N. agencies, the FAO was designed specifically
to deal with problems of food supply throughout the developing world.
Among its main functions, according to its own description, is "to
predict food shortages as well as to assist in planning and assessing
food aid requirements." U.N. development aid to the area remained
low and there was only token relief aid from the United Nations in the
initial years of the drought. But from 1968 to 1972, in the period
when the Sahelian drought worsened so visibly, the FAO maintained
every year more than one hundred officials working on agricultural
or livestock improvement programs in the region, with several
representatives in each of the six countries.

    Everywhere in the Sahel, say many sources, these numerous
USAID and FAO officials encountered African bureaucracies largely
unequipped to recognize or to cope alone with the accumulating problems of the drought. "Their administrative quality was very thin,"
said a high-ranking USAID official. "These are fragile, weak governments," observed another U.S. policy maker, "severely limited in
their technical resources and data on their countrysides."

    American and FAO officials in the Sahel, on the other hand,
reported to formidable headquarters bureaucracies. USAID cables
from the area, according to many who read them, went not only to
the agency's African Bureau with its administrator and deputy administrators and its desk officers and directors for each country, but also
to several other offices and bureaus ranging from the USAID foreign
disaster relief coordinator to USAID Offices of Technical Assistance,
Planning, Nutrition and Health, to senior USAID administrators
overseeing the entire agency, and beyond USAID to the State Department's Bureau of African Affairs and the Departments of Agriculture
and Defense. "Telegrams on something like a major drought," recalled one former U.S. aide, "can go into a hundred in-boxes all
over the government. But that doesn't say how much they're actually
read." It was this Washington bureaucracy that decided on the
emergency aid given each year after 1968—with requests originating
in U.S. embassies in the Sahel, filtering through USAID desk officers
and directors for each country, "cleared" by the State Department
and Agriculture, eventually to be approved, depending on the amount,
by a senior USAID official at the bureau or some higher level. Of
the existence and mounting severity of the drought over four years,
there could have been little doubt among responsible USAID officials
at all levels.

    In 1972-73, there were a number of USAID officials responsible
for drought relief, either by bureaucratic circumstance or by statute.
All sources agree that the main authority lay with the established
hierarchy in USAID's African Bureau—from assistant administrator

for Africa Samuel Adams—to Deputy Administrator Donald Brown, to
Director of Central West African Regional Affairs Fermino Spencer,
to finally the officer in charge of the Sahelian drought emergency,
Hunter Farnham. It was this hierarchy that was the center, initially
and still, of various operational and planning activities. By statute,
responsibility was to be shared by USAID Foreign Disaster Relief
Coordinator Russell McClure. Created in 1964, the Office of the
Foreign Disaster Relief Coordinator was designed to act as a focal
point for the full range of international relief activities participated
in by the U.S. government. But by all accounts, the office has never
in fact played that role, its policy and operational prerogatives remaining, along with bureaucratic power, in the various regional
bureaus. In any event, McClure's weakened bureaucratic position
was further eroded by the appointment in March 1973 of Maurice
Williams as special presidential relief coordinator. Though Williams
became the chief negotiator and a public figure in the U.S. relief
effort, he was still dependent upon the regional bureau for policy
advice and operational control. The drought for Williams was only
one among many major concerns, including disaster relief in
Bangladesh, the rehabilitation of North Vietnam, and his duties as
deputy administrator and sometimes acting administrator for USAID.
All the above officials are career officers either in USAID or the
Foreign Service of the Department of State.

   FAO field employees similarly reported to the officialdom in
Rome numbering some 3,000 and divided regionally and functionally.
"It's a huge operation," said a U.S. diplomat who deals with the
FAO, "like a major foreign ministry with lines running all over."
And like USAID, the FAO bureaucracy in Rome presided over field
reports, yearly budgets for programs, and a thickening collection of
specific evidence on the drought.

   Meanwhile, the medical data gathered by the U.S. public health
experts was duly stored in the computers and files of the Center for
Disease Control in Atlanta, documenting tens of thousands of children
and adults saved from measles or smallpox. The CDC also knew there
would be a continuing need to sustain the measles immunization program with each new generation of vulnerable children, particularly
among the nomadic peoples of the Sahel.

   Yet none of the organizations had clear lines of responsibility—
either internationally or self-assumed—with regard to the course of
the disaster in the Sahel. Both USAID and FAO knew the African
states would require major outside help to cope with any calamity.
At the same time, there seem to have been only the vaguest expectations in Rome or Washington with regard to who would do exactly
what. These vast bureaucracies with their "lines running all over"
had no effective lines of coordination or joint planning to deal with

the onrushing devastation of the area in which they were so substantially involved from 1968 to 1972.

To the USAID and FAO bureaucracies from 1968 onward came
significant and ever-increasing intelligence on the catastrophe over-
taking the Sahel. The scope, depth, and momentum of the drought
year by year were methodically recorded in the annual public reports
by USAID on disaster relief. The 1969 report spoke of the "prolonged
drought across West Africa," of "drought conditions . . . general"
throughout the region, "complete crop failure" in Senegal. By 1970,
there were more than three million people requiring emergency food.
"This was not a new disaster," the document that year explained for
Mali, "but a continuation of that which was reported" in the previous
report. Famine in Upper Volta, continued the report, "was brought
on by the same drought problem which was plaguing other countries
across West Africa." "Hunger, if not starvation, has become increasingly frequent [and] emergency imports have become the rule
rather than the "exception," concluded the 1970 report. A year later,
the description had become almost perfunctory: "Many African countries are plagued by droughts year after year" observed USAID's
1971 disaster relief report in describing emergency aid to over half
a million victims in the Sahel.

Other intelligence reports coming into Washington, such as
accounts of West African crop failures by agricultural attaches in
U.S. embassies in the Sahelian countries, consistently bore out
USAID's accumulating evidence of the extraordinary severity and
duration of the drought. From April 1969 to December 1973, for
example, Department of Agriculture statistical reports repeatedly
detailed the "severe droughts," the "consecutive poor harvests,"
and the "prolonged period of drought" crippling Senegal's peanut
crops.

Speaking to the FAO Council in Rome in February 1972, a
senior official from Chad portrayed vividly the environmental
destruction of the drought: "Our country is already half desert and
our arable lands left are extremely reduced, but even these are
threatened by the inexorable advance of the desert sands from the
north." On the basis of numerous field reports, the director-general
of the FAO told an intergovernmental committee of the United Nation's
World Food Program later that spring of 1972 that drought in the
Sahel had become "endemic," making it necessary to give the area
"special treatment" in providing emergency food aid. Both the
speech of the Chad official and the director-general's remarks to the
intergovernmental committee were duly cabled to USAID in Washington
by the U.S. embassy in Rome. But not until September 1972,
according to an FAO document, did the organization's field reports
signal in Rome an "early warning" of disaster. There was, said the

FAO, "an acute emergency situation developing in large areas due
to exceptionally poor harvests in the Sahel."

As these reports gathered in Washington, as people and livestock
in the Sahel began to die in the autumn of the fifth year of drought,
USAID produced in October 1972 what it called an "in-house report"
on the area. An outgrowth of another USAID study earlier in August
on desert encroachment on arable land, the report represented, in
its own words, no more than a "general overview" conceived "only
as the initial vehicle for stimulating and guiding future discussions."
It was not a plan for specific actions or needs. It did not recommend
particular "programmatic responses." Yet, in retrospect, the
October report seems in many ways an extraordinary document.

In 160 pages of figures and understated bureaucratic prose,
the study depicted a region of 22 million people in a mortal and
losing battle with environmental destruction. In the process, the
study became a lengthy indictment of past aid programs in the area
by the United States and others, and foreshadowed many of the problems that would beset the international relief effort in the months
that followed. "Man's intervention in the delicately-balanced ecological zones bordering desert areas has been narrowly conceived
and poorly implemented," began the report. "Past levels of development assistance have been inadequate to make more than a dent
in the situation." Moreover, the bureaucratic intervention and poor
planning reduced effectiveness even of the limited aid available to
the region. There had been "a major obstacle to progress" in the
"lack of coordination and cooperation" between those engaged in
development projects "because individuals and institutions are content with—and in fact have shown a preference for—carrying out and
protecting their own specialized discipline-oriented programs."

Among the most serious problems of coordination, the study
found, was a failure to assemble and use the available information
on the crisis. "The very first need is for a functioning data retrieval
system," said the report. "It is incredibly wasteful to repeat again
and again surveys whose results lie—often unanalyzed—in our own
files." There was also an urgent requirement for "better pre-project
planning and integrated approaches to project design and implementation" since development projects in the past had often had "undesirable
side-effects which reduce or offset anticipated benefits." The survival
of the Sahel required, too, the application of "much of the available
scientific information and technologies [which] have not been applied
successfully in the past."

The USAID report clearly recognized as well the schism between pastoral and sedentary peoples in the Sahel that would lead to
harsh inequities in the distribution of relief in 1973. Most colonial
and post-independence development had benefited "primarily the

urban sector." "Thus large elements of the rural population," the
study observed, "have become estranged from their urban com-
patriots." The report's summary on the region was chilling. "Continuing neglect and misuse of the land and water resources of the
Steppe/Savannah zone south of the Sahara," the study concluded, "is
resulting in a rapid and extensive deterioration of the subsistence
base for millions of people in the region." In short, the Sahel was
dying.

        The October report remained an obscure internal USAID docu-
ment, never widely circulated within the government or published.
It seems noteworthy now as further evidence of how much USAID
knew, or could have known, before the drought crisis culminated in
late 1972 and 1973 in thousands of deaths. The study was apparently
the first serious attempt to look critically at the character and organization of previous efforts to combat the drought. But it was two years
too late. In the fall of 1972, there was no time left in the Sahel for
a "general overview" or for more study. Wells were long since dry,
the earth cracked at jagged angles, the nomads' cattle dead or dying,
the famine among an already weakened people worse and more widespread than in any of the four years before. By October 1972, indicate
several sources, children and the elderly had already begun to suc-
cumb.

        Yet months were to elapse before the emergency international
relief effort was marshalled and functioning. Even then, much of the
rescue operation was improvised and ill-planned. Having chronicled
the drought for five years, with repeated documentation of its severity
and cumulative devastation, neither USAID nor the FAO had contingency plans ready that autumn to help the Sahelian countries deal
with the first huge wave of hunger and disease breaking over them.

        This failure to prepare for the crisis of 1972-73 was at once
an illustration of the very problems USAID's October report had
ascribed to lack of coordination and the neglect of scientific tools.
"Everybody thought that it was just a temporary climatic aberra-
tion," explained one U.S. relief official. "Nobody anticipated that
the drought would last this long." Another observer saw the same
mentality among USAID officials in Washington in the period 1968-72,
"They just kept thinking that each year would be the last," he said.
The Grain Stabilization Program had been seen by many officials as
something "to tide them over," said the source, as if the drought
were somehow a brief episode.

        From data recorded on the water tables of the area—data
available at the World Climatic Record in Suitland, Maryland, a
suburb of Washington—there could have been no such illusion. "In
1970 there was no recharge at all. In 1971 there was less than
average recharge, and in 1972 the situation was set for disaster,"

said Norman MacLeod, an agronomist and research scientist at American University. "I don't think people thought that an examination of climatic data was really worthwhile. If it [the data] had been examined . . . the situation that developed in 1972 would have been seen."

But then falling water tables were not the only index of crisis at hand. There were the persistent crop failures and the visible shrinking of lakes and rivers. Obvious, too, was the growing population of people and animals which had been made possible, ironically, by outside assistance such as the U.S. smallpox eradication program and cattle vaccination projects. That population was making unprecedented demands on grazing land and wells precisely at a time when the water and forage of the Sahel were being exhausted as well by climate—what the October report had called one of the "undesirable side-effects" of the unplanned development aid of the past decade.

In the months before mass famine hit the Sahel in late 1972, these realities were variously known and understood by disparate parts of the USAID bureaucracy, by other agencies in the U.S. government, by private authorities, by the FAO, by other donors and by the Africans themselves. Donald S. Brown, USAID deputy assistant administrator for Africa, told the Senate Subcommittee on Africa on June 15 that, "the conditions which prevail in the Sahel today are the cumulative effect of several years of inadequate rainfall, capped by a particularly poor season this year." USAID had been "involved for several years," said Brown, in programs in the area. As a result, Brown went on, "our technicians then observed areas where farmers planted six or seven times without results. We observed nomadic herdsmen searching in vain for forage and water in traditional areas and being forced to move their livestock into disease infested areas where forage was available." But why USAID or other relief agencies had not acted sooner on these ominous eyewitness reports, Brown did not tell the senators. Nowhere—in Washington, Rome, Paris, or the Sahel—were these facts assembled and analyzed to form the basis of coherent planning. As the October report reminded its readers, there was no data retrieval system, no effective coordination of policies and projects. There was no international mechanism to be triggered into emergency action by the numerous warnings from the Sahel.

Nor was the failure to plan in advance for the crisis merely another instance of the long-standing international neglect of the Sahel. Many had recognized the enormous magnitude of the problem, the danger to lives in the short run and the threat to the long-term survival of a community of millions. But the relief bureaucracies waited, as in other disasters, on events—in part out of institutional ignorance, in part for lack of a common instrument with which to act.

"Full understanding of the process underway took time," Brown
testified to the Senate. The result was a relief operation in 1973
that would be marred by lack of planning and constricted by the
particular bureaucratic and organizational limits of USAID and the
FAO, which had inherited the relief responsibility in the Sahel, as
elsewhere, by default.

Explaining the failure of the African states to anticipate the
crisis, one ranking U.S. official spoke what seemed a bitter epitaph
as well for the larger failure of the international community. "It
sneaked up on them," he said, "over a five-year period."

NOVEMBER 1972–JUNE 1973

Outwardly, U.S. relief to the Sahel in the crisis of 1972–73
was impressive. Of the $50 million contributed by October 1973, a
large part went to supply over 300,000 metric tons of food grains.
There was also emergency aid to the African states for livestock
feed and medicine, to augment surface transport, and for a number
of other relief actions. Most dramatically, there was an airlift.
Beginning in May, three U.S. Air Force C-130 transports flew
desperately needed food to outlying regions of Mali, Chad, and later
Mauritania. Largely beyond public view in USAID, however, was a
record of hesitation and delay. Unprepared, the USAID bureaucracy
lacked either necessary data or money, and sometimes both, to
respond swiftly to certain pressing needs. Critical new appropriations for Sahelian relief became entangled in congressional and
bureaucratic politics. And the vagaries of relief administration in
Washington inevitably had their effects on the blighted savanna in
West Africa—in special rations that were not there, in vaccines that
arrived too late, in food that starving people could not eat.

The first formal USAID response to the drought crisis in the
fall of 1972 was the formation of an interagency "working group,"
with representatives from the Departments of State, Defense, and
Agriculture, as well as from various offices in USAID. The group
was to be only a first attempt by the bureaucracy to "study" a crisis
by then five years in the making. Without contingency plans or even
an up-to-date collection of available data on the on-rushing calamity,
there would be no emergency measures ready to order in USAID or
in West Africa when the alarms sounded from the Sahel late in 1972.
Before the study group was formed, as one senior official remembered, "we just stumbled around trying to get hold of the problem."
Charged to "put the problem on paper" and to "design what [the
U.S.] role should be," the November task force was to provide, at
last, contingency planning for a disaster that had already happened.

From that study, over the following months came the first
systematic appreciation in Washington of the enormous dimensions
of the drought, and of the formidable obstacles to relief—possible
transport problems, famine-related health dangers and decimation
of livestock and seed supplies, the manifold difficulties of storing
and protecting grain in transit. The November group was also the
forerunner of later planning efforts within USAID, and eventually
within the United Nations as well, to examine the middle- and long-
term needs of the Sahel. Officials generally credit the task force
with generating bureaucratic interest in the crisis and beginning
some degree of interagency coordination inside the American government. "It enlightened some people around here who hadn't thought
about the problem," said one USAID source who observed the group's
work.

But the fact would remain, as officials unanimously acknowledged, that there had been no contingency plans or effective early
warning until November. It took months—months when the starvation
was already acute in the Sahel—from this initial survey of the tragedy
to the large-scale U.S. relief efforts that finally took shape in West
Africa during the summer of 1973. Though the November group
pointed up the need for massive emergency shipments of grain to
the stricken area—and USAID later claimed that it had "committed"
156,000 metric tons of food aid for fiscal year 1973—by mid-June
1973 only some 66,000 metric tons had actually been delivered. Of
that, more than 30,000 metric tons had already been programmed
as part of the routine grain stabilization assistance and were thus
unrelated to the accelerated crisis perceived in November. Not
ordered until there was finally some specific bureaucratic attention
to the drought in autumn 1972, most of these first "emergency"
shipments were then tied up during the ensuing winter and spring in
what an official USAID memorandum termed "myriad obstacles to
getting the grain moved from the fields in the United States to the
recipients in Africa."

Several sources indicated that by the end of 1972, food aid to
the Sahel, as for other needy areas such as South Asia, was hampered
because large commercial purchases by the Soviet Union had already
absorbed transport capacities—and to a large degree, the available
grain. As a result of the Soviet transaction, a small crop, and
general instability in the U.S. market, the Agriculture Department
subsequently suspended purchases of grain for international food aid
during July and August 1973. USAID officials stressed that the sus-
pension did not then affect specific purchases for the Sahel. In the
fall of 1972, however, the delay in procuring and shipping relief
grains presented "a real problem," as one American ambassador in
a Sahelian country remembered the wait for food aid. "It seems that

grain for humanitarian relief always takes a back seat to cash purchases," he concluded.

Food aid was not the only relief conditioned by the belated planning in USAID. Over the winter of 1972-73, there were critical needs for animal feed and medicines to stem the annihilation of livestock, for vitamins and medical supplies for the debilitated population, for transport or shelter or blankets. Assistance of this kind might well have enabled the six countries to cope with suffering and disease before the calamity reached (again in the words of USAID documents) "devastating proportions" in February and March 1973. Yet it was not until that same winter that USAID began to design a plan of action for such aid. Even then, according to official memoranda, it was mid-April, "after numerous discussions in-Agency, and with other donors," before USAID cabled the U.S. embassies in the Sahel on the use of contingency funds for nonfood assistance. It was to be May 1973 before the agency obligated $1.9 million in relief other than for food for the six nations. As needs were recognized and relief planned, U.S. nonfood aid to the Sahel rose rapidly to more than $4.5 million by the end of June, with over half of it in the costs of the emergency airlifts in Chad and Mali, beginning in May.

Senior USAID officials later complained that the African states in the Sahel were slow to recognize the crisis. "They didn't fully realize the gravity of the situation immediately to the extent of making official declarations of disasters," said a policy maker. Several other observers agreed that the Sahelian governments seemingly ignored the worst effects of the drought.

U.S. officials had long understood the weaknesses in the ability of the African states to deal with the drought. The October study had warned explicitly of the schism between urban-based governments and the countryside. About U.S. diplomatic approaches to inform the Africans of the magnitude of the problems after November 1972, however, USAID officials were vague. Several internal documents show there was no concerted effort to alert the Africans. "We couldn't get access to the officials who had the information," complained one high-level source. "They were simply too busy or they had no data available." At the same time, an American ambassador recalled that at least one African government had been aware of the problem and "had its request [for help] in by October or November while some others didn't until March or sometimes later in the spring." "I started work notifying Washington in August 1972," he added. But when asked what had happened in USAID as a result of his August report, the ambassador replied, "Probably nothing." The insular character of administrative difficulties of African regimes would not explain the failure of a more experienced

and well-equipped officialdom in Washington to heed the warnings of
four years or to convey them with authority and urgency to the
victims.

Yet African confusion may have accounted in some sense for
a further pause within the American government even after a joint
meeting of Sahel ministers on March 23-26, 1973, had formally
pronounced the zone a disaster area and appealed for international
help. Under U.S. Foreign Service regulations, American ambassadors abroad may respond to tragedies in their host countries by
declaring them a "disaster area," thereby instantly releasing an
ambassador's relief fund of $25,000 and establishing the country's
eligibility to receive further USAID contingency assistance. In the
spring of 1973, amid widespread suffering in the Sahel, there seemed
needless delays between the African appeal for relief and the U.S.
declaration of these disasters. The U.S. embassy in Niger declared
a disaster March 27, a day after the meeting of Sahelian ministers.
But Mali was not made eligible for emergency funds until April 6,
Chad not until April 21, Upper Volta only on April 28. Mauritania,
later discovered to be one of the states worst hit, was not declared
a disaster area by U.S. officials until May 4. Senegal followed on
May 8. And for Mauritania, Senegal, and Niger, there was nearly
a week between the formal declaration and USAID's ostensibly
"automatic" obligation of ambassadorial contingency money.

Officials explained that U.S. ambassadors, usually anxious to
maintain untroubled relations with their hosts, are generally reluctant to declare disasters without the approval of the regime in the
country, regardless of the severity of the situation. "An ambassador
can declare a disaster no matter what the host government says," a
State Department desk officer explained, "but of course no ambassador would declare a disaster without chekcing with the government."
Both senior and middle-level officials were at a loss, however, to
account for the delays of one to five weeks in the declaration of
disaster in 1973, or the subsequent wait of one week for some embassies to receive emergency funds.

If there was diplomatic hesitation among some U.S. ambassadors in the area to designate the Sahel a disaster area, there was
nonetheless harsh criticism by State Department and embassy Foreign
Service officers of what was seen as inertia and red tape in USAID
in Washington as the missions attempted to secure relief for the
famine. Several sources describe how the American embassy in
Mali, perhaps the neediest of the Sahelian states, anticipated the
lack of contingency planning and data retrieval in USAID. Under
Ambassador Robert Blake, the mission began on its own initiative
early in 1972 to assemble the information that would eventually
unlock disaster relief in Washington. "They really forced the decision

in USAID," remarked one official reading the embassy's cables.
"All the substantive officers were sent off to different regions to do
extensive research, and they got data on grain supplies and even
such things as temperatures at air fields at different times of the
day." At that, say inside observers of this bureaucratic process,
there were several months of "intense" telegram exchanges between
the mission in Bamako and USAID, from autumn 1972 to spring 1973,
before a decision was made to meet embassy requests which included
an emergency airlift to ravaged areas not served by rail transport.
"For every foot-dragging objection from USAID," as one U.S. diplomat put it, "that embassy came up with an answer."

Its ambassador to Mali having won this lengthy bureaucratic
battle, the State Department then reportedly encouraged the other
five posts in the Sahel to take advantage of the precedent. "We sent
out a cable to all missions saying now's your chance, and get in your
requests even if they're lacking some data," recalled a desk officer.

Such were the unseen realities, according to many officials,
of the American reaction to the drought in 1972-73 in the absence of
systematic contingency planning. There was USAID in Washington
slowly, insistently, eking out its information needs in the midst of
a serious crisis. U.S. embassies in starving countries had to
maneuver to "force" help from their own government's relief agency.
Life-and-death matters in West Africa were transformed into—and
dependent upon—a bureaucratic jockeying for advantage in Washington.

The effects of the basic lack of readiness for the catastrophe
were self-reinforcing. In large measure, the apparent USAID reluctance to respond to embassy requests seems to have reflected
the fact that in the final months of fiscal year 1973—the critical
period in the worsening of the situation in the Sahel, from January
to June 1973—there was little money left in USAID emergency contingency funds. Just as there were no specific plans or targets for
drought relief prior to the end of 1972, and no contingency provision
for emergency grain purchases and transport before Soviet commercial purchases absorbed the market, there had been no particular
allowance for the Sahel in USAID disaster relief budgets for fiscal
year 1973—nor, for that matter even 1974. "USAID did have real
money problems," sympathized one official critic, citing other
disasters in 1972-73, "Nicaragua and the Philippines and Bangladesh
had drained the barrel."

According to one high-level officer involved in funding, there
were bureaucratic negotiations late in 1972 between USAID and the
White House Office of Management and Budget to seek more emergency money for the Sahel. "They had a real workout over there
last year," he recalled. Yet observers in the State Department
contend that such an initiative was perfunctory, if it took place at all.

Those sources say USAID saw its bureaucratic position steadily
eroding as a result of dwindling congressional appropriations for
foreign aid, the relative neglect of USAID programs (especially in
Africa) in the Nixon administration, and the overall weakness of the
foreign affairs bureaucracies with the concentration of policy-making
authority in the White House under Henry Kissinger. In this setting,
the agency was reportedly hesitant to press for additional budget
money, at least until the drought had gained public notoriety and
congressional sympathy. "They didn't feel for many reasons, that
they would go to the OMB level for funds," said one official who
followed USAID's decisions. "They felt they couldn't kick and scream."
Analysts in the Office of Management and Budget confirmed that there
was no USAID pressure for supplemental funds for fiscal year 1973.
But as suffering deepened in the Sahel in the spring of 1973, and
urgently needed American relief seemed inhibited by lack of money,
officials in Washington and the U.S. embassies in the area found
little consolation in USAID's time-honored bureaucratic strategy of
waiting on public and congressional concern to extract new appropriations. "Never have a disaster," one State Department expert
advised bitterly, "at the end of a fiscal year."

Even when a special authorization of relief money for the
Sahel was formally sponsored in June, it became a political football,
its amount apparently an arbitrary figure which some U.S. relief
officials at once judged to be insufficient. As part of an increasingly
visible administration response to news reports and rising public
concern about the drought, the new funds were originally planned,
according to official sources, to appear as a White House initiative.
But because the catastrophe in West Africa happened to coincide with
President Nixon's veto of other congressional money bills, including
funds for disaster relief within the United States, the assistance for
the Sahel was soon viewed by the White House as a politically damaging
contrast in presidential priorities between foreign and internal
spending. With its popular and congressional support already showing
signs of erosion by the Watergate scandal, the White House quietly
dropped the relief initiative as yet another potential liability. USAID
then encouraged Senator Hubert H. Humphrey (Minnesota Democrat)
and Congressman Charles Diggs (Michigan Democrat), chairmen of
the Subcommittees on Africa in the Senate and the House respectively,
to introduce a bill for the money. "Since the projected release [of
the relief proposal] followed closely on the heels of Nixon's veto of
the domestic disaster funding item," recalled one policy maker, "it
was decided that discretion at that point was the better part of valor,
so they gave it to Humphrey."

It would seem that USAID also "gave" to Senator Humphrey
the $30 million figure, though officials acknowledged later that this

amount could only have been a "rough estimate" given the rudimentary
state of U.S. planning and data in mid-1973. The amount was reportedly based in part, for instance, on projections of 1973-74 food
needs in the six countries of 500,000 metric tons. But the USAID
document that argued for this tonnage in June 1973 was a vivid
illustration of the imprecision, if not illogic, of the projection. This
figure "seems defensible," read the official memorandum, "because
imports at this level plus local production has apparently been sufficient to sustain human life, albeit at an unadequate (sic) level."
For the 100,000 who perished in the Sahel and the two million nomads
starved into refugee camps, the level had indeed been "unadequate."
An international food survey mission to the Sahel, sponsored by the
United Nations, would report in November 1973 that the region needed
some 660,000 metric tons of food through September 1974.

 "It will get us back to point zero," one senior USAID official
remarked of the $30 million amount, "which is nothing too great."
His colleague quickly added, "I don't think it will even do that when
you consider the damage done to livestock." In any case, the capricious politics and random character of this funding process were yet
another outcome of the failures in early warning and contingency
planning. Assuming USAID overcame its bureaucratic inhibitions in
approaching budget officials, the agency might have gone to the
Congress for a more carefully estimated supplemental relief bill
before the Sahel became hostage to White House politics. But none
of that was possible without planning. "We never put together a
package," said a high-ranking USAID officer. "To put together such
a package, you better be sure that you can justify it. This means
data [and] the first overall development needs were being assessed
only last summer [1972]."

 Together, the absence of pre-crisis planning and the lack of
contingency funds had immediate practical effects on the initial U.S.
response to the drought in May and June 1973. When the FAO asked
the United States in late May to airlift 1,000 metric tons of sorghum
and millet seed from the Sudan to Chad, USAID refused the request,
citing both a shortage of funds and lack of information. "We do not
have FY73 disaster relief funds available for this purpose," replied
the USAID cable to Rome. The telegram went on to enumerate the
other "major reasons" for the rejection: no information on how the
seeds would be used or on logistics such as runway conditions and
navigational aids, the absence of specific requests for seeds by U.S.
embassies in the area as distinct from the FAO observers, and a
number of "other unanswered logistic questions."

 To the USAID bureaucrats receiving the seed request, the
proposal for an airlift somehow seemed preposterous. On the margin
of the original FAO telegram, one official scribbled to another a telling

note: "Nehemiah [a senior FAO official] has got to be kidding."
Unfortunately, he was not. As the October USAID study had warned,
the drought had devastated the entire agricultural economy. Again,
the FAO study mission was to report in November 1973 the exhaustion of seed supplies and recommend establishing "a revolving
stock of seed supplies totaling more than 36,000 tons." Later, in
June, USAID would contribute $300,000 to the FAO, which went to
support the airlift of seeds from Sudan to Chad by FAO-chartered
aircraft. But in the spring of 1973, the United States was unprepared
to respond directly to this urgent request for help in the Sahel. On
June 8, 1973, five years after drought had begun to ravage the area,
nine months after the FAO had sounded its early warning of disaster,
a USAID cable to its missions in the region requested what it called
"some evidence [of] minimum programming input." As millions
faced starvation, with little more than one-third of promised U.S.
relief food having arrived by surface transport, the cable asked
with no apparent irony, "when and where are shortages of grain
projected, and why do shortages exist?"

Looking back on these episodes, some officials saw the lack of
readiness as reinforcing a natural caution and inertia in the USAID
bureaucracy. Explaining the failure of the State Department to spur
earlier action on the drought in 1972, one diplomat summed up the
crucial factor: "USAID had their data excuse." But other sources,
including several in USAID, say that the refusal of the seed airlift also
reflected a long-standing bureaucratic feud between at least some
sections of USAID and the FAO. When the FAO appealed in May for
cash donations to a Sahelian Trust Fund, for example, the USAID
reaction was decidedly unenthusiastic. "We had no intention of putting
anything in it," commented one USAID policy maker about the FAO
fund. "We knew it was going to be bungled." According to the same
source, the later $300,000 U.S. contribution to the fund was a
bureaucratic mistake, the product of an unauthorized promise made
to the FAO by a U.S. relief official visiting Rome. "We let it go
through," said the source, harshly critical of the "incompetents" in
other USAID offices who had advocated the contribution. This was
apparently the last slip of its kind. By September 1973, nearly
twenty countries, a number of nongovernmental organizations, and
various United Nations agencies had contributed over $13 million to
the Trust Fund. But the U.S. contribution remained at the initial
$300,000, out of a total of more than $6 million for U.S. nonfood
assistance to the Sahel. The figures on American drought relief
also indicate that Washington could have contributed much more to
the trust fund or to the airlift of seeds even in the face of limited
contingency relief funds available to USAID that spring. Even though
by May 1973 the United States had committed less than $2 million in

nonfood aid to the Sahel, it would eventually spend $4.6 million on such aid before the close of fiscal 1973 on June 30.

There has been no evidence thus far of what U.S. officials feared as "bungling" in the FAO Trust Fund. On the contrary, it has provided valuable help to the Sahel, and acted as a convenient mechanism for contributions from countries not previously involved in aid to the area. However, even FAO's own officials point to discernible weaknesses in its capacity to anticipate and organize a major disaster relief operation. Although clearly aware of the poor harvest and cumulative desolation in the area in September, 1972, the vast FAO bureaucracy in Rome did not act on the gravity of the situation for months afterward. It was not until February 1973 that the FAO established its "working group" on the drought, some three months after the United States began to "study" the calamity. It would be May before the FAO's director-general requested of the U.N. secretary general a "mobilization" of the United Nations system. The organization's early warning system, concluded one senior FAO official, had been at best, "informal, inadequate and ineffective."

The FAO effort seems, in fact, to mirror most of the problems evident in USAID's handling of the crisis. The stream of reports from the Sahel went largely unheeded over five years. The headquarters bureaucracy was unready with specific contingency plans or funds. The FAO confronted one of the most massive disasters in its history with what amounted to a series of improvisations. By the spring of 1973 FAO would have, as one of its officials acknowledged, "no hard statistical data of any kind" on the actual needs of the area. "We have perhaps just an estimation of the percentage of the population affected," said the same FAO official, "but [there was] no effort to make such an assessment beyond an informal ad hoc nature." Thus, when USAID insisted on precise data to support the seed airlift request in May, FAO could not supply the information that both it and USAID might have gathered in the months and years as both bureaucracies watched the drought deepen. The principal difference between the FAO and USAID seems to have been less in bureaucratic execution than in a general policy approach to the crisis once it was clearly recognized. When Rome finally recognized the powerful human reasons to respond to the drought—evidence of mass exodus and suffering, if not precise data on airfields and needs—the FAO chose to act forcefully on issues such as the seed airlift, while USAID hesitated.

The more important point, however, is that neither of the major organizations engaged in drought relief in the Sahel since 1968 was able to forecast and stave off the worst effects of the catastrophe. Though they were in a position to coordinate their actions, to mount a concerted effort enlisting the best specialized contributions of both

donors and recipients under the acceptable political umbrella of the
UN, they could not—or, in any case, did not.

The results of this failure were apparent when journalists
visited a refugee camp outside Timbuktu late in the summer of 1973.
There they found nomad children in the advanced stages of malnutrition. No longer able to digest solid foods, the children were doomed
to die without a special milk ration designed to reverse the process
of edema. It was all a familiar cycle, explained a young French
doctor to the reporters. Edema had struck down hungry and long-
weakened children in the same way in Biafra and Bangladesh and so
many other places. "But don't you have the milk by now?" a visitor
asked. "No," said the doctor looking at the long row of children,
"it has not arrived yet and will not be here in time for them."

But edema of this kind was not to be the worst killer in the
famine. U.S. Public Health experts surveying the starvation in July
and August would find that many more casualties had come, ironically,
from a childhood disease that had been almost eradicated in the
region a few years earlier—measles. Exhausted by hunger and their
long exodus, crowded together in squalid settlements, many of the
younger children of the nomads died of measles while vaccine was
still being shipped.

It was in these tragedies that the failure of contingency planning
by the relief bureaucracies became a human reality. There might
have been a systematic gathering and analysis of data from the Sahel,
and planning for the relief of the area based on experience in other
disasters. Needs might have been identified in advance of the fateful
winter of 1972-73. Special milk rations might have been available
in the camps as the starving nomad children trekked in. A measles
immunization program might have been among the preventive steps
taken in the fall, or even as the camps filled the following spring.
There might have been stores of seeds and grain ready to move with
the FAO early warning in September 1972. There might have been
an international mechanism to alert the Sahelian governments to their
plight, and to mobilize their limited resources before the disaster
became overwhelming. There might have been plans to ship emergency relief before rail cars, grain elevators, and ships were tied
up with the Soviet wheat purchases or relief for other disasters.
And there might have been relief funds planned, avoiding the political
snares into which the added American relief contribution fell in 1973.
But despite the five years of warning and the millions of dollars in
relief that preceded the crisis of 1972-73, these opportunities were
all lost.

"Harsh lessons can be drawn from the massive famine now
facing six sub-Saharan countries," editorialized the Wall Street
Journal on July 10, "but the grimmest of all is that relatively routine

relief measures, taken months ago, might have considerably reduced
this disaster." In retrospect the editorial seems accurate—except,
perhaps, for one important point. By all official accounts, the
"measures" that might have been taken—the planning and organization—were scarcely routine for the USAID, FAO, or African bureaucracies. The neglect, the inertia, the delays, the red tape, the
institutional short-sightedness—all these bore the stamp of bureaucratic routine. It was the "routine" of the present system of international relief that fixed the conditions of the halting and sometimes
tragically belated response to the drought in 1972-73.

AN UNSYSTEMATIC SYSTEM

By mid-summer 1973, the international drought relief effort
begun in the spring had become a massive and highly publicized
rescue operation. Through American and European media, the
world saw not only the images of suffering, the emaciated nomads
and dead cattle, but also the scenes of mercy, the hills of food rising
on West African docks, or the lines of refugees receiving their ration
of American-donated grain. Moreover, the relief effort appeared
visibly free of the political or military problems that had obstructed
international help to the victims of other recent disasters resulting
from civil strife in Burundi, Biafra, or Bangladesh. The stricken
African states were imploring the outside world for help and the
donors were responding. On June 20, the White House released a
letter from President Nixon to U.N. Secretary General Waldheim
enumerating the impressive quality of U.S. help and pledging that
"the United States stands prepared to commit further resources as
needs are identified."

In late July representatives from the Sahel, major donors and
private relief agencies met in West Africa. Following that meeting,
FAO officials would tell the press that "the threat of famine in sub-
Saharan Africa is under control." From that briefing the Associated
Press reported in a widely printed story that "United Nations officials
said it was doubtful that large numbers of people had died from starvation, although several thousand had reportedly died from diseases
such as cholera and measles . . . ." The officials added, the dispatch
went on, "that it was impossible to say how many had died because
. . . communications are poor within the countries affected." But
there would be no "massive starvation deaths." As these accounts
appeared worldwide, USAID and U.N. sources began to provide
similar private briefings to the Congress and press in Washington.

In the Sahel, however, there was a harsher reality. Overwhelming an unprepared transport system, the piles of food were
consumed by waste and wharf rats as well as hungry people. Many
who did eat food sent from the United States were soon weakened
further by violent diarrhea because their systems could not digest
the coarse sorghum. Not all starving people in refugee camps,
particularly the nomads, were actually given the supposedly lifesaving
rations. And early in August, as optimistic reports began to appear
in the American press, there was preliminary scientific evidence
in the U.S. government—the first results of a systematic study of
nutrition in the drought-ravaged area—that fatalities in the Sahel
would be high. The study showed clusters of nomad children suffering
malnutrition levels more severe than those recorded in the famine in
Bangladesh.

Yet there seems little outright deception in the disparity between
this official optimism and conditions in West Africa. By their own
accounts, U.S. and U.N. relief officials were simply not informed
about what was happening as millions of dollars and thousands of tons
of food poured into the Sahel in 1973. The intelligence they did
receive—such as the nutrition survey—was communicated among the
various elements of the relief effort only in a most haphazard manner.
For a number of reasons, reports which were made to the press, and
even to the President of the United States, omitted major problems
obstructing the rescue operations and important data on the severity
of the disaster. Much as the relief bureaucracies were unready to
react to the drought before it became a catastrophe, they were also
largely unprepared to monitor the effectiveness and equity of the
massive relief once it began to flow.

Problems in monitoring the progress of relief began with the
lack of a detailed picture of the transport capabilities of the stricken
countries. That ignorance was yet another price of the failure to plan.
In 1969 and 1970, three separate studies prepared for USAID by outside
consultants had stressed the primitive character of most of the rail-
ways and roads in the region. The capacity of the area to support any
unusual traffic was simply unknown. But it was not until January 30,
1973, that USAID sent a two-man team to the area to survey how the
African facilities could absorb the thousands of tons of emergency
grain shipments then contemplated. Instructed "to review port and
inland transportation capabilities," the team apparently visited only
West African ports. Its report, filed in late February, established
ton-per-month capabilities for each port, though mainly on the basis
of the volume of rail traffic in January carrying the shipments inland.
Nothing in the report warned of future shortages, or of potential problems when rail traffic was increased.

The report recorded, for example, 2,500 tons per month as the
then manageable cargo capacity from the port of Dakar in Senegal to
Kayes, a distribution point for relief in Mali. Five months later,
FAO officials would estimate Mali's needs at 20,000 tons monthly,
a figure subsequently confirmed by U.S. experts. Yet in August
1973, the railway to Mali would be found to carry at most 10,000
tons per month. As a result, in the summer of 1973 there was at
once too little and too much grain for Mali. As shipments to Mali
fell short, tons of grain piled up on the docks of Dakar. "The rats
feed well at Dakar," cabled a reporter to The Guardian on July 24.
"Some of those stocks will still be on the wharves in November," he
wrote of the transport tie-up, "if the rats—the only fat animals I
saw in West Africa—leave any at all." At mid-August senior USAID
relief officials had not seen the Guardian dispatch.

Another USAID-sponsored transport survey of the Sahel was
undertaken from July 19 to August 23, this time by a six-person team
drawn from the Department of Agriculture and the U.S. Air Force
as well as from USAID. The report revealed the obvious deficit in
shipments from Dakar to Mali, and recommended emergency truck
transport from the Ivory Coast. It also reported that U.S. C-130
aircraft flying in Mali had been grounded due to mechanical problems.
This second transport survey warned of the prospect of fuel shortages
plaguing the airlift as well. "It is understood that measures are being
taken to increase the fuel availability," the team reported. A month
later, Thomas Johnson of the New York Times reported from Mali
that the American planes had been grounded again, by fuel shortages.

Exactly what was shipped was to be as important as how much
and by what means. And here too there were few signs of planning
and only an accidental monitoring. In its report, the January-February
transport survey team had sounded an almost accidental warning.
"The team noticed in examining cargo at Dakar, Senegal," they wrote,
"that a considerable amount of foreign material was visible through
the polypropylene bags. Recognizing that Number 2 sorghum is
basically animal feed it is suggested that an effort be made to reduce
the percentage of foreign materials as this cargo is programmed for
human consumption."

There is no evidence of what reaction, if any, this observation
stirred in USAID. Months afterward, many officials seemed genuinely
surprised by an August 18 Washington Post report from Timbuktu that
nomads were unable to digest American-donated sorghum and "diarrhea
is rampant." The sorghum problem seems to have been some combination of two factors. Although sorghum has often been part of the
diet for some sedentary farmers in the region, the coarseness of
this grain made it inedible for humans. Moreover, the pastoral
people were accustomed to a high-protein diet of meat and dairy

products. But again, as USAID waited until the crisis had reached
staggering proportions to take stock of the erratic transport capacity
in the Sahel, so, too, no one in the relief bureaucracy apparently
bothered to consider the dietary habits of the people whom the millions
of tons of hastily purchased grain were to nurture—let alone whether
any human being could stomach sorghum American farmers fed their
animals. It was left to the first transport survey team to happen upon
this grotesque mistake. Even then, the problem apparently remained
unredressed for months.

The quality of relief rations reportedly mattered little, however,
to many of the starving nomads awaiting the food in refugee camps
or on the outskirts of villages. Late in July, and some sources say
earlier, USAID began to receive random reports from journalists
and private relief workers that there was blatant discrimination in
the distribution of relief supplies. "The pastoralists are getting
short-changed," said one U.S. official summarizing an August 1
cable from an American embassy in the Sahel. "There are disputes
between them and the farmers, and the farmers are getting the
grain."

The disputes were rooted, as many academic and official
experts knew, in the historic suspicion and enmity between the
sedentary agricultural peoples of the Sahel and the fiercely proud,
independent nomadic tribes. The two races and cultures had often
clashed before the colonial period. Even after independence, the
nomads remained largely beyond the administrative reach of the
modern African regimes, whose political base was in the villages
and cities. When drought drove the nomads into sedentary areas,
it left them at the mercy of people, themselves suffering, who regarded the pastoral tribes at best as troublesome aliens, at worst
as enemies.

All this was understood by USAID and State Department officials.
"We knew from the French and our own experience that there was a
major north-south, nomad versus sedentary problem," said one
American official. "No love was lost," remarked a senior USAID
officer. Yet as the distribution of food became the responsibility of
local or provincial African officials, some in areas of the deepest
historical rivalry between farmers and pastoralists, there would be
no provision in the international relief effort even to observe—let
alone ensure—equitable handling of the emergency rations. No im-
partial monitors, either African or international, were in the camps
or villages. Only late in the summer of 1973 did the reports of bias
filter back to USAID in Washington. By autumn, the U.S. Public
Health nutrition survey would document a shocking contrast between
the nutritional state of sedentary victims of the drought and the deep
starvation of the nomads. For a time, the difference might be

explained by the relatively poorer condition of many pastoralists as
they trekked to settlements. But the nutritional deficiency of the
nomads continued, sometimes in the same camps where sedentary
peoples were in much better condition on ostensibly identical rations.

"The nomads are being wiped out," concluded one USAID policy
maker by October. But many U.S. and FAO officials were clearly
reluctant to confront the issue of discrimination out of concern for
relations with the African regimes in the Sahel. "I can't give you the
information I have," said one State Department analyst, "because it
would have disastrous effects on our relations with these governments." The same USAID officials who were anxious that American
embassies in the Sahel provide precise details on airlift requests
somehow were uninterested in pinning down perhaps fatal discrimination against the pastoralists. "I honestly don't know [about discrim-
ination]," said one senior USAID relief policy maker in mid-August,
though other sources confirm that several such reports had by then
crossed his desk. "I'm sure that it's being dealt with by someone . . .
we've left it to our ambassadors . . . they know the local political
situation."

As relief supplies gathered in West Africa and the contributions
mounted over $100 million from more than twenty donors, there was
no coordinated effort from any quarter to identify and cope with problems such as the bias against pastoralists. Of the USAID monitoring
attempts, one policy maker quickly acknowledged, "It's an unsys-
tematic system . . . we make use of whoever the hell is on the
ground." A Foreign Service officer following the relief operation
commented simply, "The monitoring is inadequate and incomplete."
Officials indicated that monitoring responsibilities lay with the African
government, yet cautioned no bureaucracy could reasonably be expected to perform, in effect, an objective assessment of its own
efforts or political decisions. USAID apparently relied heavily on
reports of journalists, missionaries, or other observers from the
area, anyone who had visited affected areas or refugee camps.

U.N. officials recount that the FAO efforts to monitor relief
were similarly vague and random. "Our information is highly subjective," said one FAO official. "We have no hard statistical data
of any kind," added an FAO official responsible for coordination of
the organization's program with other governments. "There was no
estimate, or perhaps just an estimate, of the percentage of the population affected, but [there was] no effort to make such an assessment
beyond an informal ad hoc nature." FAO sources said they too were
dependent for information about relief on random reports of journalists,
pilots, "or anyone on the scene." Asked if the FAO had considered
the potential or existing problems of feeding grain to nomads in Mali
accustomed to milk and beef, a senior organization officer answered

only, "No." The FAO was studying, the official said, the "findings" of an American television crew that had recently visited refugee camps in Mali and Niger.

The bureaucratic results of this official myopia on the relief effort were hidden from public view—the lack of any systematic basis for planning further relief, the unrecognized waste and injustices, the accounting for lives, food, and money that would never be possible. But the information gap became visible as officials in Washington or New York began to speak publicly on the basis of such scanty official intelligence on the drought. On August 1, for example, Under-Secretary General Bradford Morse would tell a group of U.S. congressional aides, in the presence of responsible USAID officials, that, as one listener remembered, "the threat of famine is under control." Stories echoing that statement followed within days in both the New York Times and Washington Post. But almost immediately afterward, there came a counterstatement from the League of Red Cross Societies in Geneva (LICROSS), citing 12 million "severely affected" drought victims with no end of the crisis in sight. It seems clear both statements were made in good faith, each from an effort to convey to the public and concerned legislatures an accurate picture of reality in the Sahel. But it seems equally clear, according to a wide number of official and private relief sources, that neither statement was based on reliable data. If "mass" starvation (no more than 100,000 deaths?) had in fact been under control on August 1, neither the FAO nor USAID had a system to yield that judgment with certainty. And both should have known—as at least many of their officials did know—that they lacked such knowledge.

In fact, as officials spoke their claims, scientific data was accumulating on the extent of malnutrition in the Sahel and on the areas of most severe need. A reliable computation of the death rate in the drought was made and evidence of the incidence of drought-related diseases piled up. But an added casualty of the disarray of the relief effort, however, that information would go largely unnoticed for the next four months.

THE NUTRITIONAL SURVEY

There are conflicting bureaucratic versions of how the nutritional survey originated. Various USAID offices claimed that it began at their request, one of the results of the autumn study group. Much evidence suggests, though, that the initiative belonged to the Public Health Service itself. In February 1973, as the first press reports began to appear on yet another bad harvest in the Sahel,

American doctors at the Center for Disease Control in Atlanta drafted a formal recommendation that the United States sponsor a survey of existing and potential malnutrition in the area, particularly the susceptibility of the population to disease. Their proposal was a natural outgrowth of an ongoing project at CDC on the epidemiology of famine, a study of the spread and control of starvation based on both historical research into great recorded disasters—the blockade of Leningrad, the Irish potato famine, the starvation in the western Netherlands in 1945—and firsthand observation in recent catastrophes in cases such as Biafra and Bangladesh. Many of the CDC physicians and technicians were also involved in the U.S. smallpox and measles eradication programs in West Africa in the mid and late 1960s, bringing to the drought singular experience in the area as well as in the general subject of famine.

Yet, by all accounts, this extraordinary resource was brought to bear on the tragedy of 1972-73 almost by chance. No early warning had mobilized the experience in CDC, summoned its recommendations, or automatically shared its expertise with the governments of the Sahel about to feel the full force of the disaster. The Public Health doctors had not been included in USAID's November study group. Nor had they received regular official reports from USAID or the FAO on the Sahel. Sources remember that the CDC experts in Atlanta gleaned most of their information on the current crisis from returning colleagues and "usually the New York Times." But by February 1973 even these fragmentary signs were clear enough.

The doctors proposed a survey of samples of the population in four of the six Sahelian states—Mali, Mauritania, Niger, and Upper Volta—based on an authoritative medical research technique using comparative measurements of the proportion of weight to height. Employed in Bangladesh, the weight-height survey is regarded as providing a reliable index of malnutrition among a given population. Those falling below a designated borderline, 80 percent of median weight for height, were found to be badly undernourished, or below what CDC called the "acute malnutrition threshold." The median standard took into account relative differences in the nutrition and stature of various populations due to traditional diets, and thus measured malnutrition relative to the customary health of a given group, rather than as an arbitrary standard. In March 1973, a memorandum urging such a survey in the Sahel duly wound its way from Atlanta, through the CDC's parent Washington bureaucracy in the Department of Health, Education and Welfare toward USAID. "We had our own bureaucratic protocol to observe," said one of the participants in the survey. "But by the time the memo got through, the crisis was on us."

Whatever the origins of the CDC survey, it too was belated. The first U.S. doctors arrived in West Africa only in late June and and early July, with the first summary report issued July 20. Over the next eight weeks, in nine reports, the survey clinically recorded a portrait of the calamity in the Sahel. This gathering evidencè, duly sent to USAID, was sometimes in sharp contrast to the official public optimism of the same period.

On July 30, the survey reported measles cases in Mauritania during the first quarter of 1973 as three to fourteen times greater than previous quarters. One in every ten stricken children was dying. On August 6, the survey reported areas of Upper Volta where malnutrition was more severe than that measured in 1972 in Bangladesh. On August 13, the doctors found nomadic camps in Mali where 70 percent of the children were below the "acute malnutrition threshold," as compared to 11.6 percent in the historic famine in Bangladesh. Sedentary villages had 47 percent below the threshold. Throughout the Gao Cercle, a large affected area in Mali, the survey found the people to be on a "starvation diet" of less than 400 calories daily. In Mauritania, the same report documented acute malnutrition rates of 18 percent, 25 percent, and 22 percent in various villages and camps.

On August 20, the survey reported that "food supplies are nearly depleted in Mauritania," "food distribution is erratic" in Niger, and from Upper Volta that "food distribution vehicles are no longer able to reach" three villages whose children were suffering high rates of malnutrition. In one of those villages, said the report, "no food distribution has taken place since June, and the villagers' diet has consisted primarily of leaves and roots."

By August 27, the Public Health experts reported from Mali that "very few young children have been immunized" against measles, despite rising incidence and deaths. And from Mauritania, as in other countries, the survey found that, "in all areas, a striking contrast in nutritional status between nomadic camps and sedentary populations has been observed, even when both groups live in the same cities." The figures from Mauritanian villages and camps were telling. For one area, 3 percent of sedentary farmers was below the threshold, 30 percent of the nomads were acutely malnourished. In another sector, 11 percent of village children were below the borderline, as against 17 percent of the pastoralist children. For still another, there was 10 percent malnutrition among farmers' children, 52 percent among the children of nomads. Again, the report warned of poor food supply: "In all of the areas surveyed it was found that while the Mauritanian government distribution system is relatively effective, its effectiveness is severely hampered by a lack of adequate quantities of food." This while British reporters found grain fattening rats on the docks in Dakar, Senegal.

On August 31, the survey reported one nomad camp of 10,000
near Timbuktu where nearly 75 percent of the children surveyed fell
below the threshold, almost seven times worse than the malnutrition
recorded in Bangladesh. More hopefully, the report indicated that
death rates in the camp, earlier estimated at 182 to 365 per 1,000,
were judged to have been reduced to 10 to 16 per 1,000, or below the
normal annual crude death rate for Mali.

On September 10, the survey reported once again the "provision
of food extremely difficult" in Mauritania, with areas still suffering
high rates of malnutrition. By September 14, in concluding the survey,
the U.S. doctors returned to five villages in Mali's Gao Cercle they
had visited during July, but still measured some 40 percent of the
children below the malnutrition threshold. The Public Health teams
then returned to Atlanta to correlate and analyze their data for a final
report on the nutritional state of the four countries.

In the Sahel, the survey had some immediate effect. The
governments of Upper Volta and Mauritania urgently diverted relief
shipments to feed areas in desperate need. "Almost all the [African]
ministers of health made changes in feeding and transportation,"
recalled one of the experts. For the Africans, of course, this was
the first authoritative information they had received on the actual
human impact of the drought on specific areas and elements of their
population. In the vast multimillion dollar relief effort, with literally
hundreds of foreign "specialists" in the area for five years, it would
be the only planned, coherent appraisal of starvation, food distribution,
and the threat of disease.

In Washington, however, the survey seemed less appreciated,
if noticed at all. Some USAID experts apparently understood the
ominous implications of some of the findings. "That data can predict
the nutritional state for the overall nomad population," said one
analyst of the high malnutrition rates recorded from the refugee
camps. For a bureaucracy admittedly dependent on the random reports
of journalists for its intelligence on the drought, the CDC survey
might have been eagerly received, as the basis for current policy
as well as middle- and long-term planning. It was not. Though the
regular reports filed through Atlanta were sent to USAID's foreign
disaster relief coordinator, many USAID officials, including ironically
enough the offices of health and nutrition, had not even heard of the
survey by late August. Responsible officials in USAID's Africa
Bureau seemed ignorant or indifferent regarding the survey findings.

Not surprisingly in this context, there was no systematic effort
to distribute the reports beyond USAID. By September, the responsible
official for African affairs on the National Security Council staff in
the White House had never heard of the survey. As late as November
1973, five months after it was begun, officials working intensively on

the drought at the United Nations in New York were unaware of the reports. "I haven't seen it, what is it?" asked one U.N. official, whose main source of data on the Sahel had been U.S. and British press clippings.

For the FAO, supposedly a central coordinating institution for drought relief, the story was similar. The FAO Washington liaison office was told of the existence of the survey and its potential importance by the authors of this report in August. Asked early in October what had been done with the data, an FAO official replied, "I think I called them and got on their mailing list . . . I really don't know whether it went to Rome—or stayed here . . . it was fairly pertinent information, but I really don't know." In late November, the FAO would call the Carnegie Endowment to ask the meaning of the final CDC report. "I've got this document on my desk and it seems to be relevant data," said the official, "but what is it, and who sent it?"

The failure in communication was at all levels. Though CDC knew above all the importance of the data in human terms, it apparently made no special bureaucratic effort to ensure proper distribution. "We hope they [the findings] have some impact," said one Public Health official, "but we can't guarantee it." USAID had no mechanism to analyze and act on the reports as they came in, much less see that the international relief effort—the United Nations in New York, FAO in Rome and West Africa, other donors, or even the Africans themselves—was systematically informed. Many who did receive the reports, say a number of sources, apparently lacked the knowledge or time or inclination to grasp their meaning. For the functioning of the international relief effort, however, the precise reasons for the communications failure seem less important than the fact that it happened so completely.

The day after CDC's fifth report from the Sahel—with evidence in hand of extreme malnutrition and dwindling food supply in many areas, of unmistakable discrimination against nomads in relief distribution, of famine more acute in some regions than in Bangladesh—USAID released to the press a formal report on the drought sent to President Nixon from relief coordinator Maurice Williams. According to USAID officials, there was no further classified section of the memorandum. The version made public was the complete report given to the President. That memorandum embodied much of the confusion and official self-deception that had grown out of the basic failure to plan and monitor the Sahelian relief effort. Whether the product of ignorance or oversight, the report showed the relief bureaucracy unable to compose a candid, accurate picture of the crisis even for its own chief executive.

The memorandum began with the dramatic assertion that
"mass famine—which threatened millions some weeks ago—has been
averted." That claim was based on a calculation that the "625,000
tons of food already delivered or on the way" (emphasis added) "is
adequate to meet basic calorie needs and avoid widespread starvation
throughout the next sixty days before the harvest." USAID officials
admitted later, however, that their calculations of relief distribution
as and against calorie needs had been (not surprisingly, given their
internal information) "very rough." "They're not very proud of it,"
said a senior USAID policy maker of the estimates made by the
drought desk.

The USAID calculations underlying the claim to the President
have not been made public, but it seems clear they were based on
an assumption that drought victims were receiving a maximum relief
allowance of 10 kilograms of grain per person each month. Yet the
CDC team—the only systematic survey of the distribution system then
or later—had nowhere found relief consistently at 10 kilograms, and
in most locations it was at best 5 kilograms per person monthly.
Moreover, even assuming the maximum delivery—and it could only
have been a USAID assumption—the basic calorie yield from the
sorghum (presuming one could digest "animal feed") and millet would
be less than the internationally recognized "basic calorie needs" of
small children as well as adults.

The CDC survey, for example, would record a sedentary village
of 400 people in Niger receiving some 4,700 kilograms of grain during
a 31-day period. ("Nomads in the same area," observed the team,
"received one bowl of powdered milk.") But that 4,700 kilograms,
assuming equitable distribution among the sedentary victims, would
provide less than one-half the calorie needs of a male adult, and only
two-thirds of a female adult. In Mali's Gao Cercle, the teams found
camps with a 400-calorie-a-day ration, in Mauritania settlements
receiving about 560 calories daily—compared to "basic calorie needs"
of 1,250 for children, 2,800 for male adults, and 2,000 for female
adults. Whatever its origin, whatever the "rough" arithmetic, USAID's
calculations of meeting needs in the Sahel scarcely reflected the only
hard stistical data available on the subject.

The memo did go on to say that there were "pockets of severe
malnutrition" (apparently a reference to the areas surveyed by CDC)
and observed "the four years of drought that preceded present emergency relief efforts had a cumulative weakening effect." There was
no explanation, of course, of why that "cumulative" process had not
been dealt with more vigorously before it had become the "present
emergency."

Of the bureaucratic rivalries and deadly African political problems that shrouded the relief effort, the President and American public

were allowed no glimpse. The FAO, which USAID suspected of "bungling" and believed to be inefficient in planning or monitoring, was described in the memo "as doing a fine job." So were the Africans, "responsible for the final distribution of food . . . doing a remarkable job under difficult circumstances." There was no word in the report of the gathering evidence of discrimination against the nomads, of the cables that "couldn't be shown," or of the harsh contrasts in CDC reports between children in the same camps assigned to live or die by the accident of birth. "Our response has been timely and effective," concluded the memo, "and has been in the great humanitarian tradition of America to help people sustain their lives in the face of catastrophic disasters beyond their control."

The memorandum for the President referred to the ongoing CDC survey almost in passing. There were U.S. epidemiologists in the Sahel, it said, "to guide special medical and food relief efforts" and to identify "pockets of acute nutritional and medical distress for special attention." But the impression was that the teams were only one more "special" effort among many, with no general significance for the drought or relief policy. Nearly three months later, in November 1973, after some six weeks of reportedly heated bureaucratic efforts by USAID to expunge certain sections, the Public Health Service produced its final report on the nutritional survey. Far from the incidental activity described to the President, the survey represented, in its own words, "the most objective data received to date on the nutritional status of populations living in the drought affected zone in West Africa." Also appended to this study, the CDC summary reemphasized and enlarged upon the findings of the nine periodic reports. It was a very different view of reality than USAID's self-congratulatory memorandum to the White House.

Summary data confirmed again the disparity between nomads and sedentary farmers. Of 3,500 children measured, "children from nomad clusters ranged on the average 10 to 17 percent below the threshold while those from sedentary or southern groups were approximately 3 to 7 percent below." These figures were, said the report, "conservative, since they do not take into account the large number of children whose weight for height values fall very close to the malnutrition threshold, but are nonetheless above it."

The survey found that a major killer in the drought had been measles. And again, the nomads had suffered enormously. In Niger, the survey found "deaths attributed by villagers to measles and/or famine accounted for 73 percent of the total among sampled nomads as opposed to 32 percent of the total among sampled sedentary peoples." Most of the victims, of course, had been children. "A well-planned measles immunization campaign among these groups," concluded the U.S. doctors, "could have reduced measles morbidity and mortality." The report went on:

Nomad populations, camped near urban centers,
could be vaccinated more conveniently than ever
before. However, past experience has demonstrated
the importance of maintaining low levels of sus-
ceptibles through the continued immunization of
newborns. A contributing factor in the current
measles epidemic is the large reservoir of susceptible children which accumulated following a
decrease in emphasis on measles immunization
after the mass vaccination campaigns recently conducted in West Africa.

It was this stinging indictment of USAID's lack of planning,
albeit delivered in almost oblique bureaucratic rhetoric, that had
delayed the USAID "clearance" of the CDC summary for several
weeks. The measles epidemic had been all too clear, even in public
documents released in mid-summer. A State Department press
release in July had stated: "Malnutrition is responsible for increasing
the death rate from measles in Mali and Niger." A UNICEF memorandum dated July 21 reported that "measles has reappeared in
epidemic form in the affected areas," and indicated that a request
for vaccine was "under consideration" in USAID. And the agency, as
the report to the President duly noted, had "promptly sent 370,000
doses of vaccine to the region." But the inescapable point of the CDC
findings was that the critical period had indeed been much earlier,
in the winter and spring before the epidemics began among famished
children. The most telling word in the CDC memo was "planned."
        For weeks, USAID was "adamant," as one participant put it, that
the CDC passage on measles be deleted from the final report. But the
Public Health experts were apparently equally forceful. "We will not
make any accommodations in the substance of the report in order to
make certain individuals in USAID more comfortable," said a CDC
source. "That's an ethical and professional position from which we
can't and will not deviate." Late in November, the summary was
completed—with the conclusion that the measles deaths might have
been avoided.
        The CDC summary report contained other striking findings as
well. The epidemiologists estimated "the maximum number of deaths
due to famine this year" at 101,000 for four of the six countries. It
was much less than many had feared, and only a fraction of the
"millions" mentioned in early sensational press accounts of the
tragedy. Yet in proportional terms, for the 2 million nomads and
the 22 million of the entire region, it was clearly a human disaster
of cruel magnitude.

Country by country, the CDC final data was a measure of the depth of the catastrophe beyond the death rate. In Mauritania, "famine can be considered as adversely affecting the majority of this nation's people," with more than a threefold increase in measles for 1973 over 1971. "Not enough food is available for distribution by the government," the CDC found in Mauritania, a fact omitted from USAID reports on the country. Most ominously for the future, the teams found by interviewing nomads that 66 percent "would remain in or near the cities even if they had animals again." The drought had not only ravaged the land, but had also wrought a social revolution, creating a new rootless mass in urban areas with which the overwhelmed regimes could hardly deal, if at all.

For Niger, measles had gone from 2,886 cases in 1971 to over 29,000 in 1972 and over 35,000 in 1973. The death rate, averaging 23 per 1,000 for 1965-71, had skyrocketed in 1972 to 54 per 1,000 for sedentary farmers, and a total death rate nearly double the previous average—44 per 1,000. "Distribution of food," reported CDC from Niger, was "erratic." Then the by now familiar observation:

An example of one sedentary village receiving adequate calorie supplies for one month and an adjacent nomad encampment receiving only one bowl of powdered milk per person points out the need for a specialized distribution system that deals directly with nomad encampments.

In other words, the international relief effort would have to confront the problem. "Traditional enmities between nomadic and sedentary populations," said the CDC summary, "make it unrealistic to assume that sedentarists will feed nomads from a food allotment to a village."

For Mali and Upper Volta, as elsewhere, the survey found measles at the old pre-immunization levels. In Mali, cases had more than doubled in 1973 over 1970, with deaths in 1972 and 1973 more than ten times greater than in 1971. In Upper Volta, measles cases tripled between 1972 and 1973; deaths were more than five times greater.

As with the earlier periodic reports from June through September, the CDC summary findings were routinely distributed from Atlanta to USAID in Washington, but with no particular system from that point onward. Copies were eventually given to the FAO (at the request of the authors), to African diplomats in Washington, and reportedly to governments in the Sahel. By early December 1973, however, more than a year after the drought became a recognized crisis, several officials in USAID had not seen the CDC data. White House officials were still unaware of its existence.

"It seems strange," said the Wall Street Journal, reflecting on the failures of the relief effort, "that a situation like this could develop in a world which has the largest bureaucracy in history devoted to international good deeds." The answer lay not alone in mechanical failures of performance, or in the impersonal malfunction of the international relief effort. As the participants in U.S. and UN relief activities recalled events, and as documents became available, more and more visible was the capricious influence of bureaucracy— the rivalries and clashes of individuals and organizations that can shape policy or action quite apart from the substance of issues. There seemed little readiness to recognize common mistakes or to cooperate more closely in the future.

To USAID, as one official characterized them scornfully, the Public Health doctors in the Sahel were "yellow berets." It had been "like blasting them out of bedrock," he said, "to get them to complete the measles/smallpox programs and leave West Africa." What the doctors found, the singular nature of their contribution, apparently mattered less to some in USAID than the fact that CDC was thereby trespassing on USAID's bureaucratic domain. To the CDC experts, on the other hand, the USAID officers were simply "programmers," with little real concern for the people of the Sahel.

There was similar disdain in USAID for the United Nations and the FAO in particular. "We are terribly concerned," said a USAID briefing memo on June 14, "that the UN will turn this process into a bureaucratic monster." As for the FAO, one responsible U.S. official summed up its contribution tersely: "They were making a lot of noise, and they wanted to do everything by airlift." Bureaucratic bickering was no less concealed within the U.S. government, where the Africa Bureau in USAID is said to have jockeyed for power with McClure and the Office of the Foreign Disaster Relief Coordinator. The State Department's Bureau of African Affairs reportedly lost its bureaucratic struggle with USAID for earlier and more urgent action in the crisis. Even where bureaucratic battles were fought over policy rather than perogatives, the results were no more helpful to the relief effort.

In November, officials say, the telltale signs of bureaucratic success and authority began to appear in the West African Office of USAID, the locus of new public concern and—most important in an institution where power is measured by money to dispense—potential new appropriations. There would be carpets on the floors, new desks, more staff. "It's time we started paying attention to amenities," said an official.

It seems unlikely, however, that the flaws in USAID relief
efforts—whatever their character—were singular to the United States.
The British government had received all the relevant information on
the developing disaster, including the FAO's early warning data and
appeals over the winter and spring. But it was months before London
contributed 300,000 pounds (sterling) to the Sahel. There were reports
in August that German and Belgian aircraft had been withdrawn by
their governments from vitally needed airlifts for a NATO military
exercise. The French, so long the dominant outside power in the
region, once so closely aligned to its peoples, seemingly played a
hesitant role in relief. By late August, Paris had contributed only
$7 million of the world total of over $76 million in food aid to the
stricken countries. In any case, U.S. officials thought the French
would participate in relief only on their own terms, in an arrangement "that gives full cognizance to French interests." A USAID
briefing memo warned in June: "They [Paris] will not permit themselves to be 'coordinated' by the U.N." Later in the summer of 1973
the relative indifference of the French government brought criticism
in the French press, and eventually also from opposition ranks in the
National Assembly.

U.S. congressional interest in the crisis was led by the two
chairmen of the Subcommittees on African Affairs, Senator Humphrey
and Congressman Charles Diggs and by Senator Edward M. Kennedy
(Massachusetts Democrat), who presided over the Senate Subcommittee
on Refugees. As recounted earlier, there were congressional hearings
on the disaster in June and July, and both Humphrey and Diggs subsequently introduced bills for special aid to the Sahel. After a series
of congressional maneuvers, in which disaster relief became involved
in other controversies surrounding the Foreign Aid Bill, assistance
for the Sahel finally emerged from a Senate-House conference at $25
million, which was then to await final Senate passage.

Beyond the initial hearings in June, however, neither the Senate
nor House would continue close oversight of the relief operations in
USAID. Deputy Assistant Administrator Brown had assured both
Senators Humphrey and Kennedy in June and July that relief was
proceeding satisfactorily, that African regimes were doing an "excellent" job of distribution, and that the United States had responded
well, including a "speeded" delivery of measles vaccine, "the demand
for which has become more urgent." Brown avoided a Kennedy question about the low U.S. contribution to the Sahel Trust Fund in mis-
taking the U.S. nonfood aid as $5 million at a time when it was scarcely
over $1 million. In any event, Brown assured the senator, "we had
worked closely with the FAO." Ten days earlier in hearings before
the Subcommittee on African Affairs there had been a few probing
questions from Senator Humphrey, but no revealing answers. "He

was critical of USAID's efforts in certain places," said a Senate staff
consultant who watched the Humphrey hearings. But USAID saw the
episode differently. "Together with State we have participated in
several congressional hearings," said a USAID internal memorandum
on June 27. "The Humphrey hearing in particular was very favorable
to USAID," the memo concluded.

After those hearings, the Sahel largely disappeared as a
congressional issue. In December, neither Senate nor House staff
members on the African Affairs Subcommittees had heard of the
CDC nutritional survey. Congressman Diggs and Delegate Walter
Fauntroy did visit the Sahel, however, in official trips late in 1973.

A year after USAID's November group had first examined the
drought, the crisis had brought planning suddenly into bureaucratic
vogue. There was a group at work within USAID (albeit with uncertain
funds) to plan medium- and long-term projects. At the United Nations
in New York was a staff of planners under Under-Secretary Morse
reportedly addressing some of the same problems.

Not even this belated planning effort, however, would be free
of some bureaucratic undertow. USAID remained concerned, as a
June 14 briefing memorandum had told senior policy makers, that
the United Nations effort be limited to "organizing studies of long-
term development needs," and seeing to an "exchange of information. . . on what is being done"—the latter effort, as the memo puts
it, to be "more sketchily staffed." There should be, after all, no
"bureaucratic monsters."

The problems facing these planning groups were enormous.
Most immediately, there was the question of how much assistance
the Sahel would need simply to stay alive through another year of
drought and crop failure. The $25 million U.S. contribution emerging
from congressional bargaining was only half of what Washington had
contributed in 1972-73. It would make possible, as relief officials
had warned, barely a return to "point zero." At year's end the
contribution of other European donors was uncertain.

Beyond daily survival were the questions of how to begin to
arrest the fatal decline of the region. Had development aid hastened
the calamity by sinking wells that exhausted the water table in areas
adjacent to the desert? Were projects planned as the October study
charged and as many CDC experts thought, without an appreciation
of the overall ecological impact? There were no ready responses
to this in planning bureaucracies that had only begun to assess the
problem.

Over the summer and fall of 1973, two professors from American University, Norman MacLeod and Darrell Randall, made what
seemed an extraordinary discovery. Working from satellite photographs of the sub-Saharan region, the two scientists found an area of

land that had retained its vegetation and moisture amid the encroaching desert. On examination in Niger, the area turned out to be a French-run cattle and sheep ranch, with its grass growing behind the protection of barbed wire fencing to prevent aimless grazing by nomadic herds. At once, there seemed an answer to the tragedy of the Sahel in simple range management. "Millions of dollars should be put into barbed wire and enclosures," Randall told a reporter. But that straightforward solution would clash, as USAID's October study indicated, with the traditional freedom of the nomads. Even if such a massive social change could be effected with the pastoralists now in no condition to resist, there remained formidable problems of "managing" a range stretching more than 2,000 miles across territory previously beyond the political authority of Sahelian regimes, much less their meager development budgets.

And even if there existed a practical and affordable solution to the invasion of the desert, the planners still have to reckon with the bureaucratic inertia of donors and recipients. To some Africans, the solution lies in more wells, to others it is a massive "Marshall Plan" for huge dam and irrigation projects, which many Western experts oppose vigorously.

"Despite the urgency of the crisis," wrote David Ottaway, the Washington Post correspondent in Bamako, "there remained the danger that each African state will pursue its own particular priority project and that regional development efforts will splinter even as foreign nations are gearing up to make a sizeable joint investment." There were also doubts that the international community would ever make the large, sustained investment necessary to move the Sahel from emergency to self-reliance. "Some of the donors are more comfortable with a recurring welfare situation," said one ranking aid officer who had just canvassed European officials. "They feel the costs of a recurring welfare situation are better than the substantial investments needed for program planning."

Looming over all the plans and schemes was a problem for which there was no swift answer—the social and economic dispossession of as many as two million nomads. The CDC survey found two-thirds of the nomads refusing to return to the range even with herds restored. Yet there appeared no place for them in the economy or culture of the sedentary settlements, even if the countries of the Sahel could somehow be restored to their pre-crisis poverty, which seems now a major improvement. Many observers warned that the historic cost of the drought, regardless of the process of recovery, may have been the creation of a vast new "Palestinian" problem in West Africa.

Finally, as if these perils were not enough, the Sahel became a potential hostage to the volatile politics of oil in the wake of the

1973 Middle East war. One of the innocent casualties of the energy
shortage among the wealthy nations, warned Senator Humphrey and
others, would be international food aid. As Western economies became depressed, they would lose the capacity to produce grain surpluses of the kind sent to drought-stricken nations. The oil embargo,
Humphrey predicted to the U.S. Senate on November 21, "will lash
back upon millions of the poor in Africa and Asia." It was against
this background that the Sahel would enter its sixth consecutive year
of drought in 1974.

Relief Coordinator Williams met several times with African
officials in the autumn of 1973, and sources say he did so with unusual
effectiveness. "Everybody has been terribly surprised at our success,"
said one source of Williams's efforts to prod the African governments.
"We even have the French coddling up to us." But other sources say
that it required little diplomacy by autumn 1973 to persuade anyone
of the gravity of the situation. If public attention had waned and the
bureaucracies had turned to planning, the crisis in the Sahel was still
immediate. An FAO crop forecast for the fall was alarmingly pessimistic, according to those familiar with it. With roads impassable
and new crops failing in Mauritania, there was finally a response to
the CDC warnings since July of inadequate food distribution. An
"emergency" airlift was scheduled to begin in October.

Williams visited the Sahel on September 8-21, and returned,
according to several sources, "very shaken" by the situation. "It's
about the worst disaster I've seen," he told an associate. In December
the United States announced another grant of 150,000 tons of grain to
the Sahel, bringing to $80 million the U.S. share in drought relief.

There would be another memorandum to the President on September 27 reporting the need for further food shipments, but reportedly
saying no more about specific problems than the August 21 memo.
That memo was never released. "It was the usual stuff," said an
USAID press officer about the September 27 memo. "No one seemed
very interested anyway."

TOWARD A SYSTEM OF INTERNATIONAL MERCY

Taken singly, none of the failures in the international relief
effort in the Sahel seemed at the time irreparable. None alone seemed
decisive. Together, however, they formed a pattern of neglect and
inertia that made the rescue operation far less effective than it might
have been. An administrative and bureaucratic disaster was added to
the natural calamity—inevitably at a higher cost in human lives and
suffering.

Like the impact of the drought, the effects of the relief failures
in USAID and the FAO were cumulative. Because there was no contingency planning, there was no ready information on airfields, and
no prompt response to a request for airlifts. Without airlifts, food
supplies further dwindled—straining surface transport, affecting
shipments elsewhere, aggravating shortages in which discrimination
against nomads became more likely and more acute. Without effective
monitoring of the distribution of relief, without an early assessment
of nutrition and food needs in certain areas, the bureaucracy had
little basis for planning an airlift, or for making specific changes to
augment surface transport, or for providing special rations and vaccines. The discrimination against the nomads was also selfreinforcing.
Once it had happened, it became politically difficult at every level—
local village chiefs, provincial authorities, central governments,
international meetings—to confront the issue. Bias, waste, and inefficiency discredited every level of the relief effort. None would
admit responsibility. And once the U.S. or U.N. officials had publicly
decreed success it seems to have become impossible for them to
admit that their claims were premature, or exaggerated, or more
truthfully, simply without hard factual basis.

Most of all, the process of malnutrition itself was insidious.
Time lost by bureaucratic vagaries in Washington or Rome or Bamako
became an irredeemable loss in the fading vitality of children and
adults. Indigestible sorghum appeared in USAID documents as lifesaving relief; but in the refugee camps of the Sahel it was cramps and
diarrhea, and a further drain on strength and hope. From a certain
threshold of weakness, as the CDC doctors documented, there was no
turning back from disease or terminal starvation.

The failures of 1972-73 can be traced to more than a decade of
foreign aid policies that had ignored the destitute countries of the
Sahel. For the United States, France, and other donors, international
assistance in Africa was largely the product of political calculations
not unlike the earlier colonial policies of the European powers. Nations
and regions were given priority not for what they needed in humanitarian terms but for what they could yield in tangible advantage to
the giver. As U.S. aid to Africa diminished in the 1960s, Washington
clung to its original "investments," by then fortified by powerful
bureaucratic interest. In 1971, as the United Nations released its
shocking statistics on the poorest nations, there was new attention
by the World Bank and other lending institutions to countries so
blatently bypassed by the so-called "decade of development." USAID
publicly pledged special remedial attention to the poorest, but this
belated effort came with foreign aid cut to its lowest in the U.S.
Congress. There was no realistic prospect that Washington could
right in the 1970s the imbalance of the choices compelled a decade

earlier by congressional cuts and codified in the Korry Report. "It would have cost money to help put the Sahel on its feet before the drought," said a former official, "but no more, and maybe a lot less, than we'll have to put in now just to keep them from going down the drain for good."

The most conspicuous failure of the relief efforts from 1968 through 1973 was the failure to gather, retrieve, and use information. At every stage of the disaster, every piece of information missing added up to yet a larger void. The absence of information paralyzed planning. But it was not only the lack of data. There was the data, as the USAID October study complained, "lying in the files," knowledge and time wasted because a bureaucracy ostensibly living by facts and figures could not organize its institutional memory. Even when the intelligence came in, it was treated with sometimes astonishing casualness. Yes, admitted the USAID officials, the CDC data was extraordinary. The FAO officials thought it "looked" important. But what does some other bureaucracy's study have to do with what we are doing?

The information failure flowed from the further failure of coordination. Responsibility for warning, for communication, for planning, for monitoring, for transport belonged to everyone—and no one. The United States and the FAO acquired their major roles in drought relief almost willy-nilly by their continuing presence in the region since 1968. That process of drift left the Sahel uniquely dependent on USAID and FAO, with neither organization formally recognizing or acting on the responsibility circumstances had imposed, for better or worse. The point is not that such a process was fair or orderly, but that both the Washington and Rome bureaucracies knew very well their importance to the relief effort. They accepted authority without responsibility. Someone else would have to answer for the discrimination against the nomads, for the transport blockages, for the late vaccines.

In the autumn of 1973, it is true, there were publicized U.S. efforts to encourage a cooperative planning venture for future projects among Africans and donors under the aegis of the United Nations. But USAID officials and their documents made clear in private that this was essentially an exercise in political patronization. Let the United Nations pass along information. Let the Africans believe they were "consulted." Washington, and certainly Paris, would make their own decisions, as always, by the goals and priorities of their bureaucracies. "Everybody is trying to do his own little thing," said columnist Carl Rowan after his visit to the area. At the beginning of 1974 the Sahel remained literally at the mercy of governments and organizations to whom its 22 million people were of marginal concern.

Within the U.S. government, coordination was scarcely better. Though the President appointed a "coordinator" late in the crisis, his other duties—as acting USAID administrator, as director of other relief efforts—left little time for the Sahel. However vigorous Williams's efforts in any case—and by many accounts his dedication is clear—there was no systematic coordination of the CDC survey, no critical examination of the basis for the August 21 memorandum to the President. The drought was left to a bureaucracy that obviously had failed to anticipate it over four years, had reacted with bureaucratic lethargy and public defensiveness when the crisis struck, and had spurned (and privately ridiculed) the cooperation of CDC, USAID's own foreign disaster relief coordinator, and the United Nations. Effective coordination in USAID would have begun with a clear recognition of those failures. And it would not have issued, as in the late fall of 1973, in new rewards and status for that same bureaucracy. But then responsibility for relief policy did not stop with USAID. The bureaucracy was left to conduct the relief operations by a leadership in the State Department and White House which apparently had no time or interest in ensuring the faithful execution of President Nixon's pledge to ease suffering in the disaster.

Behind the organizational flaws were the most serious and complex issues of policy for an international relief operation. There was an unresolved dilemma between the demands of urgency and speed in the delivery of relief and the need for some monitoring and accountability. Would not systematic monitoring merely add to red tape, slowing relief shipments still more? Was not the first obligation of USAID and other donors to rush food to the docks of West Africa, accepting waste, rats, corruption, or even unchecked bias in distribution as the price of saving millions? Or would planning and coordination have made plausible both urgent shipments and international monitoring of the relief, much as the World Health Organization ships and supervises the use of vaccines or medicines to stem epidemics in nearly every corner of the world? Those questions were never posed in USAID testimony to the Congress, press handouts, in speeches at international conferences, or internal memoranda. To have inscribed such issues on the agenda would have been to begin to admit the magnitude of the failure in the Sahel.

There were also the political dilemmas that haunt international relief efforts. The disaster in the Sahel seemed remarkably free of political complications. No blockade or civil war or clash of great power interests shackled relief. Relief was not a partisan policy issue in the United States or in any other donor country, save perhaps France where the opposition deplored the regime's inattention to the tragedy. In the United States, relief for the Sahel enlisted united support from the black community as few other foreign policy issues

had. The Sahelian states were pleading for help. Yet there were
political issues beneath this surface. What responsibility did the
Africans have to distribute relief supplies equitably? What international presence, if any, did massive outside relief obligate the
Africans to accept in order to assure the international community
that the aid was used properly? Was it possible, in the midst of
crisis, for the African states to suspend for a time some of their
sovereignty to help save their own people? Or would the unpleasant
political subjects, as for USAID policy makers, have to be "someone
else's" problem? Again, these questions were nowhere on the agenda
of USAID or the international gatherings on the Sahel.

At root, each of the inadequacies and mistakes in the rescue
operation was a failure of will within the relief bureaucracies. The
unspoken truth in USAID and the FAO was that no one had raised the
issue of the Sahel before the drought became a catastrophe. Officials
watching the vivid signs of collapse hewed to the bureaucratic line of
survival—to continue present, approved, cleared policy. It was not
altogether too late for officials to compensate for this inertia when
the crisis was at last recognized in 1972-73. That meant a readiness
to face past failures, and to cut through red tape in the spring of
1973, to act rather than pause. But even then, the bureaucracy's
instinct was to continue what it had been doing, to justify inaction, to
ignore unpalatable facts.

The tragedy in the Sahel revealed again what many officials and
nongovernmental relief experts have long known from other disasters—
that international relief is too important and too complex to leave so
largely to a USAID or FAO, organizations for which disaster aid is
obviously neither a major function nor a special competence. The
organizational and functional attributes of an effective system of
international relief are clear:

● An information system combining a watch on areas vulnerable
to disaster, an early warning mechanism reaching both donors and
victims, data retrieval and analysis of current intelligence, a communications system—such as that of the World Weather Watch—
capable of rapidly conveying this information as well as the early
warning among involved parties, and not least, a public information
function that provides a flow of full and accurate reports on the disaster and the relief efforts to the media and national legislatures.

● Closely linked to the information system, a planning and
operations function responsible for the application of latest science
and technology for disaster relief or prevention, the prompt mobilization and shipment of relief supplies, and sustained coordination with
the recipients to ensure adequate transport, minimal waste, and
effective and equitable distribution of relief.

● Independent of operations, yet an integral factor in policy
and further planning, a monitoring system, which prepares for the
relief effort with full access to the information system, is on the
scene as relief flows, and faithfully reports any abuse or malfunc-
tioning in relief.

● Often as important as any technical function, a political
advisory system that alerts every element of the relief effort, from
planning to monitoring, of political or social problems that may hinder
or prevent altogether certain measures necessary to the relief effort.

It is a catalogue of what was missing in the Sahel, and of what
has been lacking in some measure in every great disaster of the
postwar world. Perhaps what distinguishes most an organization
integrating these functions is the promise that relief of death and
suffering would be its sole mission and responsibility. To the array
of national and bureaucratic interests and clients that crowd upon any
disaster would be added an institution whose constituents were the
victims themselves, whose primary purpose was mercy, whose un-
divided loyalty would be to the integrity of that mission.

Such an organization could fix for the first time too the burden
of responsibility in international relief—a burden now borne by a few
though the obligation rests with every nation. Ultimately, the failure
in the Sahel belongs to the entire international community, rich and
poor, which has neglected to organize itself to deal with a problem
that now needlessly claims thousands of lives each year. The most
important attribute of a new relief system, then, is that it be truly
international—staffed and funded with representative contributions
from every region.

Of all the tasks on the international agenda, it is true, none
invites more cynicism than disaster relief. And on the evidence of
the last decade alone, the disillusion seems justified. Often enmeshed
in civil wars, great power politics, or simply local corruption, relief
has seemed the one expendable interest of nations. But even that
apparently inherent inhumanity in world politics has been altered under
the impact of mass communications. Whatever the callousness of
governments, their populations, particularly in Europe and America,
now see the suffering of the Sahel or Bangladesh or Biafra more vividly
than ever before through television and newspapers—and with the
seeing there has grown a rising public intolerance with governmental
indifference. That correlation of knowing and feeling among an international public by no means ensures the success of a new approach
to disaster relief, but both U.S. and UN officials believe that it has
made such an approach at least more plausible than many have thought.

No international bureaucracy will be immune to the problems
of bureaucracy simply for being international, or new, or for having
the benefit of past experience in USAID or the FAO. The creation of

a new system of international relief begs a score of formidable questions: Under whose aegis? With what sustained funding? With what
political power to deal with the opposition of nations or whole regions
to humanitarian relief? Where does national sovereignty (and indifference to suffering) stop, and international humanitarianism begin?
All these and many more.

The tragedy in the Sahel offers no facile guide through these
dilemmas. It does demand a beginning to address the problem in all
its complexity. The initiative toward a new system of international
relief clearly lies with the governments and international organizations (including the private relief agencies which will work with it)
whose political support will shelter it and whose money will sustain
it. But there is also a role for nongovernmental support. The
premise on which all else in a new relief system comes to rest is
the existence of an international group of disaster relief experts—
men and women from throughout the world trained to deal with the
special problems of relief from the epidemeology of famine to the
logistics of an emergency food airlift to the infinitely delicate political problems of negotiating relief in the midst of civil war. Without
this resource, all the courage and generosity of governments will
still be ensnared by the bureaucratic vagaries that plagued the relief
of the Sahel.

This study concludes with the recommendation that nongovernmental organizations and foundations in the United States and Europe,
in close coordination with governments and private relief agencies,
begin to explore the establishment of an international center for the
training of such experts in disaster relief.

It would be unrealistic to assume that any initiative to change
the present amorphous administration of international relief will be
swift or easy. The horror of the Sahel may be repeated more than
once before governments choose to recognize the problem and act.
The creation of a new international institution deliberately designed
to avoid the foibles of those, in effect, who create it will demand
all the genius and good will the world community can muster. There
are precedents for success—the World Health Organization and its
fight against epidemics across the obstacles of sovereignty and
politics may be the most relevant. There are all too many and
obvious precedents for failure.

Only the alternative to a new beginning seems clear. Without
a bold, fresh approach to disaster relief, innocent children seem
doomed to go on dying around the world because bureaucrats fail to
plan, or because officials remain ignorant, or because no one cares.
And many will die though the means to save them are at hand.

Early in 1974, when this report first appeared, there began
again, after months of silence by the press and governments, the all

too predictable reports of continuing disaster in the Sahel. In late January, Director General Boerma of the FAO told the New York Times that the drought "is worse this year than ever before, while pledges of aid have fallen far short of needs." On February 11, David Ottaway reported in the Washington Post the warning of African relief officials that "without fast emergency relief 200,000 people may die of starvation in remote corners of the Sahel." The loss of cattle in 1972-73, said the FAO, had been more than 3.5 million head worth $400 million, or a quarter of the total cattle of the region. U.N. officials estimated the grain shortage in the Sahel at 1.2 million tons, over twice what U.S. planners had assumed the previous summer. By February, wrote Ottaway, food stocks had been exhausted in Chad, Mali, Niger, and Mauritania, and conditions "generally are described as grim." The drought was spreading. The Post reported that it had reached crisis proportions also in the northern regions of Nigeria and Cameroon.

U.S. relief contributions by the beginning of 1974 approached $100 million, and on January 23, USAID announced another 100,000 metric tons of sorghum for the Sahel, this time presumably an edible variety. But when senior USAID officials appeared before Congress in February to seek a badly needed supplemental $50 million for the Sahel, there would be no candid admission of the bureaucratic failures that had so aggravated the crisis. Toward major rehabilitation projects for the area, reported Ottaway, USAID was taking a "wait and see attitude." In February 1974, as the Sahel was plunged into its seventh consecutive year of disaster, USAID was waiting on a "study" of the region's "development options." The project would not be completed for two years.

For its part, the U.S. Congress voted early in 1974 to reject a contribution to the development loan fund of the World Bank designed specifically to help impoverished regions like the Sahel. Throughout the wealthy countries, said officials, the distractions of domestic economic problems brought a similar turning away from international disasters.

But in the Sahel, there was simply no more time for hesitation or neglect. The 22 million people of the region seemed about to drift apart from the rest of the international community, much as Dag Hammarskjold had described in Markings the growing separation of the living and the condemned:

Between you and him is distance,
Uncertainty—
Care

He will see you withdrawing,
Further and further,
Hear your voices fading,
Fainter and fainter.

3

**A REASSESSMENT
OF INTERNATIONAL
RELIEF PROGRAMS**
Mohamed El-Khawas

The recent drought in the Sahel has seriously affected six West African countries—Chad, Mali, Mauritania, Niger, Senegal, and Upper Volta—which together have a population of 25 million people. This is not the first drought to be experienced in the area in the twentieth century; a famine occurred in 1910-14 and the years 1941-42 were abnormally dry. The recent drought, however, is the worst in 60 years because of the loss of millions of livestock herds and the exceptionally severe shortage of grain over several years affecting countries where the great majority of the population is engaged in subsistence agriculture (Niger, 96 percent; Chad, 92 percent; Mali, 90 percent; Upper Volta, 84 percent; and Senegal, 74 percent). [1]

For the sixth straight year, the Sahel countries received too little rainfall to produce an adequate harvest. The drought has most gravely damaged two major areas of activity, stock raising and the cultivation of wet season crops, both principal sources of revenue and export earnings. It is estimated that the loss of cattle is extremely high throughout the region (Chad, 100 percent; Upper Volta, 50-100 percent; Niger, 80 percent; Mauritania, 76 percent; and Senegal, 50 percent). In addition, harvests have been cut by 40 percent to 60 percent of normal. [2] There are no available figures on the number of deaths among the population, but the toll is undoubtedly high.

The continuing drought reached its most disastrous proportions in 1972-73, with a decrease in rainfall of over 50 percent throughout the area. The immediate results included water shortages, a sharp decline in agricultural production, and further encroachment of the desert on arable land. The Niger and Senegal rivers, for example, were shrunk in many places to shallow streams, while Lake Chad was reduced to one-third its normal size. Under these circumstances,

the Sahelian governments were confronted with the harsh reality that
their 1972 harvests had fallen far short of essential need. It was
then that they turned to the world community for help, seeking international assistance to help make up for the grain deficits of the 1973
and 1974 crop years. They were desperate for food since their grain
reserves had been exhausted.

In order to respond, the international community was faced
with two major tasks. First, rich nations, particularly those with
grain surpluses, had to make massive food deliveries and to make
transportation available in order to guarantee timely delivery to the
affected countries. Second, economically advanced countries had to
provide the Sahel with technical know-how and capital to salvage the
region by setting up self-help programs designed to meet future
emergencies resulting from natural calamities.

For this second task, international assistance might be needed
for a long time. The drought so severely dislocated the economy of
the Sahelian countries that many believe they have lost their ability
to support themselves for some time to come. It should be remembered, moreover, that Chad, Mali, Niger, and Upper Volta were
identified by the U.N. Economic and Social Council in 1971 as among
the least developed nations, with per capita gross national products
of less than $100 and also less than 10 percent adult literacy. [3]

A number of criticisms have been directed toward the international relief efforts that have taken place thus far. Hal Sheets and
Roger Morris have raised two serious questions regarding the international relief efforts in the Sahel, particularly those of the United
Nations and the United States. First, they argue that the relief has
seemed "haunted by rudimentary failures to heed early warnings, to
plan in advance, and to monitor and coordinate the rescue efforts."
Second, they deplore the way that the various "bureaucracies [were]
often unprepared, or unable, to take measures that might have further reduced the tragedy."[4] In addition, Elliot Skinner, former U.S.
ambassador to Upper Volta, has claimed that "the response of the
world was too little and almost too late."[5]

Other allegations were that the donor countries focused attention on the sensational aspects rather than on the substance of the
problem. They have been criticized for dealing only with the symptoms rather than with the causes of the disaster. There has been a
growing concern in the Sahel area over the need to concentrate international efforts on longer-term planning to gradually make these
countries less dependent on foreign help and to make it possible to
keep a natural phenomenon from becoming such a major disaster.

In order to assess the significance of the international relief
program, it is necessary to review the nature and extent of assistance.
The purpose of this chapter is to provide such a review of the response

of Africa and the major powers to the drought in the Sahel. It has
four specific objectives: (1) to examine and describe African relief
efforts; (2) to determine the scope of the U.S. emergency relief
programs; (3) to compare American assistance with aid programs
of other major powers; and (4) to discuss problems of delivery and
distribution in the drought-stricken countries.

EMERGENCY FOOD SHIPMENTS

As early as 1968, Mauritania warned of possible drought in the
Sahel. In succeeding years, there were many signs to demonstrate
the accuracy of this prediction. Some Sahelian governments, however,
were slow to acknowledge publicly the seriousness of the problem.
Under these circumstances, the world community had neither the
incentive nor the necessary information to initiate emergency measures
to combat food shortages. [6] This is reflected in the small amount of
foreign assistance ($50 million per annum) that the Sahel nations
received in 1969 and 1970. [7]
    Up to the fall of 1972, the Sahel governments made every effort
to use their own resources to deal with the crisis and to avoid relying
on outside assistance. However, when the 1972 harvest was exceptionally poor, they finally directed a request for additional aid to the
World Food Program (WFP). In response, 55,000 MT (metric tons)
of food grain, at a total value of almost $9 million, were approved
quickly for shipment to the Sahel. [8] This was the largest single contribution ever made to any drought-affected area from WFP resources.
Yet it was not large enough to meet the estimated 80,000 MT deficit
for that period.
    The Sahel crisis first began to attract worldwide attention in
the spring of 1973. In response to an appeal made by the ECA Conference of Ministers (Accra, February 1973), the representatives of
Mali, Mauritania, Niger, Senegal, and Upper Volta met in Ouagadougou
in March 1973. At this important meeting they declared the Sahel a
disaster area and called for international assistance to combat the
famine, which had already reached disastrous proportions. [9] They
called attention to other problems, noting that, in addition to the
threat of starvation, "the inhabitants also were threatened with epidemics, nutritional deficiencies, and unemployment problems in the
urban areas created by the influx of people." [10]
    The African governments hoped that the immediate task of the
world community would be to ensure a steady flow of relief materials
to the affected countries without further delay. Pierre Claver Damiba,
Upper Volta's deputy to the National Assembly Economic Counsel of

the Presidency, outlined the immediate objectives of the international
emergency relief program in the following terms:

1. To feed men in order to save them from dying
   of hunger or the vicissitudes of the exodus;
2. To provide drinking water for the population;
3. To heal the sick and renew the strength of those
   who are anemic;
4. To save the livestock through water, fodder and
   appropriate care;
5. To set up stockpiles of indispensable items in
   these countries and in the heart of the affected
   zones; and
6. To establish means of transportation and communication (roads) by which the supplies can be
   moved to the countries concerned and then dispatched to the localities affected (planes, heli-
   copters, trucks, light all-terrain vehicles, . . .
   etc.).[11]

In May 1973, the World Food Program took up this call and
issued its own urgent appeal for donor countries and organizations
to expedite delivery of food and medicine to the Sahel and to contribute cash to the FAO Sahelian Zone Trust Fund in order to finance
the purchase and transport of badly needed commodities.[12] In response, some African states provided gifts of food and equipment to
the Sahelian countries. Nigeria gave $3.75 million to the six countries
affected. Algeria dispatched to Mali, Mauritania, and Niger some
48 trucks of cereals, dried vegetables, jam, rice, powdered milk,
oil, and medicine. Libya sent 71 trucks to Niger, each loaded with
between 18 and 26 tons of food, in addition to running a relief road
to northern Chad.[13] Table 3.1 gives details on the nature and source
of African relief efforts. The list is probably incomplete because
many donations were small and some might not have been reported
in the press. Nevertheless, the figures show that, while a good
number of African countries made food and/or cash contributions to
one or more of the affected nations in the Sahel, the overall size of
their effort was small, mostly a symbolic gesture of support. With
the exception of Nigeria and Libya, the African donors are economically poor and could not provide the massive level of aid necessary.
   Because of the small scope of the African relief effort, the
burden of the emergency relief program fell on the shoulders of
countries outside the African continent, especially Western Europe
and North America. The initial effort was not easy since the world
community had not prepared to meet the mounting problems of the

TABLE 3.1

Status of African Contributions to the
Sahelian Relief Operation

Donor	Tons of Food	Cash Contributions (dollars)
North Africa		
Algeria	3,240	22,000,000
Egypt	7.5	—
Libya	1,562	2,000,000
Morocco	2,200	—
Sudan	10,000	—
Sub-Sahara Africa		
Botswana	—	20,000
Ivory Coast	300	44,675
Kenya	—	846
Liberia	—	20,000
Nigeria	6,000	3,750,000
Somalia	—	16,051
Swaziland	—	8,720
Togo	—	69,543
Zaire	—	223,350
Total	23,309.5	28,153,185

Sources: West Africa, nos. 2918, 2922, 2931, 2975, 2979,
2997 (May 1973-November 1974); FAO Office for the Sahelian
Relief Operations (OSRO), Reports 14 (1973) and 11 (1974); World
Hunger, Health, and Refugee Problems Part 1: Crisis in West
Africa (Washington, D.C.: U.S. Government Printing Office, 1973);
Victor D. DuBois, The Drought in West Africa, Part II: Perception,
Evaluation, and Response, American Universities Field Staff
Reports, West Africa Series, vol. 15, no. 2 (May 1974).

Sahel. Emergency efforts were hampered by a lack of appropriated
funds in each country's foreign aid program to assist the Sahel countries. The problem was compounded by the fact that the crisis had
already reached massive proportions by the spring of 1973, when
mobilization of relief finally began. Another obstacle was the need
to ensure the delivery of food and emergency supplies to many of the
affected countries before the rainy season disrupted internal transportation.

Within months, assistance began to flow to the Sahel countries. The United States and the European Common Market were the most responsive in terms of food shipments; they alone provided about five-sixths of the international relief in 1973, with the United States by far the major contributor. [14]

Indeed, the United States had begun to prepare for substantial increases in food shipments to the Sahel back in 1972 following the poor harvest of that year. By the time the Sahel was declared a disaster area in March 1973, the first American pledge of 156,000 MT of food (worth $21 million) began to arrive. In addition, the United States provided $3.5 million in contingency funds to speed food delivery to rural areas.

Other nations quickly joined in these relief efforts to provide food, medicine, and other assistance. The total international effort in 1973 was over $120 million. [15]

Through mid-1974, international relief commitments reached the high mark of $361 million. The United States had contributed about one-third of the total worldwide donation, with $100 million of the total $130 million of American assistance being in food aid (including related costs for trans-Atlantic and inland transport in West Africa). [16] Tables 3.2 and 3.3 show that American food shipments in a two-year period reached a total of 504,213 MT, representing approximately 46 percent of the world food contribution, by tonnage, to the Sahel and consequently the largest contribution of any single donor in the two years of relief operations.

The level of the U.S. effort was followed by that of the European Economic Community (EEC), whose food donations increased in volume from 92,500 MT in 1972-73 to 110,000 MT the following year. To meet the urgent need for food delivery, the EEC rapidly increased its relief efforts to include all costs for transportation of food.

Among the EEC countries, France and Germany made substantial contributions in emergency food shipments and special aid for reconstituting feed stocks, for speeding up existing well drilling, and for combatting animal malnutrition. Their contributions through the EEC were large and amounted to 90 percent of the EEC's total aid effort. In the first year of operations, France alone accounted for a little under half of the EEC donations; it contributed 49,500 MT of grain and milk powder plus a cash donation of 3.5 million francs to the European Development Fund for the Sahel, representing a third of the fund's total monies. In addition, France made a bilateral contribution to the Sahel countries of 54,500 MT of grain, worth 22 million francs, while paying for all transportation costs to the African capitals. West Germany donated 34,555 MT of grain at a total value of 47 million German marks; this comprised about one-third of the EEC's total assistance. Moreover, West Germany made a bilateral donation of 31,630 MT of grain. [17]

TABLE 3.2

Donor Food Aid Commitments to the Sahel, Crop Year 1973 (October 1972 to September 1973)
(metric tons)

Donor	Mali	Niger	Senegal	Upper Volta	Mauritania	Chad	Total
United States	55,250	68,250	45,000	41,250	33,250	8,000	251,000
EEC	35,000	14,500	17,000	15,000	5,000	6,000	92,500
France	10,000	10,000	8,000	9,500	8,000	9,000	54,500
West Germany	5,210	7,420	7,000	3,000	9,000	–	31,630
Canada	5,000	5,500	4,000	4,500	5,000	2,000	26,000
USSR	13,000	2,500	2,000	2,500	3,000	2,000	25,000
People's Republic of China	10,000	10,000	10,000	5,000	8,000	4,000	47,000
Subtotal	133,460	118,170	93,000	80,750	71,250	31,000	527,130
Others*							74,370
Total							613,500

*Major other donors in 1973 were the Sudan, 10,000 MT; Nigeria, 6,000 MT; Pakistan, 10,000 MT;
Italy, 10,000 MT; and Argentina, 10,000 MT.

Source: World Hunger, Health, and Refugee Problems, Part V: Human Disasters in Cyprus, Bangladesh,
Africa (Washington, D.C.: U.S. Government Printing Office, 1974), p. 61.

TABLE 3.3

Donor Food Aid Commitments to the Sahel, Crop Year 1974 (November 1973 to October 1974)

(metric tons)

Donor	Mali	Niger	Senegal	Upper Volta	Mauritania	Chad	Nonallocated	Total
Pipeline from November 1973	63,524	27,782	52,570	38,877	39,269	17,360	—	239,382
United States	69,000	83,804	4,940	17,525	34,734	20,000	—	230,003
EEC	26,000	30,000	15,000	15,000	14,000	10,000	—	110,000
France	10,000	10,000	6,000	9,000	10,000	8,000	21,500	74,500
West Germany	10,000	10,000	—	3,000	10,000	—	2,000	35,000
Canada	11,917	8,298	2,458	4,580	6,060	4,878	—	38,191
USSR	10,000	—	—	—	—	—	—	10,000
People's Republic of China	—	—	—	5,000	6,000	—	—	11,000
WFPa	8,000	15,946	5,060	2,475	—	—	—	31,481
Denmark	4,000	2,000	10,000	2,000	5,000	—	—	23,000
Belgium	3,000	5,000	1,900	2,000	1,500	—	—	13,400
Othersb	15,217	4,402	1,927	—	7,250	966	7,000	36,762
Subtotal	230,658	197,232	99,855	99,457	133,813	61,204	30,500	852,719
Government purchases	101,184	23,000	109,700	20,000	10,000	3,024	—	266,908
Total	330,842	220,232	209,555	119,457	143,813	64,228	30,500	1,119,627

aUnited States donated 24,210 MT to WFP.

bMajor other donors in 1974 were United Kingdom, 10,000 MT; Sweden, 8,000 MT; Iraq, 6,811 MT; Hungary, 5,000 MT; and Algeria, 3,240 MT.

Source: FAO Office for the Sahelian Relief Operations (ORSO), Report 11 (10 September 1974), p. 6.

Relief activities by Communist countries generally have been minimal throughout the two years of relief operations. This is largely due to the fact that neither the Soviet Union nor China has a wheat surplus. China has its own pressing responsibility for feeding its huge population of approximately 800 million. The Soviet Union has had to conclude sizeable wheat purchase arrangements with the United States because of its own poor harvests. Despite these adverse circumstances, both countries managed to participate in the international relief effort to some extent. China was more generous than the USSR, donating 47,000 MT to the Sahel in the crop year 1973 in comparison to 25,000 MT contributed by the Soviet Union. However, the contributions of both countries fell off sharply the following year: China contributed 11,000 MT and the Soviet Union 10,000 MT of grain. Another country, Hungary, contributed 5,000 MT of grain in the 1974 crop year.

The actual distribution of the international relief donations has been largely coordinated by the World Food Program, although some countries have made direct bilateral shipments of food. As Tables 3.2 and 3.3 show, emergency food shipments have been distributed in various quantities to the individual Sahel countries over the last two years. The largest amount of aid has gone to Mali and Niger, two of the three nations hardest hit by the drought. The third country, Mauritania, received a smaller share, probably because the relief effort there was disrupted by major transport and administrative problems. It should be noted that Chad received the least aid during the first year; aid to Chad increased slightly in the second year, but the government of Chad has complained that the international relief effort has failed to meet its needs.

ADMINISTRATIVE AND TRANSPORT PROBLEMS

In the first year of operations, the international relief program ran into innumerable administrative and logistic problems causing unnecessary delay in the delivery of food and other materials to the affected countries in West Africa. This was due to several factors, including lack of information, the limited capacity of West African ports, and the lack of rail and road infrastructure to move food inland to the drought-stricken areas. [18]

Four of the Sahelian countries—Chad, Mali, Niger, and Upper Volta—are landlocked and have to depend almost entirely on road and rail links to one of the West African ports to transfer grain to their distribution centers. In most cases, the railway capacity is far from adequate to handle substantial tonnage on a monthly basis and over a long period of time. In Mali, for instance, railway capacity between Dakar and Kayes or Bamako has been increased to accommodate 15,000 MT of grain per month since the emergency food shipments began. This represents a more than 100 percent increase over the normal monthly load prior to the drought but still is not sufficient to meet that country's needs.

The international relief programs to Chad and Niger encountered many unforeseen problems during the spring of 1974. A breakdown in Nigerian railway operations and strikes by railway and port workers dangerously threatened the movement of foodstuffs into Chad and Niger, both heavily dependent on Nigerian ports for transfer of grain. [19]

To overcome transportation problems, supplementary trucking was widely utilized for the transfer of food shipments into Niger, Mauritania, Mali, Chad, and Upper Volta. Because Mauritania's main port, Nouakchott, has limited facilities for handling large shipments, food deliveries have had to be arranged through Dakar (Senegal) and transported by truck-ferry or rail-barge to Rosso, the major storage point in Mauritania. [20]

In all, foreign donors provided 361 trucks during 1974 for the delivery of grain and other supplies by land before the rainy season began. With the exception of the trucks provided by the FAO Office of Sahelian Relief Operations (OSRO), all contributors were from Western Europe and North America. The EEC has been the most responsive in providing trucking service to the Sahel area. Although utilized only in Mauritania and Niger, the EEC contribution represented a little over one-fourth of total foreign trucking assistance. West Germany, the United States, and Britain provided another 40 percent of the trucking aid. [21] Thus, the burden of trucking assistance has fallen on the same countries that contributed most of the emergency food shipments to the Sahel.

Although the additional trucks resulted in substantial improvement in food movement, they also created enormous problems, including a dispute between the trucking associations of Nigeria and Chad regarding movement of grain on the last 80-mile stretch from Nigeria to Chad. Because Chad truckers insisted that they alone were entitled to carry food shipments past the Chad border, the delivery effort encountered unnecessary delay as Nigerians were forced to unload their trucks at the border to be reloaded by Chad truckers. [22]

Furthermore, donor countries found it necessary to provide not only trucks but also mechanics, spare parts, and fuel. William Price, Britain's parliamentary secretary to the Ministry of Overseas Development, remarked upon his return from a nine-day tour of Chad, Mali, and Upper Volta:

There is no point in sending lorries without supplies
of spare parts (which, after such a journey, they will
need at once) and perhaps without directly ensuring
their fuel supplies. . . . in Chad, for example,
twelve lorries . . . were meant to be distributing
relief food but were immobilised by shortage of
fuel. [23]

Administrative red tape within the African countries also has
been a factor in the failure to ensure a steady flow of relief materials
to drought victims. Foreign trucks and mechanics, for instance, have
not been allowed to move outside the Chad capital without a permit
from the minister, who at one point delayed shipments when he was
away from the capital of Chad for ten days. [24]

The USAID Report to Congress on Famine in Sub-Sahara Africa
(September 1974) summarized the enormous problems of transport
and communication in the following terms:

In 1973 there were times when ships were hard to
obtain because of massive, world-wide grain
movements. Ports in West Africa are poorly
equipped to handle huge shipments and there have
been port congestion problems, particularly this
year. Railroads were often inadequate to move
foods inland on a timely basis. There are few
paved roads. Ferries are slow and inefficient.
River transport is important but capacity has been
inadequate for the amounts involved. Roads leading
to many outlying distribution points where nomads
are congregated are difficult at best, impassable
when the rains come. Few trucks, and problems of
their maintenance, have often caused difficulties.
Airlifts have been needed and provided by several
donors. . . . Lack of storage has been a problem.
The complexity of managing relief operations of
this nature, involving six recipient governments
and a number of donors under extremely difficult
physical conditions, is without precedent. [25]

Despite all these problems, it was still essential to speed up
the movement of large quantities of food and other supplies from
West African ports—Abidjan, Dakar, and Lagos—to the landlocked
countries, particularly remote and distant areas that have no rail
links and are not easily accesible by road transport. Because of the
dislocation of the road transport system in northern Niger and in the

sixth region of Mali, airlifts became increasingly necessary to make
sure aid got through on time. Three operations were needed: "the
airlift of bulk supplies from ports to the main airports in the interior;
the airlift by smaller planes for distribution centers and airstrips;
and special arrangements for airdrops in isolated areas with urgent
needs."[26]

As the WFP warned, "there will be widespread starvation and
likely a high death rate among the human population, particularly in
the remote areas, unless the evacuation of available grain can be
expedited by an airlift from the ports directly to inland destinations."[27]
Claude Cheysson, international delegate to the EEC, urged his colleagues to make every possible effort to ensure the delivery of food
on time even if it meant the use of military aircraft to transport food
to the interior.[28]

In response, a dozen countries made 63 aircraft available for
airlift operations in the Sahel—a service by which over 20,000 tons
of food grain, milk powder, seeds, and animal food were transferred
by air in the Sahel between May and October 1973. As shown in
Table 3.4, France provided 28 percent of the total foreign aircraft,
the largest single contribution. On May 26, France made available
to each of the six Sahel countries, for a period of two weeks, two
large transport aircraft to carry food and other supplies to the
disaster areas, placing them at the disposal of local authorities. In
the next two months, it provided an additional five Nord-Atlas aircraft for airlift operations in Mauritania. This French assistance
was closely paralleled by West German and Belgian assistance, which
jointly accounted for 37 percent of the aircraft made available.

The U.S. airlift operations, which mainly involved extensive
airlifting from Bamako to the sixth region in Mali, carried about
6,500 tons of food in five months. In the summer of 1974, the United
States airlifted 5,000 tons of grain to such inaccessible regions as
Gao, Goundam, Tessalit, and Niori.[29]

All in all, thirteen countries made air transport available to
the Sahel. Among them were three African countries—Libya, Ghana,
and Zaire. With the exception of China and the Soviet Union, each of
which contributed one aircraft, the remaining participants were from
Europe and North America, the same countries that had already
substantially contributed to the international food relief program.

On the whole, it must be noted that the international airlift was
rather small. Thirteen countries provided air transport, but only
for a short time. By the time the summer rains began, vast amounts
of food and other supplies still had not been moved to the drought
victims. Delay in the delivery of food resulted in an accumulation
of stocks in the ports, some of which were spoiled by the rain because they were stacked in the open air. Also, the rains dislocated

TABLE 3.4

Number and Type of Aircraft Used in Airlift
Relief Operations, May-November, 1973

Donor	Type	Mauritania	Niger	Upper Volta
France	Nord–Atlas	7	2	2
West Germany	Transall	4[a]	4	2
Belgium	C 130 H	—	3	7
United States	C 130 H	2	—	—
Canada	C 130 H	—	5	—
United Kingdom	C 130 H	—	—	—
Netherlands	Fokker	—	—	—
Spain	DC 3	2	—	—
Libya	C 130 H	2	—	—

Donor	Type	Mali	Chad	Senegal	Total
France	Nord–Atlas	2	2	2	17
West Germany	Transall	2	—	—	12
Belgium	C 130 H	—	1	—	11
United States	C 130 H	3	—	—	5
Canada	C 130 H	—	—	—	5
United Kingdom	C 130 H	2	—	—	2
Netherlands	Fokker	1	—	1	2
Spain	DC 3	—	—	—	2
Libya	C 130 H	—	—	—	2
Others[b]					5
Total					63

[a]This figure included three C 160.

[b]Ghana, Zaire, Switzerland, China, and the Soviet Union
provided one aircraft each to the Sahel.

Sources: FAO Office for the Sahelian Relief Operations
(OSRO), Report 7, (November 30, 1973), pp. 9-12; The Drought
Crisis in the African Sahel (Washington, D.C.: U.S. Government
Printing Office, 1973), pp. 69-70.

the communication system before sufficient supplies had been delivered to the interior regions hardest hit by the drought. For this
reason the WFP used camel caravans to distribute food in the interior
after rains cut off the existing communication system. In the fall of
1974, about 2,000 camels were used to carry 5,000 MT of food to
north Niger.[30]

INTERNATIONAL RESPONSE ON MEDIUM-
AND LONG-TERM PROGRAMS

The continuing drought of the last seven years and the strong
probability that future droughts will occur has led to an awareness
of the need to initiate medium- and long-term recovery and rehabilitation programs to ensure that severe emergencies like those
of 1973 and 1974 can be more efficiently and effectively met in the
future. After President Lamizana of Upper Volta thanked the international community for their "generous and effective assistance" in
averting a possible catastrophe in West Africa, he pointed out "the
need to prevent a recurrence of such a disaster; not only must steps
be taken to conserve existing vegetation to check the advance of the
desert, but the people must see to it that more trees were planted
than were felled."[31] In addition, President Senghor of Senegal told
his people that they might have to cease to own goats in the year
2000, a measure against desertification.[32]

Pierre-Claver Damiba of Upper Volta outlined the African
view of needed international assistance in medium- and long-term
development:

1) reforestation and selection of seeds through the
   creation of nurseries;
2) construction of rural dams;
3) supplying equipment to dig deep wells;
4) direct financing of deep-well digging;
5) improving bottom-land, plains or land downstream
   from dams;
6) efforts regarding stock-raising (ranches, pasture
   land, hydraulics, etc.);
7) financing of educational efforts on behalf of the
   peasantry through organization and rural extension
   work backed up with the necessary equipment;
8) scientific research, various kinds of studies and
   experiments (meteorology, agronomy, hydrogeology,
   mines, etc.).[33]

The African views are in agreement with those of Robert Gardiner, executive secretary of the Economic Commission for Africa, who emphasized the need for "a coordinated strategy for agricultural development in the Sahel zone under the U.N." Attention should be given to the development and maintenance of water supplies, the replanting of crops and pastures, replacement of livestock, and measures to halt the Sahara's encroachment. 34 Thus, it is imperative that medium- and long-term recovery and rehabilitation activities be carried out over the next five to seven years.

Because the Sahel countries are not equipped to deal with the area's long-range problems, the industrialized nations must make significant commitments if the economies of these countries are to be restored. Only in this way can the Sahelian countries bring an end to their dependence upon food inputs and external assistance. As President Diori of Niger pointed out, "this part of the world really does need the Marshall Plan." 35

In September 1973 the Sahel governments met in Ouagadougou and worked out a common strategy for long-range development. They formed the Inter-State Committee for the War against Drought to organize and coordinate planning activities; they approved "a first-priority list of projects" prepared by African and foreign experts. Their list contained 123 projects whose total costs might run as high as a billion dollars; it included emergency measures (such as distribution of food to isolated nomads) and long-term projects (including construction of earth dams to collect rain in the valleys). The African governments asked the foreign donors to act as a group in financing the medium- and long-term development programs. The latter agreed and pledged to support some of the programs. 36 However, little has happened in a year's time, largely because the difficult world economic situation has posed immense problems for even the most affluent of nations.

Although the international community is well aware of the Sahel's need for longer-term recovery and development programs over the next several years, the industrialized nations have not yet committed themselves to any comprehensive development program in the Sahel. They have, however, initiated various scientific studies to determine possible development approaches for the Sahel. The United States has given the Massachusetts Institute of Technology a $1 million grant to assess development alternatives available to the Sahel, possibly including application of remote sensing and space technology to resource planning, improved varieties of grain adaptable to the region, as well as climatology studies. 37

Until these studies are completed, it is not expected that any major power will get involved in a comprehensive development plan. However, it should be noted that certain donors have supported some short-term recovery and rehabilitation programs aimed specifically at improving agricultural and livestock production. Some projects involve development of the various river basins. The European Economic Community, for example, contributed $40 million, in addition to another $10 million from France and $15 million from the United States, to finance some programs during 1974-75. Furthermore, the World Bank committed $15 million for the same period. Most of these projects are aimed at stimulating better utilization of rivers in flood plains or for construction of new storage facilities, rental of temporary storage, and provision of tarpaulins and other coverage for storage in remote areas as well as improvement of cargo handling equipment and supply of new motors for barges in the Niger River, an attempt to facilitate the movement of food into the interior.[38]

In an effort to attract foreign assistance, Mali, Mauritania, and Senegal have worked out a joint plan for major improvements in the use of the Senegal River waters and have invited other nations to participate in a multiyear river basin development program. In September 1974, M. Tioule Konate, Mali's finance minister, visited Bonn to discuss German participation in the Senegal River Project of OMVS (Organization for the Development of the Senegal River). This project includes the construction of dams and harbors in the countries on the Senegal River as well as measures to correct the river course. Although Germany promised to contribute 40 million marks in capital aid, no arrangement had yet been made, pending finalization of the contributions to be made by several Arab countries and by the World Bank.[39]

The longer-term development programs have represented a serious challenge to the world community since these projects require substantial financial contributions and multiyear commitments. None of the potential donor countries appears willing to make such a commitment, for a good number of reasons. First, there is disagreement between the Sahel governments and the European donors on the overall planning and programming and long-range kinds of development that might prevent future drought. The foreign donors have not yet approved the joint priority list worked out by the African governments for long-term development programs; they seem to have serious reservations on some projects. The foreign governments have preferred to conduct their own studies to determine the programs best suited for development in the Sahel and to decide themselves on the elements of the medium- and long-range plan that fit within a comprehensive and integrated strategy. This means that they cannot act immediately on the proposed African programs since such studies would take at least six to twelve months to complete. Consequently, they are not ready to finance other long-term projects that the Sahel

governments feel are needed to rebuild their badly dislocated economies. In the African view, the longer the donor countries take to
determine the development projects that they will finance, the longer
the Sahel countries will need to depend on external assistance to feed
their people.

Furthermore, because of the world economic situation, Western
European countries are reluctant to make any substantial financial
commitments for long-term development in the Sahel, nor have
prospective donors yet worked out a coordinated plan for medium-
or long-term development. Such efforts are necessary to ensure that
plans go forward in coordinated fashion. Ultimately, several international banking institutions, including the World Bank and the African
Development Bank, must be involved.

As a further difficulty, it appears that the Sahel governments
are still reluctant to work together in a joint regional development
plan despite public pronouncements regarding their readiness to
work collectively on the drought problem. Even though interregional
committees and commissions have been created, there is no evidence
of increased cooperation among the Sahel governments. On the contrary, certain governments have been individually active in soliciting
international assistance to support their own development proposals.

ASSESSMENT

A careful assessment of international relief efforts in the
Sahel must be predicated on an understanding of several important
characteristics of the crisis. Among the most salient is the fact
that the Sahel governments waited until the drought reached a critical
stage before they called for international assistance. This delay was
largely responsible for another important factor, that the world
community was caught off guard and lacked sufficient information to
determine the magnitude of the problem or the most efficient response.

With regard to the relief effort itself, any appraisal must recognize two other general characteristics of the situation. First, the
lack of transportation infrastructure in the Sahel severely hampered
relief activities while raising considerably the costs of food shipment.
Second, there was little coordination of effort among either the donor
countries or the Sahel governments. [40] While undoubtedly due to the
haste with which relief efforts had to get under way, this meant that
the potential benefits of effective coordination were lost.

Above all, the sheer scope of the problem must be recognized.
Whereas the Ethiopian drought of 1973 affected two to six million
people, the Sahel crisis threatened the lives of twenty-five million

people. Furthermore, the Sahel crisis was aggravated by the fact that
it came on the heels of six previous dry years that had already caused
hunger, malnutrition, and severe loss of livestock.

Each of these characteristics of the crisis posed its own
obstacles. Together, their combined impact was to present a number
of severe constraints on the efficiency and speed of relief operations.
Given this context, some problems encountered by the international
relief program were almost inevitable.

The insufficient volume of aid during the first year, when the
assistance efforts met only half the projected need, was to a great
extent due to logistic problems caused by the belated call for assistance and by the need for emergency coordination among many
nations. The lack of coordination—not only among the donor nations
and organizations and the Sahelian governments but also with neighboring African countries whose ports and transport systems were
needed to reach the landlocked countries of the Sahel—caused innumerable administrative and logistic problems during the first
year of the relief effort. Moreover, for such a large-scale crisis,
the lack of previous planning and of detailed information on the problems severely limited the type of response that donor nations could
make. Thus, for instance, international commitments already made
by countries with grain surpluses undoubtedly acted as a constraint
on the quantity of grain that they could ship to the Sahel. The U.S.-
Soviet grain deal, for example, had greatly depleted U.S. grain
supplies and driven up grain prices. Also, lacking prior information
on the extent of the problem, many governments had to attempt to
provide last-minute relief without appropriate budget allocations
earmarked for the Sahel. Similarly, because of the scarcity of
information, some countries at first thought that the drought problem
would be over once the next rainy season arrived.

The net result was the inability of donor governments to make
commitments in sufficient volume to meet the Sahel's needs. Whereas
the Sahel grain deficit for the 1973 crop year stood at 900,000 MT,
only 471,000 MT of relief assistance reached the Sahel countries
in that year. This figure represents 52 percent of the total needs
for the human population in the drought-striken areas of the six
Sahelian states.[41]

Hal Sheets and Roger Morris, in Disaster in the Desert, are
very critical of the emergency relief operations. They single out the
United States and the FAO in particular, alleging that "maladministra-
tion of aid to the region has been more serious and prolonged than
has been previously claimed."[42] Such a charge is difficult to sub-
stantiate or refute. Some administrative problems probably were

unavoidable, given the scope of the problem, the number of countries involved, and the haste with which the relief supplies had to be shipped. Whether such problems were excessive or could have been avoided—and whether certain donors were more at fault than others— is difficult to determine and necessarily subject to differing interpretations.

A point on which the United States does appear to be vulnerable is whether a larger effort could have been made, despite the difficulties imposed by the situation. The United States was the largest donor to the Sahel, with a total of $130 million contributed during the 1973-74 crop year. Yet this amount is relatively small in comparison with the $2.2 billion of emergency military aid airlifted to Israel during the Yom Kipper War in October 1973. The amount of Sahel assistance also is much smaller in size and scope than the considerable amount of American aid given to the Thieu regime in South Vietnam for a similar period. During fiscal year 1974-75, the U.S. Congress approved $700 million for South Vietnam, only half the total requested by the Nixon administration. President Ford later requested an additional $300 million in assistance for Vietnam.

From this comparative perspective, it could be argued that U.S. priorities rather than actual constraints played an important role in determining the amount of assistance extended to the Sahel. The record unfortunately shows that the United States was willing to spend huge amounts of money to sustain the war effort in Vietnam and could give great urgency to mounting a hurried but massive airlift of military equipment to Israel, while much less funding, attention, or urgency was directed to the humanitarian effort to extend assistance to the drought-stricken Sahel.[43]

With regard to another major problem affecting the relief program, the delays in transporting food inland to the drought-affected areas, the difficulty of coordinating relief from many nations was a very serious obstacle. The biggest difficulty was the absence of adequate transportation infrastructure. In particular, the lack of road and rail links connecting drought areas with West African ports prevented speedy delivery of emergency food supplies. Several other problems, including port strikes and bureaucratic red tape, also hampered delivery efforts. As Table 3.5 shows, the result was that large quantities of emergency grain remained stockpiled in West African ports during the height of the relief effort, and the evacuation rate to the Sahel countries was slow and much behind schedule.

In many specific instances, certain African governments might be faulted for contributing to delays or for failure to resolve particular problems hampering delivery of food supplies. While the donor nations bear no direct blame for such delays, they might be criticized for failing to respond to the problem by developing alternative delivery

TABLE 3.5

Food Grain Accumulations in West African Ports
(metric tons)

	Dakar/Abidjan: Destination Mali	Dakar: Destination Mauritania	Adibjan: Destination Upper Volta	Lagos: Destination Niger
July 1, 1973				
Stock	45,000	4,000	1,000	12,000
Arrivals	29,000	8,500	3,000	15,000
Evacuation	15,000	5,000	4,000	12,000
August 1, 1973				
Stock	62,000	7,500	—	15,000
Arrivals	17,500	5,000	3,000	12,000
Evacuation	15,000	5,000	3,000	12,000
September 1, 1973				
Stock	64,500	7,500	—	15,000
Arrivals	3,000	3,000	3,000	5,000
Evacuation	15,000	5,000	3,000	12,000
October 1, 1973				
Stock	52,500	5,500	—	8,000

Source: The Drought in the African Sahel (Washington, D.C.: U.S. Government Printing Office, 1973), p. 97.

plans. Foreign donors were aware of the transportation difficulties but failed to initiate any large-scale operations to speed the transfer of food. Airlifts were clearly needed, but foreign donors were slow to provide either trucking or airlift operations prior to the beginning of the rainy season. The airlifts that did occur were relatively modest, short-term operations, and could be rightly criticized as "too little, too late."

Fortunately, foreign donors were able to increase considerably their contributions during the second year of operations. The international relief program for the 1974 crop year met 76 percent of the projected Sahelian need for food grains and cereals. Out of a total need of 1.12 million MT of food grains for the period November 1, 1973, to October 31, 1974, some 852,719 MT were donated. It was reported that by August 1974 the bulk of the food supplies had arrived in the Sahel areas; 784,000 MT, both donations and commercial purchases, had reached the affected countries, with another 129,000 MT in West African ports and railroads.[44] There also was some improvement in the movement of food and other supplies to the countries affected by the drought. This was largely due to advance planning and sufficient time to work out the logistic and administrative problems concerning the transfer of food across the Atlantic and inland on the African continent. Thus, foreign donors generally have provided stepped-up assistance to meet the basic needs of the Sahel, substantially helping to prevent further large-scale loss of life.

At this time it is difficult to predict the future for the Sahel. Although the 1974 rainfall has been relatively good, the drought problems are far from over. It will be several years before the Sahelian countries can feed their populations without external aid. The expected crop for the 1974-75 year, for instance, will probably be inadequate to meet the needs of the Sahel people. Several factors are involved: (1) farmers who wandered away from their villages during the dry years have not returned to their farms; (2) foreign donors have not provided sufficient supplies of seed; and (3) the Sahel countries have extremely low reserves of grain. The immediate result has been a reduction in the amount of acreage planted throughout the Sahel area.[45]

For this reason, the Sahel countries will probably need 382,000 tons of food and cereals between November 1974 and October 1975, notably a much smaller quantity than needed in previous years. Preparations already are being made to get early commitments from foreign donors in order to allow adequate timing so that transport can be accomplished by conventional means (rail and trucks) without need for airlifts.[46]

A different type of danger lies in the fact that foreign donors have so far concentrated on trying to relieve the immediate crisis and

have shown little readiness to initiate longer-term measures to
prevent a similar disaster in the future. Despite the fact that foreign
countries are well aware of the need for a more comprehensive
approach to economic planning in the Sahel, they have not thus far
been able to finance longer-term development. The plan proposed
by the Sahel governments is an ambitious one, including new agricultural planning, development of water holes, building reserves of
animal feed, management of water resources, and surveying the
natural resources of the area. For its success, the program depends
on cooperation among the Sahelian governments and on large amounts
of external aid. Several meetings of donor and recipient nations have
been held to promote such a program and to coordinate the financing
of the long-term rehabilitation and development program, yet no
results have been seen because none of the major donors has been
willing to make a sizeable financial commitment covering several
years in advance. This is largely due to the problems of the world
economy today. Western European nations, the United States, and
Canada are currently suffering from major inflationary pressures
amid sluggish economic growth. In the process, they are trying to
balance their budgets and reduce deficits, undoubtedly at some cost
to programs of international assistance.

Another factor is that Africa apparently rests at the bottom
of the list of priorities for some countries. The United States, for
instance, has recently allocated less than 10 percent of its total
foreign aid appropriation to Africa; further, its aid is largely given
to only ten of the forty-two independent African states. If the United
States and other industrial nationa are to help make the Sahel self-
sufficient in food production, they must readjust their priorities to
pay more attention to the region. In this period of economic troubles,
this is a large challenge to the industrial nations. Without their
financial and technical assistance, however, the suffering of the
Sahelian people will continue and these countries could lose their
long uphill struggle to survive as nations.

NOTES

1. Development and Management of the Steppe and Brush-Grass
Savannah Zone Immediately South of the Sahara, in-house report
prepared by USAID, (October 1972), p. 45.

2. Statement of Thomas A. Johnson, West Africa correspondent
of the New York Times, in The Drought Crisis in the African Sahel
(Washington, D.C.: U.S. Government Printing Office, 1973), pp. 3-4.

A higher estimate was reported in "Oxfam Report on Drought,"
West Africa, no. 2966 (April 22, 1974): 474.

3. Report of the U.N. Committee for Development Planning,
March 22-April 1, 1971, Official Records of Economic and Social
Council, 51st Session, E/4990, Supplement no. 7, p. 17.

4. Hal Sheets and Roger Morris, Disaster in the Desert:
Failures of International Relief in the West African Drought, Special
Report, Humanitarian Policy Studies (Carnegie Endowment for
International Peace, 1974), p. 2.

5. Elliot Skinner, "Suffering in the Sudan-Sahel: A Void to
Fill," Community Newsletter (Center for Black Studies) 4, no. 4
(December 1974): 2.

6. For more information on "Negligence-Charge and Counter-
Charge," see Victor D. DuBois, The Drought in West Africa, Part II:
Perception, Evaluation, and Response, American Universities Field-
staff Reports, West Africa Series, vol. 15, no. 2 (May 1974), pp. 2-4.

7. Sheets and Morris, Disaster, p. 9.

8. Du Bois, The Drought, p. 1.

9. FAO Office for the Sahelian Relief Operation (OSRO),
Progress Report 1, (June 4, 1973), p. 1.

10. U.N. Official Records of the Economic and Social Council,
28th Session, A/9003, Supplement no. 3, p. 111.

11. Pierre-Claver Damiba, "The Drought in Tropical Africa:
Analysis and Policy," paper delivered at the Nineteenth International
Conference of the Banque Internationale pour l'Afrique de l'Ouest,
July 15-20, 1973, Lome, Togo, p. 13.

12. FAO/OSRO, Progress Report no. 1, (June 4, 1973), pp. 2-3.

13. West Africa, no. 2975 (June 24, 1974): 777; "Le drame
de la secheresse en Afrique Sahelienne," Marches Tropicaux et
Mediterraneens, August 10, 1973, p. 2445.

14. Africa Report, November-December 1973, p. 36.

15. Maurice J. Williams, "On U.S. Assistance to Parched
West Africa," New York Times, February 16, 1974.

16. USAID Report to the Congress on Famine in Sub-Sahara
Africa, September 1974, pp. 5-6.

17. The Drought Crisis, Appendix 8.

18. "Drought in Sudano-Sahelian Region of Africa," U.N. Official
Records of the Economic and Social Council, E/ICEF/L. 1291/Add. 2,
12 December 1974, p. 7.

19. USAID Report, September 1974, pp. 9-11.

20. Ibid., pp. 14-15.

21. FAO/OSRO, Report 11 (September 10, 1974), p. 8.

22. West Africa, No. 2974 (June 17, 1974): 743.

23. West Africa, no. 2968 (May 6, 1974): 519.

24. West Africa, no. 2974 (June 17, 1974): 743.

25. USAID Report, September 1974, p. 6.
26. The Drought Crisis, p. 27.
27. Ibid., p. 69.
28. West Africa, no. 2920, (May 28, 1973): 720.
29. FAO/OSRO, Report 7 (November 30, 1973): 5; West Africa, no. 2975 (June 24, 1974): 774.
30. West Africa, no. 2988 (September 23, 1974): 1174.
31. West Africa, no. 2983 (August 19, 1974): 1029.
32. "Stopping the Sahara," West Africa, no. 2931 (August 13, 1973): 1102.
33. Damiba, "The Drought," pp. 28-29.
34. West Africa, no. 2931 (August 13, 1973): 1102.
35. World Hunger, Health, and Refugee Problems Part IV: Famine in Africa (Washington, D.C.: U.S. Government Printing Office, 1974), p. 16.
36. West Africa, no. 2989 (September 30, 1974): 1203.
37. USAID Report, September 1974, p. 11.
38. World Hunger, Part IV, pp. 60-61.
39. West Africa, no. 2989 (September 30, 1974): 1203.
40. Victor D. DuBois, The Drought in West Africa, Part III: The Logistics of Relief Operations, American Universities Field-staff Reports, West Africa Series, vol. 15, no. 3 (May 1974), pp. 1-8.
41. FAO/OSRO, Report No. 8 (January 31, 1974): 1; Le Point sur la Secheresse, Comite Catholique contre la Faim et pour le Developpement (Paris, June 1973), p. 16.
42. West Africa, no. 2968 (May 6, 1974): 517.
43. Jean-Pierre N'Diaye compared the drought-induced emergency in Africa with the war in Vietnam (Jeune Afrique, May 19, 1973), while Robert Lambotte drew a comparison between the international emergency relief efforts for the Sahel and the Anglo-American response to the Berlin Blockade (L'Humanite, May 11, 1973).
44. FAO/OSRO, Report 11 (September 10, 1974): 1.
45. Ibid., p. 5.
46. FAO News Release, 26/74 74/98.

4

AN INTERNATIONAL PERSPECTIVE ON THE AFRICAN FAMINES
Laurie Wiseberg

The famines that struck the Sudano/Sahelian region of Africa these past years, climaxed in the 1972 drought, are frequently described as natural disasters or acts of God (just as are other recent famines, in southern Asia, southern Africa, or Central America). Yet, in the 1970s, to talk about famine in such terms is what George Orwell called newspeak; it is intended to absolve us of responsibility for the death and suffering that accompanied the failure of the rains. Specifically, the reference to natural disaster deliberately obfuscates critical socioeconomic and political dimensions of the famines such as the following:

1. Drought (or any other climatic factor that impacts negatively on the availability of food supplies) results in starvation deaths only in the underdeveloped countries of the world, and in pockets of poverty in the industrialized northern hemisphere.
2. The condition of underdevelopment, which limits the capacity of third world nations to effectively respond to crop failure or herd decimation, is perpetuated by the technologically advanced nations (and, increasingly, by multinational corporations) that are politically, economically, and ideologically hegemonous in the global power structure.

―――――――――

This chapter is based on a paper presented at the African Studies Association Annual Meeting, Chicago, October 1974. A summer fellowship granted by the University of Illinois at Chicago Circle enabled me to research the study and I would like to acknowledge that support.

3. Political elites in afflicted countries are often slow to acknowledge their incapacities and/or to appeal for international aid for fear of tarnishing their image, weakening their domestic power base, or further undermining their national sovereignty, and they are not always above utilizing a disaster situation for reasons of self-enrichment or political gain.

4. Because humanitarian interests are so low in the priority scales of governmental elites, the response of the international community, in terms of disaster relief, is generally belated and inadequate.

5. Even where humanitarian motivation is strong, relief and rehabilitation programs are often deficient (even counterproductive) because too little attention is paid to the sociopolitical impact of economic aid and because technical "solutions" are given preference over sociopolitical ones.

6. The famines of the 1970s portend a global Malthusian crisis unless political action is immediately taken to confront the world food problem in an effective and equitable manner.

An examination of the Sudano/Sahelian and Ethiopian famines will amplify these points.

THE INTERVENING VARIABLES BETWEEN DROUGHT AND FAMINE

Analyses of the African famines generally begin with a discussion of the climatic drought that scourged Africa in the early 1970s.[1] However, too many studies erroneously suggest a causal linkage between drought and famine and ignore the intervening variables that determine what consequences a drought will produce. A half-century ago, it may not have seemed simplistic to argue that starvation was caused by climatic disaster, particularly for societies remote from the technological centers of the world. At that time, the rudimentary global infrastructure (communications and transportation) inhibited surpluses from food-producing regions from being shipped rapidly enough to food-deficit areas to avert disaster.[2]

Yet, even before the modern age, technology was less critical than some would suggest. For example, if we examine the Irish famine of 1845-49, it becomes clear that British indifference, as well as the time it would have taken to send food over from England, or the potato crop failure, contributed to the death rate.[3] Nothing dramatizes the political dimension of that famine better than Jonathan Swift's Modest Proposal, although the satire was written about Irish starvation of an earlier century.[4]

The Bengal famine of 1943 was, likewise, sustained by an incompetent and callous colonial administration and by speculation and hoarding on the part of the indigenous aristocracy.[5] Moreover, the U.N. Relief and Rehabilitation Administration (UNRRA), created in 1943, might have prevented at least some of the three to four million Indian deaths, yet it gave no aid to the starving Bengalis. U.S. Secretary of State Dean Acheson explained UNRRA's nonresponse with the argument that UNRRA's activities were limited to war victims liberated by the allied forces in countries belonging to the United Nations; a more meaningful explanation of the American (and, hence, UNRRA's) position is that the United States regarded India as part of the British sphere of influence and therefore had no desire to intervene.[6]

Finally, one also can consider the hundreds of thousands who died in China's Honan Province in 1943. In this case, the drought as cause seems almost insignificant in the face of the corruption and brutality of governmental officials, army officers, and rich landlords who extracted the last grain of seed and the last acre of land from the starving peasants.[7] It appears that the political, not the technological, factors were the determining ones.

In the last third of the twentieth century, generally characterized by its technological prowess, we have the capacity to send men to the moon, to transplant hearts, and to communicate instantly over thousands of miles via manmade satellites. Surely existent technology can be utilized to ameliorate the impact of hazardous climatic fluctuations—to provide disaster relief—if the political will to act is present. Thus, for example, during the Nigerian civil war, U.S. Senator George McGovern correctly asserted that getting food airlifted to Biafra was a political, not a logistical, problem: "if we find the logistical skill to drop weapons [on Indochina], we should be able to find a way to drop some of our abundant food where there is starvation."[8] In 1948-49, when the West Berliners were menaced by blockade, neither the logistics nor the cost were obstacles to the American and British governments. To supply 2.1 million people over a ten-month period, their air forces flew in approximately 185,000 planeloads of supplies amounting to 1.5 million tons,[9] as compared with the relief airlifts to Biafra, which only brought 85,000 tons of aid, to feed two to three times as many people for twice as long a period.[10]

One dimension of the problem is, therefore, that in the face of the ever-widening disparity in the technological capacity and wealth, as between the top third and the bottom two-thirds of the world,[11] the industrialized nations lack the political will to effect an adequate response. The significance of this can hardly be overstated: When tragedy strikes an industrial state, it can generally respond with its own resources to ameliorate the situation, but when tragedy strikes in the third world, the poor must depend on the charity and technological prowess of the rich. Thus, the ruination of corn and soybean crops in Iowa and Nebraska means higher food prices for most Americans, hardship for farmers, and suffering for the poorest strata of U.S. citizens; and, given the precarious world food balance (to be discussed below), it means higher world prices for foodstuffs and less food aid to be distributed abroad. But it does not mean widespread starvation in the midwestern United States. By contrast, drought, flood, or pestilence for farmers who live on the margin in Africa, Asia, and Latin America means increased mal-nutrition or death unless there is a positive response from the first or second world.

Despite the fact that the current petroleum and ecological crises have made the industrialized nations conscious of their own dependence upon the resources of the developing states, and despite talk about "interdependence" and the "spaceship earth,"[12] it remains to be seen whether an ethic of responsibility will advance beyond platitudinous proclamations. If we are not blinded by the newspeak of "natural disaster," it must be clear that the privileged elite bears a responsibility for famine and starvation because the elite has the capacity to intervene. To cite Denis Goulet, the responsibility "of rich classes and nations for creating justice does not rest on a scape-goat theory of history which would brand them 'guilty' of the unequal distribution of riches." Rather, "the rich are now 'responsible' for abolishing absolute want in others even if they have not been 'guilty' of producing it in the past."[13] Moreover, as we move from the development decades into the quality-of-life decade, there is an expedient as well as a moral imperative for action.

THE STRUCTURE OF WORLD POWER

To pursue Goulet's argument further, the vulnerability of the poor—and the full significance of the inequalities in the world—becomes clear if we distinguish between two categories of change processes:

> The first processes concern production, mastery
> over nature, rational organization, and technological
> efficiency; the second concern structures of power
> and ideology. Historically, processes of both types
> have been launched and disseminated by societies now
> termed "developed." The two categories remain closely

interrelated. Technologically advanced nations also
wield dominant political power and influence in the
world. Consequently, entry into technological
modernity can only be obtained on terms set by those
who already master both series of processes—those
relating to technology itself and those which pertain
to power, political and ideological. [14]

If the less developed countries (LDCs) are not to remain in perpetual
dependence upon the rich, at the mercy of charity whenever they are
confronted with environmental challenge, they also must alter the
structure of power so that they gain some influence on critical
international decision making. At present, their attempt to do so
is largely blocked by the powerful; the United States and the USSR
are willing to dispense limited amounts of aid and technological
know-how, but only on their own terms.

Thus, the meaning of the African famines can be fully understood only in the context of the poverty and powerlessness of a region
such as the Sahel. Despite the Sahel's "liberation" from colonialism,
and despite nearly two development decades, four of the six Sahelian
countries—Chad, Niger, Mali, and Upper Volta (as well as Ethiopia)—
are among the core of least developed countries, as designated by
the U.N. General Assembly in 1971, with a per capita GNP of less
than $100 per year. (The other two are slightly better off, Mauritania
with a 1970 per capita GNP of $154 and Senegal with $178.) Thus, the
Sahelians are among the 800 million who Robert McNamara (president
of the World Bank) described as subsisting in poverty at 30 cents a
day;[15] their children are among the 400 to 500 million whom Henri
Labouisse (executive director of UNICEF) considered under the
threat of severe malnutrition and starvation. [16] Of the Sahelian population of about 23 million in 1970, some 88 percent of the total labor
force was in agriculture, largely subsistence farming or herding.
What little foreign exchange the region earns derives from a few
cash crops (such as peanuts) and the foreign-controlled exploitation
of its few mineral deposits (such as Mauritanian iron ore); all but
one of the Sahelian states have unfavorable balances of payments and
are still heavily dependent on France. [17] Because it must import
food, fertilizer, and oil, the Sahel has been critically wounded by
the current world inflationary situation.

The poverty of the Sahel is related to its powerlessness.
Exploited during the colonial era, the Sahel continues to be exploited
through the neocolonial nexus. France controls what little wealth
there is in the area (Mauritania's iron ore, Niger's uranium mines,
Senegal's peanut trade) as well as the region's ideological orientation.
Nor has this resulted in any significant payoffs for the Sahel in terms

of aid or trade. Indeed, had the Sahel been able to attract more aid to make up for the years of colonial plunder and/or neglect, had it been able to command better terms of trade for its commodities, the economic plight of the region would not have been as severe as it was when the drought struck. But what power did independence give the Sahelian states?

With other states, the Sahelian nations each received one vote in the General Assembly of the United Nations; however, the General Assembly makes vacuous pronouncements and not effective policy, as should be clear to anyone who has followed its attempts to change the apartheid situation in South Africa or the equally reprehensible status quo in Namibia and Rhodesia. With respect to situations of international conflict, the arms race, the protection of human rights, and, especially, with respect to the international structure of trade and aid, the LDCs have had negligible influence. The Sahelian states were among the 77 third world countries that banded together in 1963 to force the creation of the U.N. Conference on Trade and Development (UNCTAD), over the opposition of the industrial nations (both communist and capitalist); and they thought they had achieved a substantive victory. In fact, since UNCTAD's establishment, few concrete concessions have been gained: There has been no agreement on a general preferential system for commodities; the rich have moved from a conservative free trade position to a reactionary protectionism (manifested especially in such nontariff barriers as restrictive business practices[18]) to prevent their markets being "flooded" and their labor being undercut by low-wage products, and to prevent a loss of control over technology "transferred" abroad by multinational corporations (MNCs); the MNCs have grown in both size and number while LDCs have been unable to regulate either their terms of entry or their operations—witness what happened to Allende when he challenged ITT and Anaconda; and there have been organized efforts to resist attempts to reform the monetary structure to provide LDCs with relief for their balance-of-payments problems.[19]

Notwithstanding the recent muscle flexing of the oil nations—the first real instance of unity in action among a part of the third world—the Special Session of the General Assembly on Raw Materials and Development, in April-May 1974, provided little encouragement for those who hoped for fundamental change. The one concrete achievement of the assembly was approval of an emergency relief program for the countries hardest hit by the rising costs of food, oil, fertilizer, and other necessities they import. Concerning the demands embodied in the "Declaration on the Establishment of a New International Economic Order," one must agree with President Senghor of Senegal that the session was a failure and will not meet Africa's needs.[20] Simply stated, the industrialized countries are not prepared

to make concessions that might jeopardize their power hegemony.
They are willing to dole out limited aid, as long as this involves
no sacrifice on their part and as long as they can set the priorities.
The countries in desperate need, like the Sahel or Ethiopia, have
little choice but to acquiesce, or to starve.

CHARITY BEGINS AT HOME

Clearly, the capacity of the Sahelian and Ethiopian governments
to respond to the drought conditions with their own resources has
been limited. Nonetheless, as Ruth First wrote in another context,
one cannot consider all the ills of the third world as visited upon it
by outside forces, although many of them are.[21] Real economic
power may lie outside the continent, and it certainly lies outside the
drought areas; yet, the African elites in power must bear responsibility for their actions. Judging the performance of African leaders
under the shadow of Watergate may seem insensitivity to the maxim
that "People who live in glass houses . . . ." However, the issue
must be openly stated: While much of the suffering wrought by the
drought was beyond the control of the concerned African governments,
not all of it was.

Ethiopia

The shabbiest performance, and one that was dearly paid for,
was the performance of Haile Selassie and the Ethiopian ruling class.
Ethiopia is a nation in which 90 percent of the population is in agriculture or stock raising, but where nine out of ten people live as
subsistence tenants on feudal estates (about a third of the land was
owned by the emperor, a third by the aristocracy, and the remainder
by the Church). The elite's first response to the drought was to hide
it and to capitalize on it. Drought conditions first manifested themselves in provinces north of Addis Ababa in 1970-71 and went virtually
unreported for over two years. That the emperor, who visited Wallo
Province in late 1972, could justify his lack of action in the face of
the creeping disaster by saying that he was not informed of the drought
or the severity of the situation until March 1973, is a severe indictment of his regime.[22] When rulers become so insulated and isolated
from the ruled, when they cannot recognize intense suffering and
starvation, ignorance is rationalization—not justification. Interviewed about the situation in June 1973, the emperor callously
observed:

> Rich and poor have always existed and always will.
> Why? Because there are those that work. . . . and
> those that prefer to do nothing. . . . We have said
> wealth has to be gained thru hard work. We have
> said those who don't work starve. . . . Each individual
> is responsible for his misfortunes, his fate. It is
> wrong to expect help to fall from above, as a gift:
> Wealth has to be deserved! 23

Until a systematic study of the situation has been completed, it
is difficult to be authoritative about governmental responsibility for
the thousands who succumbed to hunger. However, a damning picture
is being pieced together from newspaper coverage. 24 For example,
according to David B. Ottaway (Washington Post, August 29, 1974)
one of the major findings of a 1974 special civilian commission set
up to investigate corruption and abuse of power in Ethiopia was the
fact that, as early as August 1970, Mamo Seyoum, governor and
special imperial envoy in Wallo Province, had written the emperor
asking that action be taken to save the lives of thousands of starving
peasants. This was three years before the peak impact of the drought,
indicating that there had been some pressure on the emperor, the
prime minister, and the Crown Prince Asfa Wossen (the nominal
ruler of Wallo, who owned an entire valley and some of the most
fertile land in the province) to take action to alleviate the situation.
The requests went unheeded.

Charles Mohr (New York Times, November 18, 1973) reported
that the Ethiopian Ministry of Agriculture was aware of the dimensions
of the problem at least as early as November 1972, after the completion of its annual crop survey. That survey predicted serious
harvest failures in Wallo and Tigre provinces consequent upon two
years of drought. The survey was apparently suppressed by the
Ethiopian cabinet. Moreover, the man who succeeded to the governor-
ship of Wallo, the heart of the famine area, when the situation was
becoming even more serious, claims that he, too, knew nothing about
the situation and that he was too tied up with administrative matters
to tour the province. He never left the provincial capital of Dessye
during his three years in office. In fact, the governor may have
known nothing, for he appears to have paid little attention to reports
of famine submitted to him by his junior officials. In March 1973,
the head of a subdistrict of Wallo is reported to have been so frustrated
by the indifference of his provincial superiors that he traveled to
Addis Ababa to personally apprise the central government of the
magnitude of the existing catastrophe. The same month, some 1,500
Wallo peasants marched to Addis Ababa to beg for help and were
turned back by the police. When the minister of the interior asked

the governor for a report, he admitted to "a problem of drought" but
assured the ministry that the situation was under control. Not until
April 1973, when famine rumors began circulating in the capital,
did the government send an inspection team to the interior.

Furthermore, whether the Ethiopian government was afraid
of tarnishing its international image or because it believed itself
capable of dealing with the situation through its own resources, the
magnitude of the starvation was not made clear. According to Charles
Mohr (New York Times, February 18, 1974), the Ethiopian government
requested international aid but minimized the situation. The government was not receptive to a meeting between relief donors and
Ethiopian ministers to discuss the coordination of relief. When it
was finally pressured into such a meeting in mid-August 1973, con-
frontation rather than cooperation resulted. The Ethiopians were
outraged by a private UNICEF report claiming that 50,000 to 100,000
had died of starvation.[25] As Mohr suggested, the Ethiopians apparently felt that "such events could not occur in the great Empire of
Ethiopia." National pride is understandable, particularly under the
shadow of the "foreign meddling" of relief actors as occurred in the
Nigerian civil war. It is, however, hardly commendable if the result
is a magnification of the tragedy.

Less acceptable was the Ethiopian government's position on the
cholera epidemic that swept through weakened refugee populations.
According to the official line, there was no cholera in Ethiopia, only
"gastro-enteritis C." The Ministry of Health informed the World
Health Organization that it would not appeal for aid even though the
government could not take preventive measures needed to retard the
spread of the disease. It did accept free cholera vaccine donated by
WHO, but much of this was reportedly sold at $2.00 a shot to destitute
and starving peasants (Martin Walker, New York Times Magazine,
June 9, 1974). In addition, when the government finally mobilized a
relief effort by establishing a Relief and Rehabilitation Commission
in late 1973 (even though the drought areas were not officially declared
"disaster areas" until September 7, 1974, at a time when the military
was firmly in command), it was plagued by all the inefficiencies and
corruption characteristic of the emperor's administration. Relief
food found its way more readily onto the black market than into the
hands of the peasantry. Officials used their power for self-enrichment.
Landlords, church, and aristocracy refused to lower rents, which
could amount to as much as 75 percent of the crop[26]; nor would they
distribute free relief grain until the last grain of their own harvests
was sold at a 300 percent inflation price.

An interesting sidelight was provided by a delegate to the
International Conference of Africanists, which met in Addis Ababa
in December 1973.[27] Despite the fact that a keynote speaker raised

the question of the famine at the opening session, the emperor ignored
the issue in his responding address. Despite the dire food shortage
just outside the capital, the emperor saw fit to bestow his imperial
hospitality on the conference by "commanding" the delegates to a
sumptuous banquet at the Jubilee Palace, where six different wines
and countless delicacies were served. [28] It is, consequently, not
difficult to understand why the legitimacy of the Lion of Judah was
finally challenged by posters juxtaposing a photograph of starving
children with one of the emperor feeding his dogs meat from a silver
platter (Ottaway, Washington Post, September 3, 1974). The famine
was not the underlying cause of Hailie Selassie's fall, but it was the
catalyst that served to magnify the injustice and ills of the archaic
Ethiopian system.

The Sahel

        The response of the Sahelian political elites was more humane
and more commendable than that of the Ethiopian elite. For example,
a USAID report notes that, over the past two years, the government
of Senegal has made severe sacrifices in its own use of transport
facilities in order to assist Mali and Mauritania to meet their cereal
import needs, much of which pass through Dakar to be sent north
over Senegalese road and rail. [29] Also, the Mauritanian government,
in January 1973, established an emergency fund to which each wage
earner was expected to give one day's pay per month, and every
company 1 percent of its monthly turnover, toward famine relief. [30]
Nigeria, just south of the Sahel but affected by the drought in its
northern states for more than two years, not only committed $75
million for Nigerian famine relief but also gave $15 million toward
relief in the Sahel. [31] Finally, the Sahelian governments have exhibited considerable generosity toward refugees, permitting nomads
to cross national boundaries in search of food and frequently sharing
their own meager resources with the refugees.
        However, mixed with generosity have been greed, corruption,
and unnecessary inefficiency. In examining the capacity of the
Sahelian elites to respond to the crisis, one must remember the
limitations under which they operate, and the fact that their frail
infrastructures and administrative resources were often strained
beyond their limits. Therefore, Martin Walker is correct in
deemphasizing the inevitable "horror stories, the kind of anecdotes
white South Africans like to tell to 'prove' the inadequacy of independent black governments":

Yes, the customs authorities in Upper Volta
refused to let a Canadian plane unload its cargo
of gift medical supplies until import duties were
paid. Yes, cotton seed was being exported from
Bobo at a time when FED officials were hunting
for this precious high-protein animal feed throughout
West Africa. Yes, the Sahel governments once asked
for enough chemical fertilizer to poison every acre
and river for a decade. . . . This kind of stupidity
happens in every army in every bureaucracy in
every crisis. We are, after all, talking of the
poorest countries on earth. [Emphasis added.][32]

But vagaries notwithstanding, systematic corruption and systematic greed, false pride, and the deliberate manipulation of the
disaster for political advantage cannot be excused. Thus, evidence
suggests that the political elites of the Sahel, representative (except
for Mauritania) of the sedentary as opposed to the nomadic populations,
knowingly biased relief distribution against the Tuareg and other
politically "rebellious" groups.[33] Evidence also suggests that certain
elements of the elite were indifferent to the fate of drought victims
and were involved in hoarding or black-marketeering.[34] The response
of the government of Chad to a New York Times article charging
corruption and inefficiency in the distribution of aid by persons close
to the Chad leadership was to ban further American food relief on
the grounds that President Tombalbaye felt insulted "and if taking
food means taking insults, he'd rather do without the food."[35]

Such evidence, which strongly implies that elites were more
concerned with protecting their power bases and wealth than with
making the governmental and societal changes so essential to development, is no more excusable in West Africa than it is in Ethiopia
or the United States. Thus, if one facet of the development problem
is the rich/poor dichotomy between states, another facet is the rich/
poor dichotomy within states. The third world may have little leverage
against the industrialized world, but there is even less hope that
third world nations will acquire the requisites for development and
independence in the absence of strong moral leadership.

THE INADEQUACY OF THE INTERNATIONAL
RESPONSE

It is a well-documented fact that governments respond to
international events primarily in terms of their own perceived

political and economic interests and that humanitarian concerns
rarely move them to action.[36] Governments adopt humanitarian
postures and can be mobilized either if there is a convergence between their "vital interests" and a humanitarian one, or if there is
a political cost (frequently in terms of domestic pressures) to a policy
of inaction. The former explains the Berlin airlift, while the latter
explains the response to the famine in Nigeria during that civil war.
This notwithstanding, the ideologies professed by both the Western
capitalist and Eastern socialist states, and the fact that modern
communications make it possible to spotlight disaster areas, and
the fact that there exist relief and development-oriented national and
international bureaucracies as well as nongovernmental organizations,
increases the likelihood of an international response to disasters
such as the Nicaraguan earthquake, the monsoonal floods in Bangladesh, or the drought in India. These considerations might be used
to explain the fact that there was an international response to the
famines in the Sahel and Ethiopia. However, the depth of relief efforts
varied from case to case.

AMERICAN RELIEF IN THE SAHEL

The Sahelian relief operation, and particularly the role played
by the American government, has been lauded. It is pointed out, for
example, that while more than 100,000 people may have died of
starvation in the Sahel last year,[37] hundreds of thousands were kept
alive because of the rapid response to the emergency by relief donors.
It is emphasized that, since 1972, the United States has provided
approximately $129 million in food (600,000 tons of grain) and nonfood
aid in the largest relief program it has undertaken in Africa.[38] USAID
officials note that, while there were administrative and logistic difficulties experienced in 1972-73, many were overcome by careful
planning in 1973-74.[39] And it is noted that the U.S. contribution to
the Sahel represented 40 percent of the total international contribution.[40]

Not everyone concurs in this appraisal. Critics of the U.S.
role raise serious questions about the magnanimity of the American
government. Bruce Oudes, an Africa Report correspondent, recently
wrote:

in comparison with the U.S. food programs in
South Asia those in Africa are a drop in the
bucket. During the past two years in Bangladesh
alone the United States has contributed more than

$440 million in food relief. This is far more than
the $334 million that is the combined total of all
U.S. food given to black Africa from 1954 through
1972—the first 19 years of the Public Law 480 food
program.[41]

Considered on a per capita and real need basis, U.S. programs to
Africa and South Asia amount to little more than two drops in a very
big bucket.[42]

Senator George McGovern, chairman of the Senate Select Committee on Nutrition, held hearings in June 1974 on the international
food situation.[43] Reporting on those hearings,[44] McGovern and his
staff underlined the recent steep decline in American food aid and
the strategic/political bias of the Food for Peace Program. They
noted that:

● Compared to the 6.1 million metric tons of wheat the United
States gave in food aid in 1970, it provided only 2.5 million tons in
1973, with less than a million tons projected for 1974.

● In fiscal year 1974, more than 50 percent of the Food for
Peace shipments went to "security-related countries" such as
Vietnam, Cambodia, Laos, Malta, Jordan, and Israel.

● While Congress has acted to end the practice of giving food
aid for military purposes in South Vietnam, that aid cut was offset,
in part, by the commitment of 100,000 tons of grain to Egypt and, in
part, by a $34 million increase in aid to the Chilean military junta.

An important point to remember is that last year's shipments
were less than half what they were during the 1960s and early 1970s
when the United States had large food surpluses. Even if Congress
did increase the April 1974 Food for Peace allocation of $891.7
million to the $1.6 billion that the State Department requested, food
aid would be no more than the 1972 level, considering the increased
cost of grain.[45] In November 1974, Secretary of Agriculture Earl
Butz announced that the United States would make only $1 billion
available for food aid this year.[46]

Taking a somewhat different perspective, Donald F. McHenry
wrote that, in 1973, the United States spent $49 million for the
resettlement of 33,461 Soviet Jews (approximately $1,500 per capita)
while spending only $90 million in emergency relief on 22 million
Africans affected by the Sahelian drought (approximately $4 per
capita)—"an indication of the tragic imbalance in U.S. priorities."[47]
Moreover, for those who might be impressed by the magnitude of the
American dollar commitment to USAID in a tight balance of payments
situation, it must be pointed out that almost all of these dollars remain

in the United States, to purchase American commodities, to pay
American salaries, and for American services.[48] In some instances—
as with the financing of the U.S. airlifts in the Sahel, at a rate of
$1,300 per flight hour[49]—the aid is, in effect, a bookkeeping pro-
cedure, transferring dollars from the account of USAID to the account
of the U.S. Air Force.

It is true that PL-480 food feeds hungry people and can be the
critical determinant between life and death, but it also should be
remembered that in its conception it was a measure designed primarily to assist American farmers by having the government buy
up their agricultural surplus and dispose of it without depressing the
world price of grain.[50] Therefore, it is hardly surprising that now,
when grain is no longer abundant and when farmers can get higher
prices by selling abroad than by turning to the State Department, the
PL-480 program has been drastically cut. Similarly, the forces of
the free market economy explain why the United States, in 1973,
completely cut its dried milk allocation upon which millions of children
depended in the Food for Peace program.[51] Nor is it surprising that
the government's representative in the agricultural sector, Secretary
of Agriculture Butz, attempts to play down the seriousness of the
world famine situation and seeks to leave the management of U.S.
grain supplies in private hands.[52] In other words, the Food for
Peace program, at a time when the United States is making billions
through the commercial export of agricultural produce, is cut to
below $1 billion mainly because it is no longer profitable to an im-
portant domestic interest group.[53] This, too, must be taken as a
measure of American generosity.

It can be and is argued that none of these points detract from
the positive contribution made by the United States with respect to
the alleviation of famine in the Sahel. This argument would be well
taken if there did not exist evidence to support the view of the Sheets/
Morris Carnegie study, which noted that the drought in the Sahel

revealed serious flaws in the organization of the
international relief efforts. Behind humanitarian
intentions and official claims of success lay
bureaucracies often unprepared, or unable, to
take measures that might have further reduced
the tragedy. Despite decades of international
experience in dealing with mass famine, relief for
the Sahel seemed haunted by rudimentary failures
to heed early warnings, to plan in advance, and
to monitor and coordinate the rescue efforts. . . .
Over the entire episode, in spite of the dedication
of many officials at all levels, there was the shadow

of bureaucratic factors in the U.S. or UN scarcely
related to human suffering in Africa—programs
continued or initiatives neglected out of institutional
inertia, rivalries between offices and agencies, an
unwillingness to acknowledge failures to the public
or even within official circles.[54]

In December 1973 USAID's auditor general completed a report
on the agency's performance in the Sahel, reaching conclusions
similar to those of the Carnegie study.[55] However, even if one were
to discount the inadequacies of the 1972-73 relief effort, it would be
relatively more difficult to excuse similar shortcomings in 1973-74.
U.S. Senator Edward Kennedy, addressing the Senate on July 29,
1974, noted:

Last year's logistical bottlenecks and administrative
delays in the movement of food and medicine continues. . . . the sense of urgency dramatized by
conditions in the field is not fully reflected in the
policies, priorities, and programs of AID. Although
the record shows some meaningful progress in recent
months, the fact remains that our Government's
actions are often too belated and bogged down in
bureaucratic redtape and indecision. The administration has known since early this year that additional
disaster relief funds would be available for famine
relief in Africa. Yet, not until the last few weeks
has there been any serious effort to plan for the use
and obligation of these funds.[56]

One might also note that, in late March 1974, four months after
U.N. Secretary General Kurt Waldheim made an urgent appeal for
$30 million in cash for relief, only $4.6 million was raised, of which
the U.S. pledge was $1 million.[57] Although a large percentage of the
total, the American pledge is small by any other standard and reflects
American reluctance to use dollars to adversely affect the U.S.
balance of payments; one could argue that it also reflects American
reluctance to give aid multilaterally. Again, despite the planning
time available for the 1973-74 relief effort, it was reported in
October 1974 that the United Nations and the donor nations did not
start shipping relief in large quantities until May 1974; thus, it
arrived at the beginning of the rainy season when transport difficulties
are magnified by mud-clogged and washed-out roads. At the end of
June, 67,000 metric tons of relief food intended for Mali were still
on the docks in Dakar, Senegal's capital. Three American transport

planes flew grain from Bamako, Mali's capital, to isolated areas at
a cost of $900 a ton; had the grain arrived early enough to be sent
to the interior over land, the cost would have been $80 a ton. The
United States committed 20,000 metric tons of grain to Chad in
1973-74, but only 7,000 tons had actually arrived in the country by
the end of the summer. Therefore, a Chicago Tribune report concluded:

> How many people have died . . . in Africa this year
> is impossible to calculate. . . . The fact is that they
> are dying because 900,000 tons of food, much of it
> grown, shipped and paid for by American taxpayers,
> did not arrive in time to save them.[58]

AMERICAN RELIEF IN ETHIOPIA

The U.S. response to the Ethiopian famine raises different but
equally disturbing questions. They were brought into focus during
the March 1974 hearings of Kennedy's Senate Subcommittee to Investigate Problems Connected with Refugees and Escapees. They are
perhaps best illuminated by quoting directly the chairman's ques-
tioning of Donald S. Brown, deputy assistant administrator, Bureau
for Africa, USAID:

> Kennedy: I do not know whether you saw this, the
> article that appeared in the Washington Post
> yesterday . . . the theme of it was that the
> situation in Ethiopia was sort of a Greek tragedy,
> that even if we were to provide food it is almost
> really too late to get it where it is needed right
> now . . .
> Brown: I must say we all felt uncomfortable at
> times about what was happening in the Sahel, but in
> general it seems to me that because of the very great
> attention of the governments of the Sahel and of the
> donor community, we really have accumulated a
> fairly decent understanding of what is happening
> and what are the problems there. That simply is
> much less true in Ethiopia. . . . I think the
> Ethiopian Government simply reacted much too
> slowly and much too inadequately. And the donor
> community as a whole recognized and realized the
> depth of the situation in Ethiopia much more slowly
> than they did in the Sahel.

Kennedy: Well, this is pretty much true of our own reaction to it, isn't it? . . . The U.N. Development Program office issu[ed] a report in October of 1973 calling the drought in many parts of Ethiopia "catastrophic." And then I wrote to the Secretary of State . . . in November asking for a reaction; and the State Department issued a rather optimistic sounding response. . . . originally, AID estimated the food importation needs to Ethiopia . . . [at] 150,000 tons. Now, just 2 months later, we hear talk about the need for 250,000 tons. How do you account for this kind of inconsistency?

Brown: The estimates . . . in the period October, November, December were related primarily to the requirements of Wallo and Tigre provinces, which were at that time the most hard hit. . . . In the meantime, the problems of the south developed. These are related but occurred on, if you will, a second time phase. They are related to different failures of rain and are apparently . . . spreading rapidly and becoming very difficult. Nobody at this point has a meaningful assessment of what full requirements for the problems in southern Ethiopia will be . . .

Kennedy: Is not the real reason for our slow response that we just did not want to blow the whistle on the Ethiopian government? Is that not really the bottom line of it? Perhaps you cannot say it; but that seems to me to be the bottom line. We did not want to expose it. We were not prepared to blow the whistle on it because of our relations with them. As a result, a lot of people starved to death.

Brown: I do not think that is really the response. There obviously has been a concern . . . to bring the Ethiopian Government to greater recognition. We tried to do this in ways that would lead to cooperation and willingness by the Ethiopian Government to take steps on its own. And there was feeling . . . that raising this to too public an issue, embarassing the government, could in fact harm the kind of cooperation we see as needed on their part. In that sense perhaps the whistle was not blown loudly enough.59 [Emphasis added.]

For many years, the United States has regarded Haile Selassie's Ethiopia as a "free world" ally to the extent that, in the years following

the 1953 bilateral mutual defense assistance agreement between these
governments, a Military Assistance Advisory Group was attached to
the Ethiopian Ministry of Defense. In addition, the United States gave
military aid to Ethiopia to the sum of $74 million, virtually half of
the 1953-63 American military aid to Africa. Also, the United States
considered Kagnew, an American base near Asmara, to be of strategic
importance in the tracking of satellites, the monitoring of radio
broadcasts from the Middle East and East Europe, and as a diplomatic
and military communications relay point. [60] Thus, humanitarian
considerations could not be permitted to jeopardize this special
relationship, particularly when the emperor's position was being
undermined by social unrest. The United States, therefore, said
little about the emergent famine situation, although U.S. personnel
in Ethiopia were aware of the dimensions of the tragedy.

UNINTENTIONAL FLAWS IN RELIEF
AND REHABILITATION

Yet, even when the humanitarian impulse was real and there
has been a sincere effort to provide a solid relief and rehabilitation
program, frequently the relief efforts have been misguided and have
failed because of an inadequate understanding of the sociopolitical
dimensions of development. A prime example is the case of the
Sahel, where an ecological breakdown was exacerbated by the well-
intentioned drilling of boreholes, the widespread use of vaccines and
medicine for animals and for man.
There is now widespread agreement that the famine in the
Sahel must be understood not only in terms of natural factors such
as the shifting south of the Sahara but in terms of Western intervention during a post-independence period of abnormally good rainfall.
The latter resulted in large increases in both the human and animal
population, which in turn strained the delicate ecosystem to the
breaking point. [61] Thus, technological benefits intended to ameliorate
the conditions under which the nomads lived in fact sowed the seeds
that currently threaten them with destruction. By making it possible
for a rapid expansion in herd size from 18 million to 25 million
cattle between 1960 and 1971, developers set the stage for overgrazing
and desertification. An article in Science points out: "Not foreseen
was the fact that cattle are the nomads' only means of saving, and it
in fact makes good sense—on an individual basis—for a nomad to keep
as many cattle on the hoof as he can."[62]
A second and more general example is provided by the "green
revolution." The new strains of wheat and rice and the new techniques

of cultivation that won the Nobel Peace Prize for Norman Borlaug have frequently contributed to the misery of the masses, although Borlaug intended the opposite; that is, where the green revolution was launched without regard to the sociopolitical implications of the new technology—the fact that the new strains of grain require extensive fertilizer and pesticides, that they require a capital investment in irrigation and mechanization, and that they therefore work to the advantage of the large landowner who can raise the money for the new seed, fertilizer, and tractors—it has reinforced the power position of rural aristocracies and increased the number of landless peasants.[63] A third example is provided by the birth control and family planning programs for third world countries that the United States has so heavily invested in. They have been totally unsuccessful because they have relied on technical devices—the pill, the IUD (inter-uterine device), injectables, prostaglandins—rather than socioeconomic solutions.[64]

Each of these attempts to provide developmental assistance—boreholes for the Sahel, the green revolution, and population control strategies—exhibits the same fatal flaw: the tendency to think of development in strictly technical terms, ignoring human and, particularly, sociopolitical dimensions. Additionally, those involved in crises, always under the pressure of the cataclysm on hand, seem unable to learn from past mistakes. In terms of disaster relief, we have had in a few short years such spectacular cases as Bangladesh, Biafra, Peru, Nicaragua, the Sahel, and Ethiopia. Indeed, U.S. records show 430 "natural disasters" in the world during the past ten years resulting in 3.5 million deaths and in damage estimated at $11 million.[65] Yet the United States constantly repeats the same errors with respect to relief distribution and appears to be just muddling through. In terms of development, the United States has had two decades of experience and the results have often been "anti-development."

Consider the Sahel. Social scientists acquainted with the sociopolitical development of the area might have been more aware of the problems caused by a persistent pattern of antagonism between the sedentary population and the pastoralists. In addition, they might have been more aware of the fact that the sedentary peoples are in control of each Sahel government except Mauritania, and that the pastoralists have been treated as political "outcasts" in their own countries. They have been either benignly neglected or forcefully subjected to the rule of the sedentary elites. This outcast status has been reinforced by the historical legacy of Tuareg conquest and the rebelliousness of the nomads, seeking an autonomous existence. In fact, the pastoralists have been traditionally viewed as a threat by those in power. Under such circumstances, it is hardly surprising that relief distribution, if left exclusively to Sahelian governments, would have resulted in distribution in favor of the farmers and to the disadvantage of the pastoralists. Perhaps, if foreign relief administrators had been sensitized to this dimension of relief distribution, relief efforts might have been monitored to ameliorate the position of the nomads.

Defenders of the U.S. relief effort will argue that to influence the internal affairs of a sovereign state is a violation of international law. Clearly, such influence would be intervention. Yet it could be shown that nonintervention also is a form of intervention. Nonintervention in most cases favors the incumbents. The question, therefore, is not whether to exert influence but what type of influence to exert.

It is of critical importance that social scientists focus their attention on the sociopolitical effects of the famine and of the relief operations in the Sahel and Ethiopia. Although USAID and other agencies have intruded into numerous disaster areas, rarely have they been sensitive to the interface between relief and the people to whom relief has been given. The current African tragedies provide ample evidence that sociopolitical, economic, and cultural patterns in West and East Africa have been profoundly disturbed by refugee migrations, by the decimation of the nomads' herds, as well as by the fostering of attitudes and relationships of dependency where none previously existed. If reconstruction and rehabilitation are to have any real meaning, and if aid donors are to cooperate effectively with African peoples in the development of these areas, those concerned with development must have more than just economic or technical data. They will need an understanding of the sociopolitical forces that must be contended with. Furthermore, if one is concerned with questions of economic justice and economic independence—true development—one must find methods for ensuring that rehabilitation plans are more than programs of the elites, by the elites, and for the elites. The groups most deeply affected by the famines in the Sahel and Ethiopia, the pastoralists and the landless peasantry, respectively, must be given some voice in the definition and implementation of development goals. How this can best be effected in a cooperative relationship between donors and recipients of aid is not easy to specify, but it is undoubtedly a problem that requires close and careful attention.

THE MALTHUSIAN POSSIBILITY

The Sahelian and Ethiopian famines, which can be viewed as isolated episodes, take on a different meaning if they are seen as symptoms of the malaise of the world economic system. One could argue that they are warning lights that portend a collapse of the international economic order and a degeneration into Malthusian politics[66] unless there is an effective response to the problems caused by chronic hunger, chronic underdevelopment, population growth, resource depletion, environmental pollution, and double-digit inflation. As Lester Brown, of the Overseas Development Council, has been warning for several years, "if our society is to survive and progress in the seventies and eighties, we need a new ethic, a reordering of global priorities."[67] This alone can forestall a collapse of the world ecosystem, which would mean that we would all become Sahelians—people living on the margin. Most particularly, the African famines dramatize the critical nature of the current world food situation. Unless there is better management of our human and natural resources, the struggle for bread may produce a cataclysm as awesome as nuclear holocaust.

U.S. Secretary of Agriculture Butz is correct in one regard: "Food is power," in the current situation of grain scarcity.[68] Since North America is presently the major grain-exporting region, the United States becomes, not by virtue of its atomic arsenal but by its control over grain production and exportation, a superpower with a determining voice in decisions about which nations will survive and which will perish.

The FAO/U.N. Conference in Rome, in November 1974, was a great disappointment because it failed to produce either a world security reserve system or expected aid pledges. All that was agreed to was the establishment of a World Food Council, a coordinating body without meaningful decision-making authority or economic power. Furthermore, those who hoped the United States would make a pledge for a specified amount of immediate relief aid had to be satisfied with Henry Kissinger's rhetoric—"No tragedy is more wounding than the look of despair in the eyes of a starving child"[69]; and with Butz's explanation that a public commitment could not be made because of budget restraints, tight supplies, and the bullish effect a pledge would have on the market, with its consequent impact on American consumer prices.[70] Hence, the father of the green revolution, Norman E. Borlaug, concluded that the World Food Conference did nothing and that millions would die from hunger during the coming months: "It was nonsense and you can quote me."[71]

If Borlaug is right, we have perhaps already entered the Malthusian age where evaluation of the efficiency of relief has no meaning because there are too many disasters and too few relief resources to ameliorate the tragedy. From this dismal perspective, the Sahelians and Ethiopians were fortunate this time around—they got some aid, even if relief distribution was mismanaged and inadequate. The next time disaster strikes, they may receive nothing.

Hopefully, however, Borlaug is wrong and there is still time to forestall the Malthusian possibility. This will require a drastic reordering of the priorities of both the rich nations and the elites in the third world. It will require a commitment to true development, a modification of the power structure in accordance with the requisites of development, a commitment to the efficient management of the world's resources, and a preparedness to provide disaster relief where humanitarian considerations demand it. If we fail in this regard, if there are more Sahelian and Ethiopian deaths, we can no longer deny our culpability for mass human suffering.[72] The Sahelian and Ethiopian famines, like the general world hunger problem, are outcomes of sociopolitical and economic forces that we direct and for which we must accept responsibility.

NOTES

1. There is some disagreement among climatologists on when the drought actually began in the Sahel. Poor rainfall is considered by some to have begun in 1968. However, the MIT group (working on a USAID study, a 25-year future perspective on Sahelian development) argues that the 1968-69 rains were more or less normal; they only appeared low by comparison with the pluvial early 1960s, which detracted attention from the cyclical nature of rainfall in the area. Interview with John Paden, Northwestern University, who served as a consultant to the MIT study.

2. This notwithstanding, one must also note that sophisticated analysts recognize that no society (or network of societies) no matter how "underdeveloped" is passive with respect to its environment. Even the most "primitive" human orders have adaptive mechanisms that determine their survival capability in the face of hostile natural forces. Human action, therefore, always intervenes between drought and its consequences. See Jeremy Swift, "Disaster and a Sahelian Economy," in David Dalby and R.J. Harrison Church, eds., Drought in Africa (London: Centre for African Studies, School of Oriental and African Studies, University of London, 1973), pp. 71-78.

3. Cecil Woodham-Smith, The Great Hunger, Ireland 1845-9 (London: Hamish Hamilton, 1962).

4. Dean Jonathan Swift, A Modest Proposal for Preventing the Children of Poor People in Ireland from Being a Burthen to their Parents or Country and for Making Them Beneficial to the Public (1729).

5. B.H. Bhatia, Famines in India, 1860-1965 (Bombay: Asia Publishing House, 1967); Kali Charan Ghosh, Famines in Bengal, 1770-1943 (Calcutta: India Associated Publishing, 1944).

6. Transnational Institute, "World Hunger: Causes and Remedies" (Amsterdam, Holland: Transnational Institute, October 1974), p. 40.

7. Theodore H. White and Annalee Jacoby, Thunder Out of China (New York: W. Sloane, 1946, 1961), pp. 166-78; Edgar Snow, Journey to the Beginning, (New York: Vintage, 1958, 1972), pp. 7-11.

8. Congressional Record, Ninetieth Congress, Second Session, vol. 14, pt. 17 (August 2, 1968): 25007.

9. Great Britain Air Ministry, The Berlin Airlift (London, 1949), p. 39.

10. Laurie S. Wiseberg, "The International Politics of Relief: A Case Study of the Relief Operations Mounted During the Nigerian Civil War, 1967-1970," doctoral dissertation, University of California, Los Angeles, 1973, p. 286.

11. On the nature of the technological gap, see Zbigniew Brzezinski, Between Two Ages: America's Role in the Technetronic Age, (New York: Viking, 1970). On the still widening gap in wealth, see Theodore Caplow, "Are the Poor Getting Poorer?", Foreign Policy, no. 3 (Summer 1971): 90-107; James P. Grant, "Development: The End of Trickle Down?", Foreign Policy, no. 12 (Fall 1973): 43-65; Ruth Leger Sivard, World Military and Social Expenditures (New York: Institute for World Order, 1974), pp. 5-7.

12. See C. Fred Bergsten, "The Threat from the Third World," Foreign Policy, no. 11 (Summer 1973): 102-24; C. Fred Bergsten, "The Response to the Third World," Foreign Policy, no. 17 (Winter 1974-75): 3-34.

13. Denis Goulet, The Cruel Choice (New York: Atheneum, 1973), p. 135.

14. Ibid., pp. 14-15.

15. New York Times, May 8, 1974, p. 4.

16. New York Times, May 14, 1974, p. 1.

17. UNCTAD/Research Division, "Selected Statistical Tables on the Six Drought-Affected African Countries," June 27, 1973, mimeo.

18. Robert L. Curry, Jr., "U.S.-Developing Country Trade and Restrictive Business Practice Policies," Journal of International Affairs 28, no. 1 (1974): 67-80.

19. For general treatments on the rigging of the trade system against the third world, and of the power of multinationals with respect to third world countries, see the numerous articles that have appeared in 1972-75 in Foreign Policy and Monthly Review. See also Anthony Sampson, The Sovereign State of ITT, (New York: Fawcett-Crest, 1974).

20. New York Times, May 8, 1974, p. 4.

21. Ruth First, Power in Africa, (Baltimore: Penguin, 1971), p. 17.

22. New York Times, November 18, 1973, p. 3.

23. Oriana Fallaci, Chicago Tribune, June 24, 1973.

24. The two newspapers systematically scanned were the New York Times and the Washington Post. Additional information was revealed during the hearings of the Senate Subcommittee to Investigate Problems Connected with Refugees and Escapees, March 21, 1974, chaired by Senator Edward M. Kennedy.

25. According to Martin Walker, New York Times Magazine, June 9, 1974, the Ethiopian government tried to have the UNICEF report suppressed. However, it became public as a result of a leak to the Western press in November 1973.

26. Abraham Kidane, "The Political Economy of Famine: A Case Study of Ethiopia," paper delivered at the 1974 meeting of the African Studies Association, Chicago, October 31, 1974, p. 7.

27. The conference delegate prefers not to be identified.

28. The event is somewhat reminiscent of the sumptuous wedding celebrations of Governor Diete-Spieff, in Port Harcourt, shortly after the Biafran collapse. Although in the surrounding areas refugees were starving, relief transport was, nonetheless, commandeered to take guests to the wedding and to supply the banquet tables.

29. USAID, "The Drought Situation in the Sahel: Emergency Situation Throughout the Sahel as of June 10, 1974," reprinted in the Congressional Record, Ninety-third Congress, Second Session, vol. 120, no. 112, p. S13573.

30. West Africa, July 30, 1973, p. 1027.

31. Jean Herskovits, "Nigeria: Africa's New Power," Foreign Affairs 53, no. 2 (January 1975): 321.

32. Martin Walker, in The Guardian, June 30, 1973.

33. There have been numerous reports about discrimination in relief distribution. In this regard, see also Hal Sheets and Roger Morris, Disaster in the Desert, Special Report of the Humanitarian Policy Studies Project (Carnegie Endowment for International Peace, 1974), pp. 38-40.

34. The fall of the government of President Hamani Diori of Niger, while not caused by the famine, was catalyzed by it in a manner similar to the fall of Haile Selassie; that is, the corruption and ineptitude in the government's response to the famine helped to provide a focal point for discontent and provided a legitimate pretext for military intervention. The drought situation in Upper Volta, while not as clear, nonetheless played some role in the downfall of the civilian government of Gerard Ouedraogo.

35. New York Times, November 1, 1974.

36. For an expansion on this point, see Laurie S. Wiseberg, "Humanitarian Intervention: Lessons from the Nigerian Civil War," Human Rights Journal 7, no. 1 (1974): 61-98.

37. Center for Disease Control, U.S. Public Health Serivce, Department of Health, Education and Welfare, "Nutritional Surveillance in West Africa—Mauritania, Niger, Mali, Upper Volta, July-August 1973," (Atlanta).

38. USAID, "Drought Situation in the Sahel."

39. Testimony of Donald S. Brown, deputy assistant administrator for the Bureau of Africa, USAID, before USAID, Subcommittee on Refugees.

40. "Report to the Congress on Famine in Sub-Sahara Africa," September 1974, p. 6.

41. Baltimore Sun, September 2, 1974.

42. It should be emphasized that we are not arguing for a reduction in aid to India, Bangladesh, or Pakistan, where the food situation is critical and worsening at this time.

43. Hearings before the Select Committee on Nutrition and Human Needs of the U.S. Senate, Ninety-third Congress, Second Session, Part 1: Famine and the World Situation, June 14, 1974; Part 2: Nutrition and the International Situation, June 19, 1974; Part 2A: Appendix to Nutrition and the International Situation, June 19, 1974.

44. Report on Nutrition and the International Situation, prepared by the staff of the Select Committee on Nutrition and Human Needs, U.S. Senate, September 1974.

45. In line with McGovern's argument on the security-related nature of U.S. food aid, see also Lyle P. Schertz, "World Food: Prices and the Poor," Foreign Affairs 52, no. 3 (April 1974): 511-37.

46. New York Times, November 3, 1974, p. 65.

47. Donald F. McHenry, "Captive of No Group," Foreign Policy, no. 15 (Summer 1974): 148.

48. Beverly May Carl, "American Assistance to Victims of the Nigeria-Biafra War: Defects in the Prescriptions on Foreign Disaster Relief," Harvard International Law Journal 12, no. 2 (Spring 1971): 231, especially note 111.

49. Herschelle S. Challenor, "The Sahel Drought: A Continuing Disaster," RAINS Information Sheet, November 1, 1973.

50. Stephen S. Rosenfeld, "The Politics of Food," Foreign Policy, no. 14 (Spring 1974): 17-29.

51. New York Times, October 29, 1974, pp. 1, 51. With regard to the cut in the milk program, see also USAID's attempt to rationalize the harm done by the termination by focusing on its success in developing Whey Soy Drink Mix as a milk substitute: David L. Rhoad, "WSDM: Initials for Good Nutrition," War on Hunger, November 1974, pp. 13-17.

52. New York Times, July 5, 1974, p. 1; Christian Science Monitor, August 27, 1974, p. 1, among the numerous articles that

have appeared in the press on the policy of the Department of Agriculture as defined by Earl L. Butz.

53. For an extended discussion of the politics of agrobusiness, see Roger Morris and Hal Sheets, "Why Leave It to Earl?", Washington Monthly 6, no. 9 (November 1974): 12-19.

54. Sheets and Morris, Disaster in the Desert, pp. 2-3.

55. When the Carnegie study first appeared, both USAID and FAO issued statements denying the validity of its findings. USAID, four-page press release, March 3, 1974; FAO, press release, FAO/2477, ND/81, March 7, 1974. Subsequently, however, a USAID audit supported the Carnegie study's conclusions. That audit has not been made public although it was under study by Senator Hubert Humphrey. I was able to discuss the FAO Report with someone who read it in its entirety and saw parts of the report under the promise of confidentiality. Additionally, it was leaked to a reporter and an article was written on the audit: Jack Thomas, "US Food Aid to Starving Africans a Nightmare, Report Asserts," Boston Globe, June 30, 1974.

56. Congressional Record, Ninety-third Congress, Second Session, vol. 120, no. 112, p. S 13571.

57. Testimony of Bradford Morse, undersecretary general of the United Nations, to the Senate Subcommittee on Refugees.

58. Ovie Carter and William Mullen, "The Faces of Hunger: A Five-Part Series of Articles and Photographs," Chicago Tribune, October 13-18, 1974.

59. Donald S. Brown, testimony to the Senate Subcommittee on Refugees.

60. Robert L. Hess, Ethiopia: The Modernization of Autocracy (Ithaca, N.Y.: Cornell University Press, 1970), pp. 199-201.

61. Dalby and Harrison Church, Drought in Africa; R.S. Temple and M.E.R. Thomas, "The Sahelian Drought—A Disaster for Livestock Populations," World Animal Review, no. 8 (1973): 1-7; Nicholas Wade, "Sahelian Drought: No Victory for Western Aid," Science, July 1974.

62. Wade, "Sahelian Drought."

63. See, for example, Roy L. Prosterman, "Land Reform as Foreign Aid," Foreign Policy, no. 6 (Spring 1972): 138; Transnational Institute, "World Hunger" pp. 25-27.

64. Pierre Pradervand, "Africa 1974: Population, Is There a Problem?", draft paper prepared for a special issue of the Population Bulletin, April 20, 1974, mimeo., pp. 26-27.

65. New York Times, November 3, 1974, p. 20.

66. The term Malthusian politics, commonly used today, is acutally a misnomer in that Thomas Malthus, in his famous essay on population, argued that grinding poverty was the result of the natural

laws of a benevolent creator and not the result of unjust socioeconomic institutions. Moreover, Malthus fervently campaigned against the poor laws and other attempts to alleviate the poverty and suffering of the masses on the grounds that public relief would only stimulate population growth and exasperate the situation. Finally, on the basis of contemporary social science research, one can argue that birth rates are reduced as living standards go up and not—as Malthus believed—that misery was the only conceivable restraint. See, for example, Frank W. Notestein, "Introduction," On Population: Three Essays, (New York: Mentor, 1960), pp. vii-x. Yet, if interpreted loosely to mean intense and bitter struggle by people on the margin of survival, with the haves jealously, fearfully, and futilely guarding "theirs" and the have-nots dying in famine and pestilence, the term Malthusian politics is only too meaningful and a distinct possibility. It is in the latter sense that the term is used here.

67. Lester R. Brown, World Without Borders (New York: Vintage, 1972).

68. New York Times, July 5, 1974, p. 1.

69. Address by Henry A. Kissinger before the World Food Conference, Rome, November 5, 1974; release of the U.S. Department of State.

70. New York Times, November 16, 1974, pp. 1, 12.

71. New York Times, December 11, 1974, p. 13.

72. Frances Moore Lappe, "The World Food Problem," The Hastings Center Report, (Institute of Society, Ethics and the Life Sciences, 1974).

CHAPTER

5

CAN THE SAHEL SURVIVE?
PROSPECTS FOR LONG-TERM
PLANNING AND DEVELOPMENT
David Shear
Roy Stacy

The mass starvation that resulted from the Sahel drought in
1968-73 no longer threatens that region. Emergency action by donors
and specialists from developed countries throughout the world prevented the disaster from reaching even larger proportions than the
estimated 100,000 persons dead and the loss of some 40 percent of
the goats, sheep, cattle, and camels.

After good spring rains in 1974, the fall harvest was 90 percent
normal. But a human crisis remains. A deteriorating ecological
base, debilitation of herds, and social dislocation of the pastoral
peoples who farm and grace the semiarid lands of the six sub-Saharan
countries we call the Sahel, still present a set of difficult, interrelated problems. If further catastrophes are to be prevented, new
approaches to these problems must be taken.

What the United States learned through its intensified activity
in the Sahel during the drought years indicates that there are good
possibilities for the region's recovery. The challenges are complex.
The U.S. Agency for International Development's approaches suggest
new departures in planning and development. What is significant and
exciting about these approaches is that they suggest that the United
States does not undertake the burden alone. Nor is the program a
patchwork series of actions with no plan for the overall development
of the entire region.

The development and planning program that USAID now suggests
was developed from our experience working with donors from many
nations who worked together on short- and medium-term programs
in response to the Sahelian emergency. This program is a long-term
approach that coordinates worldwide efforts of national and private
agencies into a regional phase. These programs would work with the
Sahelian governments, as well as with governments of contingent states

that share the same climatic and agricultural zones, and with
international and regional organizations. With such a coordinated
approach to improve the efficiency of financial and technical assistance—for the first time in an areawide approach—USAID finds
that one of the world's poorest regions has some prospects for a
better future and perhaps for self-sustaining growth.

OVERALL DEVELOPMENT STRATEGY FOR THE SAHEL AREA

According to Section 639B of the Foreign Assistance Act:

The Congress supports the initiative of the United
States Government in undertaking consultations and
planning with the countries concerned, with other
concerned international and regional organizations
toward the development and support of a comprehensive long-term African Sahel Development Program.

In response to this congressional mandate, the Africa Bureau of
USAID is now completing a multiyear planning effort, undertaken in
collaboration with the six Sahelian states and with other interested
bilateral and international donors. This multiyear Development
Assistance Plan (DAP) entails a series of programs that donors can
collectively support to solve key regional development problems. At
the same time, the Development Assistance Plan coordinates and
unifies the thinking of all parties in an overall development goal for
a five-year period. This goal is simply to prevent food shortages,
both immediate and long term, with maximum concentration on
social and economic equity. This means creating an agriculture that
is less susceptible to drought and that has a more solid base for
increased production and increased farmer income. Because the
food shortages have been so great and have affected so many persons
in the poorest segments of these societies, the issue of equitable food
allocations is most important. However, this issue must not preempt
solutions for the overall food problem in the Sahel area. Therefore,
both extensive and intensive programs must be developed.
    A parallel and supporting goal is reversing ecological deteriora-
tion in the area. Conservation of land and water resources is an
essential prerequisite to restoring the area's ability to feed itself.
Continued environmental damage means continued food deficits and
continued demand for food from developed countries whose supplies
are shrinking. The Sahel is understandably the focal point because it

has suffered the greatest environmental damage. Further environmental damage in the Sahel may threaten the production base of the
coastal states to the south because of population migrations and
overcropping. The Sahel region is a very special geographic area
and therefore is the focus of special kinds of assistance.

The fragile environment may not be able to support "standard"
assistance approaches because some development interventions
inadvertently worsen ecological imbalances. Programs must therefore
work for both food production and ecological reclamation. In such
areas of marginal natural resources, programs cost more, are more
difficult to manage, and must be long term. The overall purpose of
this new regional planning approach is to fundamentally alter the
environment and expand the now narrow margin of survival. The
immediate return of such investments may seem unproductive when
tested by traditional cost-benefit analysis; therefore, more subjective
analysis will have to be applied in deciding on program and project
elements.

It is recommended that a strategy to achieve the above goals
comprise four concurrent main streams:

1. Programs aimed at bettering the life situation of the rural
segments of these societies, specifically the small cereal cultivators
and pastoral herdsmen who form the vast majority of the population
that has been affected by drought and by the paucity of development
opportunities. These would involve the widest possible distribution
of low-cost, low-risk, moderate technology, high human participation
inputs (extensive programs).

2. Programs aimed at converting major natural resources, in
a highly effective manner, into filling the important food deficit gap
in the region. The role of cash crops should be examined along with
food crops in multicropping schemes. These programs would be
designed to significantly transform existing environmental/productive
situations and establish a foundation for the longer run development.

3. Programs aimed at arresting and reversing the progressive
deterioration of the physical and human resource base. In the program process, people must be given a greater capacity for preserving
and enhancing their habitat.

4. Programs selectively aimed at improving the administrative
and management capacities of national and local governments as well
as local institutions to meet the priority social and economic development needs of the population.

KEY PROBLEM AREAS

It is difficult to define in any sequential priority a series of separate key development problems for the several sectors involved in these strategy streams. Such definitions cannot be so globalized as to obscure the paths to problem solutions, nor so particularized that achievements would make only a minor contribution to a broader development goal. The problems are invariably interrelated and problem articulation and solutions will differ from country to country and between regions. This overlapping will be kept in focus as the DAPs are developed. Moreover, depending on country or region, it is probable that certain sectoral problems or constraints are more critical than others and the United States may not, in some instances, be ideally suited to provide appropriate assistance.

Proposed programs also are being formulated in a balanced manner, with solutions that address multiple contributions to the several parallel streams listed above.

For the sake of categorization, the key problems that are being addressed in the planning effort will be discussed under four subsectors: food and crop production, livestock development, health and family planning, and rural education.

Food and Crop Production

To begin solving key problems in food and crop production, people must have enough food to sustain a quality of life beyond merely replacing energy expended in the inefficient production of their food. The trend in West African countries' crop production over the past decade indicates a slow overall production increase, with a marked increase in export crops and a 1 to 2 percent annual decrease in the per capita production of food crops. The relative decline of food crops (plus the prolonged drought) means that many people in the Sahel now live at the subsistence level or below. There also is a strong correlation between environmental deterioration and chronic food shortages.

There are seven elements that continue to restrict food and crop production: limited productivity of rural labor; missing elements in an agricultural technical package; insufficient exploitation of available surface and ground water resources; decreasing soil fertility; increasing animal and population pressures on good, arable land; poor planning and management of agricultural programs; and ineffective pricing and marketing systems for food crops.

1. Limited productivity of rural labor: Most food crop production in the region has been realized through hard peasant labor and, frequently, slash-and-burn cultivation. The conversion of labor energy into food is generally very inefficient, and the introduction of adaptable levels of technology are needed to assure a greater return for labor inputs.

2. Missing elements in an agricultural technical package: One reason that labor productivity has been relatively static in the region is that, for varying reasons, farmers have not had access to certain intermediate technologies. In addition, certain elements of "sure" technical packages have yet to be developed. For instance, there has been little development of improved seeds for food crops. Also, chemical fertilizers have been impossible to obtain at economic prices. The most spectacular results in agriculture research have been obtained from technological packages with fertilizer-responsive varieties and with irrigation. Yet, for the vast majority of rural farmers in this region, these inputs have not been within reach because of their cost.

3. Insufficient exploitation of available surface and ground water resources: It is certain that any major long-term increases in food production in the region will require more intensive and rational exploitation of the major regional river basins (Senegal, Niger, Volta) and of Lake Chad. More immediately, there also is great potential in the more extensive use of surface and ground water, in simple irrigation techniques, and in water spreading. Aside from the major irrigation possibilities, there are many fertile areas that flood during the rainy season and could be doublecropped at lower cost with moderate technology.

4. Decreasing soil fertility: Continued cultivation of many areas in the region will depend upon the ability of farmers to improve soil fertility and to maintain a mineral balance. Years of mono-cropping and of soil neglect have combined with natural forces to create a soil exhaustion threat to rural livelihood and food production. Agricultural programs must be devised that increase yields as well as begin the process of rebuilding the organic matter and minerals in the soils.

5. Increasing animal and population pressures on good, arable land: The most productive land in some higher-rainfall areas tends to be relatively densely populated and heavily farmed. The achievement of food production goals in the region will require the opening of new unutilized river valleys where various endemic diseases have to date foreclosed settlement and, therefore, exploitation of these agricultural resources.

6. Poor planning and management of agricultural programs: The shortage of trained manpower inhibits many aspects of development

(to be discussed later); the administrative/management gap affects the agricultural and livestock sectors. Various methods of assisting governments in training and in building institutions to implement planning are critical.

7. Ineffective pricing and marketing systems for food crops: Contrary to marketing and pricing of export commodities, the systems for food grains usually have not yielded satisfactory returns to producers. The recent Sahel drought has masked a major problem in cereals: the low prices producers get at harvest time, and ensuing fluctuations that frequently force farmers to buy food grains at much higher prices later on. Prices are traditionally low at harvest but producers frequently get prices far below normal market prices because of distortions and anomalies in the system. There will be only marginal income benefits to participants in increased production programs unless such marketing and pricing problems are solved. Building more secondary roads may be necessary to speed grain harvests to markets.

Livestock Production

Livestock in West Africa has two purposes: growing meat for sale and converting pasture into dairy produce for the herdsmen themselves. A successful livestock development strategy must recognize these purposes and successfully bridge competing interests for livestock and animal products. We think the livestock industry can and should provide subsistence for areas environmentally damaged and also a continuing source of meat transported to urban areas. This will require livestock and range development for subsistence dairy herding, as well as controlled beef production. This may raise difficult choices for governments and donors because this approach may require a strong commitment to the food needs of the herding population, as well as some limitations in commercialized beef production.

Livestock programs for this region also should emphasize that the conversion of arid pastureland into animal resources by pastoralist and nomadic groups has been a highly efficient economic activity. There are vast, remote areas of marginal lands ideally suited to labor-intensive breeding and raising of cattle that provide employment and nutrition for several million persons. There are new elements such as mixed farming or feed lots and improvements in range management being made in the system, but the basic labor-intensive structure of resource conversion should be left intact.

Generally, any sound livestock strategy or even individual project design must consider the interrelationship between the

Sahelian, Sudanian, and Guinean zones, as well as the commercial interdependence between coastal and interior states. The special potentialities and resources of each zone should be maximized in a way that does not degrade the environment. The Sahelian zone, with its fragile and variable conditions, cannot support pastoral groups and also provide sufficient meat for a rapidly growing urban demand. What is ultimately required is a planned series of balanced and reinforcing investments in all zones, including specific undertakings in coastal states. This "vertical" strategy must be the longer-term objective toward which current planning, investments, and trade relationships must be directed.

The key problems in the livestock sector vary from country to country and between zones. Listed below are the key livestock sector problems that must be addressed in any program development:

1. Deterioration of range resources relative to the balance of the ecosystem: Solutions to this problem must be consistent with the area's realities. There have been traditional principles and codes to use and conserve pastureland that were followed by pastoralist peoples. These have not assured proper range management in the recent past for a number of reasons. There are numerous approaches to range conservation and management, but the only cost-effective and realistic approach is to restore the environment so that, with some improvements and adaptations, the traditional management will work again. The methods probably cannot really be defined without a grassroots planning effort with the pastoralists themselves.

2. Rising urban demand for meat, primarily in coastal states: There will undoubtedly be a quantum jump in aggregate demand for meat in coming years. Unless ways are found to expand production and offtake throughout the region, there will be a growing disparity between supply and demand with consequent pressure on prices. Most of the governments of the region are politically committed to holding food price increases to acceptable levels; therefore, the questions of marketing and consumer pricing must be addressed in any program.

3. Excessive reliance in some countries on livestock as a source of revenue and export earnings: The necessity of relying on this sector for revenue and foreign exchange appears to limit the options of some countries in the way of approaching the development of the industry. As new growth sectors are found, it may be important to change pricing and taxation policies to encourage greater production and commercialization. Many of these issues will have to be resolved regionally, hopefully through the regional organizations that have been established to deal with such questions.

4. Limited allocation of country revenue resources to livestock services: Because the revenue base in most of the countries is limited,

and since many governmental costs are fixed (salaries), there is a
very limited amount of domestic funds allocated for operating or
capital budgets in the livestock sector. New means will have to be
devised to finance veterinary and extension services. One possibility
is to attempt to shift service payments to users if the burden of
taxation can be relieved on the sector.

5. Inadequate animal fertility, nutrition, and disease control,
which contribute to high calf mortality: Longer-term qualitative
improvements in herds and greater commercialization of the sector
are going to require improvement in cow fertility, reduction in calf
mortality, and upgrading of animal nutrition. Greater use of animal
finishing and fattening in higher-rainfall zones will only be possible
if calving rates can be increased and disease and mortality in young
animals reduced.

6. Overconcentration on cattle as a source of protein: In
response to demand for beef, and programs of assistance for cattle,
these animals have increased in large numbers relative to other
forms of livestock. One theory holds that large numbers of livestock
could be held on available land if there were greater diversity in
herd composition. Different animals make different consumptive
demands upon the environment; when their relative numbers are in
balance, it should be less degrading on the environment. Also, some
smaller animals (poultry, pigs) may be much more efficient in converting underutilized resources into protein.

7. Underutilization of rangelands in higher-rainfall zones due
to presence of tsetse fly and onchocerciasis: Large areas of potentially
productive land are little used because of the above health hazards.
Since the technology of control of the insect vectors of the two diseases
is well understood, land use planning, followed by eradication programs, could greatly increase the livestock (and crop) production
potential in the southern Sahelian states and in northern portions of
coastal states. In addition, the introduction of Trypano-tolerant
breeds (Taurin or Zebu) could be considered where vector control
is technically unfeasible or too expensive.

8. Inadequate use of animal traction in mixed-farming enterprises: There are probably numerous areas, particularly in the
Sudan, where greater use of animal traction could expand farm productivity, contribute to improved soil fertility through more intensive
use of manure, and increase farmer income through the finishing and
selling of the oxen. Following the establishment of work animals and
an increase in farm area, a larger number of livestock could be
grown and finished on the farm using wild grasses and agricultural
residues. Forage production also is possible where it does not
compete with scarce labor or land being used for food crop production.

Rural Health and Family Planning

As in many areas of the world, health and population questions are inextricably linked to the issues of food production, the quality of rural life, and environmental reclamation. If the limited productivity of labor is a key factor in restricting farm output, then poor health and nutrition standards are root causes of inefficient labor productivity. Therefore, it is necessary that any crop production program also address directly (or through other donors) the low-cost delivery of rural health services and improved nutrition.

Relative to the current land production capacities, the Central West Africa region has a serious overpopulation problem. Since most of the governments have not been anxious to actively engage in control programs, it is suggested that expanding the productivity of labor may be the best current approach to the problem until more direct approaches are acceptable. Relieving the current need for additional family units of labor (children) to produce a relatively small incremental unit of food could start the process of personal preference for smaller families.

Again, the priority development problems of the sector are likely to vary between regions and countries:

1. Inadequate and inapproapriate rural health delivery plans and systems: There has been talk about developing cost-effective health delivery systems in the region. In fact, excessive investments have been made in showpiece facilities with little or no impact on rural needs. Most of the debilitating diseases in the area are preventable, but health programs have been largely curative rather than preventative. To penetrate rural areas, preventive programs must be designed to provide services through trained but inexpensive paramedical personnel. This is the most important part of the process of directing health care to rural areas.

2. Limited financial and material resources to implement health plans: Most of the countries have health plans, but they do not have the means to adequately implement them. In the past, donors have been unwilling to invest in health programs unless those programs were integrated with other activities so that their administrative continuation was more assured. This policy has left vast areas, usually the poorest and more remote, with virtually no health care services.

The nature of the problems in this sector indicate an extensive regional approach is needed. For the foreseeable future, lower-cost

extensive programs will be needed if maximum developmental impact
is to be obtained.

Rural Education and Human Resources

The legacy of colonial education in Central/West African states
has left the countries poorly equipped to approach key problems in
education and human development. Mostly, their formal education
systems are elitest and develop only a thin veneer of skills for the
modern sector of the economy. They ignore the needs of the rural
masses. For the fortunate few who get formal education, upward
mobility is by no means assured because the modern sectors of most
countries have an annual increment of no higher than 1 to 2 percent
in new job opportunities. Still, the absence of opportunities in rural
areas and the enormous differential between urban and rural salaries
continues to attract to the cities people who, with minimum functional
literacy, are willing to take the risks. As a result, cities continue
to grow at a rate approximately three times greater than that of the
population as a whole.

To make education (formal or informal) more "relevant" will
require changes in popular perceptions regarding the rewards of
education. A shift is required away from expectations of employment
and upward job mobility to expanding the ability of people to make
meaningful decisions about their lives; to expanding their options and
supplementing their abilities in multiple resource exploitation.

Programs developed in the planning effort must seek to cut
through some of the past rhetoric and really explore alternative means
of extensively upgrading the skills, productivity, adaptability, and
resourcefulness of the masses who do not receive any formal education. It is suggested that the people themselves should be both the
ends and the means of this process. For example, the traditional
structures, (village, family) may be the only effective mobilizers
of these new skills.

The key problems of the sector are briefly listed below:

1. Inadequate means and resources to transfer more relevant
skills to rural populations: If as an overall goal we are seeking
qualitative improvements in rural life, then a part of that process
is a narrowing of the perceptions of differential attractiveness between
urban and farm settings. It is creating new opportunities for food
production and better health services, on the one hand, and the transfer
of the appropriate education and training skills necessary to transform

new opportunities and motivation into real returns (food and income) on the other.

2. Limited administrative and management capabilities at all levels of national, local, and regional government institutions: With the large influx of development assistance, particularly in the Sahelian states, the capacities of key technical and administrative personnel are being overextended far beyond capacities. If longer-term country budgetary limitations can be dealt with, it is crucial to close this development administration manpower gap as quickly as possible so that the effective absorptive capacities are expanded. It is possible that special kinds of in-service training programs will have to be designed and that selected governmental institutions will have to be supported. Unless the management gap also is addressed, other food and environmental problems could become even more intractable.

THE PARAMETERS OF PROGRAM COMPOSITION

In selecting the sectors and key problems to be addressed during the next five years, the range of policy and programmatic possibilities has been substantially narrowed. However, even within the more narrowly defined key bottlenecks, further guidelines are required as program selection criteria.

National Versus Regional Programs

The development programs should be developed with a regional strategy in mind. The key problems identified are common to all countries in the region and there is a recognition that there is a need for regional solutions to many of them. Where there is a confluence of certain factors, along with geographic and economic interdependencies, regional programs can realistically be considered. However, for the foreseeable future much of the planning and articulation of programs is going to be more national in nature, particularly now that donors (including USAID) are establishing national offices. With the exception of a few major projects, it should be expected that most programs and projects will have to be fully justified as part of the overall regional strategy although their actual implementation may more often be undertaken nationally.

We have already agreed that, developmentally, a zonal
strategy is essential, seeking to integrate the economies and potential
of the more highly productive coastal areas with the requirements
and contributions of the poorer and environmentally more fragile
areas. The timing is now auspicious to initiate a series of complementary zonal or area investments. Both recipients and donors have
accepted the zonal theories, and regional organizations have been
formed to develop and conserve shared resources.

Multinational Programs

Several major resources in the region specifically lend them-
selves to area development programs through regional organizations.
These are: OMVS (Organisation pour la Mise en Valeur du fleuve
Senegal), for the development of the Senegal River Basin; Niger River
Commission, for the Development of the Niger River Basin; and the
Lake Chad Basin Commission (LCBC) for the development of the
Lake Chad Basin.

These three great watersheds represent the major possibilities
for agricultural production over the longer run and their intensive
development over time is undoubtedly crucial to fully resolving the
key problems in the agricultural, livestock, and health sectors.

Special Multinational Bodies

Several multinational institutional vehicles will continue to
play important planning and implementation roles and should be
considered in forming new programs.

Now that a larger quantum of USAID resources is going to be
put into Central/West Africa, appropriate elements of that investment
package should be handled in a manner that will strengthen the African
Development Bank and confirm our long-term support for that institution.

To deal with a range of regional and sectoral problems (including livestock), the Entente Fund has a special role in the relationship between poorer inland and coastal states, particularly the

Ivory Coast. It can provide the focal point for additional regional planning on several regional problems.

The Lake Chad Basin Commission will begin to play a greater role in the development of the Lake Chad resources. We should support that expanding role.

The role of the Interstate Committee for the Struggle Against the Drought (CILSS) has been a very special one. Initially set up to deal specifically with the drought and to gain and coordinate support from the international community, it is now at a crossroads. It has succeeded in raising wide donor interest in the region but, due to staffing and other limitations, could not function as an effective planning or coordinating unit. This latter capacity could be rein-forced substantially depending on the CILSS relationship to the Coordinating Group (CG) for the Sahel.

Special Assistance Criteria

A series of internal USAID policy decisions have been kept in mind as this strategy becomes articulated:

1. There should be no constraint on the number of U.S. direct hire or contract personnel. However, since there are only a limited number of qualified, French-speaking personnel available, especially for rural areas, programs should attempt to maximize the use of other donors and Peace Corps.

2. We will be willing to consider the financing of sectoral and problem-related research. We will be prepared to finance local and even recurring costs when activities are revenue producing, thereby assuring that the budget support would be limited and finite in time. Balance-of-payments assistance will be considered when directly related to key problem resolution.

3. To the extent possible, elements of research, training, and project design should be accomplished through local institutions. Wherever possible, local institutional capacity should be utilized.

4. Capital projects, particularly of an infrastructure nature, should not be ruled out. However, in most cases these capital ele-ments must be an integral part of an area or production project with widespread benefits. Our preference will remain that capital and road projects be presented to other donors.

Donor Coordination

As indicated previously, development of the Sahel must take
place over the entire area if it is not to continue as a recipient of
international relief and if it is to move from being a food-deficit region
to one that is substantially self-sufficient in food production and
economically viable. Donor investment not only will be needed over
a wide geographical area but it also will be needed for a period of
time long enough to bring about an actual transformation of the Sahel.
Such an undertaking must clearly be well coordinated and institutionalized if this is to occur.

Consistent with this congressional mandate and USAID's desire
to assist in addressing the fundamental long-term problems of one
of the world's poorest regions, USAID has begun discussions with
other major donors on a coordinated approach to the fundamental
long-term problems of the Sahel and contiguous areas. Discussions
have been conducted with the Development Assistance Committee of
the OECD (Organization for Economic Cooperation and Development),
with the United Nations, and the IBRD (International Bank for Reconstruction and Development). These groups have indicated real interest
in pursuing an institutionalized donor coordinate approach to Sahelian
development. The government of France, through its Ministry of
Cooperation, has wholeheartedly endorsed the idea of a multidonor
approach to major investment in the region and, in concert with
USAID, requested the chairman of the DAC to convene an informal
meeting of donors providing assistance to the Sahelian countries to
determine their interests in formally establishing a Sahel Coordinating
Group. This initial meeting took place on January 30, 1975, in Paris.
Discussions with positive results have been held with the U.N.,
CIDA (Canadian International Development Agency), FED (European
Development Fund), and West Germany. These preliminary discussions clearly indicate that there is keen interest and a large
measure of agreement on the need for a more structured approach
to development assistance in the Sahelian region.

Useful experience in donor coordination was gained during the
massive relief effort to avert widespread famine and disease, and
during the recovery period immediately following the drought when
many short-term projects, designed to facilitate the relief process
to ameliorate the most obvious consequences of the drought on people,
livestock, and natural resources, were undertaken on a donor-
coordinated basis. Medium-term programs, undertaken on a bilateral basis and designed to meet the Sahelian countries' priority
objectives of good crop and livestock production, are being implemented in close coordination with other donors and their development

assistance activities. Although assistance to the Sahelian region has been provided without the benefit of a formally established institutional mechanism for assuring donor coordination of efforts, a number of specific instances can be cited. The IBRD has sponsored multidonor meetings to address regional transportation problems and is taking the lead in establishing a multidonor administrative mechanism for the special problem of onchocerciasis control and development in the Volta River Basin. FED has sponsored several multidonor meetings to address joint analysis and to develop a common strategy for planning the livestock sector in the Sahel and contingent areas. The U.N./FAO played a vital role in coordinating the international provision of emergency food aid during the drought. Another U.N. agency, the World Meteorological Organization (WMO), which sponsors the Global Atmospheric Research Atlantic Tropical Experiment (GATE), will assess weather patterns and atmospheric conditions in the Sahel-Sudano zone.

The Sahelian countries themselves have formed associations to deal with common problems. To deal specifically with problems directly caused by the drought and related ecological problems, the six Sahelian countries have created CILSS (le Comite Permanent Interetats de Lutte contre la Secheresse dans le Sahel). The Sahelian countries also are members of associations formed to deal with the exploitation of shared resources, for example, the Senegal River Basin Organization (OMVS); the Niger River Commission; and the Lake Chad Basin Commission (LCBC). Common sectoral problems and policies also have been focal points around which cooperative associations have been built, notably: health problems, Organization for the Coordination for the Fight Against the Endemic Diseases in Central Africa (OCEAC); livestock (the Entente Livestock community); birds and insect pests, Joint Organization of the Fight Against Insect Pests and Birds (OCLALAV); and water resources, the Inter-African Committee for Hydraulic Studies (CIEH). Each of the Sahelian states is a member of the African Development Bank, which is actively providing assistance packages for each of the affected countries.

Positive benefits have accrued from such donor cooperation, especially in minimizing duplicated effort and maximizing the impact over the medium term in key sectors such as food crop and livestock production. However, donor coordination as it exists presently is characterized by informal, ad hoc arrangements and is limited by and large to bilateral and project-specific activities.

The Sahelian states and donors alike recognize the need for a coordinated approach to development problems that cover a broad geographic area or require investments that no single donor can provide. Lacking appropriate institutional vehicles through which to channel major investments to solve the major development problems, most donors have worked on a bilateral basis with individual Sahelian states or through interstate or regional organizations.

Because of the interest in and experience gained by donors in working together on emergency, short- and medium-term responses to problems in the Sahelian regions, there is a real opportunity to coalesce worldwide concern for the area into an approach that will ensure sufficient investment to bring about longer-term development over a broader geographic area and for the long term. Specifically, this approach would involve (1) creation of a formal multidonor Sahel Coordinating Group that will work in close association with the recipient Sahelian countries to develop and coordinate investments programs; and (2) the establishment of a special Sahel development fund under the aegis of the Sahel Coordinating Group to assure that external resources are adequate to meet long-term development objectives.

The establishment of a Sahel Coordinating Group responds to the need to address fundamental long-term development problems of the Sahelian region and contingent areas. The critical problem that would be resolved by the creation of such a group is the absence of any mechanism to coordinate with concerned governments' planned and future large-scale investments in the region. This group, in close association with Sahelian governments, interstate organizations, and regional associations, would assume leadership in coordinating an investment program, in assisting the mechanization of domestic resources, and in assuring the adequacy of external resources. In exercising its coordinating functions, the coordinating group would be charged with increasing and improving the efficiency of financial and technical assistance—both multilateral and bilateral—for the long-term development of the region. Membership in the coordinating group will be open to bilateral donors and multilateral agencies that have indicated an interest in the region. These would include the OPEC countries, which have indicated their readiness to provide assistance to Sahelian countries individually or through the African Development Bank. The coordinating group would not supplant bilateral assistance but, on the contrary, would provide a more comprehensive framework within which the efficiency and effectiveness of bilateral aid could be increased.

The prospects for the Sahel, therefore, while difficult in the extreme, are by no means impossible. The fact that the Sahelian states themselves appear ready to make the difficult decisions necessary to mobilize domestic resources for development problems; the organized fashion of assistance from the industrialized world; and the natural resiliency of the peoples indigenous to the area, all combine to create a circumstance in which longer-term development can take place. Perhaps the most important factor, aside from the need of some reasonable balance of annual rainfalls, will be the determination of the donor community to provide funds over a sufficiently long period of time for the entire area to have a reasonable prospect of self-sustaining development. The technologies, the resources, and the will to solve the problems exist. Whether all these elements will come together to bring progress and real hope to the 30 million people involved rather than dust and desperation still remains to be seen.

6

THE DESERT-SIDE ECONOMY OF THE CENTRAL SUDAN

P. E. Lovejoy
S. Baier

The role of the desert edge in the history of West Africa has long been appreciated, but the recent Sahelian drought and the tragedy it has entailed for so many people has accentuated the need to understand the relationship between desert and savanna.[1] The drought, which began in some places in 1968 and continued until 1973 or 1974, depending upon location, has been the worst in over two centuries, but its economic impact on the savanna, severe as it has been, has nonetheless been minimized because of a reorientation of the savanna economy toward the coast, a shift dating to the beginning of the colonial period. With the end of the trans-Saharan trade, the redirection of overseas trade toward the coast, and the development of peanuts as an agricultural export, much of the savanna gained new independence from the economy of the desert and Sahel. Nevertheless, the area along the southern edge of the Sahara was extremely significant historically in the development of adjacent regions in the savanna before the colonial period, so it seems likely that one of the most underestimated impacts of colonialism may have been the decline of the desert-edge sector. This sector offered an extensive market for grain, manufactures, and other products imported from the savanna; was a source of livestock, several types of mineral salts, and transport services; and provided access to North African markets. In addition, it was the original home of many immigrant merchants, craftsmen, and farmers who contributed greatly to the development of the savanna. An examination of the desert-edge sector, therefore, reveals the dynamics of economic change in the precolonial era and provides a comprehensive perspective on the current crisis.

One important conclusion that emerges from a look at the desert edge and its links with the savanna is the realization that different parts of the southern Sahara were so closely integrated with adjacent areas of savanna that we can detect economic regions. These regions, subdivided into areas of localized specialization, depended upon production for the market by a majority of people within regional boundaries. In many places towns developed, sometimes in proximity to relatively densely populated rural areas, and these became centers of economic growth. The desert edge was only one part of these larger economic spheres, but the types of interaction in sub-Saharan Africa also characterized other parts of the world straddling the ecological frontier between desert and adjacent areas of fertile agricultural land. This was especially true of areas along the great desert strip from the western Sahara through the Arabian Peninsula as far as the Gobi Desert in Central Asia. [2]

The region comprising much of northern Nigeria and Niger, referred to as the Central Sudan, provides an example of an integrated desert-side economy. The desert played a unique role in the development of the savanna here, where integration enabled the desert sector to survive periods of crippling drought and to prosper in times of favorable weather. The purpose of this chapter is to explore some of the links between this desert-side sector and the larger economy in the belief that a regional perspective on economic and social history is necessary to prevent the distortion involved in localized approaches. In particular, it is argued that Tuareg and Hausa societies cannot be treated in isolation, that distinctions between the two were closely related to economic specialization and interdependence, and that movement across ethnic boundaries was frequent and necessary to economic change. This argument proceeds within the theoretical framework advanced by Fredrik Barth, although the recent work of Michael Horowitz, Johannes Nicolaisen, and others is also relevant. [3]

When applied to the conditions of the Central Sudan, Barth's approach suggests that Tuareg and Hausa interacted within a larger, composite society and economy in which cultural distinctions reflected degrees of specialization. In order to clarify this approach, the following arguments are implicit in the chapter: First, Tuareg society, constructed in a pyramid fashion with nobles on top and various levels of dependents and servile groups below, was dominated by the few aristocratic leaders who in effect acted as managers of large firms. Second, these firms invested in diverse activities, ranging from stock breeding to transport, trade in salt, dates, grain, and manufactures, land ownership, slave labor, the finance of craft production, and commercial brokerage. Third, investments crossed cultural boundaries, however defined, so that Tuareg firms were heavily committed to the economic well-being of the whole Central Sudan, not just the desert edge where the nomads concentrated. Fourth, personnel for the firms was drawn from both sides of the Hausa-Tuareg ethnic frontier, and even included people of Kanuri and

and North African origin. Fifth, movement across the frontier was
continuous and was accelerated by droughts and economic cycles,
although the absence of data prevents an estimation of the magnitude
of movement. Nevertheless, a strong correlation existed between
nomadic life and Tuareg affiliation on the one hand and sedentary
life and Hausa (or Kanuri) identification on the other. Sixth, the
Tuareg may have occasionally raided and enslaved sedentary people,
but the dominant mode of interaction was that of cooperation and
peaceful trade. A tentative hypothesis is that raiding occurred more
frequently on the eastern and western fringes of the Hausa-Tuareg
regional economy. In these peripheral areas, economic interaction
between pastoralists and sedentary people was less intense so that
the Tuareg had less of a stake in the welfare of their sedentary
neighbors than they did in the case of Kano, Katsina, and Sokoto,
all located in the center.

RECURRING DROUGHT

The recent Sahelian drought was the latest in a series of
similar dry periods that have affected the Central Sudan over the
centuries. The present analysis of climatic cycles is most complete
for the eighteenth and nineteenth centuries. Although some information is available for droughts in earlier centuries, political chronology
based on reign lengths has yet to be worked out. Hence chronology
for early droughts, especially those before the middle eighteenth
century, must be considered tentative. This is especially true for
the seven-year drought in Borno in the middle sixteenth century, the
eleven-year famine in Kano at the turn of the seventeenth, and the
seven-year famine in Borno at the turn of the eighteenth (see Table
6.1). Nevertheless, famines of these magnitudes must have seriously
affected large parts if not all of the southern Sahara in the Central
Sudan and set in motion major population shifts from the desert and
Sahel. Livestock must have declined, and related changes in political
and economic power must have altered the stratification of Tuareg
society.[4] By the middle eighteenth century the Kel Ewey Confederation
emerged as the dominant force in Air, and it accounted for a larger
proportion of darker-skinned Tuareg than its claims to a North
African origin could support. The Kel Geres and Itisen were evicted
from Air in the 1690s, but by the mid eighteenth century they were
well established in Adar.[5] These were only the broadest political
changes in the period before 1750, but the major geographical
division between the two dominant Tuareg subconfederations lasted
well into the nineteenth century.

TABLE 6.1

Central Sudan Droughts, 1540-1974

Place	Approximate Date	Severity
Borno	c. 1540s or 1550s	no indication
Borno	c. 1550s to 1560s	seven-year duration
Kano	c. 1590s or 1600s	eleven-year duration
Borno	c. 1650s, 1660s or 1670s	famine called Dala Dama, of unknown duration
Agades	c. 1690s	unknown
Borno	c. late 1690s, 1700s or 1710s	seven-year duration
Borno, Kano	1740s and early 1750s	severe drought, ten or more years duration
Borno, Kano, Agades	c. 1790s	mass emigration from Agades
Hausa country	1847	one year, called Dawara
Hausa country	1855	one year, severe drought, called banga-banga, worst of century
Hausa country	1890	fairly severe
Hausa country, Borno	1912-14	called k'ak'alaba, worst since eighteenth century
Whole region	1968-74	worst since eighteenth century

Sources: "Kano Chronicle," as translated in H.R. Palmer, Sudanese Memoirs (London, 1928), vol. 3 pp. 116-30; Diwan of Borno, in H.R. Palmer, Bornu Sahara and Sudan (London, 1936), pp. 94-95; John Lavers, Preliminary Outline, Chapter 6, Nigerian History Project (Zairia, 1975); Y. Urvoy, Histoire de l'Empire du Bornou (Paris: Larose, 1949), pp. 85-86; Polly Hill, Rural House: A Village and a Setting (London: Cambridge University Press, 1972), p. 231, who quotes William Gowers, Nigerian National Archives, Kaduna (NNAK), S.N.P. 17, K. 2151 (1926). We wish to thank Adell Patton for showing us a photocopy of the original archival source.

Besides information on droughts, some observations can be
made on periods of prosperity in this early period. The reign of Mai
Idris b. Ali of Borno, for example, was one such time. [6] He ruled
for over fifty years, beginning in about 1563. If this chronology is
confirmed, then the eleven-year drought at Kano toward the end of
Idris's term may not have affected Borno. This would suggest that
the drought was localized and not as severe as some other ones for
the region as a whole. Furthermore, for most of the seventeenth
century, until the 1690s, only one drought is reported, perhaps of
short duration since the number of years is not recorded. More
precision is impossible at present because it occurred during the
forty-year reign of Mai Ali b. Umar. The famine at Agades in the
1690s coincided with a war between different sections of the Tuareg,
at the time the Kel Ewey defeated the Kel Geres-Itisen forces in the
struggle for Air, and it appears to have been of only one or two years
in duration and may not have been a drought.

For the eighteenth century, much more can be said. A seven-
year drought hit Borno sometime between 1690 and 1720, but it is
not reported in the Hausa country, although it could have coincided
with the famine among the Tuareg in the 1690s. But the major development of the century was the drought of the 1740s and early 1750s,
and for this one much more information is available than for any
other until the present century. This alone suggests its severity.
Although Borno chronology is confused for this period, it is known
that the famine overlapped the reigns of two mai, the first who
ascended the throne in the 1730s and the second who reigned for
three years, possibly in the late 1740s but probably from 1750 to
1753. The drought lasted for most, if not all, of both reigns. It
was particularly severe for two years, probably in the 1740s, when
it acquired the name CAli Shuwa or CAli Shu. At Kano, this period is
remembered as a time of trouble, principally because of protracted
war with Gobir, but it seems likely that this is remembered in part
because of the drought. This is especially so because the reign of
Alhaji Kabe, c. 1743-53, is contrasted with the following period of
general prosperity and immigration. The great drought of the 1740s
and early 1750s swept most of West Africa, along with a series of
epidemics. It was severe in the middle Volta Basin, the Niger bend
area around Timbuktu, and in the Senegambia region. [7]

Another drought occurred in the 1790s. While it was not as
severe as the great drought of the eighteenth century, it did force the
evacuation of Agades, depleted grain stores in Kano that had been
set aside to safeguard against famine, and probably is to be identified
with a drought that hit Borno within a decade after 1793. [8] Many
immigrant merchants who called themselves Agadesawa and were
attached to Tuareg networks in the Hausa cities moved to the savanna

at this time, and at least some Agalawa immigrants trace their
ancestry to this period as well.

The nineteenth century is remarkable for the absence of any
multiyear droughts; only one severe drought of one year's duration
is reported. The period to the 1840s was remembered as a time of
great prosperity, interrupted in 1847 by a year of scarcity.[9] The
most severe drought was in c. 1855, called banga-banga, when for
thirty days at a time no grain was available in Kano and the people
were forced to eat vultures. Years of more localized scarcity or
inadequate rainfall are reported for 1863, 1864, 1873, 1884, 1889,
and 1890.[10] Dry years were reported frequently after the turn of
the century, with worsening climate culminating in the drought of
1912-14. Lake Chad was at its lowest level in living memory in July
of 1914, and by 1957 it had still not regained the high level of
1874.[11]

These climatic cycles were the chief determinants of the
direction and extent of economic change in the Central Sudan. The
low points in these cycles represented limits to the growth of the
desert-side sector, which was always more severely affected than
the savanna, where fluctuations in rainfall were less critical. Since
the desert sector could not grow beyond a certain point, the forging
of close links with the savanna and ever-expanding investments there
were inevitable. The commercial networks uniting desert and savanna
assumed a critical importance in bad times, serving as a safety valve
for people of the desert by providing a framework for their escape
from an environment temporarily unable to support them.

THE DESERT-SIDE SECTOR

Even in prosperous years the desert and savanna were bound
together through commerce, for the Tuareg secured a living from the
harsh environment of the southern Sahara and Sahelian steppe through
specialization.[12] Although the Tuareg dominated the relatively fertile
areas of the Sahel, they depended on trade with the savanna, particularly the area centering on the Hausa states. Their concentration
along the southern fringes of the Sahara placed them close to farming
villages and savanna markets, where they obtained foodstuffs and
industrial products and sold the products of the desert. The extent
of interaction clearly establishes that the Taureg were market-
oriented, not in some peripheral way as the stereotype of precolonial
Africa would suggest, but to a degree that helps to demonstrate the
importance of market forces in the Central Sudan.

The Tuareg of the Air Massif, Adar, and Azawak required considerable grain for their diet, although milk was a principal food for half the year and in some cases the only nourishment for two to three months. Recent estimates, which indicate the extent of dependence upon millet imports over the past several centuries, show that:

> In the extremely hot season . . . when milk is
> very scarce most Tuareg eat millet porridge
> with a little milk or sauce . . . , and Tuareg
> who are not very wealthy eat millet porridge to
> a great extent all the year around, so that the
> necessary amount of millet for many camps is
> about 0.5 kilo a day per person, or about 180
> kilos a year. [13]

Assuming a population of less than 50,000 nomads in the Air and Azawak at the end of the nineteenth century, and millet consumption averaging 150 kilos per person per year, then as much as 7,500 metric tons of millet had to be brought from the south. [14] It seems reasonable to assume that approximately the same was true in the distant past. In the middle nineteenth century, for example, commerce at Agades, the most important town in Air, was "nothing but a speculation in provisions principally in ghussub or kasab (millet), which constitutes the principal and almost only food of the inhabitants." [15] Even traders from such distant places as Tuat dealt in grain, and in 1850 millet was "the real standard of the market," although cowries, silver, and gold were used. [16]

The Tuareg depended upon the Central Sudan for many articles besides grain. Every item in a description of Tuareg dress in the 1790s, for example, was manufactured in Hausa centers:

> The clothing of this nation consists of wide
> dark-blue breeches, a short narrow shirt of the
> same colour, with wide sleeves, which they bring
> together and tie on the back of their neck. . . .
> They wind a black cloth round their head in such
> a manner that at a distance it appears like a helmet,
> for their eyes only are seen. . . . Round their waist
> they wear a girdle of a dark colour. . . . Their
> upper dress is a Soudanian shirt, over which a
> long sword hangs from the shoulder. . . . [17]

The swords were fashioned in Kano and other savanna towns, where draftsmen attached handles to blades imported from North Africa and

later Europe. Such luxuries as tobacco and kola also were imported
from the south. This supply pattern developed several centuries
before the 1790s and has continued to the present.

The income needed to purchase grain and manufactures was
largely derived from the sale of animals—goats, sheep, camels,
cattle, and horses—or through the extension of services dependent
upon livestock production. Consequently, the requirements of the
herds set limits on Tuareg settlement and economic activity, and
the pattern that predominated was one of seasonal transhumance that
provided a framework not only for animal husbandry but also for
trade between desert and savanna. During July and August, when
some rain fell in the southern desert, herders took their animals
to the areas with the best pastures. Rainfall in the Air Massif was
greater than in the surrounding countryside, so that pastures there
held up long enough for a large contingent of Air Tuareg, as well as
others from the south and west, to make an annual trek across the
arid Tenere in late October and November to Bilma and Fachi, two
oases north of Borno (Bornu) on the route to North Africa. Here they
purchased salt and dates and sold grain. Profits from this trade,
together with earnings gained from services extended to trans-Saharan
commerce, were important supplements to Tuareg income. In December, after the return of the salt caravan, most Air Tuareg left for
the south, selling salt and dates and pasturing animals along the way.
The Tuareg of Adar and Azawak, areas west of the Air Massif, also
moved south during the dry season, although they were less involved
in the salt trade. Some people moved as far as Sokoto, Kano, and
Katsina, although many groups used pastures slightly farther north,
just within the territory of the sedentary states along the desert edge.
In June, when the rains began again, they left for the north, for the
excessive dampness of the savanna at this time of year endangered
the health of the camels.

Transport costs at the desert edge were low because of this
pattern of migratory transhumance. Since water and pasture requirements could be met by traveling south each year, Tuareg merchants
easily transported goods regardless of cost. Millet was about twice
as expensive in Agades as in Damerghou, for example, about 250
kilometers away, so that transport costs between these points were
about 350 cowries (about one-third of a franc in 1903) per metric
ton-kilometer. For the salt trade, costs were probably higher because of the long and arduous desert crossing between the Air Massif
and Bilma. A stock of millet purchased in Damagaram, taken to
Bilma and traded for salt, then returned to Damagaram and sold
again for millet, was worth 80 times the value of the original stock,
and much of the increase was for transport expenses.[18] This aspect
of the desert-side economy explains why nomads could move bulk

commodities great distances and helps explain why many savanna marketplaces were located along livestock trails, particularly since pack oxen were used extensively in transport as well as camels, and they could be sold if necessary.

In good times, profits from salt and date sales enabled the Tuareg to purchase savanna products. In 1850, when

> almost the whole supply of provision is imported,
> as well as all the clothing-material, it is evident
> that the population [of Air] could not be so numerous
> as it is, were it not sustained by the salt-trade of
> Bilma, which furnishes the people with the means
> of bartering advantageously with Hausa.[19]

The large annual caravans of several thousand camels each carried salt and dates to every Hausa center. Salts were of several types; they were used in cooking, medicines, industry, and mixed with tobacco. The Bilma and Fachi varieties were only a few of many kinds processed for the Central Sudan market, but this was an extremely important current of trade, with up to 2,000 metric tons entering the Sudan each year at the end of the nineteenth century. The value of salt passing through Damagaram was about £40,000, or about half of the value of trans-Saharan imports to Tripoli during an average year in the 1890s, before the volume of that trade started its final decline.[20] Unlike the trans-Saharan business, however, Tuareg merchants reaped most of the profits from the salt trade.

The Tuareg participated in the trans-Saharan trade primarily as transporters, guides, and hired security forces, and they also controlled a sizeable proportion of desert-edge production destined for trans-Saharan export.[21] Exports of ostrich feathers from the Sudan increased rapidly in the 1870s, declined again in the 1880s, and by the 1890s accounted for about half the total value of exports. The finance of the feather trade was largely in the hands of North African expatriates, most of whom were from Ghadames. By the late 1870s Ghadamsi merchants had established a community at Djadjidouna in Damerghou, where they bought ostrich feathers from village heads who organized the hunting or raising of birds. The Tuareg of Damerghou taxed the trade at the level of the village, asking payment in feathers of the choicest grade.[22] Little information on other Sahelian regions is available, but the taxation of production for trans-Saharan export may have been organized along similar lines elsewhere. Few nomads possessed the capital needed to invest directly in the trans-Saharan trade; instead, camel owners received a payment for each load they carried and left organization to North Africans who had a superior knowledge of market conditions and better financial connections.

Another important source of income derived from the control
of agricultural production in the Sahel and savanna. Military
supremacy enabled the Tuareg to dominate farming communities
in the Air Massif, Damerghou, southern Adar, and parts of
Damagaram, Maradi, Tessaoua, and beyond. Itisen and Kel Geres
controlled villages as far south as an area fifty miles north of the
Sokoto River valley, while Damerghou, the Sahel region immediately
south of the Air, was the most important granary for Air nomads. [23]
Specific families of Tuareg sections had rights to widely scattered
villages, whose separation prevented political consolidation. The
nineteenth century Kel Ewey leader Annur, for example, owned the
town of Tagelel, which had an estimated 120 compounds in 1851,
while only a few kilometers away a "man who played the chief part
during the [1840s] interregnum . . . in Azben [Air]" received
tribute from the small settlement at Farara. [24] Many people in this
region were the descendents of farmers and hunters who moved
north to exploit the frontier regions where game was plentiful and
agricultural settlement sparce. Most of these people were Hausa,
although some spoke Kanuri and were called Dagera. The Tuareg of
the Sahel fought among themselves for control of villages, and Tuareg
strangers often tried to enslave farmers and steal their cattle. Although the villages of Damerghou were located on hilltops and protected by palisades, settlements on the fringe of the desert were
extremely vulnerable to nomadic raiders, whose mobility and experience in warfare gave them every advantage. For this reason,
sedentary immigrants freely submitted to a Tuareg section for protection. Hausa and Dagera archers even fought alongside their
patrons when outsiders challenged the status quo. [25]

Living among the free farmers of Damerghou and Adar and
scattered throughout the sahel were people known to their sedentary
neighbors as buga je (s. buzu, fem. buzuwa). As enslaved people or
their immediate descendants, bugaje were low in social status, had
to lodge their overlords when they passed through, and paid tribute
in millet. Distinctions between buga je and the free people of neighboring villages were minor, since both owed their patrons a portion
of the harvest. In Damerghou and Adar, buga je and free farmers
alike paid tribute to the Tuareg, just as savanna farmers paid tax
to the sedentary states. Buga je usually spoke Hausa, unless they
were newly sedentarized. Most had been enslaved from Sudanese
populations in the first place, so their assimilation to Tuareg culture
could easily be reversed, although changes usually occurred in stages.
When previously nomadic buga je became exclusively farmers, for
example, they still preserved the custom of wearing the veil like their
nomadic masters. They also employed a unique system of land use,
which involved moving the household and animal enclosure along
narrow strips of land. [26]

Although the Tuareg obtained some grain through the taxation of sedentary peoples, they traded for well over half of their requirements. In Damerghou, for example, they distributed salt and dates to Hausa and Dagera village heads and gave them instructions to collect millet and store it in granaries so that it could be picked up on the return trip in June. Some village heads, using these goods as capital, organized trading expeditions on their own. Notable in this context were the Hausa entrepreneurs of western Damerghou, who traded between their homes and the Tarka valley to the west. A sizeable proportion of the trade between Agades and the south in the late nineteenth century was carried on by these sedentary farmers as well. In the dry season they loaded millet from their fields on pack oxen and headed north to Agades, where they traded for animals. Several loads of millet purchased as many as fifteen goats or sheep, although prices, of course, varied. This trade, which began centuries earlier, accounted for as much as 1,500 metric tons of millet each year, probably about half of the grain requirements of the area served by the Agades market. [27] This quantity suggests that thousands of head of livestock were sold at Agades each year. Other commercial networks, such as those involving savanna tobacco merchants and grain sellers who traveled north to exchange their products for livestock, salt, and dates, also accounted for considerable quantities of Tuareg imports. [28]

The highly stratified Tuareg social system concentrated wealth and the power to make economic decisions in the hands of a few. Aristocratic Tuareg (Tamashek, imajeren, s., amajer) managed their affairs so that dependents fit into a series of status categories with varying degrees of freedom. At the bottom were slaves called iklan; above them were irewelen, or freed slaves; and higher still were imrad, or vassals. Status was fluid; despite the theoretical hierarchy, which functioned primarily to assure first access to resources in times of scarcity, Tuareg nobles tended to treat all dependents alike. Nobles constituted not more than 10 percent of the nomadic population, but they made the important decisions. [29] They assigned some dependents, primarily irewelen and imrad, the task of herding, and sometimes sent them far away from the main camp. When nobles made contracts with North African merchants to provide transport animals and escorts for trans-Saharan caravans, imrad and irewelen did most of the traveling. Nobles accompanied them when caravan movements coincided with the annual descent toward the savanna and the return to the desert, but few nobles traveled across the Tenere with the salt caravans. They left this hard work to their dependents.

Besides those directly attached to noble camps, the aristocracy also controlled other nomadic and sedentary dependents. A noble or his lineage might have nominal control over a whole section of imrad Tuareg who had lost their claim to noble status after suffering defeat in battle or loss of herds. Imrad sections took charge of surplus animals belonging to nobles, but they had to surrender them in times of scarcity. Noble Tuareg also controlled independent sections of iklan and irewelen most of whom were sedentary. These were the buga je of the Sahel and savanna; Hausa-speaking people knew all dependent Tuareg by this name, which can be confusing because it lumps together nomadic and sedentary people of the lower-status categories. By calling all Tuareg of low status buga je, Hausa speakers reflected their own unfamiliarity with the theoretical hierarchy.

Although some nomadic and sedentary dependents were technically slaves, nomadic life prevented the constant surveillance of servile labor. In addition, the possibility of drought in the Sahel meant that people had to be free to emigrate to save themselves. These conditions affected buga je and Hausa or Dagera farmers alike, as the observations of the nineteenth century scholar and diplomat Heinrich Barth suggest. In describing slave conditions at the Tessaoua estate of Annur in 1850, Barth wrote:

> The estate is very extensive, and consists of a great
> many clusters of huts scattered over the fields, while
> isolated dum-palms give to the whole a peculiar feature.
> The people, all followers and mostly domestic slaves
> of Annur, seemed to live in tolerable ease and comfort,
> as far as I was able to see, my companion introducing
> me into several huts. Indeed every candid person,
> however opposed to slavery he may be, must acknowl-
> edge that the Tawarek in general, and particularly the
> Kel-owi, treat their slaves not only humanely, but even
> with the utmost indulgence and affability, and scarcely
> let them feel their bondage at all. Of course there are
> exceptions.[30]

But even the exceptions are instructive for, once Tuareg owners left, mistreated individuals fled south, where they joined existing communities of northern immigrants. This course of action also was open to servile nomadic Tuareg, although they relied primarily on an institution whereby they changed masters by cutting the ear of another noble's camel should they be maltreated.

As can be seen from the above description, ethnic identification in the Sahel and southern Sahara was characterized by a division between farmer and nomad, between Tuareg and Hausa or Kanuri; hence, ecological specialization was at the basis of ethnicity.

Furthermore, within each cultural division, other distinctions were recognized, each of which had a foundation in the relative economic, political, and social position of the people involved. Noble Tuareg were the highest in status and power and considered themselves the most "Tuareg" in culture. Their language was, in effect, a specialized tongue identified with specific occupations as well as a distinctive lifestyle. Under them were various nomadic groups that identified closely with the dominant status system but were treated as subordinate and servile members of the society. These people, who constituted the majority of the nomadic population, were often relegated to pastures where only goats or sheep could be raised or to areas further south where cattle became the specialty. Since political and economic power was related to the number of camels, status distinctions corresponded very closely to economic stratification. But environmental conditions limited the numbers of nomads and size of herds. In times of prosperity, demographic increase threatened to outdistance the resources for survival, but localized and periodically widespread droughts checked this tendency. In times of scarcity, many nomads lost their livestock and were forced to emigrate, so that population declined until conditions attracted new immigrants, both slave and free. Although the rate of flow across ethnic boundaries cannot be calculated, the number of nomads with dark skin, some as dark as savanna inhabitants, demonstrates that this population drift has been continuous over the centuries.

In the case of the sedentary population of the Sahel and Air Massif, ethnic distinctions primarily related to the process of immigration, time and conditions of settlement, and relationship to Taureg overlords. Land effectively belonged to the nomads, a right secured through military conquest, the expulsion or destruction of such early sedentary states as Gobir, and the continued insistence that tribute be paid to specific drum groups or individually powerful Tuareg leaders. Since most people in the marginal lands of the Sahel invested in animals in addition to raising millet and other food crops, distinctions between people were much closer to being on a continuum than was the case between the most nomadic Tuareg and the sedentary population of the savanna. It seems probable that many farmers, who often were livestock dealers as well, found it advantageous to invest in animal husbandry because land was neither alienable nor profitable over the long run. Famines were too great a danger, tribute payments reduced the size of agricultural surpluses, and livestock could be moved or sold if necessary. It seems likely that the optimum size of herds for sedentary people was about six cattle and probably larger numbers of sheep and goats. Beyond that point, it was more profitable to follow the herds and abandon or reduce the commitment to agriculture. This pattern explains the existence of seminomadic buga je,

permanently settled buga je, and other people who appear to fall
midway between nomadic Tuareg society and sedentary Hausa-
Dagera society. The movement across the ethnic frontier and its
correspondence with economic activity, therefore, appears to fit
into a pattern that characterized similar regions in the Sahel, particularly in Dar Fur and even closer to home, in Muniyo, where
distinctions between Fulani cattle herders and Manga agriculturalists
have been continuously manipulated to permit people to cross the
ethnic boundary. [31]

SAVANNA INVESTMENTS

Ethnic distinctions assumed an even more complicated pattern
than the analysis has so far permitted, for the Tuareg maintained an
elaborate commercial infrastructure in the savanna that enabled
people to move throughout the Central Sudan. Tuareg investment was
so extensive by the early 1850s that the observant Heinrich Barth
found it

> astonishing how much property is held in these
> fertile regions [Hausa country] by the Tawarek
> of Asben, and to what consequences this may
> eventually lead every body will easily conjecture. [32]

Barth was thinking in terms of political influence, but he was perceptive enough to recognize that cultural distinctions were not
isolating features in the Central Sudan but instead were the means
through which social and economic relations were regulated. This
network more closely approximated the commercial diasporas
analysed by Cohen, Curtin, and others, but seen within the context
of a larger social and economic system the Tuareg diaspora appears
less isolated and more an integral part of a multiethnic Central
Sudan society and economy. [33]

The commercial infrastructure included urban communities of
brokers, landlords, and craftsmen; rural grazing sites for camel
herds; as well as numerous villages and estates, often adjacent to
camp sites. The principal confederations and their component sections visited different Hausa towns, with the Kel Geres and Itisen
concentrating on markets south of Adar and the Kel Ewey visiting
areas further east. Markets overlapped, however, as an account
from the 1820s indicates:

> During the whole of the dry season they remain
> in Houssa, principally in the provinces of Kano,
> Kashna [Katsina], Zamfra [Zamfara1], and
> Saccatoo [Sokoto]. The latter are mostly Killgris
> [Kel Geres]: and Kashna and Kano are the principal
> resort of the Etassen [Itisen] and Killaway [Kel
> Ewey]: they do not live, except a few, in houses in
> the town; but build temporary huts in the woods, not
> far from them, where they have their wives, their
> bullocks, horses, and camels, the men only visiting
> the town: in this way they live until the month in which
> the rains commence, when they retire north to the
> desert. 34

The permanent grazing camps and related urban business establish-
ments that accommodated this trade not only handled thousands of
camels and pack oxen but considerable numbers of people, too, perhaps as many as a couple of thousand each year.

Urban communities associated with the Tuareg were located
in nearly every city and town. Many residents were descendents of
Agades merchants, and hence they identified themselves as Agadesawa
and Asbenawa, people of Agades and Air, respectively. Further west,
in the Sokoto area, immigrants from the north called themselves
Adarawa, or people of the Adar. Many northern immigrants ran
lodging houses (masauke), operated brokerage firms, and provided
storage facilities. Others became craftsmen or processed dried
meat (kilishi) for sale to merchants and other travelers. Heinrich
Barth, upon meeting some Agadesawa in 1850, learned that they were

> established in the northern provinces of Hausa,
> chiefly in Katsina and Tasawa, where living is
> infinitely cheaper than in Agades. All these I
> found to be intelligent men, having been brought
> up in the centre of intercourse between a variety
> of tribes and nations of the most different organi-
> zation, and, through the web of routes which join
> here, receiving information of distant regions. 35

Katsina's community was particularly important in the eighteenth
century, when its merchants diversified their activities by importing
kola nuts and exporting Borno salts, textiles, leather goods, and
other items to the middle Volta basin and Borgu.

In the nineteenth century, Tuareg merchants, including a deposed
Agades sultan, operated branch firms in the principal cities of the

Central Sudan. The Kel Azanieres, for example, a rich and powerful
Kel Ewey section with its principal dry-season base in Zinder, had
commercial operations in Katsina, Kano, Sokoto, and Hadeija. Although section members cooperated, every wealthy Tuareg had a firm
of his own, even if he lacked a network of agents with permanent
residences in the major cities. A "considerable estate" located
outside K'ofar Wombai, one of the main gates of Kano city, belonged
to one Tuareg merchant whose "company of slaves" conducted business
while he was traveling.[36] Tuareg nobles called on the services of
buga je who were empowered to act in their interest. The use of
servile employees was common in all sectors of the Tuareg economy,
and it also was common practice among the North African merchants,
the partners and backers of the Tuareg in the trans-Saharan trade.

Typical of the arrangements for bulking and distribution were
those used by the Tuareg in Zinder. Just north of the city was a
small community of settled Tuareg, and slightly farther north, not
more than a kilometer away, was the large camp or zongo of the
nomads. Nobles from a dozen Kel Ewey sections maintained dry-
season homes at this campsite and used their houses as bases from
which to sell salt and dates. They entrusted goods to their servants,
who traveled to periodic markets nearby. Other servants took herds
to pasture and returned from time to time if grazing lands were not
far from the zongo. When the Tuareg left for the Air each year in
June, they took most of their dependents with them, but they left
servile women in charge of their houses and possessions. These
women sold salt and dates from the previous year's caravan on their
masters' account. Since they were by themselves for about half of
each year, they were able to accumulate resources by trading with
their masters' capital, and Tuareg nobles saw nothing wrong in this.
Several women from the zongo near Zinder became landlady-brokers
for stranger Tuareg belonging to sections that did not maintain camps
near Zinder. They lodged their guests, helped them sell their goods
and buy local manufactures or grain, and provided storage facilities.
Tuareg women maintained houses and performed similar functions
in Agades, Kano, Bichi, and Hadeija.[37] In a matrilocal society,
the need to provide landlord-broker services elicited a response
from those who normally maintained permanent residences, namely,
the women.

Until the early twentieth century, many of the important merchants in the Central Sudan were either northern immigrants or their
descendents.[38] In Zinder, for example, two important traders of the
late nineteenth century were the descendents of Agadesawa who settled
in Tessaoua. In the first two decades of the twentieth century, Manzo
Kandarga, a freed slave of the anastafidet, or leader of the Kel Ewey
sections, dominated the commerce of the city. When Manzo Kandarga

died, two of the traders who replaced him were Agadesawa descendents. At the end of the nineteenth century the local trader with the largest business in Zinder was Malam Yaro, the son of a servile Tuareg woman and a man who was either an assimilated North African or a Kanuri immigrant.[39] Malam Yaro's business was large enough that his financial and banking system has come to light. North Africans who did business with his firm could sell in Zinder and buy in Kano by taking advantage of an institution for the delegation of credit from one person to another. A North African or Tuareg merchant could sell goods to Malam Yaro in Zinder, but receive in lieu of payment a letter instructing the firm's representative in Kano, Malam Yaro's half-brother, to give the traveling merchant goods worth the amount deposited in Zinder. The balance was regulated by transfers of the same kind in the other direction, or by transfers of money or merchandise within the firm. This delegation of credit, called hawala in Arabic, was common practice among North Africans, too. The merchants of the Tuareg communities in Sudanese cities borrowed this practice, and undoubtedly others as well, from the commercial culture of North Africa.[40]

Outside the main cities, grazing camps were sometimes so extensive that whole communities grew up around them. A prosperous town, Bichi, developed adjacent to one campsite twenty miles northwest of Kano City:

> The town is very remarkable, as exhibiting the
> peculiar circumstances of the social state in this
> country [in 1850]; for it belongs partly to the
> Tawarek tribe of Itisan, whose buga je or serfs—
> properly half-castes, born of free mothers, but
> slaves from the fathers' side—live here, culti-
> vating for their lords the fields around the town.
> Thus we see Tawarek every where, not only as
> occasional merchants, but even as settlers and
> proprietors.[41]

Around the town were several small servile villages founded by Tuareg merchants and immigrants. The name of one village, Damargu, reflected the origins of its inhabitants. It was settled in the eighteenth century, and perhaps earlier, and its first six village heads were from Air. The family of Madugu K'osai, the famous nineteenth century Tokarawa caravan leader and kola trader, was associated with this village. 'Yan Gwarzo and 'Yan Bundu, only a few miles away, were other buga je villages near Bichi.[42] Similar Tuareg communities existed at K'ofar Guga, the quarter near Katsina's northwestern gate, at Bebeji in Kano Emirate, at Zinder in Damagaram, and at Zirmi in Zamfara.[43]

Many Tuareg-controlled agricultural communities were not
specifically associated with grazing camps or urban centers. Most
were located in Katsina and Kano Emirates and were really an extension of the Sahelian agricultural system. Annur, for example,
had an estate outside Zinder in the mid-nineteenth century, in addition
to villages in Damerghou and near Tessaoua, while his brother Elaiji,
who headed the salt caravan of 1850, owned a place at Kazaure, thirty-
five miles north of Kano, and supported a Muslim cleric at Gezawa,
fifty miles north of Katsina. The inhabitants of these southern communities were servile in status, known as buga je to their Hausa
neighbors, but otherwise were nearly indistinguishable from others
in Hausa society. They formed the nucleus of the Agalawa, or
"southerners," whose ranks were swelled in the late eighteenth and
nineteenth centuries by immigrant farmers from the north.[44] The
Agalawa became famous through their success in savanna trade,
particularly importing kola nuts from Asante and exporting Borno
salts, textiles, leather goods, and dried onion leaves (gabu) to
Borgu and the middle Volta basin.[45] Their first concentrations were
near Katsina, the most important eighteenth-century Hausa commercial center, but after 1800 many people left these early places
for the Kano area, whose economic boom attracted other immigrants
as well. In Kano Emirate, however, the Agalawa were recognized
as fully integrated members of Hausa society with only historical
ties with the Tuareg.

Other immigrants included the Tokarawa, whose ancestors
abandoned nomadic livestock herding in the Sahel and desert in order
to exploit commercial opportunities in the savanna, and as for their
distant cousins, the Agalawa, this usually meant kola importing.[46]
Some of these people were descended from servile nomads who lost
their herds and were forced south to become farmers in the Hausa
countryside, and they naturally settled close to the Agalawa. Others
were more fortunate and saved part of their investment and used
livestock proceeds to finance new commercial ventures. In all cases
these immigrants, like the Agalawa, adopted a corporate name and
distinctive facial markings (askar) to promote their business interests.
Although the continued use of buga je as a term of reference also
assisted in maintaining a common identity, they considered themselves full members of Hausa, Muslim society. Most traced their
ancestry back to the late eighteenth or early nineteenth century, but
the pattern of immigration continued into the twentieth. Together
with the more numerous Agalawa, they accounted for a large portion
of the prosperous commercial class of Kano and other towns at the
end of the nineteenth century, and in the twentieth they commanded
enough capital to play a major role in the economy of northern
Nigeria, particularly by investing in produce buying and motor transport and by continuing to dominate kola wholesaling.

Tuareg investment in the savanna, the immigration of such
people as the Agalawa, Tokorawa, and others, and the operation of the
livestock industry, with its dependence upon scarce resources,
demonstrate the interrelationships between desert and savanna and
help elucidate questions relating to ethnicity. Not only does the
integration of Tuareg society and economy within a larger sphere
suggest that the organizational principles behind ethnic identification
were related to economic specialization, but the use of surnames,
facial markings (askar), and other identifying features accompanied
ever-increasing economic diversification. Pure Tuareg were nobles,
nomads, and closely connected with the management or operation of
livestock production, transport, and desert-oriented trade. Immigrants in the savanna were associated with one or another aspect of
the commercial infrastructure that handled Tuareg operations, or
they branched off into some other activity, such as the kola trade
in the case of the Agalawa and Tokarawa. Hence a series of ethnic
boundaries or subboundaries obtained, so that any analysis must
constantly exploit distinctions in order to unravel economic specialization and change. Through this analysis, a process emerges that was
closely related to economic cycles and shifting opportunities. Although
any treatment of these cycles must be considered extremely preliminary, they appear to relate to periods of famine and agricultural
prosperity, although such political changes as the jihad of 1804-08
also had major repercussions.

THE DROUGHT-RECOVERY CYCLE

Although no evidence on reactions to precolonial droughts is
available, a knowledge of recent patterns and the human ecology
of the Sahel suggests a model of the drought-recovery cycle. The
events of the early twentieth century represent an important source
of information on cyclical patterns, and these events must be taken
into account in attempting to reconstruct earlier cycles. The crisis
in the desert economy after the turn of the century was the result of
an interplay of a number of factors.[47] By 1911 the trans-Saharan
trade had collapsed, in part because of the completion of the railway
from the coast to Kano. The end of trans-Saharan business marked
the loss of an important source of income for the Tuareg, while the
presence of the colonial governments in Niger and Nigeria undermined their military superiority and interfered with the collection
of tribute from sedentary people. The Tuareg had the salt and animal
trades to fall back upon, but the French upset these activities as well.
French military forces in need of pack animals and remounts

commandeered camels belonging to the Tuareg, often without com-
pensation. The drought of 1912-14 compounded the problem by
causing camel losses of a magnitude about equal to those resulting
from French military operations. Further requisitions during World
War I added to the tensions, which erupted in the revolt of 1916. This
uprising seriously challenged the colonial military presence in the
desert and magnified the existing crisis in the economy. [48] The French
used severe measures to repress the uprising—so much so that the
majority of people in northern Air left for temporary exile in Nigeria.
In 1938, twenty years after the last of the fighting, the desert economy
was still in the process of recovering. In that year the size of the
salt caravans, which observers said was proportionate to the size of
camel herds, approached the pre-crisis level, but the average for
the years 1910-13 was surpassed only in the 1950s. [49] Such a long
period of regeneration can be hypothesized for severe droughts, like
the present one or that of the middle eighteenth century.

    The impact of warfare, such as that associated with the revolt
and its repression, was roughly similar to that of multiyear droughts.
Gaining a livelihood from the desert depended on a constant search
for pasture and water, but this became impossible when combatants
filled in wells, making movement extremely difficult and hazardous.
Neutral sections were often caught in the fighting, since raiding
parties were interested in the animals and grain supplies not only
of their enemies but of noncombatants as well. Many Tuareg responded
by leaving the desert until the fighting was over, moving temporarily
to the southern end of the network. This is what happened during
the revolt of 1916, when much of the Air Massif became uninhabitable.

    In 1913 among the first people to move south were the sedentary
farmers of Damerghou, whose crop failures gave them advance
warning of the impending disaster. They took their animals to Katsina
and Sokoto and traded them for millet and locust beans (dorowa),
which supplemented diets when millet prices were high. [50] Some old
people and children stayed behind in Damerghou but were resupplied
from time to time by villagers returning with provisions. Because
they left early and were able to sell animals before the price fell
drastically, they suffered less than their neighbors to the south in
Damagaram, although deaths from starvation occurred in Damerghou
as elsewhere.

    A model of the cycle of drought and recovery emerges from
this analysis of the events of the early twentieth century. When
drought occurred, the desert economy contracted, with nomadic
Tuareg and farmers alike leaving for the extreme southern end of
the trading network. Servile nomads attached to a noble's camp were
in effect members of his family, and he provided for them to the
extent this was possible. But nobles held rights of ownership over a

large proportion of the animals in the herds of imrad or vassal sections, and in bad times they claimed these animals. Consequently,
many nomads of lesser status no longer had enough animals to support
themselves. When the disturbance in the desert economy was especially prolonged, as in the drought of the middle eighteenth century,
or the upheaval associated with the 1912-14 drought and the 1916
revolt, many immigrants from the north were permanently lost to
the desert economy through sedentarization.[51] Unfortunately, it is
not possible to make even a rough estimate of the proportion of the
nomadic population that spilled over into the savanna, even in the
case of the migrations of the early twentieth century, when data are
abundant in comparison with earlier periods.

In times of scarcity, nobles and their retinues depended on the
hospitality of servile farmers settled on estates deep within the
territory of the sedentary states. In normal years they stayed only
for a short time as they passed through, primarily to collect tribute
and settle disputes. But during hard times nobles stayed until the
weather improved and herds recovered. Estates in the south were
least affected by drought, but the prolonged presence of the nomadic
master constituted a serious burden when grain surpluses were
marginal.

Just as the Tuareg social structure telescoped during hard
times, it expanded again when the weather improved or political
conditions returned to normal. Nobles collected their personal
followers and headed north. As the herds expanded and could support
a larger population, nobles called upon imrad or other servile Tuareg
who had become temporarily sedentary or semisedentary because of
the need to farm. Nobles enticed people into their followings by
loaning them some animals. The population, which had been super-
fluous and even dangerous during periods of scarcity, gradually
became necessary once again to take charge of surplus animals, to
trade, and to undertake transport and escort duties.

The assimilation of outsiders during economic recovery took
several forms. First, Tuareg participation in wars between sedentary
states, or raids on sedentary peoples, produced captives. Kel Ewey
and Kel Geres sections exchanged their captives, so that the necessity
of keeping a close watch on newly acquired slaves was reduced.[52]
Once acquired, slaves were quickly assimilated into Tuareg society.
Their status began to evolve almost immediately, and they were
given progressively greater freedom of movement.[53] This spatial
mobility was the basis of the social system, which adapted to the
cyclical nature of the desert-edge climate.

As opportunities in the north improved, free farmers left the
southern states, moved toward the desert edge, and established
tributary relations with nomads. This is exactly what happened in

Damerghou in the late eighteenth and early nineteenth centuries,
when the area was repopulated with immigrants from Katsina, Gobir,
Daura, and western Borno. This movement appears to have continued
the resettlement of the Sahel that followed the disastrous drought of
the 1740s and early 1750s, but a break in the pattern must have
occurred with the drought of the 1790s.

The cyclical pattern of desert-edge regeneration gradually
produced a situation in which some people were able to move from
the Sahel and southern Sahara because they became successful and
decided to invest in the savanna. Much immigration during the
nineteenth century, a period of relatively favorable climate, was an
outgrowth of decisions to reinvest capital acquired on the desert
edge—a response to opportunities in the savanna rather than to losses
of capital and emigration by necessity. This movement was a steady
trickle, in contrast to the larger movements of people fleeing drought
conditions, but it was an important source of capital. The investments
of successful Tuareg businessmen in southern estates accounted for
some of this demographic shift, and servile farmers from the Sahel
could move to Agalawa communities in the savanna if crops failed
in the north and conditions looked better on another estate in the
south. These northern immigrants also assumed the Agalawa identification. In the Tokarawa case, sedentarization and emigration from
the north was steady but gradual throughout the nineteenth century,
as some servile nomads were forced south through the loss of livestock while others used capital derived from livestock sales to reinvest in the lucrative kola trade. Family traditions include stories
of men who had lost everything in the north and others who moved with
their herds. Some wealthy cattle dealers successfully established
their sons in kola importing, and in two instances sons became major
caravan leaders.

THE DESERT EDGE IN THE COLONIAL PERIOD

Until recently the desert sector provided impetus for growth
and change in many areas of economic activity in the Central Sudan.
Nomads dominated commerce because of their long experience in
trade across the ecological frontier, their association with the trans-
Saharan trade, their ownership of transport animals, their ability
to accumulate surplus pack and slaughter animals in times of prosperity, and their military superiority based on wealth and mobility.
Capital accumulated in the desert sector often was invested in trade
and production in the savanna, as the examples of nomadic participation in the Sahelian leather and cloth industries and the numerous

cases of investment in grain-producing estates and serf villages
demonstrate. When nomads came to live permanently in the savanna,
they brought capital with them if they came in times of prosperity.
If drought was the reason for emigration, they brought at the very
least valuable experience in commerce.

The economies of the desert and savanna continue to be closely
integrated, but the desert is no longer the important source of commercial capital and specialized personnel that it once was. The
explanation for this change lies in the crisis in the desert following
the imposition of colonial rule. The new economic situation upset
the centuries-old pattern in which Sahelian merchants moved south
to invest in savanna trade and production. After 1920 it was no longer
true that many of the leading merchants in Hausa towns were recent
Tuareg immigrants. The reorientation of trade toward the coast
brought commercial opportunities within the reach of Hausa traders,
many of whom entered the lower levels of the distribution hierarchy
associated with exporting peanuts and importing European textiles
and other manufactures. The declining position of northern immigrants and Tuareg capital in the savanna occurred despite the unusually heavy migration from the desert in the early twentieth century.
Most buga je immigrants in Damagaram, to take an example, were
destitute, and they tended to concentrate their dry-season commercial
activities in the potash trade. They lacked the capital necessary to
deal in livestock, although it offered better opportunities. Instead,
Hausa and Kanuri-speaking farmers invested heavily in animals.[54]

CONCLUSION

The relationship of the desert edge to the economy of the
Central Sudan clearly demonstrates how flexible ethnicity can be as
an organizing principle. In this region, ethnic groups have been
categories of ascription and identification by and for the people
involved, and as such they have had the characteristic of organizing
interaction among people. Identification has been related most
specifically to ecological specialization, in which different people
exploited distinct niches in the environment and where interaction
has been primarily limited to commerce and the maintenance of
servile relationships. For the historian, these organizing principles
have had the added advantage of assisting in historical reconstruction,
not in the simplistic fashion in which the migration myths of whole
peoples are often imagined but rather by considering a regional context that allows for economic change. It is suggested that an understanding of the processes that have occurred over the past several

centuries can help evaluate the possibilities of recovery from the
present drought. Such an analysis must take into account the changing
patterns of ethnic identification, for these provide the key to the
future as they have to the past.

The 1969-73 drought was the most drastic since the 1740s and
early 1950s but, unless the most pessimistic forecasters are correct
that long-range climatic changes related to air pollution in the northern
hemisphere will continue to produce drought conditions in the Sahel,
there will be a gradual recovery. [55] The pattern can even be predicted,
if some trends that began at the beginning of this century with the
initiation of colonial rule continue. The Tuareg-dominated economy
has been in shambles twice now in the past sixty years, and nomad
control of servile villages may never recover. This will affect the
replenishment of camel and other herds, since the Tuareg will have
far less favorable terms of trade for grain acquisitions than in the
past. Hence the gradual decline of Tuareg society and economy can
be expected to continue, at least up to a certain point.

Nevertheless, the resources of the Sahel will still attract livestock investors as conditions there return to normal. Since the early
part of the century, Fulani cattle, sheep, and goat herders have
increasingly moved into areas previously closed to them. From the
Manga country north of Borno through Damerghou, and Adar, Fulani
drovers are now common, and the relationships that they establish
with sedentary farmers in the region resemble the earlier forms of
economic specialization based on ethnic stratification. And as before,
there is a continuous flow across the ethnic frontiers, as Michael
Horowitz's study of interaction between Fulani and Manga has demonstrated. [56]

Hence, it can be seen that the desert-edge sector continued to
have a resilience characteristic of its long history. Only the actors
and the social and political relationships have changed, but the nature
of these changes will prevent the desert edge from assuming the same
importance as it did in the past.

NOTES

1. We wish to thank Philip D. Curtin, Allen Isaacman, Martin
Klein, Jean Hay, Jan Hogendorn, Allen Howard, Marvin Miracle,
and A.G. Hopkins for comments on various drafts of this chapter
which was initially presented at the African Economic History Work-
shop, University of Wisconsin-Madison, August 19, 1974. This is a
revised version of a paper which is to appear in International Journal
of African Historical Studies 8, no. 4, (1975).

2. The literature on nomadism and the desert edge is extensive, but see O. Lattimore, Inner Asian Frontiers of China (New York, Oxford University Press, 1940); Philip D. Curtin, Economic Change in Pre-Colonial Africa: Senegambia in the Era of the Slave Trade (Madison, University of Wisconsin Press, 1975); William Irons and Neville Dyson-Hudson, eds., Perspectives on Nomadism (Leiden, E.J. Brill, 1972); Fredrik Barth, Nomads of South Persia (New York, Allen and Unwin, 1961); and Cynthia Nelson, ed., The Desert and the Sown: Nomads in the Wider Society (Berkeley, University of California Press, 1974).

3. See Fredrik Barth, Ethnic Groups and Boundaries (Bergen, 1969); Michael Horowitz, "Ethnic Boundary Maintenance among Pastoralists and Farmers in the Western Sudan (Niger)," in W. Irons and N. Dyson-Hudson, eds., Perspectives on Nomadism, pp. 105-14; and Johannes Nicolaisen, Ecology and Culture of the Pastoral Tuareg (Copenhagen, National Museum, 1963).

4. There has been no adequate study of Tuareg economic history, but for the main political events, see: Maurice Abadie, La Colonie du Niger (Paris: Editions Geographiques Maritimes et Coloniales, 1927); Boubou Hama, Recherche sur l'histoire des Touareg Sahariens et Soudanais (Paris, Presence Africaine, 1967), esp. pp. 339-40, 347-50; Hama, ed., Documents Nigeriens, vol. 1: L'Air (Niamey, CNRSH, 1969); Yves Urvoy, Histoire des populations du Soudan central (Colonie de Niger) (Paris, Larose, 1936), pp. 164-83; Urvoy, "Chronique d'Agades," Journal de la societe des africanistes 4 (1934): 145-77; Murray Last, The Sokoto Caliphate (London, Longmans, 1967), pp. 24-36, 107-13; Irmgard Sellnow, "Der Einfluss von Nomaden auf Wirtschaft und Politik der Hausastaaten," in Sellnow, ed., Das Verhaltnis von Bodenbauern und Viehzuchtern in Historischer Sicht (Berlin, Deutscher Verlag, 1968), pp. 185-205.

5. Sources conflict on the struggle between the Tuareg factions. Boubou Hama (Touareg Sahariens et Soudanais, pp. 347-48, 391) suggests that Tuareg pressure in Adar began in the seventeenth century, continued into the eighteenth, and included wars with Kebbi, Gobir, and Zamfara. Hama suggests 1770 as the date when Kel Ewey gained complete control of Air. Urvoy (Soudan Central, pp. 183, 269) also argues that Kel Ewey supremacy was consolidated between 1750 and 1770. Nicolaisen (Pastoral Tuareg, p. 412) accepts an eighteenth century date but provides no proof. Hornemann (Journal, pp. 181-82) learned at Fezzan in 1797-98 that the "Kolluvi [Kel Ewey] possess (from recent conquest, it would seem), the country of Agadez; which, with other provinces adjacent forms a state named collectively Asben." Heinrich Barth, Travels and Discoveries in North and Central Africa (New York, Harper and Brothers, 1857), vol. 1, p. 278, estimated that the Kel Ewey conquered the Air around 1740.

6. Tawarikh Salatin Barnu, Deutsche Morgenlandische Gesellschaft, ms. arab. 53; photocopy, Northern History Research Scheme, Ahmadu Bello University, Zaria, uncat., trans. Abdullahi Smith.

7. On the great drought of the mid-seventeenth century, see Curtin, Economic Change, appendix I; Sekene-Mody Cissoko, "Famines et epidemies a Tombouctou et dans la Boucle du Niger du XVIe au XVIIIe siecle," Bulletin de l'IFAN 30, no. 3 (1968): 815; Kitab Ghunja, as translated in Jack Goody, The Ethnography of the Northern Territories of the Gold Coast, West of the White Volta (London, Colonial Office, 1954), p. 41.

8. Paul E. Lovejoy, "The Hausa Kola Trade (1700-1900): A Commercial System in the Continental Exchange of West Africa," Ph.D. thesis, University of Wisconsin-Madison, 1973, pp. 132, 144. In 1846 Agades contained an estimated 8,000 to 10,000 inhabitants but was much smaller than it had been in previous years, for a "great number of the people have emigrated to Soudan, where less labour is required to till the soil, and nature is more lavish in her productions;" see Richardson, Travels, vol. 2, p. 144. Four years later Barth learned that the immigration had taken place at the end of the eighteenth century (Travels, vol. I, p. 371).

9. "Kano Chronicle," p. 128.

10. Hill, Rural Hausa, p. 231.

11. A.T. Grove, "Desertification in the African Environment," African Affairs 73 (1974): 143.

12. The best introduction to the Tuareg economy is Nicholaisen, Pastoral Tuareg.

13. Air Tuareg need eight to ten litres of milk a day when living solely on milk, but they "claim they get weary from constant milk drinking"; see Nicolaisen, Pastoral Tuareg, pp. 209, 213.

14. Nicolaisen, Pastoral Tuareg, pp. 8, 213; Francis Rennell of Rodd, People of the Veil (London, Macmillan, 1926), p. 402; Camille-Charles Jean, Les Touaregs du Sud-Est, l'Air (Paris, Larose, 1909), pp. 100-17.

15. Heinrich Barth in August Petermann, "Progress of the African Mission, Consisting of Messrs. Richardson, Barth, and Overweg, to Central Africa," Journal of the Royal Geographical Society 25 (1851): 146-47. Also see Barth, Travels, vol. 1, p. 374; M.J.E. Daumas and Ausone De Chancel, Le grand desert: Itineraire d'une caravane du Sahara au pays des Negres—Royaume de Haoussa (Paris, N. Chaix and Co., 1856), p. 172; C.A. Walckenaer, Recherches geographiques sur l'interieur de l'Afrique septentrionale (Paris, A. Bertrand, 1821), p. 449.

16. Barth, Travels, vol. 1, p. 374.

17. Friedrich Konrad Hornemann, The Journal of Frederick Hornemann's Travels, from Cairo to Mourzouk, the Capital of the Kingdom of Fezzan, in Africa, in the Years 1797-98 (London, G. and W. Nicol, 1802), pp. 109-10. Also see Barth, Travels, vol. 1, p. 519.

18. Transport costs in the savanna, between Zinder and Zungeru, at the same time averaged 50 percent higher. See Henri Gaden, "Notice sur la residence de Zinder," Revue des Troupes Coloniales 2, no. 17 (1903): 650, 652, 790; Archives du Department de Zinder, "Notice politique et commerciale sur l'Azbin," August 1903. Also see Stephen Baier, "African Merchants in the Colonial Period: A History of Commerce in Damagaram (Central Niger), 1880-1960," Ph.D. thesis, University of Wisconsin-Madison, 1974, p. 127.

19. Barth, Travels, vol. 1, p. 291.

20. For the salt industry of Bilma, see Abadie, Niger, pp. 274-75; Hama, Touareg Sahariens et Soudanais, pp. 362-63; Nicolaisen, Pastoral Tuareg, pp. 214-15; Etude du Capitaine Lefevre sur la question de Bilma (about 1904), 11 G 2 no. 4, Archives de la Republique du Senegal, Dakar; James Richardson, Narrative of a Mission to Central Africa Performed in the Years 1850-51 (London, Chapman and Hale, 1853), vol. 2, p. 117; Henry Beaufoy, "Mr. Lucas's Communications," Proceedings of the Association for Promoting the Discovery of the Interior of Africa (London, Frank Cass, 1967), vol. 1, p. 169.

For the volume of trans-Saharan trade between Tripoli and the Central Sudan during the last quarter of the nineteenth century, see Baier, "African Merchants," pp. 19-20, 52-57.

21. There has been no adequate study of trans-Saharan trade, but see Hornemann, Journal, p. 64; James Richardson, Travels in the Great Desert Sahara in the Years of 1845 and 1846 (London, R. Bentley, 1848), vol. 2, p. 17, 115-17; Barth, Travels, vol. 1, pp. 159-469. The major secondary sources are A. Adu Boahen, Britain, the Sahara, and the Western Sudan, 1788-1861 (London, Oxford University Press, 1964); Boahen, "The Caravan Trade in the Nineteenth Century," Journal of African History 3, no. 2 (1962): 349-59; C.W. Newbury, "North African and Western Sudan Trade in the Nineteenth Century: A Re-evaluation," Journal of African History 7, no. 2 (1966): 233-46. See also Baier, "African Merchants," pp. 48-78.

22. Baier, "African Merchants," pp. 52-57, 60-61.

23. For Tuareg-controlled agricultural villages in Adar and Damergu, see Pierre Bonte, L'elevage et le commerce du betail dans l'Ader Doutchi-Majya (Paris, CNRS, 1967), pp. 44-59; Stephen Baier, "The Trade of the Hausa of Damerghou, 1900-1930," paper

172   THE POLITICS OF NATURAL DISASTER

presented at the fifteenth annual convention, African Studies Association, Syracuse, New York, 1973. For earlier references, see Hugh Clapperton, Journal of a Second Expedition into the Interior of Africa (London, J. Murray, 1829), pp. 195-96; Barth, Travels, vol. 3, pp. 97, 101, 103.

    24. Barth, Travels, vol. 1, pp. 321, 420, 422; Richardson, Mission, vol. 2, p. 170.

    25. Account of Haruna Biriam, interviewed at Malam Tilum, October 14, 1972 (Baier Collection, tape 41, African Studies Association Center for African Oral Data, Archives of Traditional Music, Indiana University, Bloomington). Also see Baier, "The Trade."

    26. Richardson considered buga je to be "Tuaricks, who having settled in Soudan, have forgotten their own language, speaking only Haussa. . . . On the south, they are scattered in villages and towns, or wandering in tribes, along the north banks of the Niger. [And] . . . they are scattered . . . through the extensive provinces of Housa, subjected to the Fullahs." (Mission, vol. 2, p. 165). Also see Baier, "The Trade"; Bonte, L'Ader Doutchi-Majya, pp. 44-59; Barth, Travels, vol. 1, p. 431.

    27. Henri Gaden, "Notice," pp. 650-54; Guntu Nomo of Gangara (Baier Collection, tape 40). According to the prices observed by Gaden in 1902, from two to four sheep could be traded for a load of millet weighing about 100 kilograms. Nicolaisen's estimate for the 1950s was that three to four camel loads of grain were worth about fifteen goats or sheep (Pastoral Tuareg, pp. 213-14). For an account of the Agades-Damerghou trade, see Baier, "The Trade"; interviews with Usman Saidu of Gangars and Issafou Mamadou of Tanout (Baier Collection, tapes 40 and 41).

    28. Baier, "The Trade," pp. 2-4.

    29. Rennell of Rodd, People of the Veil, pp. 136-38; Nicolaisen, Pastoral Tuareg, pp. 10-12; E. Bernus, "Les Touaregs du sahel nigerien," Cahiers d'Outre-Mer 19 (1966): 12-16; J. Clauzel, "Les Hierarchies sociales en pays Touareg," Travaux de l'Institut des Recherches Sahariennes 21 (1962): 136-48; Henri Lhote, Les Touareg du Hoggar (Paris, Payot, 1955), pp. 185-212.

    30. Barth, Travels, vol. 1, p. 439.

    31. For Darfur, see Gunnar Haaland, "Economic Determinants in Ethnic Processes," in Barth, Ethnic Groups, pp. 58-73; Fredrik Barth, "Economic Spheres in Darfur," in Raymond Firth, ed., Themes in Economic Anthropology (London, Tavistock Publishers, 1967). For the Manga and Fulani, see Horowitz, "Ethnic Boundary Maintenance."

    32. Barth, Travels, I, 481.

    33. Curtin, Economic Change; Abner Cohen, "Cultural Strategies in the Organisation of Trading Diasporas," in Claude

Meillassoux, ed., The Development of Indigenous Trade and Markets in West Africa (London, Oxford University Press, 1971), pp. 266-81; Paul E. Lovejoy, "The Kambarin Beriberi: The Formation of a Specialized Group of Hausa Kola Traders in the Nineteenth Century," Journal of African History 14, no. 2 (1973).

34. Clapperton, Journal, p. 229.

35. Barth, Travels, vol. 1, pp. 359, 372. Kilishi is a speciality of the inhabitants of Agadesawa ward in Kano.

36. Barth, Travels, vol. 1, p. 526; but also see p. 438; vol. 3, pp. 73, 564; Richardson, Mission, vol. 2, pp. 170, 179, 194; Lovejoy, "Hausa Kola Trade," pp. 93-95. For the operations of the Kel Azanieres in Zinder, see Roberta Ann Dunbar, "Damagaram (Zinder, Niger), 1812-1906: The History of a Central Sudanic Kingdom," Ph.D. thesis, University of California at Los Angeles, 1970, pp. 196-98.

37. See accounts of Muhaman Kane, Illali Ali, and Cillo Alassan (Baier collection, tapes 20, 36, 37, 38); Barth, Travels, vol. 1, p. 486.

38. Lovejoy, "Hausa Kola Trade," pp. 87-177; Baier, "African Merchants," pp. 15-38, 69-73, 214-34; Muhammad Uba Adamu, "Some Notes on the Influence of North African Traders in Kano," Kano Studies 1, no. 4 (1968): 43-49.

39. Andre Salifou, Le Damagaram ou sultanat de Zinder au XIXe siecle (Niamey, CNRSH, 1971), pp. 160-61; Dunbar, "Damagaram," pp. 87, 202-8, 224n; Fernand Foureau, D'Alger au Congo par le Tchad: Mission saharienne Foureau-Lamy (Paris, Masson, 1902), pp. 522-23, 545-47.

40. Baier, "African Merchants," p. 36.

41. Barth, Travels, vol. 1, p. 486.

42. Bichi, "Inspection Notes, 1949-1950"; Nigerian National Archives, Kaduma, Kanoprof 6/1, 33V; accounts of Malam Abubakar, born 1898, and Malam Kasan, born 1912, both of 'Yan Bundu (interviewed March 21, 1970, tape 22), and Malam Baladari, born 1920, and Malam Ibrahim, born 1900, both of Damargu (interviewed March 20, 1970, tape 22). Tape references are to the Lovejoy collection, Department of History, Ahmadu Bello University, Zaria, and Centre for Nigerian Languages, Abdullahi Bayero College, Kano.

43. Barth, Travels, vol. 1, p. 467; vol. 3, pp. 739, 797; Richardson, Mission, vol. 2, p. 179, 214-15; Dunbar, "Damagaram."

44. Barth, Travels, vol. 1, pp. 422, 438, 467; vol. 3, pp. 73, 564; Richardson, Mission, vol. 2, pp. 2-3, 170, 179, 194. Annur also had estates in Air. For examples of other estates near Gobir, Tasawa, Maradi, and Zamfara, see Barth in Petermann, "Progress of the African Mission," p. 157; Barth, Travels, vol. 1, pp. 441, 451, 456; vol. 3, pp. 97, 101, 103.

45. Lovejoy, "Hausa Kola Trade," pp. 132-38, 143-52.

46. Ibid., pp. 138-39, 150-52.

47. See Baier, African Merchants, pp. 103-28, for a complete discussion of economic crisis and recovery. Information on the drought of 1912-14 is found in Archives Nationales de Senegal, 2G 14-11, Niger, "Rapport d'ensemble, 1914"; Gilbert Vieillard, "Coutumiers du cercle de Zinder," in Coutumie-Juridique de l'AOF (Paris, Larose, 1939), p. 138; accounts of Musa Malam Sidi, Habu Taliya, and Amadu Mai (Baier collection, tapes 34, 40 and 41). See also Grove, "Desertification," pp. 133-38.

48. See Finn Fuglestad, "Les Revoltes des Tuaregs du Niger," Cahiers des Etudes Africaines 49 (1973): 82-120; A. Richer, Les Touaregs du Niger (Region de Timbouctou-Gao): Les Oulliminden (Paris, Editions Geographiques Maritimes et Coloniales, 1950), pp. 267-305; F. Nicolas, Tamesna, les Ioullimmenden de l'Est (Paris, Imprimerie Nationale, 1950), pp. 90-101. On French commandeering of camels, see Rennell of Rodd, People of the Veil, p. 205; Archives Nationales du Senegal, 2G 15-2, Niger, "Rapport politique, 1 trimestre 1915"; Archives Nationales du Niger, TC 21, Loffler, "Rapport sur les operations de Tibesti"; and Baier, "African Merchants," 105-6.

49. Data on the volume of the Bilma salt trade in the twentieth century is primarily from the Archives Administratives du Niger, Niamey; for example, J. Perie, "Carnet monographique du canton de Bilma, 1941." For a fuller discussion and complete list of sources, see Baier, "African Merchants," pp. 110ff.

The recovery of the salt trade from Taodeni to Timbuctu appears to have paralleled that of the Bilma salt trade. See J. Geneviere, "Les Kountas et leurs activites commerciales," Bulletin de l'Institut Fondamental de l'Afrique Noire 12 (1950): 1117-18.

50. And grain prices could be very high, as they were in the famine year of 1914, when a cow bought only two kilograms of millet, a price about 500 times less favorable than in good years. Baier, "The Trade," pp. 10-11; accounts of Amadu Mai, Haruna Biriam, and Habu Taliya (Baier collection, tapes 40 and 41).

51. For the immigration of the early twentieth century, see P. Gamory-Dubourdeau, "Etude sur la creation des cantons de sedentarisation dans le cercle de Zinder, et particulierement dans la subdivision centrale (arrondissement de Mirria), Bulletin du Comite des Etudes Historiques et Scientifiques de l'AOF 8 (1924): 239-58. See also accounts of Ibrahim Mahaman and Alhassan d'an Madugu Muhaman (Baier collection, tape 29).

52. Gaden, "Notice," p. 622.

53. Johannes Nicolaisen, Structures politiques et sociales des Touaregs de l'Air et de l'Ahaggar, Etudes Nigeriennes no. 7 (Paris, CNRS, 1962), pp. 100-7.

54. Accounts of Alhassan Muhaman and Ibrahim Muhaman
(Baier collection,tape 29); Archives du Department de Zinder,
"Rapport commerciale, 2e trimestre 1909."
55. For the argument that permanent climatic change is likely,
see Reid A. Bryson, "Climatic Modification by Air Pollution, II:
The Sahelian Effect," Institute for Environmental Studies, Report 9
(1973). See also H.H. Lamb, "Some Comments on Atmospheric
Pressure Variations in the Northern Hemisphere," in David Dalby
and R.J. Harrison Church, eds. Drought in Africa: Report of the 1973
Symposium (London, University of London, School of Oriental and
African Studies (SOAS), 1973), pp. 27-28.
56. M. Horowitz, "Ethnic Boundary Maintenance." It is possible
that a close study of the segmentary aspects of eastern Tuareg
lineage organization and the role of Islam in the social structure may
modify some of the approaches and conclusions of this paper. The
authors hope that such a study—long overdue—will soon be forthcoming.

7

INNOVATION TECHNOLOGY
TRANSFER AND NOMADIC
PASTORAL SOCIETIES
Randall Baker

Most people in the "developed" world would speak with a
justifiable pride about the record of livestock and rangeland improvement over the last two centuries as living proof of the application
of science to satisfying our basic needs. Having overcome the winter
food problem it was no longer necessary to slaughter large numbers
of animals annually to be laid down as salt meat. From the eighteenth
century in particular, the science of genetic engineering accentuated
the productive capabilities of animals bred for milk, meat, or wool.
    With the opening up of the great rangelands of Australasia and
the Americas, mainly during the following century, the record of
advancement accelerated. Hydraulic technology made available the
water formerly trapped in deep aquifers, which in turn opened up
great expanses of grazing and provisioned the stock routes; new
vaccines and control methods were developed to counteract enzootic
and epizootic diseases that had formerly destroyed great numbers of
domestic animals; new bloodstock was imported from the old world
and improved in situ to match the peculiarities of the local physical
environment while pastures were upgraded by research into varieties,
seed selection, evaluation of stocking rates, and the introduction of
leguminous rotations. At the same time that these innovations were
being perfected and diffused, the related infrastructure also was
being improved in such areas as marketing, credit, extension
services, and management training.
    The critical factor in the success of the transfer of modern
livestock production methods to these areas of white colonization
lies in the fact that they were introduced in vacuo. That is, no
attempt was made to incorporate the indigenous people or their
land use systems. They had viewed the same environment through
the eyes of a different level of technology and had developed an

advanced hunting and gathering economy. The fate of the Plains
Indians and the aborigines is too familiar to repeat here, but the
disdain that characterized most contemporary evaluations of their
"primitive" lifestyles is, perhaps, the key to our understanding of the
disastrous experience of technology transfer in the pastoral areas of
tropical Africa.

It is no exaggeration to state that the very developments that
did so much to improve livestock production in the "developed" world
have played a major causal role in the environmental destruction of
much of Africa that lies along the margins of cultivation. Until this
point is fully appreciated and steps are taken to assess the appropriateness of alien technological innovations in the social, economic,
and political context of the proposed recipient areas, there would
seem to be little hope of halting, never mind reversing, the present
downward trend. For such countries as Niger and Botswana, where
livestock production and export is the mainstay of the economy and
the basis for future growth, the position could hardly be more critical.
During recent months the truly terrible conditions associated with the
drought and, in particular, its impact on the 2,500 miles of the Sahel,
have received considerable coverage in the world press and this should
have brought home quite clearly the vulnerable state of grazing lands
in most of Africa.

However, to this writer at least, it would seem that the cause
and effect of the recent drought have been confused to some extent
so that, in many accounts, the major causal elements are identified
as the "creeping Sahara" or the major "shifts in the world pressure
systems," with the inevitability that either or both of these would
involve. These two explanations have occurred with great regularity
over the last two generations following each period of "unusual
dryness" and some of these statements have been treated critically
by R.M. Prothero.[1] On one occasion climatic change was identified
as the cause of the rapid change of vegetation to ever more xerophytic
forms in Karamoja (northeast Uganda); oddly, this trend faded out
toward the boundary of the pastoral system and no such change was
occurring in neighboring districts.

A recent symposium in London made it clear that there was no
firm evidence of climatic change, an idea upheld by the WMO representative at a recent FAO/UNEP panel on arid and semiarid rangelands held in Rome in April 1974. On the other hand, the evidence
of mismanagement, system breakdown, and a crisis of technology
transfer has been plain to those who wish to see for many years;and
such human factors offer at least a significant causal element in
explaining the "creeping Sahara." However, few of those who make
the planning decisions, disburse the research or aid funds, or
formulate political guidelines for investment perceive the true nature

of the problem in its entirety—or so it would seem. Individual research workers, on the other hand, have been presenting convincing
evidence for many years. The tragic result is that the same mistakes
continue to be repeated decade after decade, for—in the development
game unlike almost all other forms of expenditure—there seems to
be no meaningful periodic audit.

Botswana now is sliding down the same spiral that Karamoja
moved along thirty or forty years ago and, worse, plans are being
formulated now for investment programs in West Africa that could
perpetuate the errors into the future. There appears to be a failure
to recognize any merit in the traditional land use system as a form
of ecological adjustment, and the growing frustration with the failure
of technological packages introduced into these traditional systems is
threatening to throw the baby out with the bath water. Almost no
consideration is given to the fact that other peoples have completely
different economic systems, social values, and survival strategies
that will influence their perception of a situation and their response
to any given change. As a result, the introduction of what is indis-
putably a technological "good thing" in the sociotechnological mix of
the "developed" donor area may turn out to be the beginning of an
ecological nightmare in its new context. Rather than come to grips
with this fundamental problem and give the context the study it
deserves, efforts now seem to be concentrated upon bypassing this
fundamental aspect of the problem altogether and creating contextual
islands to suit the innovation, such as seizure of large areas of
grazing for government ranching schemes run by rich or influential
citizens. In such circumstances, the pastoralist, more bewildered
and angry than ever, finds himself under increased pressure with
the option of struggling on, working as a paid ranch hand if jobs are
available, or joining the drift to the bidonvilles. The visiting expert,
it seems, is anxious only to deal with or create that which is re-
assuringly familiar.

Immediately, however, one would wish to emphasize that this
chapter is not a slur on experts—far from it. Instead, it seeks to
question the whole basis of project or program planning and the
shortcoming of spacelessness from which economics is now awakening.
The expert is, after all, an expert: a man with a proven reputation
in his own field. The hydraulic engineer or management specialist
does not, as the Greeks believed, lose his reason on crossing some
point of the Tropic Sea. He does, however, carry with him a
specialism with built-in response assumptions that he either does
not consider at all or holds to be constants or universal truths. To
some, these are simply "outside my brief." Thus, the man who
drills wells does not ask what will happen to all the animals that
survive as a result of his activities any more than a doctor working

in the tropics questions the future of all the extra babies he is adding
to the population problem. In his own country, the expert would know
that his activities would form part of a management-marketing complex that would direct the extra production into the marketing network
with no depletion of productive resources. Problems would be handled
by a specialist extension service and, at the end of the day, the
energy equation would be balanced at the improved level by the use
of supplemental inputs.

In the context of traditional pastoralism, the same innovation
is fed into a completely different response mix, based in all probability upon a search for subsistence security and social standing
dependent upon retaining the maximum number of productive animals.
The implicit assumptions break down immediately because there may
well be no adjustment of increasing cattle numbers resulting from the
innovation to the capacity of the communally held rangeland. This
is particularly critical when it is recalled that most of the innovations
that have been taken up are of a type designed to keep more cattle
alive: improved deep-water wells, veterinary health programs,
reduction in raiding. In addition, the improvement in human health
projects has meant that more pastoralists now require animals so
that ultimately the problem is one of overpopulation.[2] Pressures to
increase offtake have been far from effective and the marketed offtake
in many countries has barely changed over the last ten years. Such
countries as Tanzania and Uganda have seen the failure of meat-
packing enterprises because the increased flow of animals has just
not been forthcoming. As a result, the energy equation has been
thrown out completely and is being adjusted by nature, but this time
downward—through the increasing efficiency of natural calamity. The
energy shift is borne very largely by the grazing resources of the
areas concerned, since ruinous overgrazing is now widespread.
Desertification, which results from overgrazing, works its way
outward from the new water points—a fact vividly revealed to the air
traveler flying over Botswana's cattle posts—and continues as gullying
and sheet erosion eventually laying bare the substratum. The normal
response to this has been to dig more wells, "ease the pressure," and
"spread the load." On September 17, 1973, the Guardian reported:
"President Hamani Diori of Niger, who has called for a Marshall
Plan of recovery for the six drought-stricken areas, seems to think
that wells are the answer. He wants the international aid community
to drill 2,500 wells. . . . to an average depth of 900 feet." Some
writers see hope in the long-term figures of cattle offtake, pointing
to rises in average totals marketed. These averages, it should be
pointed out, are arrived at by incorporating the increasingly frequent
disaster years.[3] In such times, pastoralists would naturally try to
sell any stock that is threatened and nonproductive in the absence of

grazing, in order to convert it into food or cash with which to purchase food. It is also the writer's contention that these disaster years are accentuated by the erosion of the resiliance of most pastoral areas to resist shortfalls in precipitation. There is no doubt that this has been the case in Karamoja, where annual grasses were gaining on the Hyparhenia/Themeda perennials at a rate approaching one mile per year during the 1950s and 1960s and where large areas had been stripped bare and gullied. If this can happen in an area of 20 to 30 inches (500 to 600mm) of rainfall annually, then it requires little imagination to detect at least one major causal element in the parallel case of the creeping Sahara.

Clearly, the priority now is to stop the present disastrous trend. Some 72 percent of Africa's land surface is permanent pasture or waste. This expanse should be producing much-needed proteins and structural lipids required for the growth of body and brain, for many parts are potentially as productive as many Western rangelands. At the present time we are faced not with an insufficient and erratic offtake but with a rapidly moving process of destruction that will prevent these rangelands from playing any significant role in the future. There is, for instance, at the moment a great danger that when the rains come in the Sahel and the millet grows again, then the "problem" will be considered over until next time. Undoubtedly certain lessons will be learned regarding the distribution and storage of relief supplies, and possibly even drought prediction, but it seems unlikely that there will be a rethinking of the whole question of appropriateness of technology and planning methodologies. Already France is considering new assistance programs for well drilling in West Africa. Despite all the terrible evidence that Karamoja laid bare, one West European government still was supporting a major water "development" program for livestock with no complementary management or control inputs as late as 1969.

Where does the real problem lie? There would seem to be several causal elements contributing to the longevity of this situation:

1. The fragmented nature of responsibility: There is rarely any governmental planning, policy, or implementation body in a position to view the "problem" in the holistic context of human ecology. Water resource sections drill wells, markets come under another body, and so forth. Nobody, in all probability, considers social values or aims. Range management divisions, where they exist, tend to be dominated by veterinary considerations and are poor relations of ministries which, themselves, have little real power. It is almost impossible for these units to conduct multidisciplinary research; if they do, they have no way of ensuring a commitment by other ministries to an integrated program.

2. Where social values are studied, all too often this is within
the framework of anthropology, where a temporal and spatial line is
drawn around the relevant group and it is studied as a closed system.
Little work has been produced on the dynamic aspects of pastoral
societies, their response to change, and where it has then it is all
too often buried in journals that are themselves closed systems. The
current program in Darfur is an encouraging exception.

3. There is an attraction in capital-intensive packages: To the
recipient they are prestigious, have a high initial political payoff,
and are outward manifestations of modernity (the tractor cult of the
1960s exemplified this); to the donor they are familiar, easily costed
and staffed. In this way it is easier to explain why governments that
are aware of the consequences of indiscriminate water provision will
still support a well-drilling program. All too often that is what the
local people want, and in the short run it reflects well on the image
of the government in power which sees little immediate kudos in any
alternative investment.

4. The research centers, which have done such excellent work
in Africa, very often perform in a cultural vacuum. As UNESCO
stated: "much more scientific attention has been given to the understanding of relations between grazing animals and their substrata
than has been given to the relations between Man and grazing animals. . . . Too often the animal user's view of his animals does not
relate to the scientist's understanding of the animal's relationship
to its habitat."[4] Many people have observed the situation whereby
the results of research do not get beyond the boundary fence of the
research station unless it is onto the farm of some businessman or
civil servant.

5. Holistic disciplines such as geography and ecology fail
to make their mark on applied research and decision making.
This has perpetuated single-sector thinking and the failure to detect
interrelationships. It would be fruitless to present this argument
without some proposals for change and action. The UNESCO Man and
Biosphere Program (MAB 3), shining as a light in a dark firmament,
recently stated: "Studies are needed of the process of diffusion of
knowledge and of the human and technical factors constraining the
transfer of technical knowledge on grazing land management. These
studies should not be confined to the land-using population but should
also include the study of the constraining factors in the technically
advanced group attempting the transfer." To this should be added
immediately that the problem is not so much to get the indigenous
population to accept the change, that it does swiftly enough; instead
it is to sharpen our predictive capacity regarding the outcome of the
innovations in the new environment. The work of the MAB 3 program
will, however, be successful only if it finds its way into development
planning and decision making.

From the above it would seem that the immediate priorities are:

- A provisional emergency code of planning based on the principles of ecology involving traditional land-use systems and the indigenous social values, aims, and constraints. This would incorporate social values and responses and would serve as a foundation for all project research and planning. One also has to recognize areas in which people are in fact in balance with their ecosystem but where interference with aid and development programs would be destructive. The balance between destruction and rebuilding has to be carefully weighed against building on existing tradition and practices.

- A realistic research program on dynamism in pastoral societies that would provide, at least, methodological guidelines for all future project or program planning. Ideally, this should be organized on a regional basis.

- An evaluation of the rationale of each pastoral system before any change is contemplated. Thus the experience hard won over centuries may be, where advisable, preserved and built on, and appropriate innovations introduced after sufficient research.

- Most essentially, to try to get the message across to donor agencies, multilateral agencies, and recipient governments so that some structure of integrated regional planning or coordination of effort will ensure a holistic approach to change in pastoral areas. This will almost certainly involve administrative innovation so that resistance and jealousies should be expected. However, this is the most important part of the task and can be achieved only by lobbying with well-substantiated argument. Academic discussion will never achieve change. In general, it would seem that some form of regional planning structure is essential, with all ministries contributing to the formulation of the regional plan to which they could then be committed. This would overcome jealousies, provide a vehicle for basic ecological principles to be adhered to and for cooperative implementation.

- Parallel research should be carried out into the prospects for utilizing the indigenous flora and fauna, which are far more efficient in their use of the vegetative cover than the narrow range of domestic livestock. Similarly, if ranching is the answer then attention should be focused on the maximum local participation. People already eat wild species of plants and animals and would be interested in the controlled utilization of their own natural resources. Recently the government of Mali has shown an interest in hosting a pilot research project on the management of indigenous farming in semiarid areas. This project has received support from Belgium and its activities should parallel the continental program of the International Livestock

Centre for Africa proposed for Addis Ababa. The situation is as yet
far from encouraging, and it seems to a great extent that we are
dealing with an administrative trap. It is necessary to recognize the
nature of the trap rather than to continue searching for more refined
methods within the existing framework.

POSTSCRIPT

Since this essay was first drafted in 1973, FAO and the United
Nations Environment Program (which resulted from the Stockholm
Conference on the Environment) convened a panel to consider guidelines for the management of arid and semiarid rangelands of Africa
and the Middle East. The draft document produced by the panel
(FAO/UNEP 1974) embodies many of the ideas incorporated in this
essay including: range management units with "teeth"; the need for
a regional planning framework; the necessity to research and involve
traditional range management and social factors, and the urgent
requirement for an action program. Most important, at least in
this writer's opinion, is the preparation of a set of basic planning
guidelines based on ecological principles and a recognition of social
factors, which it is hoped governments will adopt as policy and which
will form a sine qua non of future aid and assistance programs. If
these ambitions become reality, this could represent the most
significant advance in range management in the third world since
the beginnings of the colonial presence.

NOTES

1. R.M. Prothero, "Some Observations on Dessication of
Northwestern Nigeria," Erdkunde 16 (1962): 112-19.
2. R. Baker, Development and the Pastoral Peoples of
Karamoja: An Example of the Treatment of Symptoms, paper
presented to the symposium on pastoral societies in tropical Africa,
Niamey, Niger, 1972 (forthcoming, Oxford University Press).
3. R. Baker, "Problems of the Cattle Trade in Karamoja,"
in H. Berger, ed., Ostafrikanische Studien, band 8 (Nuremberg:
Wirtschafts und Sozialgeographisches Institut, 1968).
4. UNESCO (MAB) (1973) Final report of an expert panel on
Project 3. MAB Report Series No. 6 SC/72 Conf. 143/3, Paris.

APPENDIX: SUGGESTED WEAKNESSES IN A
SECTORAL PROBLEM-PERCEIVING-
AND-SOLVING FRAMEWORK

Figure 7.1 seeks to show a commonly occuring pattern of
sectorally oriented planning and administration and the main ways
in which such a structure defies any attempt at holistic or ecologically
based planning. The real problem, rangeland management, is shown
encompassed by a circle that represents the boundary of the problem.
The circle is divided into segments or symptoms of the problem, the
boundaries of these symptoms being fixed by the terms of reference,
fields of action, and, thus, perception of the various ministries. The
largely neglected social factors are shaded differently to emphasize
the fact that usually no ministry or department chooses to incorporate
these into their terms of reference in rangeland management. Weaknesses occur at the following numbered points:

1. As a consequence of limiting terms of reference, no branch
of government perceives or deals with the problem holistically. The
body concerned will extract the area of symptoms over which it has
some control.
2. The approach to the "problem" depends upon its perception
by what is often an urbanized elite drawn from an agricultural background and educated in Western techniques and norms.
3. The national plan may introduce blanket policies that have
a widely varying impact depending on the regional socioeconomic and
physical circumstances in the country; it does not necessarily ensure
intersectoral cooperation.
4. A request for technical assistance will lay down terms of
reference based on what the client ministry thinks is appropriate.
5. The response could incorporate fashions and fancies of
the aid scenario at the time, political expediency, accounting convenience, and so on.
6. The research will be limited by time, the terms of reference
of the client's brief, the perception of the "problem" conditioned by
the researchers' background and time available.
7. The suggested program or project to deal with the symptom
is subject to ministerial revamping including the possibility of expediency, political kudos, and corruption.

This pattern is repeated for all the departments and ministries
concerned, which frequently suffer from an almost total lack of contact with each other. The advantages of regional planning or special
area planning are self-evident.

FIGURE 7.1

A Sectoral Path to Problem Solving
(Sequence Repeated for Each Pie Chart Segment)

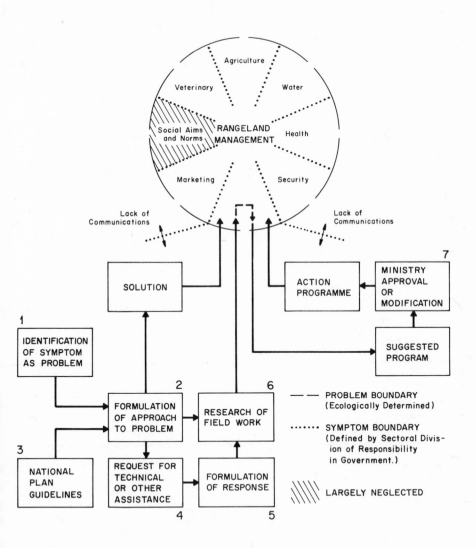

8

CLIMATIC CHANGES
AND THE FUTURE
OF THE SAHEL
Derek Winstanley

Sahel is derived from an Arabic word meaning border—border of the desert. Ecologically, it can be defined as the semiarid zone with mean annual rainfall between 200 and 600 mm sandwiched between the Sahara Desert and the tropical rain forest. Although this ecological zone extends across the broadest part of Africa from the Atlantic coast to the Red Sea, the word Sahel is here used loosely (as it has been by the international news media) to embrace the six countries of West Africa most severly affected by the recent drought: Mauritania, Senegal, Mali, Upper Volta, Niger, and Chad. Included in these so-called Sahelian countries is the more humid Sudan zone to the south, but through popular usage the word Sahel today probably has more political than ecological meaning.

Drought has revealed the continuing vulnerability of human activity in the twentieth century to changes in the physical environment. It also has revealed obscene disparities between affluence and absolute poverty in our world. It is therefore with the dual theme of climatic variations and the widening gap between the developed countries and the fourth world (third world countries that are not major oil exporters) that I review the recent drought and venture to look at the future of the Sahelian countries in a global context.

CLIMATE

The main aspect of the climate of West Africa is the alternation between dry and wet seasons: in the zone 10 to 20 degrees north, about

---

I wish to express my gratitude to Joseph Lai for assistance with data collection and analysis and to Melodie McDonald for cartographic work.

95 percent of the annual rainfall occurs in the months from May to
September, while virtually no rain falls in the somewhat cooler
winter months (see Figure 8.1). The rains penetrate progressively
farther north from May to August and then retreat; the length of the
wet season, and hence the growing season, decreases from about
five months at 10 degrees north to two or three months at 18 degrees
north. This is the so-called "normal" pattern of rainfall distribution
to which patterns of food production and human activity have been
adapted and on which good harvests depend. The relationship between
yields of sorghum, one of the main food grains, and rainfall is shown
in Table 8.1

FIGURE 8.1

Normal (1931-60) Seasonal Rainfall Distribution
over North Africa
(mm)

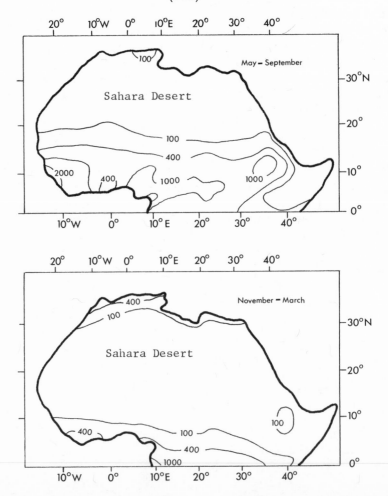

TABLE 8.1

Degree to Which Water-Soil Moisture Is an
Agricultural Constraint in the Sahel

Water Available (mm)	Average Sorghum Yield (Kilograms per hectare)
230	0
255	120
305	900
355	2,000
405	3,750
455	5,800

Note: The results were obtained from field tests on soils of
moderate to good fertility, using an improved variety of sorghum
with modern agricultural practices, including fertilizers.
    Source: U.S. Department of State, "Central/West Africa
(AFR/CWR) DAP Substitute Strategy Framework," mimeo.
(Washington, D.C.: USAID, 1974).

Whether or not it rains is determined not only by the amount of
water vapor in the atmosphere but also by vertical air currents;
clouds form when moist air is lifted to condensation level, whereas
downcurrents (subsidence) in the atmosphere inhibit rain-making
processes. The seasonal north-south shift of the isohyets (lines of
equal rainfall)—amounting to some ten degrees of latitude (Figure
8.1)—is closely related to seasonal changes of the pressure and
wind patterns over the earth, that is, the atmospheric circulation.
In winter the Sahelian zone is under the influence of anticyclones in
the subtropical high pressure belt; subsidence and dry northeasterly
winds from the Sahara provide extremely unfavorable conditions for
rain. In summer the subtropical high-pressure belt shifts northwards,
and moist air from the Gulf of Guinea penetrates inland thus providing a more favorable environment for rain-producing processes.
Even so, the daily distribution of rainfall is not random but is associated with organized pressure systems, which in West Africa move
from east to west.
    The Sahel in general is a marginal area in terms of large-scale
human occupance. Both sedentary agriculturalists and nomadic
pastoralists exist in a delicate balance with their environment.

HISTORICAL PERSPECTIVE

Drought is a relative rather than an absolute condition and is therefore difficult to define. However, a distinction can be drawn between normally low rainfall in desert climates (over the Sahara, for example) and in well-defined dry seasons (for example, November-April in the Sahel zone), and abnormally low rainfall (that is, a sustained period of below-average rainfall in regions that normally receive appreciable amounts). The case of normally low rainfall can be termed aridity, and the case of abnormally low rainfall drought. Drought must therefore be considered with reference to some normal or average conditions. In general, marginal areas with low rainfall concentrated into a short wet season are most drought-prone. There also are different aspects of drought: atmospheric (climatological and meteorological); soil; hydrological and agricultural (Subrahmanyam 1967).

The distribution of rainfall shown in Figure 8.1 is for the period 1931-60. By international agreement this 30-year period was designated as a standard reference period for climatological data throughout the world; mean values of temperature and precipitation over this period were considered "normal." But evidence from various sources indicates that in the past patterns of rainfall distribution have been considerably different from those in the twentieth century. The latest really wet phase was probably a few thousand years ago, but even in the Middle Ages there were farming villages requiring at least 400 mm of annual rainfall in areas that can now be remembered only as desert. On the other hand, geologists have found that there have been living sand dunes hundreds of kilometers farther south than those at present existing and that old sand dunes lie beneath the present water levels of Lake Chad (Davy 1974, pp. 19-20).

These changes of rainfall distribution in the tropics, and ice ages in higher latitudes, are evidence of changes of climate. Theory postulates that such changes of climate have played an important role in the evolution of species—including man. It seems that man can adapt to long-term climatic changes by changing his land use patterns and by migration. What seems to be disastrous to the population dynamics of biological species is not the magnitude of climate change per se but the rate of change. Short-term climatic fluctuations or even seasonal climatic anomalies can have disruptive effects on populations that have adapted to certain climatic conditions. These populations, however, do not have adaptive responses to cope with rapid environmental change.

Lovejoy and Baier (1975, p. 26) have produced a chronology of droughts in West Africa since the sixteenth century. Nomadic pastoralism is portrayed as a way of life functionally adapted to a great extent to the marginal and fluctuating climatic conditions, which determined a characteristic drought-recovery cycle. Droughts and famines set in motion changes in economic and political power and resulted in increased death rates and regular movements of people across ecological and ethnic frontiers. The close interdependence between nomadic and sedentary agricultural economies and societies provided a safety valve for the nomads, but nature maintained a population equilibrium.

Rainfall records this century (see Figure 8.2) show that rainfall fluctuations continue to be a recurring and characteristic feature in this transitional zone between humid climates to the south and desert climates to the north. Periods of below-normal rainfall (drought) occurred at the turn of the century, around 1913, in the 1940s, and in the late 1960s and early 1970s. One aspect of the time series of rainfall data in the Sahelian zone, in common with almost every other part of the world, is the nonexistence of reliable periodicities in the occurrence of droughts.

CLIMATOLOGY OF THE RECENT DROUGHT

As already stated, drought must be considered with reference to normal or previous rainfall conditions. Figure 8.2 shows that rainfall in the zone 10 to 20 degrees north decreased by more than 40 percent from the early 1950s to the early 1970s. Droughts, unlike floods, do not develop overnight; they are usually the culmination of a set of weather sequences that require extended periods of time to develop. One method of investigating the nature, severity, and geographical extent of the drought is to map the changes in the rainfall distribution patterns from 1952-56 to 1968-72. It is evident from Figure 8.3 that during this 20-year climatic fluctuation the isohyets across the breadth of Africa shifted south by one to two degrees of latitude. Such a change may sound small, even insignificant, but this is all that has happened to produce a devastating drought over some five million square kilometers.

Analyzing the data in another way gives a different angle on the same situation. Figure 8.4 shows that the severity of the drought was primarily a function of latitude. Rainfall during the period 1968-72 was in fact considerably above normal along the Guinea coast and decreased to 60 percent below normal along the desert fringe; the climatic zones in West Africa have been squeezed together. Plotting

FIGURE 8.2

Regional Rainfall Index: Mean Percentage of Normal (1931–60)

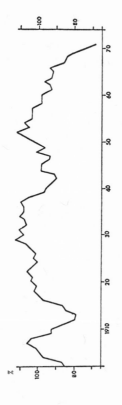

Note: Figure shows May–September rainfall in the zone 10°–20° N in Africa (five-year moving averages).
The number of stations used in the analysis increases from 6 to 78.

FIGURE 8.3

The Decrease of May-September Rainfall from 1952-56 to 1968-72

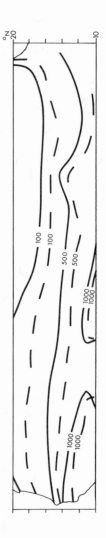

Note: Decrease is indicated by the southward shift of the isohyets (mm) from 1952-56 (———) to
1968-72 (— —).

FIGURE 8.4

Distribution of Mean Percentage of Normal (1931–60) May–September
Rainfall in West Africa During 1968–72

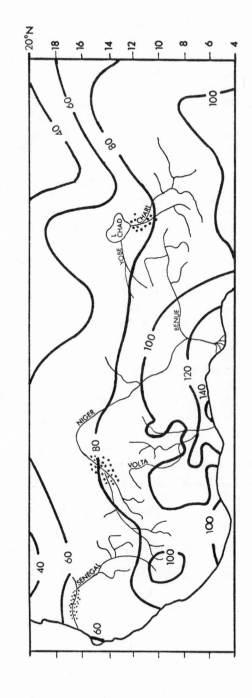

Note: Flood Plains are indicated by dots.

the departures from normal rainfall on an annual basis shows that
Mauritania and Senegal were the first to be severely gripped by
drought in 1968 and that the drought became more severe and spread
south with time. Inclusion of 1973 data in Figure 8.4 merely increases
the predominantly north-south differences and causes the normal
isopleth (100) to shift south slightly. The patterns in Figures 8.3
and 8.4 appear so systematic and organized that one is immediately
led to think that some coherent large-scale atmospheric changes
must be responsible for the changes in the rainfall distribution
patterns.

The above rainfall analyses certainly explain why the nomads
along the desert fringe suffered most during the recent drought and
why the more densely populated agricultural areas and urban centers
farther south were less severely and only later affected.

Thus, when transformed into percentage deviations from normal
rainfall, the apparently small climatic shift shown in Figure 8.3 takes
on a different meaning (Figure 8.4). Because there is such a tight
north-south rainfall gradient (a northward decrease of about 1 mm
per 1.4 km), a slight latitudinal shift of the climatic zones causes,
for example, places that ordinarily receive 200 mm to receive only
100 mm, and so forth. A southward shift of the isohyets of only one
or two degrees of latitude results in widespread drought and starvation. But the fact that this is only a fraction of the normal seasonal
shift of the climatic zones of some ten degrees of latitude illustrates
the distinction made earlier between normal seasonal aridity (Figure
8.1) and drought (Figure 8.3).

The above rainfall analyses certainly explain why the nomads
along the desert fringe suffered most during the recent drought and
why the more densely populated agricultural areas and urban centers
farther south were less severely and only later affected.

Not only does mean annual rainfall decrease from south to
north (Figure 8.5, part A), but it also becomes much more variable
from year to year (Figure 8.6). Figure 8.5, parts B and C, however,
shows another interesting feature of the precipitation climatology of
this semiarid zone: that is, variations of rainfall over time scales
of about ten to twenty years also increase with latitude. If this model
is representative of historical climatic fluctuations in this zone, then
it could help explain the age-old drought-recovery cycle of the nomads
and their traditional interdependence with settled agriculturalists
farther south. During these climatic fluctuations, rainfall anomalies
along the desert fringe seem to be inversely correlated with rainfall
anomalies to the south of about 10 degrees north—at about 10 degrees
north there is relatively little variation. During wet years in the
Sahel, nomadic society prospered and the nomads migrated northward
with the rains. When the rains failed for several consecutive years,
mortality rates increased and the nomads migrated to the extreme
southern end of their trading network, where agricultural estates
would be least affected by drought and might even experience higher-
than-normal rainfall. It is possible that the traditional north-south

FIGURE 8.5

Zonally Averaged Rainfall Analysis for 71 Stations in the Zone 10°–20°N in Africa:

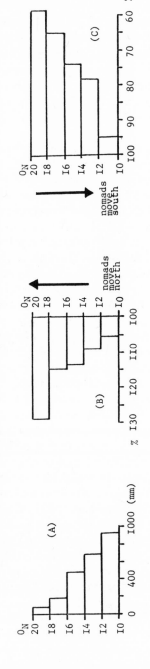

Note: (A) normal May–September rainfall (mm); (B) mean percentage of normal May–September rainfall 1952–56; (C) mean percentage of normal May–September rainfall 1968–72.

FIGURE 8.6

Coefficient of Variation of May–September Rainfall (1951–72)

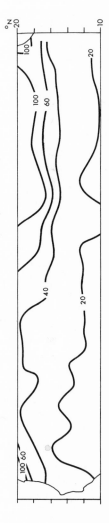

197

migration of the nomads is an adaptive response that has evolved to take advantage of the geographical variations in rainfall anomalies during these climatic fluctuations—if drought had been as severe in the more southern agricultural areas as in the northern pastoral zone, there would have been no point in migrating southward.

RECENT TRENDS IN THE SAHEL

Numerous physical, social, economic, and political factors have combined in producing the disastrous situation in the Sahelian countries, and it is difficult to isolate cause and effect. The impact of drought on these countries, however, can only be understood by taking into account developments over the past few decades.

It is evident from Figure 8.2 that since the 1940s there has been a climatological drought-recovery/drought cycle, which is characteristic of this zone. An important point, however, is that the 1940s drought was not very severe; the recent drought was the first widespread and severe drought for some 60 years. During this time both nomads and sedentary agriculturalists expanded northward, and the nomads in particular slowly regenerated their resources after the earlier droughts and the 1916 revolt. Superimposed on this traditional drought-recovery cycle have been social, economic, and political changes associated with French colonial rule and the slow intervention of the Western world. Political independence in 1959 and 1960 thus came after 10 years of particularly good rainfall and 45 years after the last major drought—with hindsight, drought in the 1960s and 1970s seemed inevitable. Since 1960 these countries have become politically independent, but increasingly economically dependent upon the outside world.

Until 1965 total food production in the Sahelian countries was increasing at the same rate as for the world as a whole (Figure 8.7, part A). Total food production was in fact increasing at a faster rate than population, permitting an increase in the amount of food per capita (Figure 8.7, part B). There was very little external aid at this time; in fact, few people had even heard of Mauritania or Upper Volta.

But 1966 seems to have marked the turning point in the recovery cycle—two years before it is generally thought the drought started. Looking at the regional rainfall index in Figure 8.7 part C, however, who is to say when the drought started? Annual food production from 1965 to 1973 (with the exception of 1971) is very closely correlated with the fluctuations of annual rainfall (Figure 8.7, parts A and C), which is not surprising considering the almost total dependence of agricultural production on the summer rains. Figure 8.8 shows that, over the region as a whole, rainfall during the drought period has been below normal in every month of the wet season (although this does not mean that rainfall has been below normal every month at every station). In this case, severe food shortages were caused by an average decrease of monthly rainfall of between 20 and 40 percent. The largest deficits were at the beginning and end of the wet season, when rainfall is particularly important for the planting of the seeds and for the maturation of the crops. Fluctuations of the generally higher rainfall in July, August, and September are probably less critical to crop growth than variations of the normally lower rainfall in May, June, and October.

From 1967 to 1972 the index of corn production (1963 = 100) for the six Sahelian countries plunged from 164 to 76, and the sorghum and millet index dropped from 111 to 84. The production of cash crops also decreased dramatically during the drought: the index of groundnut production, for example, fell from 114 in 1965 to 87 in 1972. Taking Mali as an example (Szabo 1974, p. 5), there was a deficit (compared with the 1968 figure) of 124,000 tons of millet and sorghum in 1969, a further 126,000 tons in 1971, and 190,000 tons in 1972. The Mali government was faced with a total cereal deficit in 1972 of about 33 percent of the requirements of 800,000 tons. Inland fish production also decreased dramatically during the drought (Figure 8.7, part E). This was because the virtual disappearance of the annual floods on the Niger and Senegal flood plains disrupted the normal reproductive and growth cycle of the fish and their numbers declined rapidly (Winstanley 1975).

The loss of export revenue from cash crops, cattle, and fish, compounded by the skyrocketing prices of imported food, fertilizer, and oil, has been the root cause of economic stagnation and the widening trade deficits since 1968: The combined trade deficit for the six countries grew from 19,000 million francs CFA in 1968 to 45,000 million francs CFA in 1971 (Africa South of the Sahara 1972).

From 1960 to 1970 animal populations increased by 46 percent and human populations by 21 percent (Figure 8.7, parts B and D), resulting in deforestation, overgrazing, extensive bush fires, monoculture, and general degradation of the environment. Unlike crops, which respond to rainfall variations year by year, animals can obviously withstand a period of water shortage. However, mortality only results from the cumulative effects of a sustained water shortage. This has been evident since 1970 (Figure 8.7, part D), although the greatest losses undoubtedly occurred in 1973. Although it is almost impossible to estimate the animal losses accurately, figures quoted in the press range from about 20 to almost 100 percent, dependent upon the region. In Mali, for example, it is estimated that 5,571,000

FIGURE 8.7

Recent Trends in the Sahelian Countries

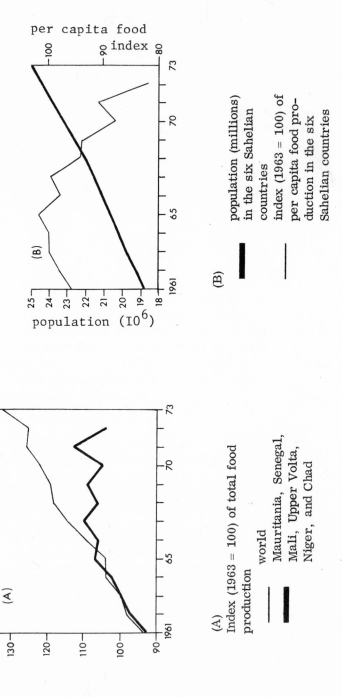

(A)
Index (1963 = 100) of total food
production

——— world

━━━ Mauritania, Senegal,
Mali, Upper Volta,
Niger, and Chad

(B)

━━━ population (millions)
in the six Sahelian
countries

——— index (1963 = 100) of
per capita food pro-
duction in the six
Sahelian countries

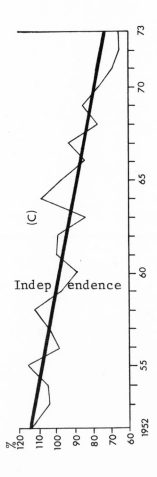

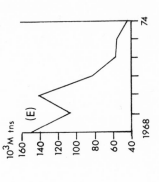

(C)
Mean percentage of normal (1931–60) May-September rainfall in the six Sahelian countries. The best-fit trend line is shown. The Sahelian countries gained their political independence in 1959, 1960.

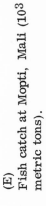

(E)
Fish catch at Mopti, Mali (10^3 metric tons).

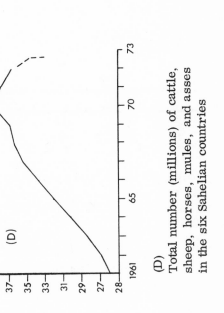

(D)
Total number (millions) of cattle, sheep, horses, mules, and asses in the six Sahelian countries

FIGURE 8.8

Analyses of Monthly Rainfall at 47 Stations
in the Sahel

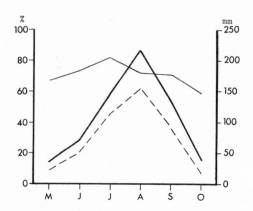

Note: (▬▬▬) normal (1931-60) mean monthly rainfall.
(— — —) mean monthly rainfall 1968-73. (━━━) mean percentage
of normal monthly rainfall 1968-73.

sheep and goats and 1,740,000 head of cattle perished in the Gao and
Mopti regions alone. These losses are equivalent to 30 years of
normal beef consumption in Bamako, the capital of Mali, and 77 years
of normal sheep and goat consumption (Szabo 1975, p. 5). The FAO
estimated that the total loss of cattle in the six Sahelian countries in
1972-73 was 3.5 million head worth $400 million, and that the grain
shortage was 1.2 million tons (Sheets and Morris 1974, p. 43).

It is interesting to compare and contrast the drought in the
northeastern United States in the 1960s with the Sahelian drought. In
the northeastern United States, annual precipitation was some 70 to
80 percent of normal during the four to five years of drought (Palmer
1968, p. 41). From Figure 8.4 it is obvious that during the five years
1968-72, mean May-September rainfall (which is virtually synonymous
with annual rainfall) was as low as 40 percent of normal; when 1973
data are included, the drought is even more severe. But whereas the
Sahelian drought caused severe hydrological, agricultural, social,
economic, and political problems, agriculture in the northeastern
United States actually fared better in the severe drought year 1965
than in 1964; this is because the climate ordinarily supplies more
rainfall than the crops require, except during July and August (Palmer

1968, p. 41). By contrast, climate in the Sahel is marginal for crop production and pastoralism at the best of times, and persistent drought extending over entire countries has a disastrous effect on national economies. The point is that the magnitude of the impact of a climatological drought is dependent upon many regional physical, social, and economic factors—which emphasizes the relative rather than absolute nature of drought.

Good rainfall in the Sahel in 1974 brought an end to the drought, but a shortage of seeds meant that cereal production was only 80 to 85 percent of the pre-drought level (Sumary 1974). It will obviously be many years before the herds are restocked.

CAUSES OF THE DROUGHT AND CLIMATE
TO THE YEAR 2000

The view that one takes of the future climate of the Sahel depends largely on how one views the causes of the drought. Merely to identify the existence of a climate change requires the skill to separate changes in the long-term mean (the signal) from the shorter-term weather fluctuations (the noise). Then to attribute cause and effect necessitates separation of internal and external forcing factors quantitatively, a step that requires a theory of climate (Kellogg and Schneider 1974). I propose to outline the different hypotheses that have been put forward on the causes of the drought, without critical comment, and then to outline a number of possible scenarios for the future. The hypotheses fall into three main categories: that drought is a random phenomenon; that it is related to natural trends in climatic factors over large areas of the earth; and that the Sahelian drought is anthropogenic.

Drought as a Random Phenomenon

From a statistical viewpoint, the study of climatic fluctuations is a problem of time series analysis. According to the stochastic model of a stationary, normally distributed random variable, precipitation variations from one year to the next occur at random and climatic fluctuations and anomalies need no further explanation; a run of six consecutive years with rainfall below the median value, as from 1968 to 1973, can be expected about once every 70 years (El-Sayed and Landsberg 1974; Bunting et al. 1974).

But in climatology we are concerned with identifying as clearly as possible the precise nature and extent of nonrandomness in time

series of meteorological observations (Mitchell et al. 1966, p. 2).
Nonrandomness can take the form of persistence, trend, periodic or
aperiodic fluctuations, or perhaps some combination of these. The
length of the time series also can influence how the variations are
interpreted; for instance from Figure 8.2 the decrease of rainfall
from the early 1950s would be interpreted as part of an irregular
fluctuation, whereas in Figure 8.7, part C, it would be interpreted as
a downward trend.

Drought Related to Natural Trends

Any such hypothesis requires a forcing factor, or dynamic
cause, either external to the climate system (fluctuations in solar
emission, for example), or in some way coupled to the climate
(changes in cloud and ice cover, or in the chemical composition of
the atmosphere, for example). Climate is determined by a complex
interplay between the atmosphere, oceans, land surface, and
cryosphere. So far, the highly nonlinear, interactive system has
defied a complete quantitative description. Variations in one part
of the system can be expected to be coupled to variations elsewhere.
Although we do not fully understand the physical basis for these
"teleconnections," it has been suggested by a number of scientists
that the Sahelian drought may be a regional manifestation of macro-
scale changes in the general circulation of the atmosphere.

Winstanley (1973a) showed that the belt of upper-level westerly
winds that circles the earth in middle and high latitudes—the circum-
polar vortex—has expanded since the 1950s. He suggested that the
abnormal penetration of the pressure troughs could have restricted
the northward extent of the tropical circulation systems controlling
monsoon rainfall, thus pushing the desert climate farther toward the
equator. Rainfall to the north of the Sahara, along the Mediterranean
coast, and in the Middle East increased during the 1960s.

Further evidence that the Sahelian drought was related to changes
in the larger-scale components of the general circulation was presented by Namias (1974) and Winstanley, Emmett, and Winstanley
(1975). These investigators showed that blocking (persistent high-
pressure areas) over northwestern Europe played a role in the sub-
Sahara drought. Based on an analysis of surface pressure and 500
millibar height anomalies over the northern hemisphere during the
period 1968-73, and on positive correlations between rainfall in the
Sahelian zone, a circulation index over western Europe, and global
mean surface air temperature, Winstanley (1974) and Winstanley,
Emmett, and Winstanley (1975) further suggested that the sub-Sahara

drought was a regional manifestation of a weakening of the general atmospheric circulation. During the early 1970s severe droughts also affected parts of central America, northern Colombia, Venezuela, northeastern Brazil, Sudan, Ethiopia, southern Arabia, and India—all within the same latitudinal zone and perhaps all symptomatic of changes in the general atmospheric circulation.

Whereas geographical patterns of rainfall anomalies in mid-latitudes seem to be associated with changes in the position and amplitude (north-south extent) of long waves in the westerly circulation, the Sahelian drought (Figure 8.4) can be interpreted as associated with changes in the meridional (north-south) circulation in the tropics. For example, the droughts in the American midwest in the 1930s and in the northeastern United States in the 1960s extended over some one million square kilometers and rainfall was above normal over neighboring regions in the same latitude. But in Africa the drought extended over some five million square kilometers from the Atlantic ocean right across the continent to the Red Sea (Figure 8.3) and there were north-south rather than west-east differences in rainfall anomalies (Figure 8.4).

Perhaps the oldest and one of the most frequently postulated explanations of precipitation fluctuations relates to variations of solar activity during the quasi-regular eleven-year sunspot cycle, although the physical basis for such a relationship remains obscure. A number of investigators have found positive relationships between rainfall at individual stations in the sub-Sahara zone and the variations in sunspot number (Weller 1931; Wood and Lovett 1974; Landsberg 1974), although spectral analysis of annual rainfall at 11 stations failed to reveal a significant maximum of spectral energy at close to eleven years (Bunting et al. 1974).

Anthropogenic Drought

Human activity, both inside and outside the region, has been postulated as contributing to or causing the drought. Bryson (1973) suggests that the decrease in rainfall might be related to increasing levels of atmospheric particulate matter from industrialized nations in higher latitudes. The hypothesis is that the increasing amounts of dust in the atmosphere in higher latitudes leads to lower temperature at the surface and that the increase equator-to-pole temperature gradient strengthens the westerly circulation, which extends farther south and causes the monsoon rains to be restricted in their northward extent.

Schnell and Vali (1974), Charney (1974), and MacLeod (in this volume) hypothesize that "internal" changes in the Sahelian zone— overgrazing, erosion, deforestation, and general bad land management—could lead to drought. Different mechanisms are proposed to account for the decrease of rainfall. Schnell and Vali hypothesize that overgrazing of the land and the resultant removal of large proportions of vegetation may have led to the reduction of the supply of the ice nuclei and consequently to reduction of precipitation probability or precipitation efficiency in the region. Charney speculates that overgrazing causes the surface albedo (reflectivity) to increase and that the resulting decrease in the amount of sunlight absorbed by the land creates a "cold spot" in which increased subsidence would induce a decrease of rainfall. MacLeod follows the chain of argument that the decrease of vegetation cover leads to steep temperature gradients and local turbulence, which in turn raises dust into the atmosphere. Dust prevents the normal development of rain-producing clouds despite the presence of normal amounts of atmospheric moisture. Through supersaturation, this increases the probability of abnormally low rainfall. The above processes, once started, would tend to reinforce themselves.

Climatic Scenarios to the Year 2000

1. If rainfall in the Sahel is regarded as a stationary, normally distributed, and random variable, then a further drought with four or five consecutive years with below-normal rainfall can be expected by the turn of the century, but with no long-term climatic change.

2. Winstanley (1973b) and Lamb (1973) have suggested that the recent drought might be related to a long-term fluctuation of the general atmospheric circulation and that there might be a tendency toward lower rainfall for the remainder of the century; rainfall could be some 10 percent below the 1931-60 "normal," although there would continue to be irregular fluctuations.

3. With rapidly increasing human populations, continuing economic and industrial growth, and degradation of the environment, one must also assume a long-term climatic deterioration if the drought is regarded primarily as anthropogenic. Whether or not man has contributed significantly in causing the recent drought, it is possible that the world's climates could be changed inadvertently by human activity by the turn of the century; but it is impossible to say with any degree of certainty how rainfall distribution in the Sahel might be affected.

4. It is conceivable, though improbable, that the climate of the Sahel will be changed by planned modification, either by direct action to specifically modify the Sahelian climate or through complex interactions, indirectly from attempts to modify climate in other regions. In either case, it is impossible at present to forecast the results of any such attempts (for a discussion of climate control, see Kellogg and Schneider 1974, and Glantz and Parton in this volume).

Climatic change encompasses all forms of climatic inconsistency, regardless of their statistical nature. In concluding this section, it must be emphasized that a practically significant change of climate need not be a statistically significant change (Mitchell et al. 1966, p. 17). With a rapidly increasing demand for food production and a deteriorating economic situation in the Sahelian countries, it seems probable that seasonal rainfall anomalies within the "normal" range of climatic variability will have an ever-increasing socioeconomic and political impact. There is a great deal of uncertainty about the future climate, but as far as I know, nobody has suggested a long-term improvement.

THE FUTURE OF THE SAHEL IN A
GLOBAL PERSPECTIVE

Prior to the drought, the Sahelian countries were left largely outside the mainstream of modern agricultural and general development processes. As a direct result of the drought, however, these countries have been suddenly exposed to the outside world. For several years, hundreds of millions of dollars in relief aid have been injected into these countries and millions of people have depended for their very existence on the charity of the developed nations—they have lived on the international dole. For better or for worse, the Sahelians states have become involved in global political issues and are themselves at the center of one of those issues: the widening socioeconomic gap between the developed countries and the fourth world. In looking at the future of the Sahelian countries, we are faced with fundamental ethical issues and dilemmas.

The exponential rate of growth of human and animal populations in the 1960s was due to a large extent to the application of Western medicine, which lowered death rates. During the drought, when these populations exceeded the carrying capacity of their deteriorating natural environment, hundreds of thousands and perhaps millions of people escaped the fate of the cattle, sheep, and goats only as a result of massive international relief (in Ethiopia, relief aid, for a number of reasons, was delayed and the death toll was much higher).

The Sahelian countries have, in fact, survived a super-Malthusian
situation; food production was stagnant (Figure 8.7, part A), but the
human population continued to grow at an accelerating pace (Figure
8.7, part B). Although the drought caused untold human misery and
suffering, the number of deaths resulting from the drought was
probably no more than several tens of thousands. In fact, anthropo-
metric and clinical evidence in Upper Volta in 1973 suggested that,
although the nutritional level of the population was low, the general
situation was not unusual for rural Africans living in similar environ-
ments (Seaman et al. 1973).

As a preview to the dilemmas now facing both the donor and
recipient countries, it is eye-opening to start at the grassroots level
and look at the problems through the perceptive eyes of Faulkingham
and Thorbahn (1974) in a small village in Niger. The nearly 1,500
residents of Tudu are sedentary farmers, dependent traditionally on
fields of millet and sorghum, which they till exclusively by hoe.
Before the modern period a population equilibrium had been achieved,
involving human population declines and increases during the drought-
recovery cycles. Rainfall at nearby Madaoua declined from 448 mm
in 1969 to 156 mm in 1973 and, as might be expected, yields of millet
and sorghum fell from 123 kg per capita to 4.5 kg per capita. But
this time the death rate remained stable at 12.2 per 1,000 population,
a dramatically lower level than in the past, while birth rates actually
increased to 43.6 per 1,000. The result was a 10.4 percent increase
in population from 1969 to 1973. Although some 25 percent of the
households resorted to cooking and eating leaves from trees at least
once a day in early 1974, the drought caused very few deaths.

The two main and interrelated factors to account for the low
mortality are the increasing tendency for males to be drawn into the
cash labor market outside the village and the availability of grain,
both for purchase in local markets and through the government distribution system of donated food. Tudu has thus become subtly transformed from a closed economic entity to a part of the world economy.
But at some point in the future—whether with a population of 3,000
in the year 2000 or 6,000 in the year 2020—Tudu faces an inexorable
clash between food supply and population. And to the three basic
causes of the drought outlined above must be added a fourth: the will
of Allah.

The Sahelian countries are now faced with the problems of
demographic transition at a national level. The age-old demographic
balance between high birth and death rates has been destroyed by the
application of Western medicine, which has resulted in a dramatic
lowering of the death rate while the birth rate increases. The traditional population-controlling mechanism of drought-induced famine
has been largely eliminated by massive international disaster relief

FIGURE 8.9

Population Projections to the Year 2000
in the Sahel

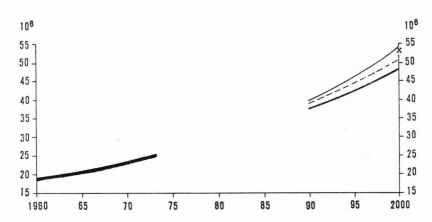

Note: The projected values diverge very little to 1990: (━━━)
actual population; (━━━) projection assuming a constant rate of
growth of 2.47 percent per annum (the growth rate from 1972 to 1973);
(────) projection based on extrapolation of trend line of population
growth rate from 1960 to 1973 (increase of 0.03 percent per year);
(─ ─ ─ ─) projection based on previous projection to 1981, on
stabilization of growth rate at 1981-82 level of 2.79 percent to the
year 1989, and then on a growth rate decreasing by 0.03 percent per
year to the year 2000; x marks the United Nations' projected figure.
     Source: United Nations. 1974. Statistical Yearbook 1973.
New York: Department of Economic and Social Affairs, Statistical
Office of the United Nations.

aid. But what will happen in the future? Will we increase our aid to
the level that our earlier involvement morally dictates; that is, at a
minimum to adequately feed the exponentially growing population? If
we, the politicians and donors in the developed countries, fail to fulfill
our commitments, even in the face of worsening domestic economic
situations, then the responsibility for the consequences must rest
heavily on our shoulders. During the next 26 years the population in
the Sahelian countries will increase from 24 million to some 50 million
(Figure 8.9)—the same increase as for the whole of Africa during the
550 years from 1300 to 1850 (Bennett 1954). We have greatly increased
the potential for unprecedented disaster during the next inevitable

TABLE 8.2

Affluence Versus Poverty

	Canada	Sahelian Countries*
Population in 1973	22,000,000	24,000,000
Life expectancy at birth	73	38
Birth rate per 1,000 population per year	16	48
Death rate per 1,000 population per year	7	24
Population per hospital bed	100	1,500
Daily calorie consumption per capita	3,100	2,100
Index of per capita food production in 1972 (1963 = 100)	120	80
Per capita GNP ($)	5,000	110
Per capita energy consumption per year (kg coal equivalent)	9,000	70
Projected population in year 2000	29,000,000	54,000,000

*Mauritania, Senegal, Mali, Upper Volta, Niger, and Chad.

drought in the Sahel—if not before. And those in North America who think that the carrying capacity of these geographically large Sahelian countries can be increased merely by economic investment and development should ask themselves whether Canada, a rich country with a present population of 22 million, could support 50 million by the end of the century.

Relief and development aid stem primarily from humanitarian and Judaeo-Christian ethics. But with a widening gap between developed nations and the fourth world, and faced with the economic and political problems associated with continued growth in a finite world, the issues go much deeper than merely keeping populations alive. The gap—the ever-widening gap—between those who have plenty and want more and those who have nothing and need more, is illustrated in Table 8.2. The developed countries (exemplified by Canada) see the depletion of the world's resources by the rapidly growing populations of the fourth world (exemplified by the Sahelian countries) as a threat to their own standard of living and overindulgent habits. The fourth world, on the other hand, sees the disproportionately high consumption patterns of the developed countries as the basic cause of the depletion of the world's natural resources and of their own continuing poverty. (Canadians spend $100 million on pet food each year—more than the Canadian aid to the Sahelian countries.) The aid recipient countries now see the standard of living and level of technological development in the donor countries as goals for themselves. But it has been calculated (Hulett 1971) that at U.S. levels the carrying capacity of the earth is about one billion people—a figure that was passed by about 1850. In a finite world, population must in time cease to grow, either by man controlling his own numbers or by nature controlling them for him. We have prevented many of the natural population-controlling mechanisms in the Sahel from operating and must now restore a balance by encouraging population control measures—before nature takes control again.

It is easy to see both viewpoints if one stands in the middle, but that is where the solutions lie. It is a global problem that demands both population control and redistribution of wealth; otherwise, we face social, economic, and political instability in an imbalanced, highly interdependent and overcrowded world. The growth of a population has considerable momentum depending on its age structure. Even with an immediate reduction of birth rate to replacement level, population in the Sahelian countries would continue to grow for at least 50 years. Clearly, population control will need to be introduced long before a decrease in growth rate can be effectively brought about simply by value changes resulting from socioeconomic development—population projections to the year 2030 are far more frightening than to year 2000. If quality of life means anything at all, then we should surely aim for a stable population level that optimizes whatever goals we have, rather than for the maximum number of people we can support at the minimum level of satisfaction (Winstanley, Emmett, and Winstanley 1975, p. 29).

The situation demands a basic change in attitude, strong political action, and sacrifices. The rich nations can no longer soothe their consciences by donating their surpluses and a modest, and in some cases a declining, amount of aid (less than 0.5 percent of GNP) to the poor countries. But it is difficult to see how concern for future generations will influence our actions.

SOURCES

Africa South of the Sahara. 1972. London: Europa.

Bennett, M.K. 1954. The World's Food. New York: Harper.

Bryson, R.A. 1973. "Drought in Sahelia." The Ecologist 3: 366-371.

Bunting, A.H., et al. 1974. "Weather and Climate in the Sahel:
An Initial Study." Mimeo. Reading, England: University of
Reading (forthcoming).

Charney, J.G. 1974. "Dynamics of Desert and Drought in the Sahel."
Mimeo. Symons Lecture delivered to the Royal Meteorological
Society, 20 March, London.

Davy, E.G. 1974. "Drought in West Africa." WMO Bulletin 23:
18-23.

El-Sayed, H., and H.E. Landsberg. 1973. "Spectral Analysis of the
Rainfall in Dakar." Mimeo. Institute of Dynamics and Applied
Mathematics, University of Maryland.

Faulkingham, R.H., and P.F. Thorbahn. 1974. "The Demographic
Impact of Drought: An Ecosystemic Study of a Village in Niger."
Paper read at Chicago meeting of African Studies Association,
1 November. Mimeo.

Hulett, H.R. 1971. "Optimum World Population." In P.K. Anderson,
ed., Omega; Murder of the Ecosystem and Suicide of Man.
Dubuque, Iowa: Wm. C. Brown.

Kellogg, W.W., and S.H. Schneider. 1974. "Climate Stabilization:
For Better or for Worse?" Science 186: 1163-72.

Lamb, H.H. 1973. "Some Comments on Atmospheric Pressure
Variations in the Northern Hemisphere." In D. Dalby and R.J.
Harrison Church, eds., Drought in Africa. London: University
of London.

Landsberg, H.E. 1974. Letter to Dr. N. Kamrany, 3 October.
Quoted in W.W. Seifert, and J.E. Soussou. 1974. "Development Planning and Droughts in the Sahel-Sudan Region." Paper
read at Chicago meeting of African Studies Association, 1 November. Mimeo.

Lovejoy, P.E., and S. Baier. 1975. "The Desert-Side Economy of
the Central Sudan." Int. J. Afr. Hist. Studies 8. In the press.

Mitchell, J.M., et al. 1966. "Climatic Change." WMO Tech. Note
No. 79. Geneva: World Meteorological Organization.

Namias, J. 1974. "Suggestion for Research Leading to Long-Range
Precipitation Forecasting for the Tropics." Mimeo. Paper
presented at International Tropical Meteorology Meeting, 31
January to 7 February, Nairobi, Kenya. Boston: American
Meteorological Society.

Palmer, W.C. 1968. "The Abnormally Dry Weather of 1961-1966 in the Northeastern United States." In Proceedings of the Conference on Drought in the Northeastern U.S.A., Sterling Forest, New York, 15-17 May, 1967. New York: New York University Press.

Schnell, R.C., and G. Vali. 1974. Letter to D. Winstanley, 10 October.

Seaman, J., et al. 1973. "An Inquiry into the Drought Situation in Upper Volta." The Lancet, 6 October: 774-78.

Sheets, H., and R. Morris. 1974. "Disaster in the Desert." Issue 4: 24-43.

Subrahmanyam, V.P. 1967. "Incidence and Spread of Continental Drought." Report No. 2 on WMO/IHD Projects. Geneva: World Meteorological Organization.

Sumary, R. 1974. "Aid Must Not Stop When the Rains Do." The Guardian, 21 December, p. 16.

Szabo, A. 1974. "Problemes de la nutrition humaine et developpement de la peche." Paper presented at Consultation of Fisheries Problems in the Sahelian Zone, 13-20 November, Bamako, Mali: Food and Agriculture Organization of the United Nations. Mimeo.

Weller, L. 1931. "La pluie a Dakar et l'activite solaire." Bulletin du comite d'etudes historiques et scientifiques de l'Afrique occidentale francaise 13: 264-71.

Winstanley, D. 1973a."Recent Rainfall Trends in Africa, the Middle East and India." Nature 243: 464-65.

Winstanley, D. 1973b. "Rainfall Patterns and General Atmospheric Circulation." Nature 245: 190-94.

Winstanley, D. 1974."Climatological Aspects of Drought in the Sub-Sahara Zone." Deutsche Geographische Blatter 51: in the press.

Winstanley, D. 1975. "Fisheries Along the Southern Edge of the Sahara." Mimeo. Ottawa: Environment Canada.

Winstanley, D., B. Emmett, and G. Winstanley. 1975. "Climatic Changes and the World Food Supply." Planning and Finance Service Report no. 5. Ottawa: Environment Canada. In the press.

Wood, C.A., and R.R. Lovett. 1974. "Rainfall, Drought and the Solar Cycle." Nature 251: 594-96.

CHAPTER

9

DUST IN THE SAHEL:
CAUSE OF DROUGHT?
Norman H. MacLeod

CLIMATIC CHANGE AND DROUGHT

The current drought in the Sahelian zone of Africa has brought
about widespread suffering, which has in turn set in motion a worldwide effort to provide both short-term relief and long-term rehabilitation assistance. A basic assumption underlying these programs is
that the drought will end. However, recent papers by Reid A. Bryson,
Hubert H. Lamb, Derek Winstanley, and others, present information suggesting that a long-term climatic change is under way. [1] The
change in global climate they suggest includes equatorward shifts of
climatic zones, which have already resulted in the droughts observed
not only in Africa but also on the Indian subcontinent and in the
Western hemisphere. The trend of climatic change forecasts a bleak
future for mankind.

The discussions and data provided by M. Diallo, director,
Meteorological Services, Republic of Niger, are gratefully acknowledged. Also, D. Kurtz, School of International Services, The American University, has been of special assistance in discussions during
preparation of this paper.

This work was supported in part by NASA Contract NAS 5-21970,
by Church World Service, and The American University. Travel
funds provided by the United Methodist Committee on Relief through
Church World Service for this trip, June 20 through July 16, 1974,
are greatly appreciated.

Several theories have been advanced to explain such a global temperature drop, among them, changes in solar output or sunspot activity, as well as an increase in terrestrial albedo (decreasing energy flow within the atmosphere) due to increased atmospheric dustiness. The effects of these postulated changes on man and societies, the droughts currently experienced globally, as well as floods and cooler weather in northern latitudes, have reduced the food production capacity of the globe. If the trend intensifies or simply continues at the present level, it also is postulated that a larger proportion of mankind will go hungry—an even larger number than at present. In the models of Bryson and Lamb, there are essentially no factors under the control of man. They are doomsday prophecies.

The doomsday is in some measure already upon millions of people in Africa and southern Asia, where there is widespread suffering from prolonged drought. For example, in the Sahel area bordering the southern reaches of the Sahara Desert in west Africa, millions of head of livestock have succumbed and, while estimates vary, hundreds of thousands of people have lost their means of food supply and thousands have died from a multitude of diseases, if not outright starvation. If models such as Bryson's and Lamb's are correct, the Sahel should be abandoned, the remaining population should be evacuated now, and international mechanisms set in motion to ease the massive effects of such a social displacement.

REVEGETATION AND DROUGHT

Bryson's arguments of global climatic change are compelling and lead to a profound concern for the future of human society. That concern has led us to analyze the Sahelian drought and to search for a method of reversing the trend to drought and famine. We conclude that there is such a means: revegetation of the Sahel through management for food production resources, and enormous and complex undertaking. Nevertheless, the restabilization of the land through establishment of plant cover is a real alternative to drought and famine.

In fact, there have been demonstrated successes of revegetation in the Sahel, including range management projects started during the drought years. These projects demonstrate that revegetation can be accomplished through plant, soil, and water management.

Reversal of the trend of long-term losses of vegetation, that is, reversing the processes of desert formation, must take into account the social as well as noncultural factors that have led to the

present situation. The management of revegetation cannot be successful without understanding these factors, for it is quite apparent to
Sahelian pastoralists and farmers that loss of vegetation and soil
fertility (called "desert encroachment" by Westerners) has proceeded
for decades, if not centuries. The cultural adaptations to ecological
conditions in the Sahel, which supported great African empires and
kingdoms in the past (Ghana, Mali, Timbouctou, Bornu) have been
destroyed by war, by colonial exploitation, and today through commercialization (specifically, cash cropping for export purposes).

ATMOSPHERIC DUST AND CLIMATE CHANGE

In Bryson's view, a principal factor in global climatic change
is a substantial increase of dust in the atmosphere. The evidence
he presents suggests that human activities may have an important
influence on the present droughts, through introduction of dust into
the atmosphere. We agree with this point of view. It is important to
analyze potential sources of dust so as to determine whether or not
corrective action is possible.

This chapter presents: (1) models of dust generation into the
atmosphere of West Africa and its dispersion within the global weather
system and (2) a set of brief recommendations for human counter-
actions that might alleviate the drought problems.

We advance some alternative hypotheses concerning the African
drought and offer some ecological perspectives that permit a model
of Sahelian climate, including drought. In this model or set of models,
there are some parameters that can be controlled by man, although
with difficulty and at great expense. If man does control these factors,
some of the outcomes of the models are the cessation of drought and
the productive greening of the desert, a revegetation of the Sahel and
parts of the interior Sahara. The revegetation of the range and crop
land of the Sahel is advocated not only as ecological rehabilitation
of Sahelian food production potential but as the method critically
needed for reversing the trend toward drought in the Sahel—perhaps
on a global scale as well. Thus, these hypotheses are to be examined carefully, for these are the very opposite of doomsday
prophecies. They are, instead, propositions for increasing regional
and even worldwide food production.

CLIMATE OF THE SAHEL

The following discussion concerns the drought in West Africa
and some recent observations of sand and dust movements, an

analysis of the cause of the movements and of the effects of dusty atmospheres on the climate of the Sahelian zone.

The climate of West Africa is dominated by seasonal shifts in the zonal weather systems, particularly the inter-tropical convergence (ITC). Moving north in summer and south in winter, the leading edge of the ITC is the location of maximum precipitation. Places located south of the maximum northern excursion of the ITC have two summer rainfall maxima, one as the ITC moves north and a second when the ITC retreats to its winter position (see Figure 9.1).

North of the ITC, climate is dominated by westerly high-pressure systems formed by descending dry, cold air. These highs produce the Harmattan, a very hot, dry northeasterly wind, which also moves in a seasonal pattern but opposite to the ITC. In recent years, the northeasterly Harmattan winds have penetrated much farther south than normal—in 1973 to the coast of the Gulf of Guinea.

Between the Harmattan airs and the southwest monsoon, easterly winds are found in a persistent low-pressure trough. At the southern edge of this trough, where the ITC is located, a series of cumulus formations—squall lines—move from east to west, the result of the interaction of wet monsoon airs and the dry Harmattan. The latter rides over the monsoon air, blocking and lifting the monsoon air and thus producing rainfall.

The system described above is the normal climatic regime in the Sahel. But for several years, and particularly for the last three years, unusual and increasing amounts of dusts in the Sahelian atmosphere have been reported. During the NASA Skylab-3 mission in winter 1973-74, the Skylab crew reported large-scale movement of smoky dust clouds out of West Africa into the Atlantic, and out of East and Central Africa into the West Indian Ocean. Another study of dust movements across the Atlantic was conducted with analysis of nimbus meteorological data.[2] This showed that the dusts were contained in a large, coherent stream of warm air (flowing between 4,000 and 20,000 feet in altitude) from the west coasts of Africa to the Caribbean Islands, which suppressed normal exchange of energy (water vapor).

In late June and early July 1974, the altitude of the dust formation was observed by the author (from commercial aircraft) to be about 27,000 feet near the southern coast of West Africa (Sierra Leone and Liberia) and 21,000 feet at 13 degrees north latitude (near Ougadougou, Upper Volta).

Rainfall since 1968 has been either scanty or poorly distributed through the summer season. While this series of years is not the only period of drought experienced by the Sahel, it is the most extended drought and also the most destructive of crops, livestock, and people.

FIGURE 9.1

Regional Atmospheric Circulation
in West Africa

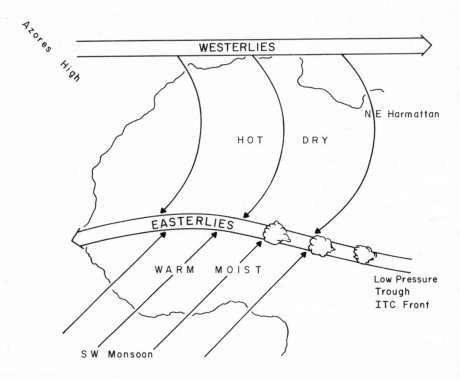

Note: Regional atmospheric circulation in West Africa is
dominated by four systems: the westerlies; the desert high-pressure
zone, which generates the hot, dry Harmattan; a low-pressure trough
in which the easterlies are found; and the warm moist winds. At the
Intertropical Convergence (ITC) northern front, maximum precipitation occurs, with lesser amounts of precipitation occurring south of
the front.

These systems "follow the sun," moving northward in summer
and south in winter. This motion gives rise to the seasonal weather
pattern of the Sahel: rain in summer, dry in winter; the length of the
rainy season is dependent upon latitude. Occasional low-pressure
systems move westerly from the Azores high. When this occurs,
monsoon airs flow north across the desert, bringing occasional
rainfall to the Sahara. Such rainfall occurs particularly in late
winter.

During the winter of 1973-74, we observed with the Earth
Resources Technology Satellite (ERTS) imagery extensive movement
of sands in western Niger. Covering thousands of square miles, the
moving sands indicated to us that the deterioration of vegetation and
soils in the Sahel had passed a critical point and that a dust bowl
condition had fully developed.

A field trip to Niger was undertaken to establish correlations
between the features observed in ERTS images and the actual conditions on the surface. During this trip, reports of unprecedented sand
and dust storms were received. These storms occurred in the same
regions where sand movements had been observed in the satellite
imagery. New extensions of sand dunes in the Tchin Tabaraden area
of Niger were photographed, as well as a new form of sand movement.

Normally, sands in the Sahel are coated with iron oxides that
give a yellow or reddish color to the dunes. Now, white quartz sand
from flat areas occupied by silty soils of hydromorphic origin are
dusting the dunes. The white sands are those not exposed to the
process of iron coating and only recently removed—separated by
winds—from the soils. The blowing of white sands is an indication
that soils that were previously protected from wind erosion by vegetated surfaces or accumulated organic matter had lost that protection
and become unstable.

We observed in June and July that when rains do occur in
western Niger, they are preceded by a relatively severe sand storm.
Two very severe sand storms occurred during the field survey. One,
in Ougadougou, preceded a torrential downpour. Extensive electrical
activity accompanied both the sand storm and the rain storm. (lightning and thunder occur during strong local vertical motions in the
atmosphere; rapid up-and-down transport of dust and water particles
produces an electrical potential that is discharged through lightning
flashes.) The second storm was observed in Niamey, Niger. Again,
electrical activity was severe—but no rain followed the storm. Such
storms are reported to have become common in western Niger.

Both the severity and the infrequency of thunderstorms in the
early rainy season suggest a slow development of a disequilibrium
between the monsoon wind and the northeast Harmattan winds. The
inversion formed by dusts in the monsoon air prevents a normal
mixing, which results in an abnormal energy potential difference.
When a breakdown across the potential gradient occurs, the flow of
energy is abnormally great. This flow of energy produces a very
severe storm.

At the ITC, in dust-free air in which a normal lapse rate
(cooling with altitude) and energy transfer occurs, storms of moderate
intensity should occur frequently. Thus, the current severity of dust
and rain storms and their infrequency suggest the importance of

dust-generated inversions in the Sahel: Their importance lies in the
reduction of storm frequency (rainfall distribution) and the increase
of storm intensity (which also causes severe soil erosion and crop
damage).

During the day, in both Ougadougou and Niamey, the underside
of clouds were a brick-red color. Some meteorologist felt this color
was due to sunlight reflected from the soil surface. As the cloud
color was uniform, and the surface color is not uniform (green in
vegetated areas, dark red on laterite plateaus, "silver" on sheet
metal roofs of urban areas), we speculated that the cloud base was
colored by dust picked up as the clouds passed along the top of a dust
layer. The brick-red color is just that of the fine dusts of the Sahel
collected on white cloth.

We also felt that if the cloud color were due to reflected light
from the land, the intensity of the cloud base color should vary with
change in the relative positions of the sun, cloud base, and observer.
Such intensity or spectral changes were not evident; rather, the red
tint was consistent in all directions. We reached the tentative conclusions that the cloud base does pick up dust, that a dust layer
extends to the base of the clouds, that the dust layer rises during
the day with diurnal heating—its upper boundary marked by the cloud
base level. Further, we hypothesize that mixing of this low-level
dust generated during the day and the regional monsoon air occurs
primarily during the night. This low-level dust layer also constitutes
a weak inversion that is frequently observed in radiosonde data obtained at Niamey (see Figure 9.2).

It is possible, then, that the peculiar cloud base colors are
related to local upward transport of dust brought into the atmosphere
by microturbulence, as discussed below. The local dust is transported from the surface to the lower atmosphere during daylight hours,
and from the lower atmosphere aloft into the regional monsoon air
during the night.

Generation of Dust: A Model

Denuded Soil as a Source of Dust

Analysis of ERTS imagery of the Sahelian zone, and the
savannas and woodlands south of the Sahel, shows a very large
proportion of the land surface to be open—that is, unvegetated.
Skylab and other space observations show the same situation. Even
without exact data on the rate of loss of vegetation, and without
thorough examination of specific causes of vegetation loss, we can

FIGURE 9.2

Radiosonde Data from Niamey, Niger

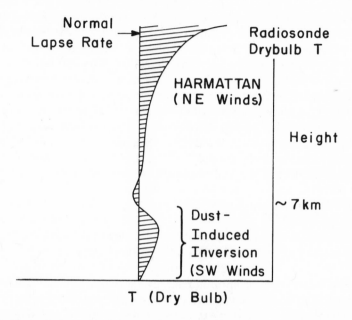

T (Dry Bulb)

Note: A radiosonde is a set of temperature, humidity, and pressure sensors sent aloft
lloon, from which the sensor data is radioed to a weather station. The course of the
on ascent is observed from the ground. These observations are used to determine wind
and direction.

This figure is a schematic representation of 1974 average values in winter, spring, and
er for Niamey, Niger. The straight line represents dry bulb temperature values found
tandard atmosphere with a given surface air temperature, and the curvilinear line
sents an average of the dry bulb actually measured temperature in the atmosphere above
ey.

The measured atmosphere is generally hotter than a standard atmosphere. The region
ich the measured atmosphere is cooler is the upper boundary of the monsoon winds,
ng from the southwest. Above this boundary the very hot Harmattan winds are found,
ng from the northeast.

Usually, these winds mix and raise the altitude of the monsoon air. Such a lifting of
air in this situation produces precipitation because of cooling below the dew point of the
oon air. The vertical motions also entrain the moist warm air below to bring about
tion of cumulus clouds.

These data can be used to plot the lapse rate—the fall in temperature with height. In this
the standard lapse rate is shown as a straight line to emphasize the difference between
the actual temperature of the atmosphere. The standard lapse rate curve should show
temperature with increased height.

In the observed situation, there is little mixing because of the inversion formed by dusty
We postulate that this is one reason for the sporadic and scanty rainfall in the Sahelien
.

observe that the terrain has become less vegetated especially in the
past few decades, and at an increasingly rapid pace.

The microclimate of bare soils in the Sahel is very different
from that of vegetated soils. The most important difference is found
in the temperature gradient, and particularly the location and size
of the diurnal temperature maxima.[3] Figure 9.3 shows these differences schematically. Obviously, the particular plant community
examined will have unique thermal characteristics. However, the
temperature maximum in a closed plant canopy is not located at the
soil surface but within the plant canopy. On bare soil, this maximum
is located at the soil surface. In addition, temperature maxima of
bare soils are much higher. Differences of 30°C have been measured
in the tropics and 10°C in temperate climates of the United States.
Further, the temperature gradient near the surface is much steeper
over bare soils than in plant canopies (superadiabatic).

A Model for Dust Generation

The implications of microclimate differences among vegetated
and open soils are profound. Microturbulence developed during
convective energy transport is easily observed near irradiated
surfaces in the form of shimmering heat waves. Because such energy
transport occurs over a vegetated soil within a plant canopy, not at
the surface, the convective air movements do not bring dusts into
the atmosphere. However, with bare soils, which contain silts and
clays, dust is brought into the atmosphere during the daily development of steep temperature gradients through the concurrent development of turbulence at the soil surface. Thus, it is not necessary to
invoke strong surface winds to conceive of a means of atmospheric
dust production in the tropics. But surface winds are higher over
unvegetated regions because of the lower surface roughness of bare
soils. This factor should intensify the production of dusts. And, as
pointed out earlier, there are high concentrations of dusts in the
Sahelian atmosphere.

Effects of Dust in the Sahelian Atmosphere:
A Model

Having analyzed the principal sources of dust, it is now important to assess the effect of dust on the Sahelian climate. Because
the source of moisture for Sahelian precipitation is the southwest
monsoon, it is this system in which the effect of dust as a cause of
drought should be examined. The lapse rate of the atmosphere

FIGURE 9.3

Temperature Gradients of Vegetated and Bare Soils

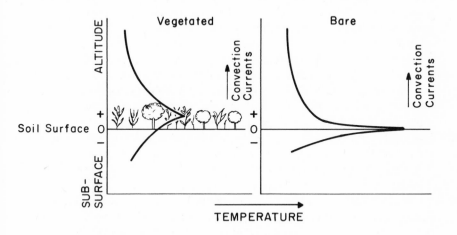

Note: Dust is easily generated from bare or sparsely vegetated soil surfaces but not from vegetated soils. Over a bare soil, the temperature gradient is very steep and the maximum temperature is at the soil surface itself. Convection currents (microturbulence) develop over both vegetated and bare soils, but they are more vigorous over the bare soils because of the steeper temperature gradient. The turbulence over a bare surface can and does pick up dust because it starts at the soil surface, not in a plant canopy. To prevent the generation of dust, the soil surface must be protected by vegetation.

observed with daily noon radiosonde at Niamey is shown in Figure 9.2. This generalized figure shows that the warm, moist air of the monsoon tends to be isothermal instead of cooling with altitude. The air above the monsoon is very much warmer than a standard atmosphere, showing the influence of the Harmattan blowing above the monsoon air and in an opposite direction. In between the hot, dry air and the moist, warm air, a small region of cooler air is frequently found.

There are several effects of the isothermal character of the monsoon air. First, precipitation will obviously not occur until the air is cooled below the dew point. The elevated and uniform temperature of this isothermal system suppresses updraft, which would cool the air. (The energy gradient in this system is opposite to that which would produce rising air.) Second, the dust aerosol is well mixed or uniform within the system. This tends to maintain the isothermal character; that is, the system is stable and tends to be further stabilized by the dust. Third, the pressure of the system is reduced because of the higher temperatures aloft. This may be the most important effect relative to regional aspects of the drought (see Figure 9.4).

It is along the ITC front that the greatest rainfall occurs in the Sahel. This is the region in which southwest monsoon is blocked by the Harmattan winds and lifted and thereby cooled. In stable, dusty monsoon air, the Harmattan wind does not mix effectively with the monsoon, although some clouds are formed along the front. Another way of describing the situation is to say that cumulus cloud formation along the ITC is suppressed by the presence of dust in the monsoon air. Therefore, rainfall along the front is also reduced, producing a drought.

Because the pressure of the dusty monsoon airs is reduced relative to nondusty air, there should be an increase in the size of the trough (intertropical depression) in which the easterlies flow. The northeast Harmattan winds should flow farther south and the monsoon more gently north. That is, the ITC should be located in a more southerly position in dusty monsoon airs than would normally be the case. If this were to occur, more northerly parts of the Sahel should experience a shorter rainy season, if any. Savannah regions to the south of the Sahel should have a longer rainy season than normal, but with less actual precipitation.

In the summer of 1974 it was observed that the ITC was approximately 6 degrees south of its normal location and that some areas in southern Upper Volta, for example, have experienced a longer period of rainfall. Thus, the effect of high dust loading is twofold: Rain-producing systems do not go as far north; cumulus (rain) cloud formation is suppressed.

Reversing the Trend: Conclusions from the Models

If the model of dust introduction and that of dust effects are substantially correct (that is, are descriptive of the actual mechanisms), then we can state that the drought is feeding upon itself—that is, it is self-perpetuating. Because enormous amounts of dust are transported out of West Africa, possibly in sufficient quantity to affect global temperature and thus global climates, the solution of the

FIGURE 9.4

West African Weather System

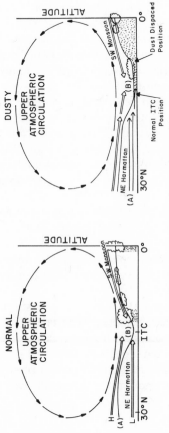

(A) ZONE OF LOWER ATMOSPHERIC CIRCULATION
(B) EASTERLIES TROUGH

Key: (A) Zone of lower atmospheric circulation
      (B) Easterlies trough

Note: This figure shows north-south vertical cuts of the West African weather system, the left side being normal, and the right abnormal with dusty monsoon air. In the abnormal case, dusty air has produced an inversion in which air temperature is uniform. This means that dusty upper-level monsoon air has both higher temperatures and lower pressure than normal. The low pressure permits the northeast winds to blow further south, displacing the normal position of the ITC front to the south. The result is a shorter rainy season in the Sahelian zone. The dust-induced isothermal state of the monsoon results in suppression of rain-cloud formation as well. Thus, if and when the ITC front does arrive, cloudiness but not rainfall is experienced.

225

Sahelian drought problem should have a beneficial global effect. We can do something to break the cycle: revegetate the Sahelian zone of Africa.

Rehabilitation Through Management of Ecological Resources

Elsewhere, we have presented recommendations for revegetation and rehabilitation of the Sahel—based on the assumption that there would be time for long-term programs. The implications of the present discussion are: (1) that an immediate regional action program is required; (2) that until the dust problem is laid to rest, there will be no long-term improvement in rainfall; and (3) that the remedial program must have priority over all other development and projects now under way or being planned in the Sahel.

Revegetation of the Sahel can be accomplished through range and crop management—including, as an essential, cover crops for the dry season and initiation of soil and water conservation measures. Revegetation does not mean setting aside the Sahel as an unproductive reserve. It does mean that range management and crop management, including cover crops, are essential. In short, immediate programs to cover the land are needed. The precious water that is available should be expended on this program. We have recommended the following actions:

1. Revegetation of surfaces through range and crop management, soil and water conservation measures of small scale but with extensive regional application.

2. Reforestation on a practical scale; but in pastoral regions, revegetation through grazing management, installation of small structures to maximize water retention (prolong growth season), introduction of suitable forages, and dune-controlling vegetation.

3. In cropped areas, maximization of mixed cropping, introduction of cover crop through direct government intervention and farmer incentives.

This should occur throughout the Sahel and sub-Sahelian zone. The principles involved are: (1) insuring a maximum year-round plant cover; (2) insuring maximum plant growth through use of water retention (soil-water conservation) techniques; (3) insuring maximum range and forest stabilization through pasture management.

(While this chapter is concerned primarily with the technical problems of the drought and of the possibilities of overcoming drought effects, we recognize that these proposals have extensive social ramifications with which we do not deal. There must be a comprehensive program of interaction with the farmers and herdsmen involved, dealing with the changes in their lifestyles that will be necessary to achieve the objectives of these recommendations and principles. Social and political factors must be an integral part of the consideration, planning, and implementation of programs fitting into this framework of objectives if they are to be successfully reached.)

From an ecological viewpoint, the limitations of water supply— from precipitation or from shallow and deep wells—and the necessity to restabilize the surface with vegetation restricts the possibilities of practical techniques to be recommended to the governments concerned. Because we have so little information on the potential natural vegetation of the Sahel (that which would form climax or mature and stable plant communities after sufficient release from cultural pressures and after sufficient time for plant and animal communities to mature), we can only infer, from a few examples, that particular techniques would be useful.

For example, in Niger a not very stringent grazing management scheme imposed for less than six years had begun to stabilize soil and permit accumulation of organic reserves and moderate the microclimate—all of these in a productive management scheme. The significance of this pasture management in the Sahel is that in a very short time a visible and positive set of changes developed—just those desired to reduce the probability of drought. We can glean clues to ecological management from space imagery, from the ancient and successful practices of nomadic peoples of arid regions, and from the many studies of arid zones available. Using these clues in conjunction with known ecological principles, we can begin to sketch the outlines of a program of rehabilitation.

Using Space View of Earth to Locate Potential Agriculture Zones

As ERTS images lay before us the present ecological situations, something of the character of land use practices in the Sahel, and something of the geographic distribution of both critical land use problems and development opportunities, the graphical representation of rehabilitation can be done directly as an overlay on a mosaic of ERTS images. Figure 9.5 is such an overlay.

There are four zones of potential agricultural use included, each related to both the ecological and the social situation. One is a zone of crop production, one of mixed agriculture, one of livestock production, and one of intensive agriculture, based to some extent on irrigation. While these zones appear as large generalized regions, they have been mapped directly from the ERTS images. The map is an attempt to look at regional potentials—and at zones where particular management techniques are considered to be most useful.

FIGURE 9.5

Zones of Agricultural Potential Derived from ERTS-1 Imagery

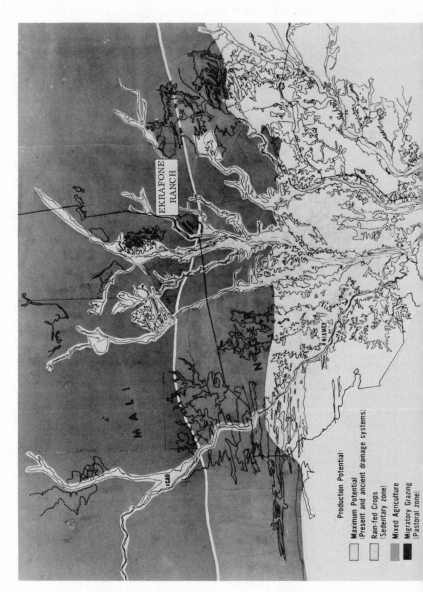

For example, in the sedentary zone, where traditional agriculture consists of the production of millet and where cash crops of peanuts and some cotton are produced, the major problem is overuse in the context of traditional rain-fed agriculture. We have calculated, with models using ERTS images as a data base, that the fallow time (the period of years during which fields are allowed to return to bush so that soil fertility may be restored) has been reduced from fifteen years to three years or less. Traditional management techniques—crop and fallow rotation—are breaking down or have already been disrupted, so that soil fertility has not been restored or maintained as in the past. A return to the traditional fallow rotation will not work, since arable land must now be put to maximum use to produce the food the population needs for its own survival.

The management objectives suggested for this sedentary zone are maximum production of food crops, maximum year-round vegetation cover, maximum addition of organic matter, and improvement of other fertility factors. These are to be attained in the minimum time—immediately, if possible. The time factor allows no delay to gather large capital and technical resources, or to train large numbers of people in new agricultural techniques. There are only the land and the people on which to base recommendations.

This does not suggest that people should completely change their traditional ways, but that certain aspects of food production be modified. These recommendations envision a more intensive use of land with more intensive management, taking into consideration the ecological dynamics of the region. The expected outcome is a moderated microclimate, better use of environmental resources, an increase in soil fertility, and, most important, a rapid increase in grain and food production.

There are techniques of water, soil, and plant control and conservation that are generally applicable to the Sahel. Their application would represent a major recovery campaign, one that should be considered prior to the implementation of major rehabilitation programs, or at least in conjunction with such programs. If satellite imagery is any guide—and we believe it is demonstrably so—then we have seen similar surface conditions throughout the northern Sahel as well as in cropping regions. The areas outside the observed dust bowl are not immune to the development of similar dust and sand storms. This, again, means that the priorities and pace of rehabilitation must be adjusted to the realities of the surface deterioration brought about by the drought.

A Plea for Specific Actions

The foregoing discussion is not presented simply as an academic report of a research project. Rather, we have presented a situation

230 THE POLITICS OF NATURAL DISASTER

report and a general action program in order to point out that it is possible to take constructive action directed at causes of the drought that will be far more effective than expensive relief programs dealing only with the symptoms.

We have seen instances during the period of Sahelian drought in which these management techniques have resulted in recovery of the soil surface and increases in production beyond that found prior to the drought. We feel, therefore, that these management techniques should be integrated into a regional recovery program under collective guidance and implementation of the Sahelian states, with major funding and technical assistance through the international community's family of development and environmental programs.

While we might agree with Bryson and Lamb in many particulars, and while we recognize that our hypotheses are more or less untried, we do not agree that drought is inevitable. We feel that every possible action should be taken to prevent the deterioration of semiarid regions, and to act positively in retaining and increasing the productive capacity of these areas.

CONCLUSION

Observations from the ERTS and Skylab spacecraft as well as from aircraft and on-the-ground studies have revealed that West African crop regions contain high percentages of open land throughout the year. Instead of the traditional fallow, capable of restoring soil fertility, much of the region is in seasonal monocrop cultivation. This situation has led to loss of organic matter, reduction of soil permeability to water, and a greatly increased susceptibility to wind and water erosion. While pastoral zones are overgrazed, the cropped soils present the greatest hazard.

A model of dust production from these open soils is presented that requires no wind initially but does require unaggregated soils containing little organic matter. The lack or absence of vegetation on open soils leads to steep temperature gradients sufficient to develop strong local turbulence, which in turn raises dust into the troposphere.

A second model is presented to assess the effect of dusts in monsoonal winds, the rain-producing winds of the Sahel. The presence of dust increases the southerly dimensions of the trough of easterly winds, which prevents the ITC from moving into a more northerly or normal position and thus prevents rainfall from occurring in the Sahel in a normal pattern; that is, this produces a tendency toward drought in the Sahel. In addition, the dusts prevent the normal development of rain-producing clouds within the monsoonal winds despite the

presence of normal amounts of atmospheric moisture, again
increasing the probability of abnormally small rains—or drought.

The rectification of these conditions is to be sought through
land management techniques appropriately applied to ecologically
defined zones of differing agricultural potential. These techniques
are directed toward a realization of maximum biological productivity
in each of the zones. They are, in essence, the techniques of revegetation, but in a mode that will produce optimum production and
maximum biological stability. They include multiple crops, managed
grazing, and, in particular, the establishment of a year-round vegetative cover in the affected areas. The year-round cover will virtually
eliminate excessive dust production and thus the problems of dust-
induced drought. These measures can only be taken through the
agencies of established governments and with the agreement, cooperation, and understanding of the people immediately affected by these
"rehabilitation" programs.

NOTES

1. Reid A. Bryson, "Drought in Sahelia: Who or What Is to
Blame?", Ecologist, October 1973, pp. 366-71; Hubert H. Lamb,
"Is the Earth's Climate Changing?", UNESCO Courier, August
1973, pp. 17-20; Derek Winstanley, "Recent Rainfall Trends in
Africa, the Middle East, and India," Nature, June 1973, pp. 464-65.

2. Toby N. Carlson and Joseph M. Prospero. "NOAA, Univer-
sity Scientists Link Sahara Dust, Tropical Weather, Pollution, and
Solar Energy Balance," U.S. Department of Commerce News Release,
January 10, 1974.

3. Norman H. MacLeod and A.M. Decker. "Controlled Soil
Temperature Field Plots: Temperature Profile Analysis," Agronomy
Abstracts, 1969, p. 148.

CHAPTER
10

AGRICULTURAL PRODUCTION
SYSTEMS IN THE SAHEL
W. Gerald Matlock
E. Lendell Cockrum

The human suffering resulting from the recent drought in the Sahel region of sub-Saharan West Africa has focused the world's attention on the needs of the developing nations there. Chad, Mali, Mauritania, Niger, Senegal, and Upper Volta, especially, felt the effects of this natural calamity, but other countries such as Sudan and Ethiopia did not escape unscathed.

In addition to the need for immediate drought relief measures (including food for humans and animals), local governmental authorities and various international groups dedicated to helping developing nations recognized the need for formulating long-term plans for the region. As envisioned, the plans help the people of the region not only to better cope with such natural catastrophes as drought but to prosper in the modern world context.

A first step in this direction was to use a systems analysis approach to natural resources utilization. A planning framework was constructed to assist decision makers in evaluating the effects on the well-being of the people of the region of alternative strategies for agricultural development. The task began with collection and analysis of background data concerning the climate, the ecology including

---

This chapter is a revised summary of Volume II of a December 1974 M.I.T. study entitled A Framework for Evaluating Long-Term Strategies for the Development of the Sahel-Sudan Region. This was a multidisciplinary study sponsored by the U.S. Agency for International Development. Citations to pertinent references as well as the details of the mathematical analysis in the application of the ISYALAPS framework are all presented in that volume and its appendix.

ecological succession rates and parameters of productivity of natural and agricultural ecosystems, and the existing agricultural production system.

The planning framework is flexible enough to permit the analysis of a broad spectrum of possible regional and/or local development alternatives for any planning area. As examples of how the framework might be applied in the Sahel region, two alternative strategies were analyzed to predict potential future agricultural production. Results from these were compared to production under the current system.

CLIMATE

The climate in the Sahel region varies from that of a hot desert to that of a dry subtropical woodland. Rainfall ranges from less than 100 mm per year in the north to more than 1,250 mm per year in the south.

Most of the region receives its rainfall from a monsoon system. Significant geographic and temporal variations of weather often occur; they are most extreme in the more arid zones. As a general rule, there is one day in the growing period (wet season) for each 5 mm of annual precipitation. Recurring droughts of varying lengths have been reported in historical records since the sixteenth century. Of the 22 droughts listed, six lasted 1 year; eight for 2 years; two for 3 years; one for 4 years; four for 5 years; and 1 lasted 18 years (1738-56).

Temperatures range from warm to hot, with only stations in the mountains of northern Chad ever recording readings below 0°C. Temperatures are low in December-January and again during the wet season (May-October).

During the dry season, the region is under the influence of dry northeasterly trade winds. At the beginning of the wet season, violent winds associated with thunderstorms are common. Later in the wet season, southerly monsoon winds dominate.

Solar radiation is high, with few cloudy days recorded other than during the wet season. Relative humidity usually is low and evaporation rates are high.

The weather patterns are such that one can define five climatic zones of variable width extending across the region from east to west, based upon rainfall and vegetation (see Figure 10.1). From north to south these zones are:

1. Desert: less than 100 mm annual rainfall, fewer than 10 rainy days per year (July-August), 36 percent of the region.

FIGURE 10.1

Climatic Zones of the Sahel Region

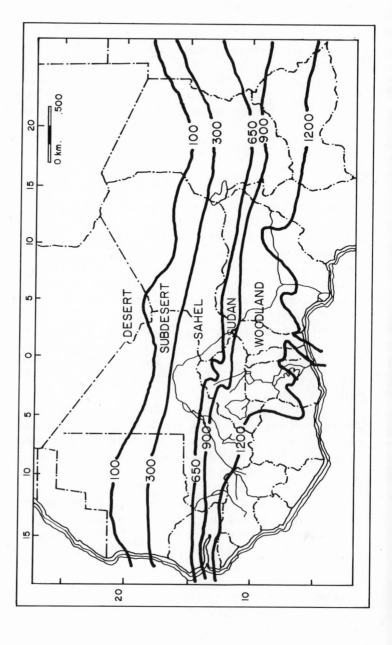

2. Subdesert: 100 to 300 mm annual rainfall, 10 to 25 rainy days per year (July-August), 28 percent of the region.

3. Sahel: 300 to 650 mm annual rainfall, 26 to 46 rainy days per year (June-September), 17 percent of the region.

4. Sudan: 650 to 900 mm annual rainfall, 50 to 65 rainy days per year (May-October), 10 percent of the region.

5. Woodland: over 900 mm annual rainfall, 65 to 80 rainy days per year (May-October), 9 percent of the region.

THE EXISTING AGRICULTURAL
PRODUCTION SYSTEM

Much of the region is arid even in periods of normal rainfall. Only 8 percent (42 million hectares) is considered arable; 25 percent (136 million hectares) is grazing land; 12 percent (61 million hectares) is forest; and 55 percent is classified as "other areas" (FAO production yearbooks). Of the arable lands, 26 percent were being cultivated in the mid-1960s. A small portion (163,000 hectares) is irrigated. High-quality deep, fertile soil is scarce throughout the region.

Since the region is inhabited by ethnic groups that differ markedly in social and cultural traits, there is no one "traditional" way of agriculture. The inhabitants of the north engage almost solely in animal husbandry. In the southern subdesert, Sahel, and northern Sudan zone are the transhumant herdsmen who keep their animals on the subdesert and the northern Sahel during and immediately after the northern rainy season. After the forage produced by the short rainy season there is exhausted, the animals are driven southward to graze on fallow lands and crop residue during the dry season.

During the dry season, animals undergo a period of little growth and, often, of actual weight loss (see Figure 10.2). The combination of genetic traits and poor environmental conditions results in slow maturation, low birth rates, extended nursing time for calves, and high mortality rates. In addition, the herdsmen depend upon milk and meat for most of their food, but the cows produce barely enough milk to support their calves. Hence, taking milk for human consumption further increases calf mortality and lowers herd productivity. The net effect is a significantly less efficient conversion of ecosystem productivity (forage) into meat than is encountered in more modern animal production systems employed in other arid/semiarid parts of the world (such as Argentina, Australia, southwestern United States).

FIGURE 10.2

Hypothesized Seasonal Variability in Weight of Cattle
Raised Under Traditional System

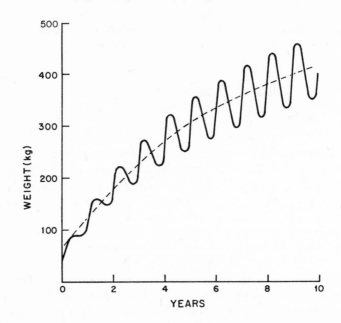

Once animals are mature and sold, they are driven to markets
in the south. This trek may involve several weeks and hundreds of
kilometers and certainly results in significant weight losses that
further reduce the net production realized from the ecosystem.
However, the cost of the resulting meat, in terms of external inputs,
is minimal. Essentially, it results from natural productivity and
poorly compensated human labor.

From the Sahel climatic zone on southward, sedentary farming
is practiced (see Figure 10.3). Most farmers appear to have some
domestic animals such as horses, donkeys, pigs, and chickens. In
the southern woodlands, few cattle are raised because of the prevalence of sleeping sickness (trypanosomiasis).

Three major types of cultivation are practiced; dry land
farming, flood retreat farming, and wadi farming. Most prevalent
is dry land farming, depending upon rainfall for moisture needs.
Flood retreat agriculture involves planting seeds on plains of rivers
as the annual floodwaters recede, where crop growth depends upon
moisture remaining in the soil. Wadi farming is a modified flood
retreat technique practiced in smaller drainage channels.

FIGURE 10.3

Distribution of Agricultural Practices in Climatic Zones

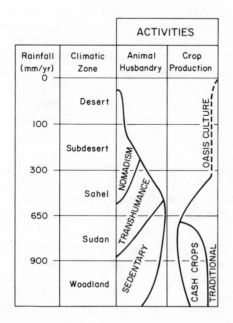

Traditionally, the soils are not tilled; rather, holes are made in the ground and the seed inserted at generally low seeding rates. Limited cultivation is usually done to control weed growth. Labor shortage for this hand cultivation often restricts the area planted. Mixed cropping is customary.

Crop farming depends on human labor and a fallow period for restoration of fertility and moisture and for pest reduction. Generally, no treatment is applied to protect the seed, plant, or stored grain, even though the crops are attacked by many pests. Animal grazing on fallow and harvested fields provides the only fertilizer (manure) returned to the ecosystem.

The disappearance of perennial vegetation in the Sahara, the development of sand seas and expanses of bare rock, as well as desertification in adjacent subdeserts and savannas, are primarily the result of misuse of the ecosystem by man. Such human activities as wood cutting and land clearing as well as overgrazing by domestic animals initiated the desertification process by destroying the native vegetation. The areas were then converted into bare rock and sand dunes by natural weathering processes.

Not only has the long-term misuse of the land resulted in desertification in the more arid zones but it has caused southward shifts of vegetation zones, even in the wetter southern area. Further, in the Sahel and woodland zones, many small streams have changed from perennial to ephemeral flow as a result of the destruction of vegetative cover.

The Sahel and Sudan zones probably received more rain between 1956 and 1965 than at any time in this century. This resulted in increased productivity in both natural vegetation and in field crops. Consequently sedentary farming activities expanded toward the north and everywhere the carrying capacity of the rangelands was increased. Simultaneously, animal health programs were increased and new wells were drilled. The interaction of these factors resulted in a marked increase in animal populations to levels that exceeded the sustainable carrying capacity of the range, even during the little pluvial decade.

Concurrently, human population continued to rise and export crops became an important part of the output, replacing traditional cereal production in more favorable areas. The resulting pressure for increased production decreased fallow time and lowered productivity (production per hectare), even though total production continued to rise as a result of a larger percentage of the land being used for agricultural activities in any given year. Further, the expansion of cultivated lands in the more moist area decreased available grazing lands. Thus, even greater pressure was placed on the exceptional forage productivity of the Sahel. Heavy cutting of trees for firewood near the urban areas contributed to the ecosystem destruction.

By the end of the abnormally high rainfall period, about 1965, the expectations of people had risen to the point that a return to average conditions was considered to be a drought. The combination of reductions in forage from decreasing rainfall and the high animal population often caused extreme overgrazing and even further reduction of forage. Desertification became common, particularly around wells, and on the northern grain fields that were abandoned when the return of normal rainfall conditions failed to provide enough moisture for crop production. Even in the more southerly part of the region, soil erosion became common. Thus both animal and crop productivity decreased throughout the region.

With the beginning of the "drought" (actually just less than average rainfall) in 1969-70, the stage was set for a major crisis. In terms of rainfall alone, the 1969-73 drought was no worse than many and not nearly as extreme as some of those recorded in the past 400 years. However, because of the all-time high numbers of humans and domestic animals, its effect was a catastrophe far exceeding most of those previously recorded. Major crop failures were widespread, as were human and animal starvation. The ecosystem was degraded by native vegetation destruction, desertification, and soil erosion to the point that abandonment for generations may be necessary for natural restoration.

Even before the drought, average agricultural productivity in the region was low, generally only about 20 percent (or less) of world averages and less than 10 percent of those of arid/semiarid agricultural systems of the southwestern United States. Cereals are the major crop; many varieties are grown on about 65 percent of the cultivated land. The 1969 production was about 5 million metric tons or about 500 kilograms/hectare (kg/h) in contrast with world averages of about 2,500 kg/h. Peanuts and cotton occupied about 25 percent of the cultivated area. Small amounts of dates, cowpeas, manioc, yams, sugarcane and tobacco were produced on the remaining 10 percent of the cultivated area.

In 1969 there were 26 million animal units (one animal unit is equivalent to a 450 kg cow and her calf) in the region including cattle, sheep, horses, donkeys, goats, and camels. Even though productivity was low as a result of the high incidence of disease and death losses, livestock production accounted for 15 to 20 percent of gross domestic product (GDP).

Fish production (inland) was about 440,000 metric tons. There were about 42 million chickens in the region and egg production was about 24,000 metric tons. Milk production was more than 1 million metric tons annually. Swine made up a minor component (281,000) of the domestic animal population. Agricultural byproduct (hides and skins, cottonseed) use was not highly developed.

Wood is the principal source of fuel energy in the region, and per capita use is 300 to 500 kg/year. Annual consumption is almost 9 million metric tons.

About 80 to 90 percent of the population is directly employed in agriculture, and nomads make up to 15 percent of that total. Less than 0.1 percent are in salaried agricultural positions.

Although the majority of the herders and farmers do not operate as part of a market economy, this primary (agriculture) sector contributes from 31 to 53 percent of the GDP in the six countries. Farm income is low, and the rural population receives only a small share of national income. On a national basis, agricultural products represent 4 to 20 percent of total imports (emergency food supplies have been imported in recent years), but the value of agricultural exports exceeds that of agricultural inputs. Investment of public funds in agriculture varies from 15 to 40 percent. Much of it is applied to export crops.

Trends in agriculture in the region show increasing land use, with greater increase for cash crops, and downward production in recent years (see Figure 10.4). Livestock numbers increased until 1970 and have decreased since then (see Figure 10.5; note that sheep, goats, and camels remained relatively constant*). Meat production has increased in recent years, probably only because of pressure to reduce herd numbers. Other animal production (milk, poultry, eggs, fish) shows modest to substantial increases in recent years. Wood production increased, largely because of increased fuel demand in urban centers. Population has grown, although outmigration has had some effect. New agricultural education and research institutions and agencies have been established, but their impact to date has been slight. Exports of agricultural products generally increased until 1969 and have declined since then. Imports do not show a consistent pattern of change.

Characterization of the agricultural production system of the Sahel countries was hampered by lack or poor quality of available statistics. Not only were many gaps present in the yearly data but different sources often presented conflicting information.

POTENTIAL FUTURE AGRICULTURAL PRODUCTION

The planning framework created to evaluate alternative agricultural development plans for the Sahel is described below, with examples of its use to determine the results of implementing an arbitrarily chosen alternative strategy for the Sahel. To provide a firm base for the framework, the nature and purpose of long-term development planning were characterized and then some of the major constraints to successful development were identified.

Planning is the essence of management and a vital part of modern life. In developing countries, its aim, generally, is to transform a subsistence economy into a modern one. Good planning must take into account constraints in the region, set priorities, and resolve

----

*Goats and camels are essentially browsers, capable of feeding on the woodier, thornier plants of a rangeland that are not suitable for grazing cattle, sheep, and horses. In general, the poorer rangelands in the region (especially in the north) have higher percentages of browsing animals. Sheep, however, also can use rangeland that cannot support cattle.

FIGURE 10.4

Comparison of Production, Cereals, and
Cash Crops, Sahel Region

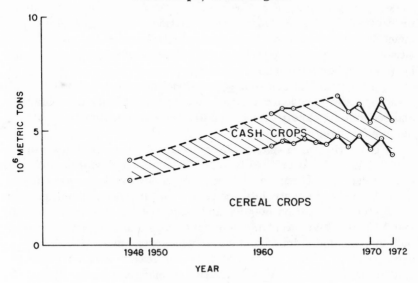

FIGURE 10.5

Livestock in the Sahel Region

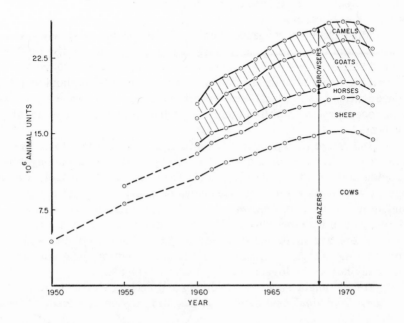

conflicts. It must not only realistically consider the human and economic situation but also adequately evaluate restrictions imposed by available resources.

Systems analysis is an approach that can be extremely useful in developing a plan. It can be used to examine the total agricultural production system, including determination of relevant factors, quantification of relationships, and calculation of effects of following various strategies. It provides insight into what ought to be or can be done and helps determine priorities.

Among the factors limiting potential development are climate, ecology, natural resources, time, energy, traditions and culture, and economics. Their effects usually are more serious in arid or semiarid areas.

Climatic constraints limit agricultural productivity; weather variability can be a critical factor. Drought and pluvial periods will occur with more frequency and severity in arid and semiarid areas.

Ecological constraints are paramount in arid or semiarid areas. Ecosystem destruction is quick and easy, but reconstruction is slow and difficult. Many arid and semiarid areas are overpopulated by both humans and animals and suffer widespread overutilization by grazing and browsing. Moist periods may lead to excessive human and animal populations and cultivation of marginal lands. Rapid ecological degradation then occurs with a return to average or drought conditions.

Natural resources (including soil, water, weather, and climate) not only are the base for agricultural production but also set its upper limits. Realistic evaluation of these parameters is necessary for successful development plans.

Most changes in agricultural development occur slowly. An evaluation of the development of agricultural systems in the western United States shows that a series of laws passed over a 60-year period (providing funds for education and research, regulating land use and conservation, and establishing credit and other assistance for farmers) was necessary to establish the present high-intensity agricultural systems.

Primitive food production systems provide from 5 to 50 food calories for each calorie of energy invested. Industrialized systems provide only about 0.1 to 0.2 calorie for each calorie of fuel. Current energy supply problems focus concern on energy use, but use of wind and animal power, animal manure and green manure crops, and limiting chemical inputs can reduce energy needs significantly.

There are many institutional and attitudinal obstacles to development. Agricultural planning must take account of human needs, but many human factors are exogenous to agriculture.

Development requires financing and resources are usually limited. Technical assistance and food aid may be required. Farmers must receive a fair share of the profit from export crops as well as other economic incentives. Demand for agricultural products is a critical factor in planning.

The ISYALAPS (Integrated Sustained Yield Arid Lands Agricultural Production Systems) planning framework is based upon quantification of the natural resources for agricultural production in a planning area. It utilizes a systems analysis approach that includes the following premises: productivity is different in different ecosystems; can be exploited without ecosystem degradation; and can be increased by technology, management, and other inputs. It is a tool for estimating long-term sustained yield that would result from implementation of various alternatives available for the agricultural production systems of the area. Results are then compared with the existing situation.

The analysis procedure that constitutes the ISYALAPS framework involves a sequence of steps. (The exact number involved depends on the complexity of the planning area.) They can be summarized as follows:

1. Division of the planning area into climatic zones and determination of their area (where sufficient water resources are available, irrigable land is considered as a separate zone): For planning purposes, some form of agricultural production is assumed to be possible in most zones, although in zones such as the desert, the arctic, and the alpine, productivity is generally so low as to be economically unjustified.

2. Definition of four activity* levels for implementation to provide alternatives for decision makers. The activity levels are defined as follows:

---

*A fifth or higher level of activity is recognized as including such capital-intensive, high-energy, and technology input activities as hydroponic, greenhouse growing of tomatoes and similar vegetables in Lebanon, Israel, the United States, and elsewhere; the algae growing projects in Japan; and the dream of cultivating the Sahara with water distilled from the sea. While such activities may be economically feasible in special situations, all appear impracticable for the large arid and semiarid areas available in many developing countries. Even in those countries, such projects might be economically feasible on a small scale under special circumstances (such as supplying fresh vegetables to a remote mining community). However, as part of long-term development, they would result in such a small percentage of the total production that further consideration is not warranted here.

- Level A: Minimum activity with impact, which seeks an ecological balance so that long-term sustained yields are possible. In general, this level simply modifies present activities (by reducing animal numbers and thus grazing intensity, or increasing fallow time) so as to prevent ecological degradation.
- Level B: Extensive management activity, which enlarges the production area. This level requires such inputs as fencing and water development to increase the area available for both grazing and farming.
- Level C: Intensive management activity, which applies technology, management, and some inputs. Animal traction, simple machinery, green manure crops, and composted animal manure, mineral supplements to range animal diets— all would be utilized where feasible.
- Level D: Maximum activity, which uses all available technology to maximize production. Use of tractors, mechanized cultivation and harvesting, chemical fertilizers, pesticides and herbicides, animal feed lots, as is common in Europe and the United States characterizes this level.

Obviously, there are benefits and costs associated with each activity level. Actual monetary expressions of these are not yet available. However Figure 10.6 shows the theoretical effects of activity levels on benefit-cost relationships as they are visualized at the present. Note that as the activity level proceeds from A to D, the cost rises sharply. Further, note that the maximum benefits possible (in terms of agricultural productivity) are so low in dry zones that high levels of activity are not economically feasible:*

3. Selection of an arbitrary agricultural strategy (or strategies): A strategy is defined here as a mix of activity levels for the different segments of the agricultural sector (crops, animal husbandry) in the various climatic zones. Many strategies are possible, but tradeoffs are involved in production factors and impacts. Generally speaking, it is advantageous to use a more intense activity level in a zone of higher rainfall.

4. Allocation of land in each climatic zone to specific agricultural purposes: Lands are classified and allocated according to their most appropriate agricultural use, keeping in mind the constraints of existing uses in the zone. Obviously, some land will not

---

*However, the ISYALAPS framework presented here would permit the evaluation of a plan that would propose the application of activity level D in the driest zone and only activity level A in the wettest zone.

FIGURE 10.6

Theoretical Effect of Activity Level on
Direct Benefit-Cost Relationships
in Three Climatic Zones

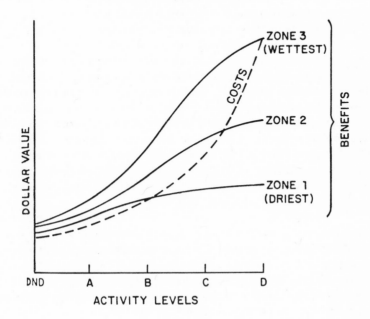

be suitable for either animal or crop production and thus must be
excluded from consideration. Steep mountain slopes, bare rock, sand
dunes, cities, and roads are examples of excluded areas.

    5. Determination of the total potential crop and wood production:
Total production under the arbitrary strategy is calculated. The
process includes selection of a fallow/cultivated land ratio, choice
of crops, and determination of effect of activity level on productivity.
Production is calculated for food crops and for nonfood and wood
crops. Total calculated output is reduced to account for domestic or
draft animal consumption.

    6. Determination of the total potential livestock production:
Livestock production under the arbitrary strategy is calculated by
estimating carrying capacity and assuming production parameters
such as fertility, mortality, and offtake (percent of herd removed
for consumption or sale). Total production is converted to calories
and protein content.

    7. Determination of potential production of milk, poultry, eggs,
and fish: Similar procedures are used to calculate calories and protein

from these sources. Quantities of agricultural byproducts (hides and skins, cottonseed) also are estimated.

8. Summation of total potential agricultural production: Production from all segments of agriculture is combined in terms of calories and grams of protein for food products, and kilograms for nonfood products, for the entire planning area under the selected strategy. Where possible, the latter are converted into monetary values for determination of contribution to gross domestic product (GDP) or other economic indicator.

9. Estimation of human carrying capacity, surpluses, and shortages: Human carrying capacity is calculated after correcting total production for losses in transport and storage. It is determined by an evaluation of the total calories and grams of protein produced in relation to the United Nations World Health Organization standards for minimum daily requirements. The number of people who can be productively employed in agriculture also is estimated. All activity levels, but particularly widespread utilization of activity level D, will require a significant number of people in indirect agricultural activities, including such infrastructure activities as education, extension, transport, storage, and marketing.

10. Comparison with existing situation: Potential production in all categories and carrying capacity are compared with that obtained under the existing agricultural production system. (Data limitations often make such comparison difficult.)

11. Determination of steps necessary for implementation: Implementation of an agricultural development strategy requires action by many groups including local and national governments, the private business sector, individual farmers, and the donor agencies. Specific actions required are a function of the activity level to be implemented. Changes are often needed in policy, legislation, programs, and the indirectly related sociocultural area. Certain inputs, infrastructure, and trained personnel are necessary for the success of a given plan. Finally, time is required for implementation. All these should be considered and estimated as explicitly as possible in any application of the ISYALAPS evaluation framework.

12. Determination of impacts: Implementing any given strategy will have obvious impacts not only on the agricultural sector but also on other aspects of the society. Cost-benefit analysis is used to evaluate quantifiable impacts, but social impacts are approached subjectively and, in final analysis, are judged as to acceptability by the people inhabiting the planning area. Certainly the imposition of unwanted impacts by donor organizations can be avoided.*

---

*However, the decision makers need to be aware that the ever-increasing world population makes the probability of long-term

13. Iteration with alternative strategies: The first trial of the use of the ISYALAPS planning framework will not answer all the questions of development; furthermore, changes over time necessitate frequent revisions. Therefore, as new alternatives become evident, they are tested for impact and acceptability through the same sequence of steps.

14. Matrix for project evaluation: No project proposal can be properly evaluated without the consideration of the interaction of a number of different factors. For completeness of analysis of action programs arising out of any selected alternative strategy being evaluated with the ISYALAPS framework, a four-dimensional matrix is suggested. The dimensions included are (1) geographic (location and climate); (2) social and/or land use arrangements; (3) activity level (an economic dimension); and (4) political. Since it is difficult to conceptualize four dimensions simultaneously, the matrix can be considered as a series of cubes, one for each political dimension (or geographic, and so on). Each cube, then, is made up of a series of subcubes, depending upon the number of divisions deemed necessary to be recognized in each of the dimensions. The matrix thus takes account of geographic variability, social diversity, and political structure, and recognizes financial and other resource limitation. Utilizing this matrix, any proposal (including local projects) that fits the framework can be further evaluated, and priorities among various projects within a given alternative can be set.

15. Evaluation criteria: Proposals for major projects or subprojects within a given alternative can be evaluated only after goals for the agricultural and other sectors of the economy have been set by the government (or peoples) concerned. Guidelines for measuring the acceptability of projects then can be set up. Obviously, questions should be asked concerning possible conflicts with goals, past success of similar projects in the area or elsewhere, financial and other demands, costs, benefits, need for inputs and infrastructure, measures of project success, time framework, and restraints to project success.

The Sahel countries of sub-Saharan West Africa previously discussed (Chad, Mali, Mauritania, Niger, Senegal, and Upper Volta) were chosen as the planning area for analysis. The long-term development alternative arbitrarily selected for evaluation with the ISYALAPS framework was an integrated strategy that combines

---

support of any ecologically inefficient (in terms of food production) social system highly improbable.

various activity levels for the segments of the agricultural sector.
It emphasizes effective natural resources management, takes advantage of all possible productivity, and can be implemented by reasonable means (in terms of donor as well as recipient capability). Activity levels A and B are proposed for the drier climate zones (desert, subdesert, and Sahel) and activity levels C and D in the wetter zones (Sudan, woodland, and irrigated). A livestock production system possible under this integrated strategy is shown in Figure 10.7.

The following premises provided a foundation for the evaluation example: (1) the region will remain predominantly agricultural; (2) energy will be available for critical operations such as land preparation; (3) government stability will increase; (4) migration to urban centers will continue; and (5) funds will be available for agricultural projects.

The sequence of steps summarized in the previous section was followed in applying the ISYALAPS planning framework to the Sahel region. (Details of the mathematical analysis are given in the final report of the MIT Sahel-Sudan project, mentioned at the beginning of this chapter.)

Land was allocated to crop, livestock, and wood production in the five defined climatic zones and an irrigated zone on the basis of available knowledge of land use in the region. An urban zone was included for milk, poultry and eggs, and fish production.

Crop and wood productivity factors were based on those found in similar climatic zones in other parts of the world. The potential production of each crop was then calculated for the region.

Livestock and other animal production factors were similarly determined, and potential production from these segments was calculated. Figure 10.8 shows the estimated effect of activity levels on livestock carrying capacity.

The total potential agricultural production of the Sahel region under the integrated strategy was then summarized in calories and grams protein of food, and kilograms of nonfood crops and wood. Totals were corrected for assumed storage and transit losses. Potential human carrying capacity was then computed on the basis of available food and employment opportunity in agriculture.

COMPARISON OF POTENTIAL AND EXISTING PRODUCTION

The potential production in the Sahel region was compared with existing production in terms of calories, which were determined to be the limiting factor. The integrated strategy used in this application

FIGURE 10.7

Schematic of Possible Livestock Production System

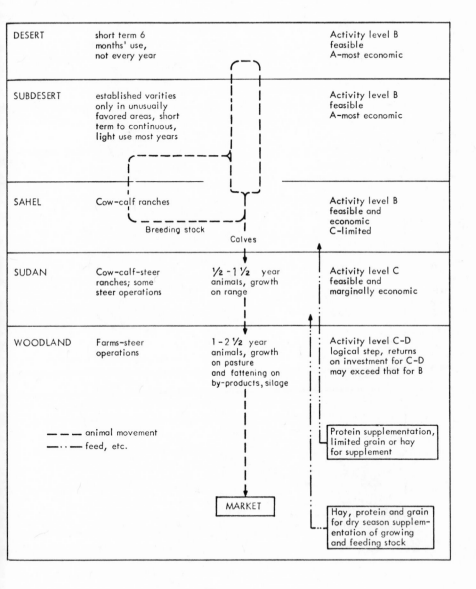

DESERT	short term 6 months' use, not every year		Activity level B feasible A-most economic
SUBDESERT	established varities only in unusually favored areas, short term to continuous, light use most years		Activity level B feasible A-most economic
SAHEL	Cow-calf ranches Breeding stock	Calves	Activity level B feasible and economic C-limited
SUDAN	Cow-calf-steer ranches; some steer operations	½ - 1 ½ year animals, growth on range	Activity level C feasible and marginally economic
WOODLAND	Farms-steer operations	1 - 2 ½ year animals, growth on pasture and fattening on by-products, silage	Activity level C-D logical step, returns on investment for C-D may exceed that for B

— — — animal movement
—··— feed, etc.

Protein supplementation, limited grain or hay for supplement

MARKET

Hay, protein and grain for dry season supplem- entation of growing and feeding stock

FIGURE 10.8

Estimated Livestock Carrying Capacity for Different Activity Levels

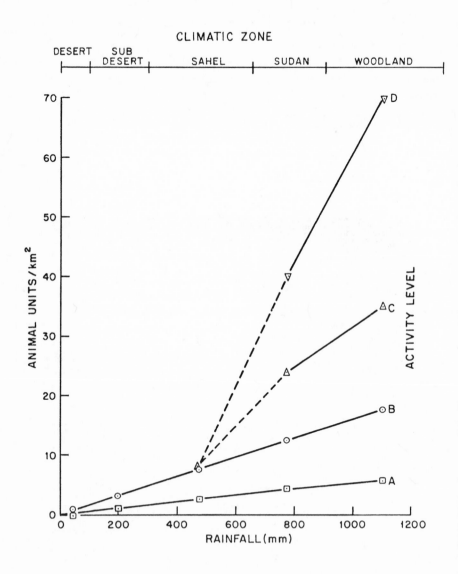

of the ISYALAPS planning framework shows the potential to increase calorie production in an average year by 30 percent.

Cash and export crop (largely peanuts and cotton) production also were compared. The integrated strategy has the potential to increase exports by more than 400 percent in the region. Potential wood production under this strategy is 140 percent greater than existing production in the region.

Comparison of human carrying capacity shows that the potential production of the integrated strategy would support a population of about 33 million in the six-country region, which is 30 percent larger than the existing population. However, population directly employable in the improved agricultural activities is about 60 percent less than the estimated population in agriculture at present. Infrastructure activities as previously described, and agricultural related industries, will necessarily absorb some of the surplus.

CONCLUSIONS

ISYALAPS is a framework for planning (not a plan), and although the study is incomplete in that much remains to be done (1) to quantify the current status and (2) to finalize values for long-term sustained yield using the activity level concept in the Sahel (or other countries), a number of conclusions can be drawn from the study and applying the ISYALAPS framework to evaluate an arbitrarily chosen agricultural strategy for the region. These include:

• The current drought is not permanent and no major climatic change has occurred in the recent past, nor is there any indication that such a change will occur in the near future. What will occur is a continuation of major multiannual variations from the mean, resulting in drought periods as well as pluvial periods.

• The existing agricultural production system is part of a vicious circle including ever-increasing human population and limited natural resources (see Figure 10.9). Agriculture has lagged behind other developments in the region and would have become incapable of supplying the nutritional needs of people in the near future even without the recent drought. Operations of this system over the past decade, but particularly during the drought, have contributed directly to the problems of desertification, reduced productivity (loss of fertility), soil erosion, and deforestation. Pressures of population and the export-oriented economy resulted in increasing use of marginal lands for food production. Animal numbers increased for the same reasons but also for lack of other savings opportunity. Both human and animal numbers were thus far beyond the carrying capacity of the region in the years immediately preceding the drought. With

FIGURE 10.9

Population-Agricultural Production-Natural
Resources Vicious Circle

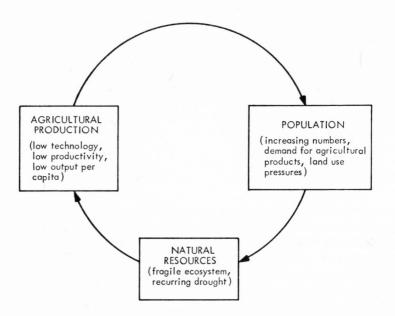

the ecosystem so badly out of balance, the consequences of drought
were inevitable. The social costs of continuing the existing agricultural production system are staggering, with recurring and
increasingly severe famine, starvation, and need for relocation of
distressed people and animals. Monetary costs also are high in
terms of requirements for assistance, massive food relief, and lost
productivity.

● Shortcomings of the available agricultural production data
make comparisons of existing and potential production questionable.
The area reported as being farmed is not really well known. More
exact data would permit accurate determination of fallow/cultivated
land ratios being used. The information regarding the population
engaged in various agricultural pursuits was extremely uncertain.
No data were found concerning the number of fishermen in most
countries nor the number of woodcutters. A significant improvement
in the data base must accompany agricultural development planning.

● Much sensationalism has accompanied the reporting of the
plight of the Sahel. Someone's unsubstantiated opinion is overheard

and picked up by a journalist. The statement then appears in print
and thereby automatically gains authenticity. The following items are
in this "no evidence" category:

1. "Vast reservoirs of easily available groundwater underlie
the region just waiting to be tapped for irrigation." Although isolated
areas with some groundwater potential occur in the region, and
consolidated rock aquifers occupy much of the subsurface, there is
no evidence of aquifers with potential for extensive irrigated agriculture development.

2. "Properly managed, the Sahel region can be a breadbasket
supplying food for half of Africa." Agricultural production from the
region can be increased, but it is extremely unlikely that production
for export, even under the best management, will increase significantly in the next few decades.

3. "The Sahara Desert is encroaching on the Sahel at a rate up
to 30 miles a year." Desertification is a process that occurs in place
as a result of misuse of land, not as the advance of an existing desert.

4. "There is no way, short of a major social upheaval, that the
nomads will consent to reduce their herds." Nomads are wise in the
ways of the desert and have evolved a system that permits them to
survive in the face of adversity, but they respond to incentives, and
as a result of the drought have indicated their willingness to change.

The region can be made more productive than it is or has been.
Application of the ISYALAPS planning framework with an arbitrarily
chosen integrated agricultural strategy demonstrates this potential.
The use of the ISYALAPS framework demands the acceptance of the
philosophy of long-term sustained yield from agriculture in a realistic
economic setting, based on the concept of living within the limits of
the natural resources. This systems analysis approach to natural
resources utilization as a basis for agricultural development planning
provides a way of organizing the agricultural sector.

Moreover the ISYALAPS framework evaluates the resources
primarily in terms of improving the quality of life of the rural poor.
The human carrying capacity factors are based on a conviction of
need to provide agricultural workers with a viable production unit.
Division of natural resources based solely on population ignores the
fact that not everyone can be a good farmer. If income per capita
is to be increased, a decline in numbers of workers is inevitable.
(Labor-intensive practices in the wetter zones may have some
modifying effect.)

Control of land use in the region and changes in the social
system will be required, but progress can be made with low-level
(and low-capital) technology. Most of the region is suited for livestock

grazing, but more intensive systems have potential in the wetter
zones. Self-sufficiency in food not only for the current population
but also for the levels predicted for the year 2000 can be realized,
and production for export also can be increased. The quality of life
for the rural population can be markedly improved, but to do this the
number of people employed directly in agriculture will be reduced.
Part of the displaced population will be assimilated in infrastructure
occupations.

A strategy of applying constant activity level B to all segments of
the agricultural sector in all climatic zones will not support the
existing population, however; much of agriculture in the region is
operating above this level and must continue to do so unless population
is reduced. Activity level A would support even fewer people, but the
entire agricultural sector must attain at least this level if long-term
sustained yield is to be achieved.

In order to break the population-agricultural production-natural
resources vicious circle, broadly conceived and adequately implemented programs will be required. Governmental emphasis on
agriculture must be increased, and incentives must be provided to
induce the herders and farmers to change.

Regional cooperation is essential. Livestock control cannot
achieve the desired reduction in overgrazing if implemented in only
one country because of movements of animals across unpatrolled
borders. The major river systems of the region lie in several
countries; water resources development thus requires international
agreements. The coastal nations to the south provide an outlet for
surplus production that must be included in regional planning.

Time will be required for implementing any long-term development strategy, but action must be taken immediately in the Sahel
region to prevent further ecological deterioration. Time is required
for range and land recovery, and some preliminary steps must be
taken now to prepare for later implementation of other necessary
actions.

SOURCES

This is not an exhaustive bibliography of either agricultural
development or West Africa; both are beyond the scope of this
chapter. Listed are quoted sources or those considered of major
importance.

Africa South of the Sahara. 3rd ed. London: Europa Publications,
    1973 (pp. xxix, 1163).

Cocheme, J., and P. Franquin. An Agroclimatology Survey of a
    Semiarid Area in Africa South of the Sahara. World Meteoro-
    logical Organization, 1967 (Technical Note 86: XV, 136).

Dalby, D., and R.J. Harrison Church, eds. Drought in Africa:
    Report of the 1973 Symposium. London: Centre for African
    Studies, University of London, 1973 (pp. 1-124).

Dregne, H.E., ed. Arid Lands in Transition. Publication 90,
    Washington, D.C.: American Association for Advancement of
    Science, 1970 (pp. xiii, 524).

Griffith, J.F. Climates in Africa, vol. 10, World Survey of
    Climatology. Amsterdam: Elsevier, 1972.

Janzen, D.H. "Tropical Agroecosystems," Science, 182 (1973):
    1212-19.

McDowell, R.E. Improvement of Livestock Production in Warm
    Climates. San Francisco: W.H. Freeman, 1972.

Rattray, J.M. "The Grass Cover of Africa," FAO Agricultural
    Studies, no. 49: v, 168.

Talbot, L.M. "Ecological Consequences of Rangeland Development
    in Masailand, East Africa." In M.T. Farvar and J.P. Milton,
    eds., The Careless Technology. Garden City, N.Y.: Natural
    History Press, 1972 (pp. 694-711).

Thomas, M.F., and G. W. Whittington. Environment and Land Use
    in Africa. London: Methuen, 1969 (pp. xi, 554).

CHAPTER

11

THE MANAGEMENT
OF DESERT
GRAZING SYSTEMS
Brien E. Norton

Pasture productivity in temperate regions has been marked by progressive improvement over the last few centuries through research developments in plant breeding, species introduction, fertilizer usage, and intensive management practices. In high-rainfall areas of the tropics, a comparable process of more recent origin is promoting the potential of tropical pastures, matched by the "green revolution" in rice and other grains on agricultural land.

By comparison, the arid and semiarid rangelands of the world lie in a state of neglect. Signs of overgrazing and mismanagement are common in desert regions: degradation of the natural forage resource, invasion and sometimes dominance by undesirable species, erosion, and poverty. Where some improvement has been achieved, as in parts of the cool desert in North America and the Rajasthan desert in India, it is through the relatively expensive establishment of introduced grasses on land recovering from a history of past abuse rather than by an attempt to increase the productivity of the indigenous vegetation. One or more of the following generalizations apply to these cases of recovery: The land is in a large measure under government control; there is strong economic motivation to market livestock or its products or both; the inhabitants are sedentary. None of these conditions pertains to desert range (grazing land with few or no fences) in the Sahel, where management is performed by nomadic peoples who do not depend for their livelihood on market connections outside their grazing grounds and are inclined to be independent of government influence. The exception to this independence is in a crisis situation such as the recent decimation of rangeland herds by drought, when nomadic peoples were forced to accept government aid handouts in order to survive.

PROBLEMS OF RANGE IMPROVEMENT

In view of the problems associated with improvement of the
Sahelian rangeland, it is not surprising that so little has been accomplished. Difficulties occur in just about every component of the
system: climate, plant production, livestock, and the social and
cultural values of the nomadic herdsmen. Each difficulty increases
the risk of failure and reduces the chance of a return on an improvement investment.

As average rainfall decreases, variability of precipitation
rises (Raikes 1969). For arid and semiarid regions, this variability
can be substantial (Noy-Meir 1973). At Saint-Louis in Senegal, where
average precipitation is 370 mm per year, the recorded range is
from 144 mm to 691 mm annual rainfall (Bille 1974). If the change
from very low to very high rainfall years always followed a gradual
progression, the uncertainty would be reduced and an appropriate
management strategy could ameliorate the problem of high variability.
Even though climatologists can recognize long-term trends using
five-year moving averages (Winstanley 1973), extremes of precipitation levels can still occur in consecutive years. On a research site of
the International Biological Program in the Mohave Desert of North
America there was a fourfold increase in precipitation from 1972 to
1973.

It is not the rainfall that the range manager is utilizing but
rather the annual production of plant material (hereafter referred to
as primary production and expressed in dry weight of plant material
per unit area), whose magnitude is dependent on the amount of available soil moisture. More particularly, the palatable fraction of the
primary productivity is the basic resource for livestock production.
In arid rangeland systems, this palatable fraction includes annual
and perennial grasses, forbs and the shoots of shrubs, and will be
referred to as available forage. The uncertainty of climate from
one year to the next is compounded by even more erratic fluctuations
in primary production. At the Mohave Desert research site mentioned
above, plant production increased sevenfold with the fourfold rise in
precipitation. High variability of rainfall and higher variability of the
vegetation response to rainfall are two characteristic features of dry
rangelands that must be taken into account in any management scheme.
The picture is, however, even more bleak, for two reasons. The
beginning of the wet season for a year of low rainfall is usually delayed
(Swift 1974), which increases grazing pressure and imposes greater
stress on the vegetation during the latter part of the dry season than
would normally occur. The livestock already debilitated by scarce
forage suffer longer, and since the commencement of calving coincides

with the wet season, mortality of livestock could increase dramatically. Second, with less input to replenish soil moisture on which shrubs depend in the dry season following rains, leaves are less persistent on the new shoots (Poupon and Bille 1974). The rangeland shrubs constitute an important forage resource during the dry season when herbaceous plants have long since withered into hay of low nutrient value, so the early leaf fall accentuates plant and animal stress at this critical time. These two consequences of a drought year, one preceding and one following the wet season, reduce the usefulness of whatever forage production does occur, and this effectively increases the variability of the resource even further.

The measure of the value of a range forage resource is in terms of the sustained livestock production that can be harvested from the rangeland. The economic return on an investment to improve that resource is the value of the increase in livestock production generated by the improvement. The zebu-type cattle that one finds in the Sahel have become adapted through centuries of breeding and natural selection in the harsh physical environment of the sub-Saharan rangeland. They have more stamina for traveling long distances in the spring heat to find feed and return for water than European breeds. They also have greater resistance to the diseases and parasites of the dry tropics. The superiority they have acquired in survival in the Sahel must be weighed, however, against their inherent growth rate and fertility in the context of our discussion. In these areas they fall behind breeds such as the Hereford, and their lower capacity for production reduces the benefit of range improvement compared to, say, range improvement in North America, where the environment is less severe and European breeds can thrive.

Although the zebu stock can live in the Sahel and are resistant to disease and parasites, they still suffer from these health problems and production is consequently affected. Isolation of the Sahelian rangelands from markets and the paucity of transport facilities create another set of difficulties. Animals lose condition, some die, in the process of bringing the product to market, which could eliminate the profit that stood on the hoof on the home range. Road and/or rail construction and provision of transport vehicles would seem a worthwhile contribution by foreign aid investment, since livestock comprises the principal export commodity of the Sahelian countries (Swift 1973).

Cattle are not the only domesticated animals in the nomadic herds. They share the available forage with sheep, camels, and goats. This herd diversification has some advantages. The diet preferences differ; while cattle and sheep graze grasses, the goats concentrate on shrubs, and camels select from both forms of forage. This means that the full spectrum of feed types is utilized. The breeding seasons are staggered so that the young do not all arrive at once. The goats tend to wander near the campsites, sheep and cattle forage farther afield, and camels can roam even farther due to their less frequent need for water. In plain range management concepts applied for economic gain, these different classes of livestock are competitors for limited forage. In a cattle production enterprise, the sheep and goats would be removed from the system for the benefit of the cow. In the Sahel, however, this brings us into conflict with the traditional customs and way of life of the nomads. In a dry time, goats give milk long after the cows have ceased production, and milk is a staple in the nomads' diet. The Tuareg enjoy a sharing and exchange of livestock between herdsmen, for which herd diversity is an essential component (Swift 1973). In an unpredictable environment, recovery from devastating drought years is made easier for the nomads if they are not entirely dependent on one type of livestock. The hardier goats and camels will be the first to build up herd size, and in a subsistence pastoral economy having herds means everything.

Perhaps the principal sociological difficulty associated with manipulating the range for improved production is the attitude of the nomads to the sale of cattle on the one hand and the maintenance of herd size on the other. The herds are kept chiefly for subsistence. Prestige derived from large numbers probably plays a part in the management strategy, and animals are used for bride price and to purchase grain and pay taxes. Apart from servicing basic needs, the nomads are on the whole reluctant to part with their livestock. Essentially, therefore, the herds are managed so as to maintain the largest number possible. This approach provides some insurance against destitution by drought since, like herd diversity, it increases the chance of some livestock surviving and facilitates recovery. To the nomad, it makes good sense, and it has worked for thousands of years. For the national economy of the Sahelian countries, it is a stumbling block to realizing the market potential and export earnings from the rangelands. To a representative from an international donor agency with a few charitable millions to dispense for development programs, it is an immense frustration. A dream to improve that vast resource of livestock is easily shattered by the problem of changing the traditional habits of the herdsmen.

ECOLOGY OF DROUGHT

There is an important corollary of the maxim to keep herd numbers as high as possible. It follows that the only limitations on the amount of forage consumed each year are the ability of the livestock to survive and breed and the availability of water. In the past—that is, before Western aid and development entered the picture about sixty years ago—herd size was kept in check by a number of different factors. Poor health and nutrition of the human population, coupled with occasional wars between tribes and factions, served to restrict the growth of the nomadic tribes and, consequently, to influence the number of animals that could be herded. Livestock diseases such as rinderpest and aggravation or death by parasites helped prevent livestock numbers from increasing. Availability of water in the dry season was a further check to growth of herd size; and of course availability of forage, especially in dry years, contributed to the battery of restraints. Natural limitations of water and feed exercized a natural culling of the herds during each dry season and kept the grazing animals and vegetation in some kind of balance. Annual rainfall variation, shifts in climatic trends and disease epidemics would all cause oscillations within that balance, but the amplitude of the oscillations was dampened by the multiplicity of controls. During the last sixty years, all but one of those controls has been largely removed and the amplitude of the oscillations magnified. Medical care and veterinary care have reduced the impact of disease and parasites and increased survival and growth rates of the human and animal populations. In the last forty years, the animal population has doubled and the human population of the Sahel increased by one-third, according to one source (Wade 1974). The drilling of hundreds, if not thousands, of new bore holes, and the conversion of temporary water sources into permanent ones, has substantially alleviated the limitation of water on survival. The only factor left untouched is the vegetation, and accordingly the forage resource alone now carries the burden for controlling livestock numbers, and partly determines the size of nomadic populations dependent on those livestock.

In the recent drought, cattle had ample water; they were dying from starvation, not thirst (Sterling 1974). The forage resource was close to exhaustion. This explanation for the drought disaster is made with a rather coarse focus. There were other contributing factors. In recent decades, migration to towns and cities from rural areas has been apparent. In addition, the sedentary segment of the population has been increasing at a faster rate than the nomadic peoples, and the area sown to crops on which the settlements depend has expanded. The spread of agriculture has been at the expense of grazing land, which has had its greatest impact on the nomads in the southern part of the Sahel in areas to which the transhumant wanderers returned to wait out the latter part of the dry season.

The traditional symbiotic relationship between the nomadic livestock and the crops, by which the cattle grazed the stubble in the dry season and fertilized the fields with their excrement, has been breaking down due to the introduction of cash crops such as cotton, which are harvested late. A natural antagonism between the nomadic and agrarian peoples, who generally belong to different tribes, has not been helpful, especially since most government offices are held by members of the sedentary tribes. The overall effect has been to force the nomads to graze their stock farther north where feed is more limiting, and the late dry season stress has been correspondingly exacerbated. When the series of drought years hit them, the nomads had little room to maneuver. There is no attempt here to catalogue all the causative factors, but one more is worth noting. The last few decades when aid and development in health care and water provision were most intense also was a period of generally above-average precipitation (Winstanley 1973). This favorable climatic regime permitted livestock numbers to rise to exceptionally high levels so that the drought, when it came, was all the more severe.

The drought period in the Sahel was relieved somewhat by better rains in 1974, and this trend will hopefully continue. The loss in terms of human lives and livestock is difficult to estimate. Censuses prior to the drought were neither up to date nor accurate for the northern, drier regions of the Sahel, which took the brunt of the impact. We do know, however, that herd sizes have been considerably reduced.

On the basis of what has been said so far, it is possible to envisage the future course of events. Livestock will gradually increase and the rangeland will be repopulated by nomadic tribesmen. After a time, the interval depending on the favorability of climate, the herds will reach the carrying capacity of the range. But livestock growth will not stop there; numbers will increase beyond carrying capacity and animal nutrition will decline. At this point, the available feed will fall short of requirements for survival and the livestock population will crash. This cycle will repeat itself whether or not the rains fail. The role of climate will be to prolong the period of population growth if it remains favorable and to hasten the collapse if drought years return. Aid for the nomads in the form of grain will reduce the human population losses but it will not save the herds. There is an apparent inevitability to this scenario. Repeated disasters could be averted if only the increase in livestock could be controlled, but that solution could involve some cultural adjustment on the part of the nomads.

A SAHELIAN APPROACH TO MANAGEMENT

In addition to pursuing opportunities for an attitudinal change by the nomads, ways of improving our information base and understanding of the range community should be explored. Successful range management plans have been implemented on fenced ranches in the Sahel. The greater challenge is to devise a management strategy for the nomadic range—and try it.

The first step is to set aside conventional ideas pertaining to rangeland management as practiced in Western countries, for the time being at least. The concept of "carrying capacity" as used in the United States can be dangerous when translated to the Sahel and utilized in government documents of donor and recipient countries. It can be interpreted as a fixed density of livestock that the range is capable of supporting and, herein lies the danger, therefore should support. For a region whose primary production can vary so much from year to year, and with the wide separation of extremes exhibited in arid and semiarid systems, carrying capacity is year-specific. As presently managed, it is not feasible to adjust livestock numbers in the Sahel to such a variable value.

In the United States, which developed the science of range management over the last fifty years, carrying capacity is calculated by a standard procedure (Stoddart, Smith, and Box 1975). First, the current condition of the range is evaluated in terms of the composition of desirable forage plants relative to a potential, which is the ideal, or climax, plant community for a particular site. In scoring for range condition, the health or vigor of the forage species is taken into account, along with the presence and vigor of invading weedy species. An assessment is then made of the trend of the range, which is a measure of evidence of deterioration or improvement. Available forage for a season of use is then determined, and finally the range manager estimates the fraction of forage that could be utilized without impairing, or perhaps even improving, the range condition and its trend. For a grassland in good condition, this fraction is usually 50 percent. This information is obtained prior to the introduction of livestock for a grazing season and is used as a basis for calculating stocking rate for the season. With several years' experience, the manager can identify the carrying capacity of his range. In practice, this procedure requires regular evaluation and inventory of the range plant communities on land management units defined by soil type and topography—range sites. Forage production on a site will vary from year to year in response to rainfall patterns. By establishing carrying capacity below the level of optimum utilization during a season of high forage production, the range manager is less vulnerable to severe reductions in herd size or the risk of overgrazing caused by low forage production in a drought year. Marketing opportunities and the establishment of feed reserves provide additional flexibility to accommodate annual variations in range forage production.

As it stands, this approach is not suited to the Sahel. There is a lack of trained field personnel to perform the necessary evaluation and assessment. The range site land unit is too detailed for use in the Sahel, where grazing is conducted on a more extensive scale, and in any case, taking the initial inventory would present a formidable task. But most important, the Sahelian rangeland has been thoroughly grazed for centuries and there is no way of knowing the nature of the ungrazed potential, which is used as a yardstick in the evaluation of range condition. Even postulating a hypothetical potential would involve a great deal of guesswork.

There is another argument against the direct application of American methods to the Sahelian rangeland. Although the range assessment procedure is employed for both high- and low-rainfall regions in the United States, in the Great Basin Desert (which is the most important arid grazing area) grazing occurs predominantly in the winter months when the vegetation is dormant. During the summer months, the stock is moved to mountain pastures. Research at the Desert Experiment Range in southern Utah has demonstrated that when grazing is extended into the spring growing season there is a tendency for the forage resource to be degraded, both by lower production and by the invasion of undesirable species (Holmgren and Hutchings 1972). In the Sahel the combination of grazing and plant growth cannot be avoided, which would suggest that the influence of livestock would be more damaging there than under the Great Basin grazing system. This effect is mitigated, however, by the preference of livestock during the wet growing season for the abundant annual grasses. The annuals can withstand intensive grazing and still set sufficient seed for the next year's crop; meanwhile, the perennial grasses and shrubs remain relatively unmolested during this period.

There is no doubt that the American range assessment methods are ideal for management of grazing lands in the United States. For more tropical latitudes characterized by monsoon or summer rainfall, however, there is a need for modification. Australian scientists are currently debating the most appropriate system for management of their arid and semiarid rangelands (for example, Graetz 1974), which bear a closer resemblance to the Sahel than the North American deserts. As with the Sahel, vague or imprecise information on the nature of the ungrazed climax community is inhibiting direct application of the American system in Australia.

SOME SUGGESTIONS FOR ACTIVITY

By constructing exclosures in the Sahelian rangeland and monitoring vegetation changes under protection from grazing,

successional development toward a climax community could be
described. One might argue that the climax thus produced in southern,
scrub regions of the Sahel would be of lower value for grazing than
the present vegetation, as a result of the long period over which the
livestock and plant communities have been interacting. Nevertheless,
it would take so many years to define the successional steps, taking
normal annual variation in production into consideration, that for now
this would be an academic rather than practical endeavor. More
urgently, work is needed to improve estimates of annual forage
production. For the herbaceous annual plants this is not difficult;
harvest techniques can be used readily in the field for annual species.
Provided moisture and nutrients are not limiting, their growth is
similar to an agricultural crop such as wheat (de Wit 1975). With
information on the soil moisture characteristics, climate and soil
chemistry, Penning de Vries and Van Heemst (1975) are working on
a predictive model for annual herbs in the Sahel based on tests conducted in the Negev (Israel). As was pointed out earlier, however,
for the months of the year when annuals are present there is either
a surplus of feed or else the forage limitation is insignificant compared with low availability of dry season forage (Peyre de Fabregues
1975).

Assessing production of perennial species, especially shrubs,
in order to calculate stocking rate for the dry season is the critical
task for range research. Breman (1975) has made an attempt in this
direction, but his estimates suffer from lack of shrub data input.
There seems to be no shortcut to measuring primary production of
shrubs. The International Biological Program has explored several
techniques (harvest and weighing; dimensional analysis of volume by
weight; shoot elongation) that are all laborious and time consuming.
Understanding the contribution by shrubs to total forage production
and livestock diets will provide a sound base for developing a range
management strategy.

With livestock herds at low levels, the nomads reduced in
number and demoralized by their suffering and losses during the
drought, there is an opportunity for cautious encroachment into their
domain—territorial domain and the domain of responsibility for
husbandry of the range. Perhaps at last areas could be set aside to
be rested from grazing for a year or two to allow the vegetation to
recover, roots to grow deeper, soil seed reserves to be replenished,
some litter to accumulate, the soil to be stabilized a little. Perhaps
at last the fires that consume half the forage at the end of each year
could be prevented, in some areas, and the hay eaten or returned to
enrich the soil. Perhaps a pattern of influence can be established
with the nomads based on demonstration of range preservation techniques and results—a pattern of influence that rewards herdsmen who
control their herd size.

With the herds now thinly distributed, perhaps some permanent bore holes could be temporarily sealed off before higher livestock densities make access imperative to the herdsmen, and a chance is lost until the next devastating drought comes along.

SOURCES

Bille, J.C. 1974."1972, Annee seche au Sahel." La Terre et la Vie, no. 1, pp. 5-20.

Breman, H. 1975. "La capacite de charge des paturages Maliens." Paper presented at the International Livestock Center for Africa (ILCA) Seminar on Evaluation and Mapping of Tropical African Rangelands, Bamako, Mali, March 3-8. 13 pp.

Graetz, D. 1974. "Range Assessment in Australia: Some Thoughts Thereon." Range Assessment Newsletter, no. 74/2, pp. 7-12.

Holmgren, R.C., and S.S. Hutchings. 1972. "Salt Desert Shrub Response to Grazing Use. In Wildland Shrubs—Their Biology and Utilization. USDA Forestry Service Gen. Tech. Rep. INT-1.

Noy-Meir, I. 1973. "Desert Ecosystems: Environment and Producers." Annual Review of Ecology and Systematics 4, pp. 25-51.

Penning de Vries, F.W.T., and H.D.J. Van Heemst. 1975. "Potential Primary Production of Unirrigated Land in the Sahel. Paper presented at ILCA Seminar on Evaluation and Mapping of Tropical African Rangelands, Bamako, Mali, March 3-8. 9 pp.

Peyre de Fabregues, B. 1975. "Problems Posed by the Evaluation of the Browse Potential of the Sahel Zone." Paper presented at ILCA Seminar on Evaluation and Mapping of Tropical African Rangelands, Bamako, Mali, March 3-8. 9 pp.

Poupon, H., and J.C. Bille. 1974. "Influences de la secheresse sur la strate ligneuse." La Terre et la Vie 28, no. 1, pp. 49-75.

Raikes, R.L. 1969. "Formation of Deserts of the Near East and North Africa: Climatic, Tectonic, Biotic and Human Factors." In W.G. McGinnies and B.J. Goldman, eds., Arid Lands in Perspective. Tucson: University of Arizona Press.

Sterling, C. 1974. "The Making of the Sub-Saharan Wasteland." The Atlantic 233, pp. 98-105.

Stoddart, L.A.; A.D. Smith; and T.W. Box. 1975. Range Management. 3rd ed. New York: McGraw-Hill.

Swift, J. 1973. "Disaster and a Sahelian Nomad Economy." In D. Dalby and R. J. Harrison Church, eds., Drought in Africa. London: Centre for African Studies.

Swift, J. 1974. "Pastoral Nomadism as a Form of Land-Use; the Tuareg of the Adrar n Iforas (Mali)." International African Institute Seminar on Pastoral Nomadism in Africa, Niamey, December 1972.

Wade, N. 1974. "Sahelian Drought: No Victory for Western Aid." Science 185, pp. 234-37.

Winstanley, D. 1973. "Rainfall Patterns and General Atmospheric Circulation." Nature 245, pp. 190-94.

de Wit, C.T. 1975. "Model Studies on Actual and Potential Herbage Production in Arid Regions." Paper presented at ILCA Seminar on Evaluation and Mapping of Tropical African Rangelands, Bamako, Mali, March 3-8. 6 pp.

12

ECOLOGICAL MANAGEMENT
OF ARID GRAZING
LANDS ECOSYSTEMS
H. N. Le Houérou

INTRODUCTION

Several workshops, seminars, meetings and conferences on arid lands and rangeland problems were held during the course of the past few months. Many of these meetings were supported by the United Nations Environment Program (UNEP). Let us note some of them:

1. Regional Meeting on Integrated Ecological Research and Training Needs in the Sahelian Regions, UNESCO (MAB 3)/UNEP, Niamey, Niger, March 11-15, 1974, Report: MAB No. 18.
2. Man and the Biosphere Project No. 3, International Working Group, UNESCO, Hurley, U.K., July 2-5, 1974,Report: MAB No. 25.
3. Expert Consultation on the Ecological Management of Arid and Semi-Arid Rangelands in Africa and the Near East (EMASAR) FAO/UNEP, Rome, May 27-31, 1974.
4. First Latino-American Arid Zone Conference. UNEP/IADIZA, Mendoza, Argentina, November 11-16, 1974.
5. EMASAR Conference, FAO/UNEP, Rome, February 3-8, 1975.

Paper presented by the author, as Senior Officer-in-Charge of the Grasslands and Pasture Group of the FAO, to the Regional Meeting on Ecological Guidelines for the Use of Natural Resources in the Middle East and South West Asia (Persepolis, Iran), May 24-30, 1975. This conference was sponsored by the International Union for the Conservation of Nature (Morjes, Switzerland).

6. Obstacles to Development in Arid and Semiarid Zones, UNESCO/ ECOSOC, Paris, January 30-February 5, 1975.
7. Regional Conference on Dedesertization, UNEP/Iranian Government, Teheran, February 28-March 6, 1975.
8. International Seminar on Evaluation and Mapping of Tropical African Rangelands, International Livestock Centre for Africa (ILCA), Bamako, Mali, March 3-8, 1975.
9. Ad Hoc Inter-Agency Meeting on Arid Zones, FAO, Rome, March 10-11, 1975.
10. Regional Meeting on the Formulation of a Cooperative Program on Research, Training and Management of Grazing Lands in North West Africa, FAO/UNESCO/UNEP, Sfax, Tunisia, April 3-12, 1975.

These are the meetings in which I have personally participated (except for 9). There may have been more, considering this one is only the eleventh within 14 months dealing with similar or closely related topics. In this paper I shall attempt to report on the main findings of these meetings and their relevance to the region we are concerned with. I shall deal with the subject in a general way without referring particularly to any specific meeting, unless expressly stated.

CHANGE IN LAND USE PATTERNS, DYNAMICS OF VEGETATION AND ECOSYSTEMS

Range depletion

It is unanimously recognized that Rangelands are being misused by overstocking, clearing for cultivation, and burning and removal of woody species for firewood, charcoal, or distillation. This results in:

1. Reduction in plant cover and biomass, mainly perennials, thus limiting carrying capacity for livestock,
2. Increased erosion which, in many low precipitation areas, leads to a more or less irreversible desert encroachment,
3. A sharp reduction in production and (far worse) in productivity of rangelands. This production is often only one-fourth and sometimes as low as one-tenth of the potential as measured on control plots,
4. An increase of unpalatable species in numbers as well as in biomass,
5. An increase of annual species which leave the ground bare and subject to erosion during the dry season,

6. Rarefaction and sometimes disappearance of the most valuable forage species, ecotypes or populations, and hence erosion of the genetic stock available for future research,
7. Rarefaction, or disappearance of wildlife and consequently impoverishment of the environment quality.

Expansion of cultivation

Cultivation of cereals is rapidly expanding over arid regions where the crop expectancy is extremely uncertain and the yield very low. This is due to the demographic explosion which characterizes the second half of this century. In the Near East and North Africa, the increase in cereal production necessary to meet the needs of an increasing population, has been obtained mostly from expansion of the cropped area and, to a very limited extent, from higher yields. This fact is clearly shown in the study of official statistic records (Le Houerou, 1973). The increase in cultivated acreage is roughly that of the same magnitude as population increase (about 3 percent per annum).

The result of this situation is that the best grazing lands on arable soils in the arid zone are progressively cleared for cereal cropping with very low and irregular yields. These newly cultivated areas are often turned almost sterile in a few years by erosion, either hydric or eolic, or both, and are then irreversibly lost for cropping or grazing.

Salination hazards

The most common remedy used to meet the food needs in the arid zone is the development of irrigation schemes. These schemes have sometimes been successfully achieved, but occasionally proved to be catastrophic—resulting in salination, alkalization and sterilization of large tracts of lands where huge investments were expended. Such hazards are due mainly to mistakes in conception and planning, by using waters and soils which should not have been utilized without strict technical specifications. Even when these specifications are planned from the beginning, they tend to be forgotten once the water is there. Very often irrigated areas are devoted to food or industrial crops, with total disregard to fodder crops and animal production, and conceived without links between stock raising and irrigated agriculture. It has been shown in many countries, for instance the USSR, that the establishment of such links is essential for the development of extensive livestock raising (fodder reserves, fattening operations for young and culled animals), and that the whole operation is globally profitable at the regional level, even when it does not seem profitable at the level of an irrigated farm.

Multiplication of boreholes and watering points

In many so called range development schemes or areas, "development" has essentially consisted of multiplying water points (boreholes, surface wells, cisterns, ponds, hafirs, and so forth).

It is then possible to use, during the dry season, rangelands which previously could not be used owing to the lack of water availability. A distinction should be made here between boreholes discharging large quantities of water (several litres per second) and low or temporary yielding water sources such as shallow wells or cisterns.

Large boreholes are, in fact, usually very harmful when they allow for important concentrations of livestock (in many cases five to ten times what the range could sustain), and in the consecutive destruction of pastures within a radius of 5 to 20 kms around the boreholes. This has produced catastrophic results in the Sahel of Africa and elsewhere.

Low yielding or temporary water sources are much less harmful. Cisterns, in particular, allow only a few weeks extension of the grazing season; when there is no pasture, there is no water either, and hence pasture depletion is rarely acute in this case.

Settlement of nomads and transhumants

Nomadism and transhumance are constraints imposed by the ecological conditions in arid zones. Climate is such that plant growth and production is too irregular in time and space to allow year round feeding of livestock. When the forage and/or the water is consumed, people and herds have to move to other areas where these are available. Hence settlement of nomads and transhumants implies two possible strategies:

1. The feed supply for livestock in periods of scarcity is insured artificially either by irrigated fodder crops or by concentrates (or both); or through deferred grazing systems, or through plantations of fodder shrubs and trees as feed reserves. That is to say that one way or another a feed supply is insured to replace the migration for search of pasturage.
2. Nomadic populations are turned to other activities: irrigated farming, trade, handicraft, tourism, industry, civil service, army, and so on.

The settlement of nomads is a general tendency usually favored by governments. Some attempts to organize nomadism, such as nomadic schools, have been successful to a certain extent, but do not seem to have been widely expanded.

In some countries like Syria and Algeria, settled graziers' cooperatives have been established on quite sizeable surfaces. However, these cooperatives need surfaces large enough to balance the effect of patchy rainfall on range production. This is also the case of modern range exploitation in arid zones of the USSR, Australia, the United States, and elsewhere which usually cover several tens of thousands, and sometimes several hundred thousand hectares.

OBSTACLES TO DEVELOPMENT

The main obstacles to development of arid zones are the lack of a global policy which would take into account and integrate all the various facets of this difficult task, and the will, or power, to enforce such a policy.

The basic cause of arid land degradation and desertization is an increase in human and livestock populations, whereby the population densities grow beyond the carrying capacity of the land under the present system of exploitation.

This situation could be improved in several complementary ways: by population control, through emigration, and from rational use of the land. It might be interesting to see why these have not usually been carried out successfully; that is to say what are the obstacles to development.

Population control

Population control has been attempted in several countries with little success (China and Japan excepted). The reasons are manifold: basically the lack of education and motivation of the people and the inadequacy of the methods (including education and advertisement) toward the mentality and traditions of the populations involved.

Emigration

Emigration is very successful in many countries, but it has some inconveniences. For example, the money sent home by emigrants is often used to buy tractors, which allows clearing of natural vegetation over vast surfaces, and thereby accelerates the desertization process.

In some countries, emigration permits population density over 100 people per square kilometer in areas with only 100-200 millimeters of rainfall and without irrigated agriculture. Such a density results quickly in "mineral landscape", where almost all perennial plants are removed.

Rational use of the land

Rational use of land is a result of numerous conditions which interact in a very complex way:

Education. The number of trained ecologists, conservationists, and range specialists is extremely small in respect to the need. In a recent meeting in Sfax, a rough estimate was that, in northwest Africa, at least 200 range-management specialists and ecologists were needed for the region; more than ten times the present number.

It is obvious that unless a sufficient number of trained specialists at all levels is made available, any large scale development plan is doomed to failure. Foreign experts, however competent and numerous they are, cannot achieve any large scale development plan.

Research and survey. Insufficient research and survey is sometimes also an obstacle to development, especially when land capabilities and carrying capacities have not been determined. In such a case, development schemes initiated with insufficient basic data may be hazardous.

Very often there would be enough data available to initiate development, but these data are not integrated, or important aspects have been overlooked, especially those concerned with social sciences.

There is also a recommendation coming out of almost all recent meetings: the need for coordination and integration of natural and social sciences with engineering and other aspects. This is especially stressed in programs such as MAB and EMASAR (Ecological Management of Arid and Semi-Arid Rangelands).

Development planning. This area is closely connected with survey. Planning should always result from an integrated survey. However, this is rare. In most cases, planning is carried out after partial and sectorial preinvestment studies where only climate, water, and soils are taken into consideration. Such important factors as vegetation, rangelands, their productivity, and social factors (such as the technical level of farmers or herdsmen, land tenure, traditions and motivations of the local population concerned) are simply ignored. As development has to be achieved through the local populations, it is not realistic to plan any action without their agreement and involvement. Although this might seem to be elementary common sense, it is often overlooked in the planning process.

<u>Legislation and organization</u>. Many countries have no modern range legislation. Rangelands are exploited under traditional customary legislations which are outmoded in the present types of societies.

In other cases, some laws exist, but are not enforced, especially laws concerning limitations to cultivation under certain circumstances of particular erosion hazards, woodcutting, and so on. This is usually due to the lack of a clear-cut government policy and/or the will and power to enforce a policy once it has been decided.

Policy- and law-making, however, is not sufficient without an efficient organization able to enforce the policy. In many countries there is, for instance, no range service powerful enough to coordinate all actions taken concerning rangeland, research, survey training, water development, land tenure, range development, health services, marketing, and so forth. This presupposes a strongly-structured organization represented at regional and local levels, and one capable enough to help local populations organize a move from a traditional subsistence economy toward a production-profit orientated system. This mutation is a very difficult one, but it is rendered necessary in the face of modern economy and a growing demographic pressure.

Establishing a well structured organization, able to deal efficiently with extension and development, requires a well-defined policy and numerous well-trained personnel at all levels. Here we come back to education, and the vicious circle of underdevelopment is closed.

GUIDELINES FOR DEVELOPMENT

Any development in arid zones should be based upon: an adequate knowledge of economic criteria and social attitudes; availability of good preinvestment studies giving a sound evaluation of the carrying capacity of the land, in respect to various development strategies and investment inputs (of all nature); and a realistic acceptance of ecological facts, which are:

- low and erratic rainfall
- unpredictable recurrence of periodic droughts
- uncertain and irregular production
- low potential per unit of land area, hence the necessity of having large land-management units
- unstable and fragile ecosystems
- erosion and salination hazards.

Training

In most of the recent international meetings, especially those devoted to range conservation and management, training has been rated as the number one top priority. As aforementioned, one can hardly see any large scale development without proper training of numerous specialists at all levels and in the various disciplines involved. Training should include learning how to work in inter-disciplinary teams. Some specialities of paramount importance to arid zones, such as ecology and range management, are usually neglected or are not given adequate importance (whereas rangelands represent usually over 80 percent of land surface in arid zones). Training is also frequently inadequate in quality—too academic, too bookish, or unsuitable for conditions in the country.

Ecology and range management in particular, ought to be taught within the countries (or the regions) themselves, using local examples. Too often, students who have been trained abroad in different environmental conditions (socioeconomic, if not physical) can hardly adapt what they have learned to the case of their own country. When they come home, they are often employed, in jobs other than those for which they have been trained.

Another aspect of training is the need to attract young people of good quality to technical careers involved in arid land development. It should be an easy governmental task to make these careers attractive by appropriate salaries and other incentives to field work, but it is usually the contrary that occurs: urban or easy bureaucratic life is made much more attractive to the young, which of course is of little help to actual development. Prior to joining the central administration, technicians and administrators should have spent several years devoted to actual field work which would make them more knowledgable of real development problems at that level.

Research and survey

Development without a minimum of research and survey is unthinkable. Research and survey should always be carried out, in an integrated way, through interdisciplinary teams involving specialists of physical, natural, social, and economic sciences. This recommendation again emerges from almost all recent international meetings. It is true that this philosophy is behind the Man and Biosphere program, as well as a basic principle in the EMASAR Program. Other recently established research institutions, such as the International Livestock Center for Africa (ILCA), are developing this same philosophy for action.

One of the bottlenecks to such integrated research and survey is the scarcity of trained manpower able to carry it out. Therefore, it would perhaps be advisable to establish regional centers, grouping together interdisciplinary training research and survey teams. Establishment of such centers has been recommended by MAB, EMASAR, UNEP, and others.

Technical improvements

Technical improvements can be achieved in complementary ways:

Range development. Range development through rotational and/or deferred grazing-adapting stocking rates to carrying capacity. One of the simplest ways is the establishment of grazing reserves, which were known in several traditional systems such as the "Hema" of Arabia, or the "Gdal" of North Africa.

Herds management. Herds management must go together with range management. This includes better nutrition conditions, better health care, adequate proportion of males, proper culling, timely selling, and so forth.

Water development. As mentioned before, water development should never be carried out alone, that is, without being able to manage this resource in conjunction and harmony with the management of other resources (such as range management, proper irrigation and drainage techniques). Some very efficient traditional systems of water harvesting (surface or underground) could be popularized in other regions.

Complementary range areas and farming areas. Improved range- and herds-management practices and the settlement of nomads or transhumants imply additional forage resources to replace the feed which cannot be found on the range in certain periods.

These additional resources ought to come primarily from farming areas either from bordering semiarid zones or from irrigated farms within the arid zone. This means the growing of fodder crops and/or concentrates to be made available to the graziers through various ways—even, if necessary, by subsidizing the farmers.

The system is not easy to work out. It supposes the establishment of buffer fodder reserves, the role of which is not only to avoid periodical hecatombs during severe droughts, but also a better animal nutrition and production in "normal times". Large scale

experiences in the USSR, Syria, Tunisia, and elsewhere show that
this is perfectly workable and economically feasible. It is above all
a matter of education by the extension services.

Use of crop and industrial residues for livestock feeding. Very often
crop and industrial residues such as cotton seeds, peanut cakes,
sugar molasses, bran, and so on, are exported at very low prices
when they should be used locally in fattening operations.

Fodder shrubs and trees. Pasture reseeding is frequently a de-
ceiving and always expensive practice in arid zones. However, the
establishment of fodder shrubs and trees on large areas has been
successful in several countries. In Tunisia, for example, over
50,000 hectares of fodder shrubs were planted during the past five
years.
        Similar results were obtained in Iran, Israel, and Pakistan,
and a program has been started in Syria. The establishment of such
reserves is rather costly ($150 to $300 per hectare). There must be
assurance that the reserves are adequately protected from the beginning, and rationally used and managed when they come to production later on. Under such conditions, this solution is economically
feasible even in areas receiving as little as 200 millimeters of
average rainfall.

Village afforestation. Because fuel gathering is one of the major
causes of range deterioration and desertization, it has been advisable
(and sometimes accomplished) to establish tree plantations for firewood production around villages which, at the same time, provides
landscape beautification and amenities. This is feasible in many
areas using fast growing trees such as Eucalyptus, Poplars, and
others. Two conditions are necessary: good soil (if possible with
water table or run-in) and effective, total protection with a rational
management. Again, it is a matter of organization.

Establishment of vegetation and wild life reserves. This implies,
of course, investments and resettlement of populations previously
living in these areas. This has been carried out very successfully,
especially in East Africa and Iran. It is the cheapest way of restoring
natural ecosystems. However, it also has its limitations, especially
on shallow soils in the desert and in predesert areas where vegetation
dynamics are almost null and desertization is an irreversible
process.

Sand dune fixation and windbreaks. Sand dune fixation techniques
are now well mastered in arid zones, even in areas receiving as

little as 150 millimeters of annual precipitation. After decades of trial, foresters have now compiled an impressive list of trees and shrubs suitable for sand dune fixation and windbreak squaring, as well as techniques of establishment. More research and experimentation is still needed, however, in the most arid areas (50-150 millimeters) in order to use some very promising desert species which are not yet domesticated, such as: Leptadenia pyrotechnica, Ochrademus baccatus, Salvadora persica, Aerva persica, Boscia, Maerua, Ziziphus, Genista, and Retama.

Monitoring and project evaluation. Monitoring is concerned both with natural undeveloped areas where ecological trends ought to be identified, and if possible quantified, and development projects to evaluate the change in the environment induced by the development process.

Monitoring should use both remote sensing (aerial photographs and satellite imagery) and ground checking. Satellite imagery (of the ERTS type), which is available regularly over a number of years, can also give extremely helpful information on spatial distribution of rainfall through successive seasons, information which is of primary importance in determining the size of the land-management units. The variables to be monitored are mainly vegetation (composition, cover, and other factors), erosion, soil loss, sedimentation, land use and migration pattern, human and animal populations. Development projects not only need to be monitored, but ought to be subject to periodical evaluation, preferably by outside appraisers with the help of the development agencies. This evaluation should be particularly concerned with:

- demographic and social changes
- range conditions and trends
- changes in soil (erosion, sedimentation, and salination)
- livestock performance
- water balance and water tables
- pests and diseases
- economic results

The objective of monitoring and evaluation is to identify and correct faults, and possibly to take advantage of them in further development or in planning new programs.

Government policies and administrative structures

Planning and execution. Before any large scale development is possible, a clear government policy has to be defined and a firm political commitment must be stated.

Development is a very complex matter involving many governmental, as well as nongovernmental, services and agencies. The
first need is good coordination at the planning level (which is often
the case), and then, at the execution level (which is not often the
case).

Normally, one single agency should be responsible for the
coordination of all actions taken in a specific domain. For example,
in range areas, all forms of development executed by other departments or agencies should be coordinated by the Range Department
(both at central and local levels), that is, actions taken in water
development, communications, marketing, housing, and other fields.
Inversely, in irrigation-development schemes, it would be to the
advantage of the water-development authority to draw upon other
agencies for execution of the parts in the plan in which it has no
competence. In other words, each department should have coordinating powers strong enough to command the support of other relevant
departments and the local administration for execution of its own
development projects.

Marketing. The major problem in the marketing of livestock
products is the extreme irregularity in prices which tend to overload
the market at some periods, and leave it unsupplied for long spans
at other times. Improved range conditions and herd management
would somewhat regularize the market through more balanced feed
supply and more regular offtake selling. Some measures could
further improve the situation:

1. improved network of routes and holding grounds with feeding and
   veterinary services
2. improved credit facilities for traders and pastoralists
   -new outlets for livestock in fattening schemes and foreign markets
   -improved purchasing power in agricultural and urban areas
   -subsidies on a sliding scale of prices to encourage the sale of
    livestock during off-peak periods and at the beginning of drought
    period before the animals damage their environment.
   -prices policy encouraging good quality meat and differential
    prices between meat cuts.

Credit facilities. Range development, forage crops, and fodder
shrubs plantation have been encouraged in some countries through
special credit facilities and subsidies. This is, of course, to be
developed whenever possible.

Legislation. In the past, legislation designed to control land use has
rarely been enforced, and legislation designed to prevent overgrazing
has not usually worked. Much of the legislation dealing with land use
has been designed for agricultural rather than for range areas.

Future legislation should be directed at enabling range users to improve their current form of management, such as securing land tenure, preventing tresspass or disturbances, and, if need be, retaining preventive safeguards against range destruction. Wherever possible, range users should be involved directly in the preparation and enforcement of their own legislation, thus insuring closer relations between them and the government.

Fiscal policies. It is desirable, in principle, that range areas contribute to the general revenue of the country. However, many different situations are encountered. For example, when:

1. rangelands belong to the state
2. rangelands are the property of the users, whether legally or by customary rights
3. the country is mostly arid and has few other assets than range livestock
4. the country enjoys a more balanced agricultural economy and range areas are of marginal importance
5. the country is oil rich

One principle should be followed and that is that any taxation collected in the range areas should be devoted primarily to financing their services. Taxes may be imposed on the number of livestock, or individual persons, or by surface of land area (in this case, on groups of individuals having land rights). In all cases, the rate charged per unit should be calculated on a sliding scale related to the potential of the land as to discourage overuse of the resources.

Payment for services (maintenance of wells, boreholes, marketing facilities) should not be equated with taxation and the money so raised used to maintain the services.

INTERNATIONAL PROGRAMS ON RANGELANDS

During the past two years, new programs on rangelands have been launched especially by UNESCO and FAO.

The MAB 3 Project

In the framework of its global program on Man and the Biosphere, UNESCO has developed a project (No. 3) dealing with the impact of human activities on grazing land ecosystems. The general objectives of the project are to secure, quantify, synthesize, distribute, and apply information on natural and social science research on grazing lands, in order to provide guidelines for the optimal management of these lands and to provide more effective means to achieve optimal management.

The project is concerned with interdisciplinary research and training involving natural and social sciences. It works through national MAB committees. A central joint UNESCO/FAO Secretariat in charge of the coordination aims at organizing meetings and workshops at subregional, regional, and global levels, where guidelines are proposed and cooperative programs established. All projects are guided by an international governing council, meeting every second year, and composed of 25 countries elected through UNESCO's general conferences and several international organizations (within and outside the UN system). Several MAB 3 meetings were already held:

1. an expert panel (Montpellier, October 2-7, 1972) which defined a general outline of the project and methods.
2. a regional meeting on research and training needs in the Sahel region of Africa (Niamey, Niger, March 9-15, 1974).
3. an international working group (Hurley, July 2-5, 1974) which defined an outline of regional programmes.
4. a regional meeting on the formulation of cooperative research training and management on arid and semiarid rangelands in North West Africa (Sfax, Tunisia, April 3-12, 1975, MAB/EMASAR meeting).

Several national MAB 3 subcommittees have been established and have started working.

One of the ambitions of the program is to help establish working links between MAB 3 subcommittees in developed and developing countries. This is being done through the MAB Secretariat, Department of Environmental Sciences and Natural Resources Research, Division of Ecology, and UNESCO (Paris).

The EMASAR Program

FAO has recently set up, with the help of UNEP, a general program on the ecological management of arid and semiarid rangelands, which takes place in the FAO general program of "Natural Resources for Food and Agriculture." The objectives and outline of this EMASAR program have been defined by a panel of experts who met in Rome, May 27-31, 1974 (FAO publication AGPC: Misc/26).

The conclusions of this panel were endorsed by a general conference held in Rome February 3-8, 1975. This conference, where

38 countries of Africa, the Near East, and the Middle East were represented, proposed a framework for the implementation of the program. The program is at present concerned with Africa, the Near East, and Middle East, but will be extended by 1976 to Latin America where similar problems exist.

The follow-up actions of the first EMASAR Conference are beginning to take shape. A coordinating officer has been appointed. Several projects are under consideration, among which is the establishment of a regional EMASAR center in the Middle East. It will probably be located in Iran, following a generous suggestion of the Iranian government.

MAB 3 and EMASAR programs have different objectives. MAB is concerned with research whereas EMASAR deals with management and development. Both programs are closely coordinated since there is a joint FAO/UNESCO MAB 3 Secretariat. Some meetings are to be held jointly, for instance the Sfax meeting, since research survey and development ought to be linked tightly.

13

HEALTH CARE SYSTEMS
IN THE SAHEL:
BEFORE AND AFTER
THE DROUGHT
Pascal James Imperato, M. D.

ECOLOGY OF THE SAHEL

The Sahel is both a climatic region and a vegetation zone that lies immediately south of the Sahara, stretching across the width of Africa from the Atlantic Ocean on the west to the Red Sea on the east. Its name comes from the Arabic, sahil, meaning shore or borderland. The Sahel begins at approximately 15 degrees north latitude on the average and extends northward in most areas for about three hundred miles to 20 degrees north latitude. The southern portions of the region receive from 10 to 20 inches of rainfall per year, whereas the northern portions receive less than 10 inches per year. Rainfall is seasonal, occurring during the months of July through September after which ensues a long dry season, characterized by relatively cool temperatures from October through January and extremely high temperatures from February through June. In contrast to this sparse rainfall, that in the savanna to the south is abundant, ranging from 20 to 60 inches and that in the rain forest of the coast above 80 inches per year. There is considerable variation in different parts of it in any given year. It is a region subject to periodic droughts of varying duration, the most intense during this century having been the 1916-17 drought and the recent drought in 1972-74. From contemporary records, it appears that the drought of 1916-17 was as catastrophic as the one now in progress. It also severely affected the cereal-producing areas of the savanna (Cissoko 1962).

The southern Sahel is favored by the presence of the Senegal River in the west and the Niger River in the east. The great Inland Delta of the Niger with its flood plains and seasonal lakes and ponds

represents an important topographic variation in the central portion
of the southern Sahel. Subsistence agriculture is practiced in the
Sahel along the banks of the Niger and Senegal rivers and around
a few scattered oases by sedentary agriculturists, the most important
of whom are the Songhoi who live along the banks of the Niger. For
the most part, various types of sorghum are grown and in a few areas
rice.

The vegetation of the Sahel consists primarily of dolm palms
(Hyphaene thebaica) found along the river banks and around oases,
and several species of thorn trees and seasonal grasses. The density
of vegetation and its average height decreases gradually toward the
northern Sahel. During the rainy season, much of the Sahel supports
an abundant growth of grasses, but during the dry season grass
becomes scarce, except along the river banks and around such permanent water sources as wells, lakes, and ponds.

ECONOMY OF THE SAHEL

The economy of the Sahel is primarily pastoral, but farming
and fishing also comprise significant economic activities. The
Tuareg and the Maure nomads have traditionally been pure pastoralists with certain classes among them, namely, serfs and captives, practicing subsistence farming. Subsistence farming also is
practiced by large groups of sedentary cultivators such as the Djerma
and Hausa in the Niger Republic, the Songhoi and Sarakole of Mali,
and the Tukulor of Senegal and Mauritania. Sedentary populations do
not practice farming to the exclusion of livestock raising. Most keep
herds of camels, cattle, goats, and sheep of varying sizes, herded
by either the young men or boys of their societies and by herdsmen
hired on a seasonal basis from among the Maures, Tuareg or Peul.
The latter are primarily pastoralists of the savanna to the south of
the Sahel. But certain groups migrate up into the Sahel with their
herds during the rainy season (Imperato 1969). The former captives
of the Peul, known as the Rimaibes, are now primarily sedentary
cultivators in the northern savanna and southern Sahel. Some own
sizeable herds of cattle, goats, and sheep that are moved seasonally
by the young men of the villages along fixed migration trails between
established watering points and pastureland (Imperato 1972). This
form of nomadism, in which certain segments of a society move
seasonally with their herds out of fixed villages is known as transhumance (Stenning 1959).

Fishing in the Sahel is a significant activity on the Senegal and
Niger rivers and their tributaries. The Bozo fishermen are the

predominant group along the stretches of the Niger flowing through
the savanna and the Inland Delta of the Niger. Within the Niger Bend,
fishing is primarily practiced by the Sorko, a special caste of the
Songhoi (Rouch 1951). During the past decade, the traditional fishing
industry on the middle Niger in Mali has adopted modern techniques
and equipment and organized successful cooperatives for the pooling
of equipment and financial resources and the marketing of dried and
smoked fish. At present, approximately 12,000 tons of dried and
smoked fish are exported annually from the market at Mopti in Mali
to surrounding African states (Szabo 1970).

The traditional Sahelian economy is essentially characterized
by interdependencies among farmers, herdsmen, and fishermen.
This traditional profile has changed in varying degrees in different
parts of the Sahel over the past several decades. Farmers now own
livestock and herdsmen cultivate fields, and beyond this central
part of the spectrum is pure pastoralism on the one hand and pure
crop production on the other. The economic diversification of individual ethnic groups carries with it the obvious political and economic advantages of lessened dependency on other polities, but it
also has placed stress upon fine ecological balances that the traditional interdependency system helped to maintain. The massive
population explosion of cattle, sheep, and especially goats in the
Sahel in recent years has been due both to the intense application of
modern veterinary health techniques and veterinary vaccination
campaigns and to the increase in the number of farmer-herd owners
and the size of their herds. Overall, it has led to a steady deterioration of the environment through overgrazing. Of all the activities in
the Sahel, husbandry stands out as the one that is the most peripheral
to the modern economic life of present-day African states. Although
milk and the products made from it are bartered or sold at weekly
fairs by pastoralists in the villages of sedentary farmers, few
animals are ever slaughtered for meat. These animals comprise the
pastoralist's capital investment, and its dividends, which are principally milk and milk products and occasionally the meat of dying
animals, provide him and his family with their daily nutritional needs.
In addition, livestock is a symbol of a man's social station, through
which he accrues prestige in the community. The pastoralist is willing
to barter and sell a portion of his dividends but is unwilling to tamper
with his capital investment. The unused modern slaughterhouse in
Gao (Mali) is testimony to this attitude. Were the fruits of modernized
agriculture, fishing, and husbandry properly exchanged in the Sahel,
the end result would be a greatly improved nutritional state for all
the peoples of the area.

POPULATION OF THE SAHEL

Precise population data for the Sahel do not exist, most figures consisting of either estimates or extrapolated numbers based on sample surveys. However, approximate numbers for various parts of the Sahel are known. The total population of Senegal, Mauritania, Mali, Niger, Upper Volta, and Chad is estimated to be 25 million. An important fact, often overlooked, is that most of this population lives not in the Sahel but in the savanna to the south of it. Likewise, many have characterized these six countries as Sahelian when in reality they possess a heterogeneous ecology. There are, according to the best estimates, about 5 million people living in the West African Sahel.

The population density of the Sahel varies greatly. There also are considerable differences in the population densities between sedentary agriculturists and pastoralists in the same area. Taking 15 degrees north latitude as the southern limit of the Sahel, most of the sedentary population is found along the Niger River, just south of the Niger Bend around the town of Gao. Here the population reaches 125 per square kilometer. Along the remainder of the Niger River, between Mopti and the Niger Bend, the sedentary population density averages 20 per square kilometer. In the western Sahel, sedentary population densities range from 35 per square kilometer around certain permanent water sources to 5 per square kilometer in less arid areas (Brasseur 1963).

The density of the nomadic population also is variable. In the western Sahel, the density of Maures varies between 0.5 and 2 per square kilometer. In most sections of the central and eastern Sahel, the density of Tuaregs varies from 0.5 to 1 per square kilometer. In most sections of the central and eastern Sahel, the density of Tuaregs varies from 0.5 to 1 per square kilometer. Among the nomad population, densities at dry season pastures, during the months of May and June, often reach 50 per square kilometer.

The nomads of the Sahel comprise two large groups, the Bedouin Arabs (Maures) and the Tuaregs. The former are found in the portions of the Sahel in the modern African states of Mali, Mauritania, and Senegal; and the latter in the Sahelian zones of Mali, Niger, and Upper Volta. At the outset it should be noted that not all Bedouin Arabs and Tuaregs live in the Sahel. Some 34 Bedouin Arab groups live to the north of the Sahel in Morocco, Algeria, Spanish Sahara, and Libya. Likewise, two Tuareg groups live in the Sahara, in Algeria and Libya.

The Tuareg are essentially camel nomads, but they also keep large herds of goats, sheep, and to a lesser extent cattle. Animals

are the property of individuals, but pasture land and water resources
are public property. During July through January, when water and
pasture are abundant, milk is also abundant and the Tuareg's diet
consists then of almost nothing but milk and some meat. When the
hot dry season begins in February, milk production decreases sharply
until by June very little to none is available. The nomads are then
obliged to eat cereals, either those produced by their captives or
those obtained by bartering some of their animals. Animal mortality
is often high during the hot dry season, and animals that die are
consumed. Even today, the Tuareg's needs for cash are few. They
include the paying of annual taxes on the declared number of animals
owned and on adult members of the family, and the buying of tobacco,
cloth, tea, salt, and sugar. In order to meet these needs, a few
animals are sold.

It is quite obvious that a Tuareg's herds constitute both his
principal source of food and his capital investment. The natural
tendency for a herdsman is to increase the size of his herd, for this
assures him of an increased quantity of milk that can be consumed
and bartered. Herd sizes are not increased with the idea of selling
the animals. The Tuareg's need for cash is low and so he sells the
minimum number of animals possible. Each herdsman then strives
to increase his number of animals. Because water supplies and
pasture are held in common by all, it is not in an individual's interest
to limit his herd size in an attempt to prevent overgrazing and
destruction of the environment. Even if he were aware of the consequences of overgrazing, and few are, he would not limit the size of
his herds. To do so would jeopardize his personal survival for the
benefit of a collectivity that might not concurrently follow his example.

In the past, periodic epidemics of rinderpest (animal viral
disease) and drought served as natural controls on herd size. Survival
under such adverse conditions was assured by the social structure in
which captives produced a supplementary food source in the form of
cereals. If these crops failed, then pillaging the villages of the
sedentary black farmers for cereals would provide the Tuareg with
a food supply.

The contemporary period has witnessed the breakdown of this
traditional social structure. Former captives are now either herdsmen like their former masters or sedentary farmers, and will provide them with nothing without payment of some kind. Likewise,
pillaging has been effectively stopped. The abolition of these two
additional sources of food supply was more than compensated for by
the increase in herd sizes brought about by modern veterinary campaigns, especially the vaccination campaign against rinderpest along
with the digging of new wells. Unfortunately, the land became greatly
overgrazed as a result.

The Tuareg of the Sahel are found to the east of 4 degrees west longitude and north of 14 degrees north latitude. Their movement during the rainy season (July through September) is one of dispersal since surface water is abundant, as is pasture land. Their dry season movement is one of concentration toward the available water supplies and pasture land. Those Tuareg living within the Niger Bend and to the north of the Niger River migrate toward the river in a gradual fashion beginning in October and arrive on its banks or on the shores of the lakes of the Inland Delta in April. Those from the north descend southward toward the river, while those south of the river move northward. As they move, they gradually use up all the available pasture. Some groups north of the river cross the river in March and April and migrate toward the shores of the lakes of the Inland Delta of the Niger. Tuareg factions living to the northeast and to the east of the Niger Bend migrate between wells on a seasonal basis. Camps are set up within a 25-kilometer radius of the wells and the animals are taken to drink at a given well every three days. If there are too many animals within the 25-kilometer radius, the available pasture will be quickly used up. Also, if the rains are late, there will be insufficient pasture for the herds. In both of these situations, a considerable number of animals die. But, curiously, this mortality reduces the herd sizes to a point where overgrazing ceases, permitting new grass to grow and the surviving animals to thrive and eventually to reproduce to the point where the former herd size is reestablished (Swift 1972).

The distance from the final dry season camp to the last rainy season camp varies from 100 to 400 kilometers. During severe droughts, this distance may be increased two or threefold, in an attempt to find water and pasture. Under these conditions, the direction of the dry season movement for some is also altered, with those groups in and around the Niger Bend moving southward into the savanna country of Upper Volta instead of northward toward the river. This occurred in 1972 and 1973, during the severe drought in the Sahel.

Like the movements of the Tuareg, those of the Maure are primarily along a north-south axis. In the western Sahel, the Maure descend as far south as 14.5 degrees north latitude, but in the eastern Sahel, in the area of the Niger Bend, they are not found below 16 degrees north latitude. At the beginning of the rainy season in July, the herdsmen start their northward trek, which in most instances covers 300 to 400 kilometers. They move along fixed paths up into the northern reaches of the Sahel. The camel herdsmen to the north of them move ahead of them up into the Sahara at the same time. At the end of the rainy season, they reverse their direction and descend into the southern Sahel, following the same paths and utilizing the

pasture and water resources as they move. This dry season descent
is slow compared to the rainy season trek (Furon 1929).

The principal groups in the eastern Sahel, in the region of the
Niger Bend, are the Kunta and the Berabish. There are, in addition,
several small subfractions in this area, the Ahel Araouane, Kel
Haousa, Tenguererif, Oulad Daoud, Joumane, and Hamounat (Said
1904). In the western Sahel the Zenaga, Trarza, and Duaish are
divided into numerous factions, the most important of which are
the Ahel Sidi Mahmoud, Laghlal, Mechdouf, Oulad Naser, Oulad
Mbarek, and Ladem. In the western Sahel, the chief paths of movement of the Maures follow the longitudes connecting the following
centers: Kiffa (Mauritania) and Kayes (Mali); Aioun el Atrouss
(Mauritania) and Nioro du Sahel (Mali); Nema (Mauritania) and Nara
(Mali). In most instances, the seasonal nomadic drift is bisected in
its center by 16 degrees north latitude.

PRINCIPAL DISEASE PROBLEMS IN THE SAHEL

Disease-reporting systems in this part of Africa suffer greatly
from underreporting. Thus, available morbidity (incidence of sickness) and mortality data do not give a very precise idea of disease
incidence and case fatality ratios. However, such data, although
fraught with deficiencies, do convey a general impression of the
major disease problems.

Table 13.1 presents data on several important communicable
diseases in four Sahelian countries, Niger, Senegal, Upper Volta,
and Mali and, by way of comparison, the data on the same diseases
in the United States. The morbidity and mortality data and case
fatality ratios for the leading 20 communicable and nutritional diseases
in Mali are presented in Table 13.2. Table 13.3 lists in order of
frequency the leading causes of death in Mali by age group for calendar
year 1972. And in Table 13.4, the results of a survey for trachoma
(a contageous infection of the eyes) and onchocerciasis (river
blindness caused by a worm parasite) in four countries are presented.

What is obvious from all these data is that communicable
diseases are the major causes of morbidity and mortality in this part
of Africa. The chief causes of death among children are malaria,
measles, diarrhea, and infections of respiratory tract and lungs
(bronchopulmonary). Malaria, dermatitis, inflammatory eye diseases,
diarrhea, bronchopulmonary infections, and measles are the leading
causes of morbidity in most of the Sahel. Some of these, such as
dermatitis and inflammatory eye diseases, while carrying little or
no mortality, cause serious morbidity.

TABLE 13.1

Annual Number of Cases and Incidence Rates for Major Communicable Diseases
in Four States of the West African Sahel and the United States, 1968

Disease	Niger Number	Rate Per 1,000	Senegal Number	Rate Per 1,000	Upper Volta Number	Rate Per 1,000	Mali Number	Rate Per 1,000	United States Number	Rate Per 1,000
Pulmonary tuberculosis	664	0.174	2,599	0.686	723	0.140	2,400	0.533	38,245	0.190
Syphilis and its sequelae	1,023	0.268	3,965	1.076	2,947	0.569	16,544	3.676	19,019	0.094
Gonococcal infections	21,736	5.711	16,381	4.445	3,361	0.649	24,486	5.441	464,543	2.311
Dysentery	n.a.*	—	80,960	21.970	n.a.	—	319,825	71.071	n.a.	—
Amebiasis	6,971	1.831	11,960	3.245	n.a.	—	61,380	13.640	3,005	0.015
Whooping cough	3,234	0.850	18,588	5.044	2,343	0.452	13,927	3.094	4,810	0.024
Measles	10,513	7.762	16,354	4.438	4,742	0.916	85,506	19.001	22,231	0.110
Chickenpox	3,069	0.806	9,152	2.183	2,440	0.471	8,459	1.880	112,655	5.560
Trachoma	2,256	0.592	3,596	0.976	69,507	13.430	650	0.144	455	0.002
Trypanosomiasis	n.a.	—	26	0.007	148	0.028	48	0.010	1	—
Total population	3,806,000		3,685,000		5,175,000		4,500,000		201,000,000	

* n.a. = data not available

Source: <u>World Health Statistics Annual</u> (Geneva: WHO, 1971).

TABLE 13.2

Cases and Deaths from 20 Principal Communicable and Nutritional Diseases, Mali, 1968

Disease	Number of Cases	Number of Deaths	Case Fatality Rate Per 100
Malaria	583,274	1,522	0.3
Dermatitis	399,184	0	0
Inflammatory eye disease	326,928	0	0
Diarrhea	319,825	898	0.3
Bronchitis and pneumonia	309,007	267	0.1
Measles	85,506	1,683	1.1
Syphilis	16,544	60	0.3
Schistosomiasis	37,280	n.a.*	n.a.
Trypanosomiasis	48	6	12.5
Onchocerciasis	1,989	1	0.1
Intestinal worms	29,089	363	1.2
Gonorrhea	24,486	n.a.	n.a.
Whooping cough	13,927	70	0.5
Chicken pox	8,459	n.a.	n.a.
Diphtheria	117	14	11.9
Mumps	9,497	n.a.	n.a.
Tetanus	828	314	37.8
Poliomyelitis	963	13	1.3
Kwashiorkor	1,799	n.a.	n.a.
Guinea Worm	1,784	n.a.	n.a.

* n.a. = data not available
Source: Ministry of Public Health archives.

TABLE 13.3

Principal Causes of Mortality by Age Group
in Mali, 1972

Infants Less than 1 Year	1-4 Years	5-14 Years	14 Years +
1. Malaria	1. Malaria	1. Malaria	1. Malaria
2. Measles	2. Measles	2. Dysenteries	2. Tuberculosis
3. Gastroenteritis	3. Malnutrition	3. Trypanosomiasis	3. Dysentery
4. Bronchitis and penumonia	4. Gastroenteritis	4. Malnutrition	4. Trypanosomiasis

Source: Ministry of Public Health archives.

TABLE 13.4

Trachoma and Onchocerciasis in Four States
in the Sahel, 1968

Country	Population Examined by Mobile Teams	Trachoma		Onchocerciasis	
		Number of Cases	Rate Per 1,000	Number of Cases	Rate Per 1,000
Upper Volta	1,615,341	44,010	27.245	54,650	33.831
Mali	584,154	673	1.152	2,939	5.031
Niger	71,681	415	5.789	25	0.348
Senegal	493,586	2,587	5.241	1,949	3.948

Source: Based on surveys conducted by the Institut d'Ophthalmologie Tropicale
d'Afrique.

Many diseases such as measles and whooping cough have a cyclical epidemiologic pattern. In rural areas of the Sahel, measles characteristically runs in a cycle in which epidemic peaks occur every two or three years. It is interesting to note that the reported case fatality ratio for measles for Mali (Table 13.2) is only 1.1 per 100. Yet it is well known from detailed studies of measles outbreaks and epidemics in this part of Africa that the case fatality ratio may go as high as 50 per 100 and is on the average 5 per 100 (Imperato 1969). The low overall case fatality ratio for measles probably reflects under-reporting.

Trachoma and other eye infections are extremely important problems among nomadic populations in the Sahel (Table 13.4). Onchocerciasis, however, is principally found just to the south of the Sahel in the wooded savanna. But it does occur among nomadic groups that venture south during their seasonal migrations. The prevalence rates presented for these two diseases in Table 13.4 are a far more accurate measure of the actual situation than data received through the regular reporting system in these countries.

Cholera occurred in epidemic form in all of the countries of the Sahel throughout 1970 and 1971 and to a lesser extent in 1972. In 1971, the peak year of the epidemic in the Sahelian countries, a total of 69,125 cases were reported to the World Health Organization from Africa. Of these, 15,887 (22.9 percent) were reported from countries of the West African Sahel (Richer 1972). The attack rate for cholera in the Sahel was on the average 80 to 115 per 1,000 population, but in some areas it rose to 500 per 1,000 population. Such rates are considerably higher than those of from 2 to 20 per 1,000 population generally found in Asia (Imperato 1975 a). During the early stages of the epidemic in the Sahel, the case fatality ratio was very high, reaching 50 percent in sedentary villages where accurate statistics were available. This high ratio gradually fell to below 10 percent as treatment facilities were organized, intravenous fluids supplied, and as medical personnel became familiar with the clinical management of the disease. In 1972, the total number of cholera cases reported in Africa dropped to 6,891 from the 69,125 reported in 1971.

Cholera initially spread throughout the Sahel along the course of the Niger River. Consequently, most cases occurred among the riverine populations of sedentary farmers and migrating fishermen. The disease first broke out in Mopti, a riverine town in Mali that is the terminus of an active mercantile route with multiple connections to the coast. The disease was brought into Mopti from the Ivory Coast by a trader. The rapidity with which the disease spread can be gauged by the fact that it rapidly moved both up and down the Niger River, reaching the Sahelian town of Gao in Mali, 806 kilometers from Mopti, in fifteen days. The disease then spread into Niger, Upper Volta, Mauritania, and Senegal (Imperato 1975 a).

The Sahelian nomadic population was spared the brunt of this epidemic wave since it was camped around water holes far from the banks of the Niger River at the time the disease spread downstream. During the latter part of 1971 and during 1972, sporadic but relatively less severe outbreaks of cholera occurred among nomadic populations in Mali, Mauritania, Senegal, Niger, and Upper Volta.

HEALTH SERVICES PRIOR TO THE DROUGHT

Virtually all of the West African Sahel lies within Francophone Africa. The health services infrastructure present in the area was largely developed during the colonial era, which accounts for its almost homogeneous nature from one country to another. From the outset, the French placed very strong emphasis on mass campaigns, since they were the most effective technique in dealing with the major disease problems of the savanna and forest areas of West Africa, namely, trypanosomiasis and onchocerciasis.

The earliest mass campaigns were organized under the direction of French military physicians in the early part of this century and were directed against smallpox (Gallay 1909). These campaigns were of a temporary nature and did not lead to the development of a permanent health services structure. They primarily reached the sedentary populations in the savanna and, to a lesser extent, in the Sahel. However, they had little or no impact on the nomads, some of whom were not completely pacified at the time. In 1931, the French created a mobile medical service, the Service Prophylactique de la Maladie du Sommeil for all French West Africa (Lhote 1960). At first this service was monovalent and directed its efforts against trypanosomiasis. As a consequence, its impact in the tsetse-free Sahel was negligible. Two decades prior to its organization, the French colonial administration developed a curative health service for all of French West Africa. This consisted of regional hospitals and dispensaries, the latter often manned by medical assistants. Over the years, the static curative health service acquired the name A.M., Assistance Medical. Although some dispensaries were built in the Sahel, they were few in number and were often located in important administrative centers such as Nioro, Timbuktu, Bourem, and Zinder. In general, they had little impact on the health of the nomadic population.

During the 1930s, the mobile medical service was expanded, reorganized administratively, temporarily integrated into the

Assistance Medical and then in 1939 made an independent and separate organization known as the Service General Autonome de Prophylaxie et de Traitement de la Maladie du Sommeil. The service was organized into geographic zones known as sectors in which mobile teams of trained infirmiers and health auxiliaries examined the entire sedentary population at regular intervals for trypanosomiasis. Therapy was provided at treatment centers for those found infected with the disease. This service had no impact in the Sahel since no trypanosomiasis existed there.

In 1944 this monovalent service was transformed into a polyvalent mobile service called the Service General d'Hygiene Mobile et de Prophylaxie. Its stated purpose was to control the endemic diseases, trypanosomiasis, leprosy, malaria, syphilis, and yaws, and such epidemic diseases as meningococcal meningitis, plague, and smallpox (Lhote 1960). While in theory this new service extended mobile health services to the Sahel, in practice it did not operate effectively in areas that were not endemic for trypanosomiasis. Although sectors were created in the Sahel, they never attained a significant level of function compared to those located in the savanna. As with the Assistance Medical, these sectors primarily reached the sedentary agricultural population. In 1959 this service was disbanded. In its place each newly independent state in Francophone Africa established its own mobile medical service, which in Upper Volta was called the Service de Sante Rurale and in Mali, Senegal, and Mauritania was called the Service National des Grandes Endemies. In Niger a new concept was tried until 1971, a mobile health service with only a few teams. These teams traveled in extremely large vehicles equipped with elaborate laboratory and radiologic equipment, and consisted of several physicians, infirmiers, laboratory technicians, and medical aides. This service known as OMNES was discontinued in 1971 because of its costliness and less than hoped for impact on the nomadic population.

In 1960 the Francophone countries formed a supranational regional organization in order to coordinate their efforts against endemic and epidemic disease. This organization, known as the Organization de Coordination et de Cooperation pour la Lutte Contre les Grandes Endemies, is presently headquartered in Bobo-Dioulasso, Upper Volta.

The static and mobile health services made a significant impact in controlling major endemic and epidemic disease problems in the savanna over the decades, and thereby established among local populations a high degree of receptivity for health programs of broader scope. This, however, was not the situation in the Sahel. There people were long accustomed to a high prevalence of infectious diseases and were unfamiliar to a large extent with modern medical services. As some preliminary pilot studies in 1968 demonstrated, there was little receiver recognition of the desirability of the services on the part of nomads. In many instances, there was active resistance (Imperato 1975 b).

THE EFFECT OF THE DROUGHT ON HEALTH

The impact of the drought upon the health of the Sahelian population can be measured by mortality data, morbidity data for various diseases, and the nutritional state of the population.

Mortality data are not easily arrived at because of the weakness and/or absence of a reporting system in many areas. Estimates of mortality have ranged as high as several millions for the six-country Sahelian area. Such estimates are farfetched, given the known data.

The Mali Sahel had a population of approximately 500,000 prior to the drought, roughly 10 percent of Mali's 5 million population. The remainder of Mali's population lives in the savanna to the south. Of the 500,000, approximately 200,000 are Tuareg and Maure nomads, the remainder being sedentary Songhoi farmers and Sorko fishermen.

The Center for Disease Control of the U.S. Public Health Service (USPHS) estimated, on the basis of reported death rates, that some 100,000 people died from famine in Mauritania, Mali, Niger, and Upper Volta in 1973. In Mali, deaths due to famine were estimated at 10,000 at a maximum.

In July-September 1973, a time when relief supplies were beginning to arrive in appreciable quantities in the Sahel, a nutrition survey was carried out in two camps, Timbuktu and Gao, and in two locations in the western Sahel of Mali, in Nioro and Nara. Children below four years of age were examined in the survey, being most susceptible to the effects of acute nutritional deprivation. Of 35 nomad children examined in the Timbuctoo camp, 80 percent demonstrated signs of acute malnutrition. In the Gao camp, 70 percent of 50 children demonstrated signs of acute malnutrition in July. But two months later, in September, only 35 percent of 51 children were found to be acutely malnourished, reflecting their greater food intake during the interval. By comparison, in Nioro only 3 percent of 126 children, and in Nara only 4 percent of 182 children, were found to be acutely malnourished, reflecting the considerably lesser impact of the drought on that part of the Sahel.

Table 13.5 indicates population ratios of adult men, women and of children in the thirty camps of the Gao region. In April 1974 a nutrition survey was conducted by Dr. J. Pele of ORANA (Office de Recherche Alimentaire et Nutritionel de l'Afrique in Dakar) in Timbuctoo and Gao (Pele 1974). A total of 851 children were examined,

TABLE 13.5

Population of the 30 Camps for Drought Victims,
Region of Gao, Mali, by Cercle, May 1, 1974

Cercle	Adult Males	Adult Females	Children 0-14 Years of Age	Total
Gao	1,780	3,600	5,486	10,866
Ansongo	712	1,593	1,624	3,929
Menaka	197	458	1,050	1,705
Gourma-Rharous	1,183	1,423	1,520	4,126
Bourem	1,452	2,897	4,495	8,844
Timbuktu	673	2,079	3,834	6,586
Goundam	1,831	2,347	3,384	7,562
Dire	518	1,024	1,593	3,135
Total	9,905	17,551	26,285	53,741

642 from the refugee camps and the remainder from the towns of
Timbuctoo and Gao. Although the results of this survey have not yet
been completely analyzed, certain findings are evident. Overt clinical
malnutrition was extremely rare among children above five years of
age. Children below five years, while in a satisfactory state of
nutrition in general, manifested occasional signs of malnutrition.

During June and July 1974, the Center for Disease Control of
the USPHS conducted a nutritional survey in certain areas of five
Sahelian countries: Chad, Niger, Mali, Mauritania, and Upper Volta
(Kloth 1974). During this survey, 3,928 children between the ages of
six months and six years were examined. Of this number, 12.7
percent were found to be suffering from acute undernutrition. As
large as this proportion is, it is considerably less than that found in
mid-1973 before emergency food supplies had made an impact on the
nutritional status of the Sahelian population.

Although press reports often warned of impending epidemics of
various communicable diseases, none actually occurred. Close to
80 percent of the population of Gao had been vaccinated against smallpox and the same proportion of children against measles in 1969-70
(Imperato 1973). Thus, the measles-susceptible population was quite
low in numbers.

Health authorities did undertake measles immunization of all
nonimmunized children in the camps, thereby negating even the least
possibility of any outbreaks. The principal disease problems encountered among the refugees have been those common to the Sahel.

It cannot be said that the drought has increased their incidence directly, except perhaps among malnourished individuals who are generally more susceptible to infectious diseases.

The major immediate effect of the drought on health in the Sahel was malnutrition.

PROBLEMS OF HEALTH CARE DELIVERY
IN THE SAHEL

Prior to the onset of the recent drought, health care delivery in the Sahel was primarily dispensed through fixed curative health facilities, of which there are very few. The majority of medical care in the area has for many years been delivered by infirmiers, individuals with the equivalent of a high school education. The ratio of infirmiers to population in the Mali Sahel, for example, is 1:7,500 on the average. In the entire region of Gao in Mali there are two rudimentary hospitals serving the population of 500,000 people. In general, because of the vast distances involved in this area, only the population within a limited radius of these facilities receives hospital service.

In view of the complexities of nomad lifestyles, it is easy to understand why the delivery of health services to them has always posed serious logistical problems. In 1969 studies were undertaken to determine the best method of delivering health services to nomads (Imperato 1975 b). The four major areas of difficulty defined in these studies, aside from the logistical ones, are as follows:

1. Nomads are generally unfamiliar with the services offered. Consequently, there is little consumer recognition of the desirability of the services.

2. Nomads view themselves as a separate polity and therefore tend to deal with the government in the spirit of an equal, much the same as they deal with other ethnic groups. Their view of government has historically been that of an adversary, a view that still persists. Both colonial administrations and the governments of independent African states have modified the traditional lifestyle of nomads in a profound fashion by putting an end to serfdom and slavery and by punishing and actively preventing pillage. Such measures have been against the vested interests of the ruling power structure of nomadic groups and have over the years resulted in loss of wealth as well as erosion of power and prestige for them. As a consequence, nomads are not overly friendly to nor cooperative with government and government-associated activities.

3. The most intense contacts between nomads and governments in the past several decades have occurred during the collection of taxes. Taxes are and have been levied not only on each adult member of a family but also on every declared head of livestock. Nomads have experienced little or no tangible benefits from such annual taxes since most of the monies go to support the machinery of modern government and to provide government services from which they are far removed. They have avoided paying taxes in several ways. Births are often not reported while deaths are reported where none have occurred. Roughly 10 percent of existing livestock is declared for taxation purposes, and every attempt is made to avoid both a human and livestock census. All government agents are suspected of being tax collectors, even health workers. This is understandable since in the past government tax collectors used any number of disguises and often attached themselves for convenience to mobile health teams. Therefore, the routine registering of names and the counting of people during the delivery of health care has been viewed as an attempt at census taking for taxation purposes. Nomads now avoid the annual groupings that were once held to celebrate the end of the rainy season. During these celebrations, large numbers of nomads gathered with their herds at either river crossings or around salt licks. Eventually, so did the tax collectors. In the eyes of the nomads, taxation is pillaging carried out by a superior force—the government. It is inconceivable to them, therefore, that government would be interested in their health and welfare.

4. For the same reason that the nomads avoid traditional congregations of any size, they also avoid assembling at a given point or at a given village in order to receive health services. The use of assembly points for delivering health services is successful in areas of extremely high population density and among sedentary populations (Imperato 1969 b). However, among Sahelian nomads it has consistently been a failure. Aside from their unwillingness to assemble for fear of taxation, nomads also are unwilling to assemble in the villages of sedentary farmers. And for their part, the sedentary farmers are unwilling to permit such assemblage. Thus, attempts at assembling nomads in one place for the purpose of delivering a health service have generally been unsuccessful.

In 1969-71, mobile health services were delivered to the nomadic population in the region of Gao. The results of this program have been described elsewhere (Imperato 1974 b). During this program, approximately 50 to 80 percent of the nomadic population in various areas was reached.

The low population density of the Sahel, the dispersion of nomads over a wide geographic area, and the long distances between

individual nomad camps necessitated the investment of man-hours
and gasoline far in excess of those invested in campaigns for sedentary
farmers living in the same areas. The operational costs for the
program for nomads was eleven-fold more than that for the sedentary
agricultural population.

Short-Term Effects

The settlement of large numbers of nomads in refugee camps
throughout the Sahel has brought this population into intense contact
for the first time with the existing health care delivery systems. In
most of the larger refugee camps, dispensaries were established to
deliver medical services equal to and in many instances more varied
and of higher quality than those delivered in rural dispensaries
serving sedentary populations of this same area of Africa. Nomadic
populations, heretofore inaccessible and beyond the reach of most
health service delivery systems, were exposed to these systems and
to their services. Therefore, the immediate effect of the drought
has been that nomads have become recipients on a large scale of
modern preventive and curative health services for the first time.
They also have received rudimentary exposure to health education
programs that seek to raise levels of personal and environmental
hygiene. Also, nomads have experienced the benefits of modern
medical care in a very dramatic way. All of this has had an immediate
effect on their attitudes toward modern medical care.
In summary, then, the immediate effect of the drought on the
delivery of health services to nomads has been as follows:

1. To bring a large number of nomads into the delivery system.
2. To demonstrate the advantages of the services that the
system can deliver.
3. To improve general levels of health and well-being.
4. To modify attitudes toward modern medical care.
5. To raise levels of environmental personal hygiene of nomads.

Long Term-Effects

The heavy rains of 1974 effectively terminated the acute drought
situation in most areas of the Sahel. The immediate effect of these
rains was to provide for an excellent cereal harvest in the Sahel and
in the savanna and to generate excellent pasture for the remaining

livestock. In Mali the 80, 000 refugees who had been present in thirty
camps in July 1974 had, for the most part, left these camps by
November 1974. Half this population consisted of sedentary Songhoi
farmers who returned to their riverine villages to plant crops
(Imperato 1974 a). The nomadic population of Maures and Tuaregs
were provided with a three months supply of food and sent out into
the bush to harvest two wild varieties of cereal that had grown with
profusion throughout the Sahel.

It is difficult to predict at the time of this writing whether or
not the nomads will resume their pre-drought lifestyle and what
proportion of them have or will have the animal resources to do so.
A small number of families, whose herds escaped in time to the
south during the drought, have been able to resume their pre-drought
existence (Imperato 1974 c). But all these nomads have now been
intensively exposed to the modern health care delivery system under
circumstances where personnel and supplies were more than adequate.
In a sense, then, they were exposed in other Sahelian countries to the
best of what could be offered. What will be the lasting impact of this
experience is difficult to predict. However, it is certain that many
of them will avail themselves of services delivered in fixed curative
facilities such as dispensaries, maternal and child health stations
and hospitals, or by mobile teams dispensing immunizations and
prophylactic medication.

The drought focused the developed world's attention on the
Sahel. A variety of multilateral and bilateral assistance programs
have enabled African governments to expand and upgrade the health
services infrastructure in the Sahel. The net effect will be to raise
general levels of health in the Sahel,to decrease morbidity and mortality among the Sahelian population. However, this improvement in
health care will not be sustained without long-term assistance from
outside donors. The principal handicap in delivering high-quality
health care in the Sahel has been and will continue to be a lack of
funds with which to purchase drugs and medical supplies, an on-going
need. At the present time, many areas have adequate numbers of
health workers who cannot function even at a minimally acceptable
level because they lack the necessary resources to dispense medical
care. This situation will be progressively aggravated as greater
numbers of medical and paramedical personnel are added to the
existing cadres.

In Mali, for example, personnel costs within the Ministry of
Public Health budget are twice the operating costs, a situation that
will worsen if ways are not found to pay for operations. The specter
of rural dispensaries staffed by adequate numbers of well-trained
personnel but devoid of drugs and medical supplies will become more
common if ways are not found to provide basic medical supplies. It

would be unrealistic to expect the governments of these countries to provide these needed resources. They simply do not possess them. Consequently, the long-term expansion and upgrading of health services in the Sahel will require sizeable long-term investments from outside donors.

SOURCES

Brasseur, G. and G. Le Moal. 1963. Cartes Ethno Demographiques de l'Afrique Occidentale. Dakar: Institute Francais d'Afrique Noire (IFAN).

Cissoko, Fily Dabo. 1962. La Savanne Rouge. Avignon: Presses Universelles.

Furon, R. 1929. "Le Sahel Soudanais." La Geographie, 51, pp. 149-63.

Gallay, H. 1909. Trois annees d'assistance medicales aux indigenes et de lutte contre la variole. Paris: Larousse.

Imperato, P.J. 1969a. An Outline to the Movements of the Pastoral Peul and the Migratory Bozo Fishermen in the Inland Delta of the Niger. Atlanta: U.S. Department of Health, Education and Welfare.

Imperato, P.J. 1969b. "The Use of Markets as Vaccination Sites in the Mali Republic." Journal of Tropical Medicine and Hygiene 72, pp. 8-13.

Imperato, P.J. 1969c. "Traditional Attitudes Towards Measles in the Republic of Mali." Transactions of The Royal Society of Tropical Medicine and Hygiene 63, pp. 236-41.

Imperato, P.J. 1972. "Nomads of the Niger." Natural History 81, pp. 60-69, 78-79.

Imperato, P.J. 1974a. Health and Nutrition Services of the Sahel Relief And Rehabilitation Program in Mali. Washington, D.C.: American Public Health Association.

Imperato, P.J. 1974b. "Nomads of the West African Sahel and the Delivery of Health Services to Them." Social Science and Medicine 8, no. 8, pp. 443-57.

Imperato, P.J. 1974c. USAID Health Sector Report, Republic of Mali. Washington, D.C.: USAID.

Imperato, P.J. 1975a. "Cholera in Mali and Popular Reactions to its First Appearance." Journal of Tropical Medicine and Hygiene 77

Imperato, P.J. 1975a. "Cholera in Mali and Popular Reactions to its First Appearance." Journal of Tropical Medicine and Hygiene 77, pp. 290-296.

Imperato, P.J. 1975b. "The Strategy and Tactic for Vaccinating the Populations of the Inland Delta of the Niger." Afrique Medicale 14, pp. 307-316.

Imperato, P.J.; O.Sow; and B. Fofana. 1973. "Mass Campaigns and Their Comparative Operational Costs for Nomadic and Sedentary Populations in Mali." Tropical and Geographical Medicine 25, pp. 416-22.

Kloth, T.I. 1974. Sahel Nutrition Survey 1974. Atlanta: USPHS.

Lhote, M. 1960. "L'Hygiene Mobile." Mimeo. Bobo-Dioulasso.

"Nutritional Surveillance in Drought Affected Areas of West Africa." 1973. Washington, D.C.: U.S. Department of Health, Education and Welfare.

Pele, J. 1974. Rapport de Mission au Mali du 6 au 20 Avril. Dakar: ORANA.

Richer, C. 1972. "Panorama General du Cholera." Afrique Medicale 11, pp. 635-37.

Rouch, J. 1951. "Les Pecheurs du Niger: Techniques de Peche, Organization Economique, Probleme des Migrations." Comptes Rendus Commaires des Seances de l'Institut Francais d'Anthropologie 5, pp. 17-20.

Said, M. 1904. "Les Tribus Arabes de la Region de Tombouctou." Revue Tunisienne 11, pp. 479-89.

Swift, J. 1972. "Nomadisme et Utilisation des Terres." Etudes Maliennes 2, pp. 49-53.

Stenning, D.J. 1959. Savannah Nomads. London: Oxford University Press.

Szabo, A. 1970. Rapport au Gouvernement du Mali sur Ameliorations Possibles de l'Utilization des Produits de la Peche. Rome: United Nations Development Fund, Report no. AT 2900.

14

WEATHER AND CLIMATE
MODIFICATION AND THE
FUTURE OF THE SAHARA
Michael H. Glantz
William Parton

This chapter discusses some of the weather and climate modification schemes proposed since 1900 for the regions in West and
Central Africa surrounding and including the Sahara Desert. These
schemes were often discussed seriously during times of prolonged
droughts, of which there have been three in this region since 1900:
1910-14, 1941-42, and 1968-74.

The schemes have been seriously proposed by their respective
authors as ways to minimize the impact of periodic West African
droughts. The authors of this chapter do not necessarily endorse or
disagree with the proposals presented. They wish to present them
so that the readers will be aware of some types of "scientific" solutions suggested for "saving" or reclaiming the Sahara region. (In
fact, some of these suggestions such as reforestation and cloud
seeding have become operational in other countries as well as in the
Sahel. The asphalt island experiment was almost carried out in

The authors would like to thank Dr. Stephen Schneider and
Dr. W.W. Kellogg, who provided useful comments as well as a
critical review of this chapter.

This paper is being published in the second edition of D. Dalby
and R. J. Harrison Church, eds., Drought in Africa, Center for
African Studies, School of Oriental and African Studies, University of
London, December, 1975. The research was undertaken as part of a
larger study sponsored by the International Federation of Institutes for
Advanced Study (Stockholm, Sweden). The study is concerned with
"The Social Implications of a Credible Long Range Climate Forecast."

Venezuela in the late 1960s.) It is suggested that, no matter how extraordinary or unfeasible the schemes may seem to the reader, they should be taken as seriously as they were proposed. There are those who believe that technological advancements will resolve many of the perennial problems of the Sahel, but technological solutions must be scientifically assessed for social as well as physical implications.

THE SAHARA

The Sahara, currently the world's largest desert, extends from the Atlantic Ocean across to the Red Sea. In Africa it touches about thirteen countries whose populations exceed 150 million. Geographically, the Sahara can be divided into five main regions, as shown in Figure 14.1.

FIGURE 14.1

Principal Geographical Subdivisions of the Sahara

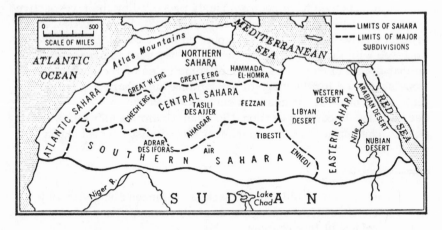

The region known as the Sahel extends from west to east and straddles the geographic border between the southern Sahara and the Sudan zones, and is part of the savanna belt, which receives a long-term annual rainfall average of 300 to 650 mm.[1] It is a marginal climatic zone in that it is subject to wide variations of precipitation in time and space. The Sahel encompasses six former French colonies—Senegal, Mauritania, Mali, Niger, Upper Volta, and Chad—states that have been suffering from the effects of six years of drought (see Figure 14.2).

FIGURE 14.2

Sahelian States

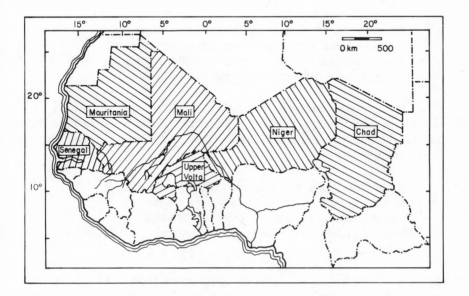

During the recent drought, precipitation in this region was considerably less than the long-term averages. The sharp reduction in rainfall has had a major impact on the Sahelian nomads, who lost the livestock on which they depended for food and transportation, forcing them to settle in makeshift camps close to population centers. Sedentary farmers unable to produce adequate, harvestable crops became dependent on the urban centers for whatever welfare their governments or international donors might be able to supply. Those in the urban centers, affected by the influx of refugees from other parts of the region, had to look to the international community for food relief.[2]

It is important to keep in mind that the regions surrounding the Sahara, especially the Sahel, are potentially productive but that poor land management practices—such as indiscriminate well drilling, overgrazing, and reduction of fallow time—have reduced the ability of this "marginal" land to withstand the impact of periodic extended dry spells and droughts.

Most of the weather and climate modification proposals for the Sahara and the Sahel have been suggested in an attempt to restore potentially productive arable land and to compensate for the tendency

of the inhabitants to destroy their land through poor land management.
With respect to the former objective, it has been suggested that there
exists a large reservoir of water under the Sahara Desert:

> men have only recently become aware of the vast
> dimensions of the subterranean reservoir below the
> Sahara . . . good soils are also available; recent
> investigations have shown that extensive tracts of
> desert land have arable (and once cultivated) soils
> overlain by a thin cover of sand.[3]

With respect to the latter, it is generally accepted that the
agricultural and animal husbandry practices of the region's inhabitants
have had a negative impact on the fertility of the land. Nicholas Wade
recently summarized this view:

> the primary cause of the desertification is man,
> and the desert in the Sahel is not so much a
> natural expansion of the Sahara but is being
> formed in situ under the impact of human
> activity.[4]

Although there have been three droughts since 1900, a major difference
in the setting of the first major drought in this century and the current
one involves technological capabilities. Interest in modifying the
weather and the climate is probably as old as man, but the developing
capability to do something about that interest is fairly recent. Research in this area has intensified since the end of World War II.

Awareness of the growing capability of the scientific and
engineering communities to modify weather and climate, and of the
political community's lack of restraint to experiment with such new
scientific endeavors, has come at a time when the global climate
appears to be undergoing some unexplainable variations. To some,
these variations mark the beginning of a transition to a new climate
norm; to others, they are just fluctuations within the current regime.
Regardless of which view proves correct, the effects of these variations are now being felt around the world: excessive droughts in sub-
Saharan Africa, India, the Soviet Union, Central America, Brazil,
and East Africa; and excessive rains in the Philippines, parts of
Kenya and Australia, and New Zealand. In addition, major grain
exporters like Canada, the United States, and Australia also were
affected by adverse climatic fluctuations in 1974, reducing the
world's available grain reserves. Coupling the impact of these
events with the revelations concerning military uses of weather
modification during the recent wars in Indochina,[5] much attention

has been drawn to the possible social and economic utility of planned weather and climate modification. While some members of the scientific community see a hope in the development of weather and climate modification techniques, others are extremely skeptical of their value. Figure 14.3 illustrates some possible engineering schemes that could be or have been proposed to modify or control the climate. An interesting discussion of the possible impact of such schemes can be found in an article by W. Kellogg and S. Schneider. [6]

FIGURE 14.3

Schematic of Engineering Schemes That Could Be
Proposed to Modify or Control the Climate

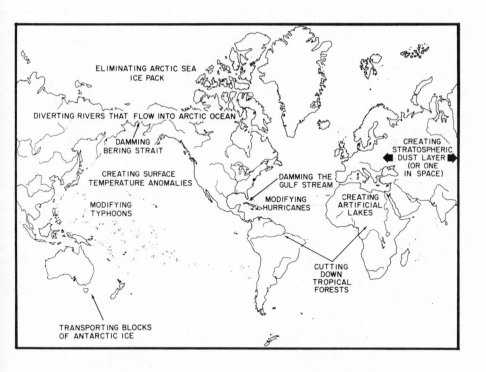

Source: Reprinted with permission of W. W. Kellogg and S. Schneider, National Center for Atmospheric Research (Boulder, Colorado).

When discussing modification schemes, it is important to distinguish between weather and climate modification. Weather modification is generally taken to mean that the impact will be of short duration. Cloud seeding operations designed to produce a change in precipitation are one example. The impact of climate modification, on the other hand, extends over a longer period of time (a month, a season, or more). The suggestion of melting the Arctic icecap by spreading black particles on the ice is an example of this type of weather modification.

Types of weather and climate modification schemes can be further divided into two categories based on the intent of the modification plan: advertent (planned) and inadvertent (unplanned). The former is intentionally undertaken to achieve a predetermined objective such as a cloud seeding operation to suppress hail. The latter refers to activities that are designed to achieve an objective (not necessarily the modification of the weather and climate) but trigger side effects modifying weather and climate. An example of inadvertent weather modification would be precipitation modification by urban areas. F.A. Huff and S.A. Changnon, Jr. "have shown that measurable enhancement of precipitation has existed for several years in and/or downwind of six large urban centers in the humid portions of the United States."[7] For convenience, weather and climate modification proposals relating to the Sahara region can be divided into three (not mutually exclusive) categories based on the techniques used for the purpose of planned (advertent) modification: (1) vegetation modification, (2) atmospheric circulation modification, and (3) precipitation modification.

VEGETATION MODIFICATION

Weather and climate modification schemes relating to a change in vegetative cover are based on the assumption that there exist feedback interactions between the biosphere and the atmosphere (see Figure 14.4). A 1950 U.N./FAO report succinctly stated this view:

> The influence of forests on climate, however, is on
> less pure ground, and leads to considerable contro-
> versy. Nevertheless, extensive areas of woodlands
> such as the equatorial forests in Africa appear to
> have a definite and positive effect on climate, and
> the destruction of such woodlands would undoubtedly
> cause climate disturbances that might eventually
> make the Continent as a whole uninhabitable.[8]

FIGURE 14.4

Vegetation Zones of West Africa

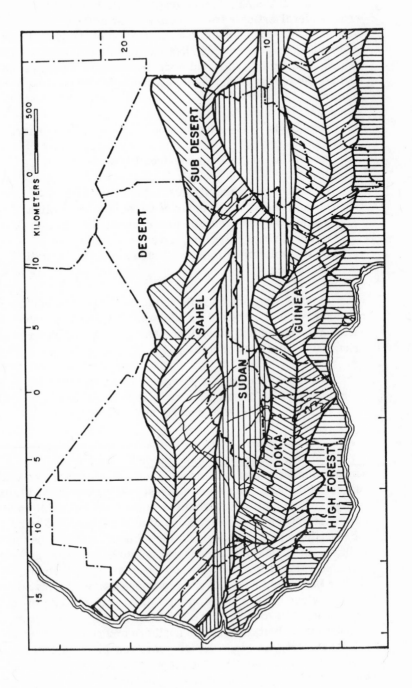

In the 1930s, E.P. Stebbing, a British forestry professor, wrote several articles based on this point of view. He suggested that deforestation, coupled with overutilization of the land through poor land management practices, has led to desiccation of the soil. This, in turn, had led to a slow but sure decrease in annual rainfall in the region. He observed the deterioration of the ecosystem to be as follows:

woodlands ⟶ savannah ⟶ Sahel ⟶ desert

According to Stebbing, desiccation of the soil

is held to be primarily due to the over-utilization
of the vegetative covering of the soil, under which
productivity is reduced, water supplies decrease
in the springs, streams, rivers and wells, the
water table sinks in the soil strata and the rainfall
decreases. [9]

In other writings he referred to a linkage between the vegetative cover and rainfall, but did not elaborate. Owen Lattimore, in an essay on geographical factors and Mongol history, referred to this linkage in a similarly general way:

Both the cultivation of marginal areas and the
overgrazing of stock in true steppe areas can
ruin the soil, create deserts and "change" the
climate. [10]

Stebbing, concerned about the shift southward of the desert sands at an estimated rate (in 1935) of one kilometer per year, suggested the construction of a forest belt across West Africa. The purpose of the belt was to stop the sands from being blown by the northeasterly winds onto arable land to the south, and to break up the hot, dry winds that desicate the soils over which they pass. In addition, the belt would encourage moisture retention in the soil and increase rainfall for some reason unexplained by Stebbing. This shelter belt would have the same purpose as the one that was to have been developed in the 1930s in the United States. With the current drought in West Africa, there has been renewed interest in a "green barrier" (tree belt) across the northern and southern fringes of the Sahara Desert. An extensive 20-year tree-planting program was begun in 1975 in Algeria. The planned barrier will be 950 miles long, 10 miles wide, and will extend from the Moroccan border to the Tunisian border. It is designed to stop the northward advance of the Sahara and to reclaim 70, 000 square miles of steppe for farming and stock raising. [11]

Recent scientific research on the feedback mechanisms between vegetation and the atmosphere suggests ways in which the feedback processes might operate. For example, Russell Schnell has stated:

> evidence has recently . . . shown that [very
> small] organic particles (i.e., biogenic nuclei)
> produced during the decay of vegetable matter
> may be important in providing nuclei in clouds
> upon which ice may form and from which pre-
> cipitation may develop. [12]

Schnell's study suggests that the destruction, natural and human, of the vegetative cover will lead to inadvertent climate modification due to a decrease in the availability of the biogenic nuclei.

Another recent attempt to analyze the linkage between the vegetative cover and its impact on rainfall and climate modification is a climate simulation experiment performed with a mathematical model by Jules Charney and his team. About this experiment they have written:

> two integrations of global general circulation
> model, differing only in the prescribed surface
> albedo (reflectivity) in the Sahara, show that an
> increase in albedo resulting from a decrease in
> plant cover causes a decrease in rainfall. Thus,
> any tendency for plant cover to decrease would be
> reinforced by a decrease in rainfall, and could
> initiate or perpetuate a drought. [13]

If the Schnell and Charney hypotheses concerning inadvertent climate modification are proven valid (they both operate in the same direction), Stebbing's idea about the linkage between deforestation and decreased rainfall would be scientifically strengthened. See also Norman MacLeod's chapter in this volume for similar reasons supporting the view that "the restabilization of the land through establishment of plant cover is a real alternative to drought and famine."

ATMOSPHERIC CIRCULATION MODIFICATION

This group of modification schemes is designed to alter the physical characteristics of the atmospheric boundary layer—the kilometer or so of the lower atmosphere that is greatly affected by conditions at the earth's surface. Three of these schemes are the asphalt island concept, carbon black dust in the atmosphere, and the creation of a large body of water in the Sahara.

Asphalt Island Concept

James Black suggested that significant additional rainfall can be produced in arid or semiarid regions by spraying a large area near a body of water with a thin coating of asphalt. [14] The surface albedo (reflectivity) of the coating would be much lower than the surrounding sand, soil, vegetation, or water. The temperature difference between the coated surface and its uncoated surroundings would lead to vertical convection of air over the blackened strip. The heated asphalt surface would heat the air column above it, and the heated air would rise. The rising air motion would promote cloud formation and, ultimately, precipitation (if moisture were present in the atmosphere, there would be no need for the experiment to be done near a body of water). [15] This technique as shown in the following schematic is designed to produce an effect similar to that caused by mountain ranges, but its magnitude would be less.

FIGURE 14.5

Schematic of Model Used to Match Thermal
Mountains to Real Ones

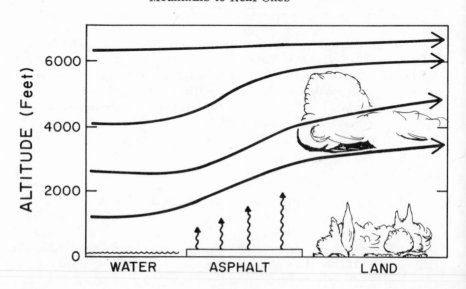

"This effect is particularly striking on the Mediterranean Coast of North Africa where a general rainfall of about 76 mm per annum increases to 500 to 800 mm in the neighborhood of mountains."[16] There is water vapor in the atmosphere over arid lands, but a mechanism is lacking to bring it out as rainfall until it reaches distant mountain ranges. Such a project could be based on other scientific investigations concerning precipitation augmentation caused by heat sources (on asphalt strip). To reinforce his proposition, Black cites as potential (heat) sources of precipitation large cities, "cloud streets" (cloud trails[17] associated with tropical islands), large fires, and large industrial areas.

It is suggested that this proposed weather or climate modification process could produce "2 or 3 acres of arable land per acre of asphalt"[18] and that "the investment cost of producing the heavy rainfall region downwind from a weather modification coating is estimated to be about $75/acre [as of 1967]" as opposed to irrigation project costs in Egypt and Australia from $300 to $600 per acre.[19]

It should be pointed out that, although other studies reinforce the heat source cloud formation proposition,[20] the idea of weather or climate modification attributed to the construction of asphalt islands has been based on intuition, theoretical considerations, and analogy, and has yet to be operationally verified.[21] It also appears that to date no country has been willing to allow hundreds of square miles of its land to be asphalt-coated for the purpose of increasing rainfall downwind of the asphalt, regardless how barren the land in question.

Carbon Dust

Although not specifically recommended for application in the Sahara, this proposal is similar to Black's asphalt island concept. The major difference is that the artificial heat source would be placed directly into the atmosphere rather than on the earth's surface. W. Gray and colleagues have proposed that "beneficial mesoscale (100-200 km) weather modification may be possible in the coming decade or two by solar absorption of carbon dust"[22] in order to enhance rainfall along tropical and subtropical coastlines or to enhance cumulonimbus (rain cloud) formation over areas in need of precipitation. This would be accomplished by placing carbon dust in the atmosphere to absorb solar radiation, which would then heat the surrounding air. The dust, acting as an artificial heat source, would increase evaporation (if released over a water surface, for example) from the water surface and promote extra cumulus convection over the land area. Gray and colleagues assume that the increased evaporation and convection would cause an increase in rainfall over the coastal area. They suggest that the carbon dust heat source is more efficient than the asphalt island source because (1) the dust is mixed in and moves with the air the experimenters are seeking to heat; (2) when applied over the ocean, nearly all the solar energy absorption by the carbon dust is extra energy gained; and (3) the area the dust can impact will be much greater (100 km^2 for asphalt as opposed to 10,000 to 100,000 km^2 for carbon dust).[23]

Although a preliminary environmental impact statement was made on the use of carbon dust for weather modification, there was no reference to the possible long-term effect of the accumulation of this dust in the environment. In addition, the experiment has to be reinitiated each time the heat source is to be created, whereas the asphalt strips would have a one-time construction. This technique of weather modification has not yet been tested.

It also should be mentioned that placing carbon dust in the atmosphere could lead to the opposite of the desired effect. It could lead to atmospheric warming at high enough elevations to suppress cloud formation. That is, the in situ heating of the atmosphere from the carbon dust could lead to increased atmospheric stability, which could occur if the dark-colored dust absorbed a significant fraction of the solar energy that would otherwise have penetrated through to the earth's surface, since surface heating drives the convective instability that causes much of the initial rainfall.[24]

Lake Sahara

Since about a quarter of the whole Sahara Desert area lies below sea level, the construction of a canal some fifty miles long through the higher land of the north African coast would immediately create a Sahara Sea equal in size to about half the extent of the Mediter-ranean. . . . All the arid regions now surrounding the desert and those parts of the Sahara which are now above the level of the ocean would be rendered as fertile as Europe. . . . Millions of human beings could then support themselves in comfort, who now lead a miserable existence on the verge of starvation.[25]

This statement was made by a Professor Etchegoyen, a dis-tinguished French scientist who, about 1910, attempted to foster interest in altering the climate of the African continent to enhance "its value as a place of colonization for Europeans." The sea, he suggested, would lead to an increase in precipitation. Differential heating of the body of water and the surrounding land would create convection, which in turn would lead to increased precipitation, in part because increased water vapor due to evaporation would exist in the area above the lake and around its edges (see Figure 14.6, which shows depressions in the Sahara).

In 1962 James McDonald challenged some of the basic assumptions behind projects like Lake Sahara. In his article, "The Evaporation-Precipitation Fallacy," he questioned the supposition that

> the creation of open water areas from which water
> would evaporate to augment the atmosphere's stock
> of vapour . . . will lead to increased local precipi-
> tations. In the driest period of a severe drought in
> any part of the world, huge masses of water are still
> drifting invisibly overhead, the principal cause of
> drought almost invariably being lack of dynamic
> processes capable of producing ascending motions
> that cause adiabatic cooling and, hence, cloud-
> formation as the indispensible first steps in getting
> any of the water down to the earth's surface. [26]

In 1974 R.R. Rapp and M. Warshaw undertook a numerical model simulation to determine the impact of a relatively small modification in surface boundary conditions (that is, modification of the earth's surface). [27] The Mintz-Arakawa model that they used divided the atmosphere into 3,240 grid points. Lake Sahara covered an area encompassing only six of the model's grid points. Globally, this modification is small, but on a regional basis it is quite large. While noting the shortcomings of the model on which the simulation was based, they concluded that there was a very low probability (<0.05) that there would be a change in the rainfall around the lake but that there was increased precipitation in a mountainous region about 900 kilometers from the lake. [28] It should be emphasized, however, that there have been many problems associated with the model used by Rapp and Warshaw; therefore, the results should be treated accordingly. [29] As they noted, their findings were consistent with those presented above by McDonald, asserting that although there may be an increase in atmospheric moisture caused by the presence of a large body of water in an arid region, there is still a need for a precipitation mechanism to release the water into the atmosphere. The moisture in the atmosphere may have to be transported 100 to 1,000 kilometers before reaching a condition favorable to the occurrence of precipitation. Peixoto and Kettani concluded that because of moisture transport ". . . the theory of the formation of precipitation from evaporation in a given place cannot be accepted." [30]

FIGURE 14.6

Depressions in the Sahara

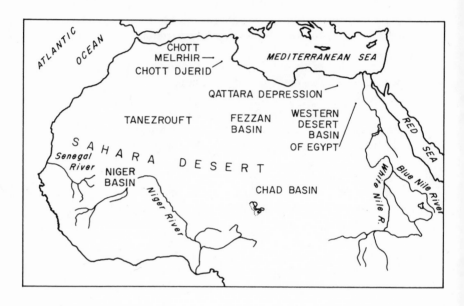

It has also been suggested that there may exist favorable side effects with the creation of Lake Sahara. Jose Peixoto and M. Ali Kettani pointed out that

> if Chott Melrhir [a large depression in Algeria and Tunisia] were flooded entirely by water from the Mediterranean, the discharge of the Great Eastern Erg [in Algeria] through evaporation would be greatly reduced, thus limiting the loss of usable underground water. [31]

It is possible that combinations of these weather climate modification techniques could be made to further enhance their goals. For example, one might combine the Lake Sahara concept with the asphalt island theory in an attempt to further increase precipitation that each of these techniques alone is (theoretically) expected to produce. Before any of these atmospheric circulation modification techniques becomes operational, an assessment of their implications should be systematically undertaken. Such questions as, "Where will the displaced descending air go?" or, "What impact will it have on the strength of the monsoonal front from which West Africa, including the Sahel, gets its annual precipitation?" must be answered at least in theory.

PRECIPITATION MODIFICATION

Perhaps the most popular form of weather modification is precipitation augmentation by cloud seeding. This technique has been widely discussed in the popular press, especially during periods of prolonged agricultural drought. After more than 30 years of experimentation with cloud seeding operations, apparently the best that a National Academy of Sciences report on this weather modification practice could conclude was that

> . . . on the basis of statistical analysis of well-designed field experiments that ice-nuclei seeding can sometimes lead to more precipitation, can sometimes lead to less precipitation, and at other times the nuclei have no effect, depending on the meteorological conditions.[32]

It has generally been accepted that there is available moisture in continental clouds as well as in maritime clouds (especially in coastal regions). For those interested in precipitation augmentation, the basic problem becomes one of increasing the clouds' efficiency with respect to processing water vapor in the atmosphere. With both types of clouds, the fact remains that only a relatively small fraction of the water vapor in an air mass falls out as rain. Cloud seeding is used to increase precipitation from cloud systems that "were already producing natural rain or were about to produce rain."

There has been growing interest in the potential uses of precipitation augmentation in general, and specifically for rain-deficient regions of the world such as the Sahel. At a recent meeting of the World Meteorological Organization (WMO) Working Group on Cloud Physics and Weather Modification of the Committee on Atmospheric Science, a "Draft Project Proposal for the Artificial Augmentation of Precipitation in the Sahelian Zone" was prepared.[33] It proposed that the project take six to seven years and be divided into three phases: feasibility study, preliminary experiments, and, if these are encouraging, an operational phase. The project would evaluate

the feasibility of precipitation augmentation in the Sahel, and the
results would determine feasibility as a weather modification scheme
for other arid regions. Although it would take at least two years, if
not several more, to evaluate the use of precipitation augmentation for
the Sahelian states, commercial cloud seeding activities have already
been carried out in the region.

For example, Weather Science, Inc., a private American firm,
was contracted by the government of Niger to undertake emergency
cloud seeding operations in September and October 1973. The seeding
design used in "Project Rain—1973" was based on research conducted
in the United States by several groups interested in this weather
modification technique. Ray Booker, the firm's president, reported
that only storms in the extreme southern section of Niger (Niamey,
Maradi, and Zinder) that had some potential for producing rain were
seeded with the hope of augmenting such rainfall (see Figure 14.7).

The process was described by Booker as follows:

the target clouds were selected for seeding when,
in the judgement of the pilot, they met the general
criteria. . . . In practice, this meant selecting
actively growing (cloud) towers which were believed
to be destined to rain in some amount. [34]

Booker's conclusions about the cloud seeding operations in Niger were
optimistic, though he noted that "no evaluation of the effectiveness of
seeding [was] possible on such a brief project." It is not clear in the
report on what he based his optimism. [35]

Cloud seeding operations have been undertaken in such countries
as the USSR, the United States (certain states), Canada, France,
Israel, Japan, and Australia with varying degrees of declared success.
Figure 14.8 indicates states that have experimented with and/or
conducted cloud-seeding operations. [36]

However, a National Academy of Sciences report has recently
raised some basic questions about the utility of cloud seeding in
convective clouds: [37]

● What is the increase in rainfall that can be expected from
cloud seeding?

● What effect does cloud seeding have on the internal dynamics
of clouds?

● What are the extra-area effects of cloud seeding?

Several important and timely questions on the feasibility and
utility of this form of weather modification have been raised. These
questions point to the need for additional scientific research, as
proposed by the WMO for the Sahel.

Recently an idea for water transfer from the water-rich tropical
parts of Africa to the water-poor regions, like the Sahel in West
Africa, was brought to light. [38] This plan would involve

FIGURE 14.7

Niger: Distribution of Annual Rain, 1931-60
(mm)

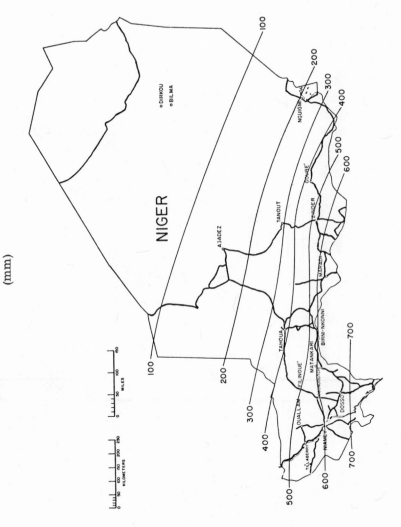

FIGURE 14.8

Nations in Which Weather (Precipitation and Hail) Modification projects
(Experimental or Nonexperimental) Have Occurred Since 1945

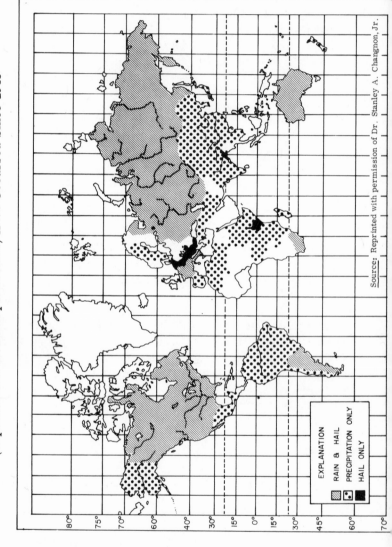

EXPLANATION

RAIN & HAIL

PRECIPITATION ONLY

HAIL ONLY

Source: Reprinted with permission of Dr. Stanley A. Changnon, Jr.

large-scale redistribution of prevailing rainfall by
displacement of the tropical front . . . resulting in
more rain in the interior of Africa than at present.
It would . . . be of interest to suppress part of
the copious rains in Cameroon, Nigeria, and other
coastal states in North Africa (sic) to keep more
moisture in the monsoon for condensation further
inland. [39]

This could be accomplished, T. Bergeron suggested, by overseeding
clouds in areas of high rainfall, along the Gulf of Guinea Coast, for
example, so that the rainfall would be suppressed, only to be precipitated out of the atmosphere further inland over the relatively arid
zones. [40]

The degree of accuracy of his assumption that the overseeding
of clouds in high-rainfall areas can cause rainfall to be suppressed
and precipitated at a later time has yet to be determined. In fact,
Bergeron recognized this when he suggested:

in order to lay a quantitative foundation for such
investigations and experiments, it would be
advisable to perform a study of the water-vapour
balance over Africa . . . and to use tritium as
a tracer for following the exchange of air in this
region. [41]

Bergeron also suggested that widespread irrigation across the
savanna and steppe of sub-Saharan Africa, using major African
rivers such as the Congo, Niger, and Nile, could provide a positive
feedback mechanism, which would purposefully modify the climate:

More water—more vegetation—more evaporation
and less runoff—more clouds and rain—more cooling
of the monsoon air (by evaporation and increased
cloudiness)—more vegetation. [42]

This mechanism would shift the arable land limit northward
and "presumably also the Tropical front itself because of increased
production of cool monsoon air."[43] As one can see, this plan somehow
involves the controversial and as yet unknown impacts of vegetation,
irrigation, and cloud seeding on precipitation modification.

CONCLUSION

Weather and climate modification may prove to be a long-term
solution for the development and reclamation of potentially arable

land in the Sahara and Sahel. At this time, however, scientific
research in the way of feasibility studies and experimentation has
not yielded enough information about the impact or the utility of such
schemes to make any of them operational. Yet solutions to perennial
problems caused in part by the variability of climate in the region
are needed now. It is strongly suggested that attention be turned to
the improvement of poor land management practices used by the inhabitants of the area. This interim solution would seek to arrest the
current deterioration of arable and grazing land, thereby making it
available for continued use in the future. It would be easier and less
costly to stop the deterioration before the land is lost to desertification and erosion, for example, than it would be to rejuvenate the
land once it has gone beyond a critical level.

NOTES

1. W. Gerald Matlock and E. Lendell Cockrum, A Framework
for Agricultural Development Planning: The Sahel-Sudan Region,
vol. 2 (Cambridge, Mass: MIT Center for Policy Alternatives,
December 1974), p. 90.
    2. For a brief discussion of the drought's impact, see Derek
Winstanley, "The Impact of Regional Climatic Fluctuations on Man:
Some Global Implications," paper to be presented at the WMO
Symposium, Norwich, England, August 1975.
    3. Robert P. Ambroggi, "Water Under the Sahara," Scientific
American, May 1966, p. 21.
    4. N. Wade, "The Sahelian Drought: No Victory for Western
Aid," Science, July 19, 1974, p. 235.
    5. See Deborah Shapley, "Weather Warfare: Pentagon Concedes
7-Year Vietnam Effort," Science, June 7, 1974, pp. 1059-61.
    6. W. Kellogg and S. Schneider, "Climate Stabilization: For
Better or for Worse?", Science 186 (December 27, 1974): 1163-72.
    7. F.A. Huff and S.A. Changnon, Jr., "Precipitation Modifica-
tion by Major Urban Areas," Bulletin of the American Meteorological
Society, December 1973, p. 1230.
    8. Quoted in J. Grant, "Some Notes on Drought in Africa and
on Control of Weather," paper presented at the University of London
(SOAS) Symposium on Drought in Africa, July 19-20, 1973, p. 1.
    9. E.P. Stebbing, "The Man-made Desert in Africa," Journal
of the Royal African Society-Supplement 37, no. 146 (January 1938):
13.
    10. Owen Lattimore, "The Geographical Factor in Mongol
History," The Geographical Journal 91, no. 1 (January 1938): 1.

11. New York Times, February 16, 1975, p. 11.

12. R. Schnell, "Biogenic and Inorganic Sources for Ice-Nuclei in the Drought-Stricken Areas of the Sahel—1974," Report to the Directors of the Rockefeller Foundation (New York, December 1974), p. 3.

13. Jules Charney et al., "Drought in the Sahara: A Biogeophysical Feedback Mechanism," Science, February 7, 1975, p. 434.

14. J.F. Black, "Asphalt Island Concept of Weather Modification," ESSO memorandum (Linden, N.J., June 4, 1970).

15. J.F. Black and B.I. Tarmy, "The Use of Asphalt Coatings to Increase Rainfall," Journal of Applied Meteorology 2, no. 5 (October 1963): 557.

16. J.F. Black and A.H. Popkin, "New Roles for Asphalt in Controlling Man's Environment," paper presented at the National Petroleum Refiners Association Annual Meeting, San Antonio, Texas, April 1967, p. 6.

17. Black, "Asphalt Island," p. 1.

18. Black and Tarmy, "The Use."

19. Black and Popkin, "New Roles," p. 7.

20. See J.F.W. Purdom, "Satellite Imagery and Mesoscale Convection Forecast Problem," in Preprints of the Eighth Conference on Severe Local Storms (Boston, Mass: American Meteorological Society, 1973), pp. 244-51; J.S. Malkus, "Tropical Rain Induced by a Small Natural Heat Source," Journal of Applied Meteorology, 1963, pp. 547-56.

21. For a critique of the asphalt island project, see W. Gray, et al., "Weather Modification by Carbon Dust Absorption of Solar Energy," in Proceedings of the Fourth Conference on Weather Modification, Ft. Lauderdale, Florida, November, 18-21, 1974, p. 195.

22. Gray, et al., "Weather Modification," p. 191.

23. Ibid, p. 195.

24. Private conversation with Dr. Stephen Schneider, deputy head of the Climate Project, National Center for Atmospheric Research, May 1975.

25. G.A. Thompson, "A Plan for Converting the Sahara Desert into a Sea," Scientific American, August 10, 1912, p. 114.

26. J. MacDonald, "The Evaporation-Precipitation Fallacy," Weather 17, no. 5 (May 1962): 169.

27. R.R. Rapp and M. Warshaw, Some Predicted Climatic Effects of a Simulated Sahara Lake (Santa Monica, Calif.: RAND, March 1974)

28. Ibid., p. 25.

29. For a discussion of the problems associated with the Mintz-Arakawa model, see W.L. Gates, "The January Global Climate Simulated by a Two-Level General Circulation Model: A Comparison

with Observation," The Journal of the Atmospheric Sciences 32, no. 3 (March 1975): 449.

30. Jose Peixoto and M. Ali Kettani, "The Control of the Water Cycle," Scientific American, April 1973, p. 55.

31. Ibid., p. 60.

32. National Science Foundation, Weather Modification: Eighth Annual Report, 1966 (Washington, D.C.: U.S. Government Printing Office, 1967), p. 123.

33. World Meteorological Organization, "Report of the Third Session of the EC Panel on Weather Modification/CAS Working Group on Cloud Physics and Weather Modification," Toronto, Canada, October 28-November 2, 1974, Appendix F.

34. R. Booker, Project Rain—1973: A Final Report to the Republic of Niger (Niamey) and to Africare (Washington, D.C.) (Norman, Okla.: Weather Science Inc., November 1973), p. 12.

35. Ibid., p. 31.

36. For an interesting discussion on cloud seeding, see Stanley A. Chagnon, Jr., "The Paradox of Planned Weather Modification," Bulletin of the American Meteorological Society 56, no. 1 (January 1975): 27-37.

37. National Academy of Sciences, Weather and Climate Modification: Problems and Progress (Washington, D.C.: U.S. Government Printing Office, 1973).

38. M. Falkenmark and G. Lindh, "How Can We Cope with the Water Resources Situation by the Year 2015?", Ambio 3, nos. 3-4 (1974): 120.

39. T. Bergeron, Cloud Physics Research and the Future Fresh-Water Supply of the World (Report no. 19, Meteorological Institution, University of Uppsala, 1970), p. 10.

40. Ibid.

41. Ibid.

42. Ibid.

43. Ibid.

satellite imagery, 217, 219, 220,
227, 229, 230, 277
savanna, the, 12, 145-68
Schneider, S., 307
Schnell, Russell C., 206, 311
"security-related countries,"
113
sedentary farmers, Sahelian,
10, 11, 37-38, 130, 283-85,
286, 298, 300, 305
Selassie, Haile, 107-117
Select Committee on Nutrition,
U.S. Senate, 113
Senegal: drought in, 196; and
France, 28; gross national
product of, 30-31, 78, 105;
health care in, 283-301;
precipitation in, 10-11;
railroads in, 17, 86, 87;
U.S. aid to, 32, 43, 52, 57
(see also, the Sahel)
Senegal River, the, 31, 77, 132,
282, 283
Senegal River Basin Organiza-
tion (OMVS), 142
Senghor, Leopold, 17, 28, 90,
106
Service General Autonome de
Phrophylaxies et de Traite-
ment de la Maladie du
Sommeil, 294
Service National des Grandes
Endemies, 294
Service Prophalatique de la
Maladie du Sommeil, 293
Service de Sante Rural, 294
Sheets, Hal, 78, 94, 114
Sherbrooke, W.C., 15
soil: erosion, 15, 238, 251,
273; fertility, 132; moisture,
191-92, 220, 222, 257, 258
Somali, 10
Sorghum, 51, 52, 53, 69, 75
South Africa, 7
South Viet Nam, 18, 19

Soviet Union: grain purchases
by, 41, 49, 94; and Mali, 28;
Sahelian aid, 28, 85, 88
Spencer, Fermino, 35
Stebbing, E.P., 5, 8, 310
Subcommittee on Africa, U.S.
House of Representatives, 45
Subcommittee on Africa, U.S.
Senate, 39, 45
surface albedo (reflectivity), 206,
215, 312
Swedish International Development
Agency (SIDA), 13
Swift, Jonathan, 102
systems analysis of Sahelian
drought, 15-16, 232-54
syphilis, 294

technology, impact in the Sahel,
19-20, 78, 104-6, 119, 132,
177-84, 242, 304
temperature drop, global, 215
temperature gradient, Sahelian,
222
Thorbahn, P.F., 208
Tigre Province (Ethiopia), 208
trachoma, 288, 292
tractor cult, Sahelian, 181
transport, Sahelian relief, 12,
51-52, 85-90, 93 ff., 110
(see also, airlifts, ports,
railroads)
tree belt ("green barrier"), 310
Trudeau, Pierre, 17
trypanosomiasis (sleeping sickness), 236, 293, 294
tsetse fly, 135
Tuaregs, the, 12, 147, 149-68,
285, 287, 295

uranium, 105
United Kingdom, the, 30, 65, 86
United Nations aid to the Sahel
(see, the Food and Agriculture
Organization)

MICHAEL H. GLANTZ is an Assistant Professor of Political Science at the University of Colorado. He has recently been commissioned by the International Federation of Institutes for Advanced Study (Stockholm, Sweden) to undertake a study of the "Social, Political, Moral and Economic Implications of a Credible and Reliable Long-Range Climate Forecast." This study is being hosted at the University Corporation for Atmospheric Research (Boulder, Colorado). While a postdoctoral fellow at the National Center for Atmospheric Research, Professor Glantz researched various social and natural science aspects of the Sahelian drought. Professor Glantz received a Ph.D. from the University of Pennsylvania in 1970.

RANDALL BAKER is Dean and a Senior Lecturer at the School of Development Studies at the University of East Anglia (Norwich, England). He spent two years in Uganda as a researcher on a grant from the Goldsmiths' Company (London) from 1966-68. He became a lecturer in geography at Makerere University College in Uganda, 1968-70. Since 1970 he has worked at the School of Development Studies though in 1971 and 1972 he was seconded to write a regional plan for Saudi Arabia's western region.

E. LENDELL COCKRUM is Mammologist and Professor of Biological Science in the College of Liberal Arts at the University of Arizona. He has served as a consultant to Massachusetts Institute of Technology, various corporations, U.S. Public Health Service and the National Science Foundation. Professor Cockrum is the author of several articles and books. Dr. Cockrum earned his Ph.D. in zoology at the University of Kansas. His research interests are concerned with populations, distribution and evaluation of desert mammals and changes associated with land use. Current projects are conducted in both the Sonoran Desert and the Sahara in Tunisia.

MOHAMED EL-KHAWAS is Professor of African and Middle Eastern History at Federal City College in Washington, D.C. He has been a frequent panelist and speaker and has written extensively on political issues encompassing the United Nations, Africa, China and the Middle East. Professor El-Khawas received his Ph.D. from the School of Advanced International Studies, Johns Hopkins University in 1968.

PASCAL J. IMPERATO, M.D., is the First Deputy Commissioner for the City of New York's Department of Health. He has lived and worked in Mali for five years as a medical adviser. He has written several books and articles on health care in Mali and has been a USAID consultant for an evaluation of the health needs of Sahelian refugee populations.

H.N. LE HOUÉROU is the Director for Environmental Sciences at the International Livestock Center for Africa in Addis Ababa, Ethiopia. Until August 1975 he served as the Senior Officer-in-charge for the Grasslands and Pastures Group in the Plant Production and Protection Division at the U.N. Food and Agricultural Organization in Rome. He is also the Scientific Coordination Officer for UNESCO's Man and the Biosphere Project No. 3 which is concerned with the impact of human activities on grazing lands. He has written extensively on desertization and desert reclamation and is the author of the forthcoming book Desert Ecology and Desertization.

PAUL LOVEJOY is an Assistant Professor of History at York University (Toronto, Canada) and Visiting Lecturer, Department of History, Ahmadu Bello University (Zaria, Nigeria), 1974-76. He received his Ph.D. from the University of Wisconsin in 1973. He is the author of several articles on the economic history of the Central Savanna and is currently undertaking research into the history of rural Kano and a study of the production and distribution of desert salts in the Central Savanna.

NORMAN MacLEOD is a crop ecologist and a specialist in remote sensing in the Biology Department at American University. He is also the director of the Drought Analysis Laboratory at American University. He is currently researching desert formation processes and the reclamation of arid regions for food production.

W. GERALD MATLOCK is Professor in the Department of Soils, Water and Engineering at the University of Arizona. He is the coordinator of all international programs in the College of Agriculture. He has consulted extensively for USAID agricultural projects in West Africa and Latin America.

ROGER MORRIS has worked in the State Department, on the National Security Council staff, and as a legislative assistant in the U.S. Senate. He was the project director at the Carnegie Endowment for International Peace for its Disaster in the Desert report.

BRIAN E. NORTON is an Assistant Professor in the Department of Range Science at Utah State University. He is also the Assistant Director for Resource Management of the U.S. International Biological Program—Desert Biome. He received his Ph.D. in Grasses and Grasslands from the University of New England, in Australia. He is currently researching the ecology of annual plants in arid areas.

WILLIAM PARTON, JR. is a member of the Natural Resource Ecology Lab at Colorado State University (Ft. Collins). He received his Ph.D. in 1972 in Meteorology from the University of Oklahoma. He is currently involved in the development of grassland ecosystems models for the U.S. IBP Grassland Programs and has presented several papers on that subject.

WALTER ORR ROBERTS has been Director and President of the University Corporation for Atmospheric Research (Boulder, Colorado) since its inception in 1960 to 1973. Currently he is Director of the Program on Science, Technology and Humanism for the Aspen Institute for Humanistic Studies. He is the leader of the Climate Project for IFIAS (The International Federation of Institutes for Advanced Study) in Stockholm, Sweden.

DAVID SHEAR is the Director of the Office of Central and West Africa Regional Affairs of the U.S. Agency for International Development. He has served with AID in Africa in Nigeria (1961-63), in Tanzania (1963-66) and in the Ivory Coast (1971-74). He has been heavily involved in AID projects (including relief efforts) in the Sahel.

HAL SHEETS is coauthor of the Carnegie Endowment for International Peace's controversial report, Disaster in the Desert. He graduated from Reed College in 1973 and is currently attending the Franklin Pierce Law Center (Concord, N.H.).

ROY STACY has served with USAID in the Somali Republic, Uganda, Southern Africa and in the Ivory Coast. He was most recently a senior planning officer for AID in Central and West Africa.

DEREK WINSTANLEY is a British climatologist currently working in the Office of the Science Adviser at Environment Canada (Ottawa). He is currently evaluating the policy implications for Canada of climatic fluctuations particularly as they affect Canadian food production. He has written extensively on climatic variability in the Sahel and in 1974 served as a consultant to the UN/FAO mission on "The Problems of Inland Fisheries in the Sahel." He received his D. Phil. from the University of Oxford and was employed as a meteorologist with the Anti-Locust Research Center of the U.K. Overseas Development Administration.

LAURIE WISEBERG is an Assistant Professor in Political Science at the University of Chicago—Chicago Circle. She has published several articles on African politics and has taught at Ahmadu Bello University (Nigeria), the University College Swansea (Wales) and at California State University (Los Angeles). She received her Ph.D. from U.C.L.A. in 1973. Her dissertation was on "The International Politics of Relief: The Case of Nigeria-Biafra Relief."

THE WORLD FOOD CONFERENCE AND GLOBAL
PROBLEM SOLVING

> Thomas G. Weiss and
> Robert S. Jordan

PLANNING FOR DEVELOPMENT IN SUB-SAHARAN
AFRICA

> Ann Seidman

CIVIL WARS AND THE POLITICS OF INTERNATIONAL
RELIEF: Africa, South Asia, and the Caribbean

> edited by Morris Davis

PLANNING ALTERNATIVE WORLD FUTURES:
Values, Methods, and Models

> edited by Louis Rene Beres
> and Harry R. Targ